# THE PSYCHOLOGICAL FOUNDATIONS OF EVIDENCE LAW

PSYCHOLOGY AND THE LAW

General Editor: Linda J. Demaine

*The Psychology of Tort Law*
Jennifer K. Robbennolt and Valerie P. Hans

*The Psychological Foundations of Evidence Law*
Michael J. Saks and Barbara A. Spellman

# The Psychological Foundations of Evidence Law

Michael J. Saks and Barbara A. Spellman

*With a Preface by Linda J. Demaine*

NEW YORK UNIVERSITY PRESS
*New York and London*

NEW YORK UNIVERSITY PRESS
New York and London
www.nyupress.org



References to Internet websites (URLs) were accurate at the time of writing. Neither the author nor New York University Press is responsible for URLs that may have expired or changed since the manuscript was prepared.

Library of Congress Cataloging-in-Publication Data
Saks, Michael J., author.
The psychological foundations of evidence law / Michael J. Saks and Barbara A. Spellman.
pages cm — (Psychology and the law)
Includes bibliographical references and index.
ISBN 978-1-4798-8004-1 (cl : alk. paper) — ISBN 978-0-8147-8387-0 (pb : alk. paper)
1. Evidence (Law)—Psychological aspects.—United States. 2. Forensic psychology—United States. I. Spellman, Barbara A., author. II. Title. III. Series: Psychology and the law (New York, N.Y.)
KF8936.S25 2015
347.73'6—dc23 2015029140

New York University Press books are printed on acid-free paper, and their binding materials are chosen for strength and durability. We strive to use environmentally responsible suppliers and materials to the greatest extent possible in publishing our books.

Manufactured in the United States of America

10 9 8 7 6 5 4 3 2 1

Also available as an ebook

*To my favorite sister, Diane Sandra Saks*

—MJS

*To my little family, Fred and Nikki*

—BAS

# CONTENTS


*Preface* ix
*Linda J. Demaine*

*Acknowledgments* xiii

Introduction: The Crossroads of Psychology and Evidence Law 1

PART I. MINDING THE JURY

1. Judges versus Juries: Trying the Facts 33
2. Balancing Acts 57
3. Instructions to Disregard and to Limit Use 85

PART II. JUDGING THE WITNESS

4. Witness the Witness 111
5. Character Evidence: Propensity and Impeachment 142

PART III. OTHER TYPES OF EVIDENCE

6. Hearsay and Exceptions 181
7. Scientific and Other Expert Evidence 202

Conclusion: The Lessons of Psychology for Evidence Law 232

*Appendix A: Table of Concepts* 243

*Appendix B: Federal Rules of Evidence (Abridged)* 247

*Notes* 279

*Index* 319

*About the Authors* 325

# PREFACE

LINDA J. DEMAINE

The NYU Press Psychology of Law book series addresses an intriguing state of affairs in legal scholarship. Although law and legal process are inherently psychological in nature, traditionally, relatively few law professors, judges, or legal practitioners have drawn on empirical psychological research to inform their perspectives and decisions. In recent years, the legal community has increasingly recognized that both substantive law and legal procedure rest on a multitude of testable assumptions about human behavior that can be informed by psychological research. Without formal training in psychology, however, it can be challenging for legal experts to identify relevant and informative psychological research, evaluate its methodological rigor, and interpret the empirical results. Consequently, in the absence of trusted resources to translate findings from psychological studies and apply them to core legal issues, psychology's potential to inform legal doctrine and practice will remain unfulfilled. Lawyers, in particular, will lack the tools that would enable them to better understand the law's effects on human behavior and how the law might be better constructed to achieve its goals.

Three important exceptions to psychology's peripheral status in legal scholarship are eyewitness testimony, false confessions, and jury decision making. In each of these realms, insights from psychological research have entered legal discussions and debates, resulting in marked improvements in the legal system's functioning. These exceptions, which developed precisely because lawyers communicated the fundamental legal issues to psychologists and psychologists introduced lawyers to informative research findings, demonstrate the potential of psychology to inform the law.

The Psychology of Law book series is intended to help make the exceptions into the rule by expanding and strengthening the intersection of law and psychology. To achieve this goal, the series applies psychology to subjects covered in the core law school curriculum. The books are designed to facilitate exchanges between lawyers and psychologists about these fundamental legal issues by introducing psychologists to the legal issues and introducing lawyers to the most pertinent research methods and findings. The books are valuable assets for law professors who desire to incorporate psychological science into their classes. To facilitate their adoption in law classrooms, the books map on to popular casebooks and are relatively brief and practical. The books are also prime resources for participants in psychology-law graduate programs, professors who teach undergraduate law and psychology courses, and mainstream psychologists who study legal issues. The books' expansive coverage of psychological research on core legal topics and their identification of areas in need of further research will provide these audiences with current knowledge and a roadmap to inspire further research. Finally, the books will be useful to legal practitioners whose work in particular areas of law can benefit from an understanding of psychology. All volumes are authored by eminent scholars who are conversant in both psychology and the law and possess the expertise necessary to identify and articulate legal issues of import, apply psychological theory and research findings to them, and identify areas of future research for psychologists.

In *The Psychological Foundations of Evidence Law*, Saks and Spellman analyze perhaps the clearest intersection between the fields of law and psychology. As they point out, in limiting the types of information on which jurors (and, in principle, judges) should base their decisions, judges (and legislatures) play the role of amateur psychologists. The rules of evidence reflect their views of how human cognition and emotion operate and which naturally occurring mental processes need to be restrained or redirected in order to provide fair outcomes to litigants. Evidence law's efforts are more likely to be successful when judges have access to psychological science, rather than merely their intuitions. In this book, Saks and Spellman provide the latest results from that science and identify areas in which psychological research is currently lacking on issues central to evidence law. They discuss the abilities and limitations of jurors and judges when engaging in the complex decision making that trials demand. They use psychology to inform the important balancing determinations of probative value versus anticipated prejudicial effects that judges regularly make. They assess how studies of instructions to disregard and to limit use of evidence can be used to enhance the likelihood that jurors will actually treat evidence as directed. Additionally, they consider how the rules governing witness testimony further the goal of providing jurors and judges with accurate information on which to base their judgments, and they discuss the psychological underpinnings of two historically challenging types of evidence—character and hearsay. They end with an assessment of a central element of modern evidence—scientific and other complex evidence provided by experts. Through their coverage of these issues, Saks and Spellman reveal an often unrecognized coherence in the many disparate rules of evidence, as well as aspects of the rules that fall short of their intended effects and areas in which we lack sufficient research findings to draw informed conclusions.

# ACKNOWLEDGMENTS

Writing a truly interdisciplinary book is difficult and we would like to thank the various people who helped us—from the law side and from the psychology side. We received useful comments on specific chapters from colleagues: Charles Barzun, Linda Demaine, Greg Mitchell, John Monahan, and Jessica Salerno. We also wish to thank our editor at NYU Press, Jennifer Hammer, for her advice, comments on chapters, and above all, patience mixed with gentle nudges.

BAS presented portions of the book in workshops at the law schools of Temple University and Cardozo University, and at both the School of Law and Department of Psychology at the University of Virginia. BAS also tortured some law students in fall 2013 with early drafts of chapters in a seminar called Evidence Law: Psychological Bases. Their feedback was especially useful because law students are a major audience for this book. Particular thanks to Elizabeth Gilbert, Kellen Galloway, Evan Mayo, and Tammi Walker. Thanks also to the fabulous reference librarians at the University of Virginia School of Law, especially Kent Olson, who, it seems, found references for us before the e-mail with the questions were sent. MJS thanks his academic home—the Sandra Day O'Connor College of Law at Arizona State University—for summer support while writing the book.

## BAS Notes

I learned evidence law twice. Once, long ago in law school, and then 25 years later when I joined the UVA law school and requested to teach it. Thanks to Greg Mitchell for letting me sit in on his class and Fred Schauer for answering many inane questions. Thanks also to two people I have never met: George Fisher and Ann Murphy. Professor Fisher's *Evidence* textbook was fun to teach from—in part because it contains some psychology but, more importantly, because it comes with a very-helpful-for-beginners teacher's manual. I am certain that I am guilty of the crime of cryptamnesia—believing that some of the ideas I have written about here are mine when in actuality they are his. I apologize in advance of discovery. Professor Murphy sends a trove of e-mails to the evidence law listserv; they typically link to useful articles or video clips that often both make me laugh and are useful in class. And, of course, massive thanks to Fred Schauer—for discussions, research, editing, blue book styling, and, especially, taking Nikki out at 7 a.m.

## MJS Notes

It took me three times. (And I am still working on it.) First, I sat in on Buzzy Baron's course at Boston College Law School when I was a faculty member in the Department of Psychology. Later I took the course when I was a student at Yale Law School. Eventually I started teaching evidence, which is, of course, one of the best ways to learn any subject.

Special thanks to Buzzy Baron, LL.B./Ph.D. (philosophy) for welcoming a novice psychology professor into legal education when he was associate dean at Boston College, showing me that law could be accessible and compatible with interdisciplinary approaches. We remain close friends, decades later. My appreciation also to Bob Hallisey (a warmly crusty Massachusetts trial judge) who also took me under his wing at an early stage of my career, and another mentor whose interest in psychology and science generally made me feel welcome in the legal world, and helped deepen my interest, my understanding, and my enjoyment of law.

# Introduction

## *The Crossroads of Psychology and Evidence Law*

The scene is familiar from courtroom trials on television: a lawyer puts a question to a witness and before the witness can answer another lawyer yells "objection," hoping to prevent some item of evidence from being learned by the jury. What rules of the courtroom game give lawyers the right to make such objections? *Why* do such rules exist? What are the psychological rationales for the rules?

The backstory of the rules of evidence begins with rulemakers: the people who created and continue to shape the rules. Decades and centuries ago these were common law judges, but today they are judicial committees, legislatures, special commissions, and sometimes still judges in their role as interpreters of existing rules. In the United States, the rules of evidence used by federal courts and most state courts are embodied in the Federal Rules of Evidence. The story also involves judges who apply the rules, lawyers who argue how the rules should be applied, parties to cases, witnesses, and jurors. And, as we describe throughout this book, the story of the rules of evidence deeply involves psychology.

When creating a rule of evidence, the rulemakers often, and unavoidably, must act as applied psychologists.[1] The rules of evidence reflect the rulemakers' understanding—correct or incorrect—of the psychological processes affecting witnesses and the capabilities of factfinders. A "factfinder" is someone who listens to the trial evidence and decides which facts to believe. In the United States that is usually 6–12 jurors, but the trial factfinder can also be a judge, and often is. In order to fashion the rule, the rulemakers need to think about the dependability of the kind of evidence under consideration, which might involve concerns about the nature of human perception and memory. Other times they must ponder the ability of factfinders to comprehend the meaning of evidence, assess its soundness, and consider its implications for the factual issues they need to resolve. In addition, rulemakers might need to consider whether certain kinds of inquiries by counsel are likely to help illuminate the strengths and weaknesses of the evidence, or whether judicial instructions can provide guidance when confronting problematic evidence. At the end of the day, rulemakers must predict how a given kind of evidence, presented and attacked in certain ways, is likely to influence factfinders, steering them away from misleading factual conclusions and moving them toward correct ones. All of these considerations put the rulemaker in the position of being a psychologist—an intuitive, amateur psychologist, but a psychologist nonetheless.

Similarly, when a trial judge, acting under an existing rule, makes a ruling on a disputed issue of evidence, often that judge, too, is acting as an applied psychologist. For example, the judge must try to predict how evidence will inform or mislead or otherwise influence the jury, and therefore whether it should be admitted or excluded. In contrast with rulemakers, however, the trial judge's focus is on a particular piece of evidence in the context of a specific trial, rather than on generic categories of evidence.

If we ask why we have the rules of evidence we have rather than other rules, a large part of the answer will be that they take into account the cognitive machinery and psychological processes possessed by witnesses and factfinders—or at least those processes as they are perceived by the rulemakers. The premises on which many of the rules of evidence are constructed, and the procedures in which they are embedded, are in large part a product of the rulemakers' beliefs about human psychology: beliefs about the way that people receive, store, and retrieve information,[2] about how people make judgments and draw inferences from verbal and other reports about objects and events in social contexts,[3] and about the organization and operation of the court[4] as well as the larger society.[5] Different underlying beliefs would have led to different rules than the ones we have.[6]

And so, we can ask what the beliefs are that rulemakers have about the capacities and tendencies of witnesses, lawyers, jurors, and others. We can ask whether the rulemakers are correct in those beliefs, and in turn whether the rules they created achieve their purposes as well as they could, or whether different rules could achieve those goals more effectively. Rulemakers, being human, and relying heavily on intuition to answer difficult questions about human psychology, will be wrong sometimes. (We are going to try to figure out which times.)

To be sure, rulemakers try to solve other problems as well. Trials are designed not only to be effective searches for truth, but also to serve other values, such as to give parties control over the presentation of their respective cases,[7] to ensure that the adversarial battle is a fair fight, to protect certain relationships, to encourage repairs of dangerous situations, and so on. Some rules reflect those other concerns. Our trial system succeeds only if its procedures and results assure the parties and the public that the process produces reasonably accurate and acceptably just results.[8]

This book focuses on the psychological beliefs reflected in the rules of evidence—beliefs about witnesses, about factfinders, and about the trial process—and how those beliefs have informed the development of the rules of evidence. It explores a number of important practices from evidence law about which psychology does, or could, have a lot to say to illuminate the underlying assumptions, and evaluates whether those assumptions are consistent with the psychological research or whether the law's goals for evidence doctrine could be achieved more successfully with a modified rule or a different rule or no rule at all.

This is a useful place to pause for a moment to address legal terminology. In this book, the noun "rule" refers to a rule of evidence: a directive to judges concerning how to treat a proffered type of evidence. Evidence "doctrine" is a widely adhered to body of principles concerning the law of a topic, in the present context how evidence is to be viewed and treated by courts. Evidence "law" is the broadest term. To borrow from *Black's Law Dictionary*, it refers to: "The aggregate of legislation, judicial precedents, and accepted legal principles; the body of authoritative grounds of judicial and administrative action; esp., the body of rules, standards, and principles that the courts of a particular jurisdiction apply in deciding controversies brought before them."

## The Psychology of Evidence Rules

Let's look at some concrete examples that illustrate the rulemakers' concerns with different psychological processes and how those concerns are reflected in several rules.

An example of a rule that makes assumptions about the cognitive capacities of people is the excited utterance exception to the rule against hearsay, Rule 803(2) of the Federal Rules of Evidence, which allows hearsay statements when the out-of-court statement is made under the influence of a stressful event. This rule is rooted in the belief that people have limited cognitive capacity and that the stress of an arousing event consumes so much of their available cognitive resources that people lack sufficient residual capacity to invent falsehoods. Thus, an out-of-court statement made by someone exclaiming something in response to such an event was thought unlikely to be fabricated due to the very stress of the occasion, and therefore was dependable enough to be exempted from exclusion as hearsay.[9] This rule—which is explicitly grounded in a cognitive theory—was suggested by John Henry Wigmore, the preeminent evidence scholar of the early twentieth century, was accepted as sound by some American judges, and later adopted by the drafters of the Federal Rules.

---

**Rule 803(2). Excited Utterance [Exception to the Rule against Hearsay]**

A statement relating to a startling event or condition, made while the declarant was under the stress of excitement that it caused.

---

If the rulemakers had believed that humans, as observers of events that later became issues at trial, had more expansive cognitive abilities, or could process thoughts and feelings in parallel—so that while part of the mind was reacting to the stimulus of a stressful incident, another part was busy constructing and evaluating advantageous lies—this hearsay exception would have found far less favor. Alternatively, if rulemakers believed that the same stress that Wigmore thought made a statement trustworthy had an even greater tendency to cause a person's perception and interpretation of an event to be distorted, and for this reason the statement was therefore *undependable*,[10] then there would be no excited utterance exception.[11] This is one example of a set of rules and rulings that are concerned with the capacities and abilities of out-of-court observers and in-court witnesses, and where the rulemakers had to employ their best (though limited) knowledge about human cognition.

Other rules seem to be concerned jointly with the behavior of people in transactions that bring them to court and with the inferential tendencies of jurors. The doctrines limiting the admissibility of character evidence—embodied in Rule 404(a)—are based on a belief that observers (in this case, factfinders) overattribute behavior to the assumed traits of the actor and overestimate the consistency with which people behave across time and different circumstances. These rules are concerned with whether, as actors, our behavior is driven by personality traits, how consistent our conduct is with those hypothesized traits; and, as perceivers of behavior, how strong our tendency is to attribute behavior to stable characteristics of people and to overlook inconsistency wrought by situational and other factors. The greater the extent to which our perceptions of consistency between traits and behavior overstate the reality of that consistency, the more sensible it is for rulemakers to adopt a rule that keeps such information from reaching factfinders. This example illustrates another class of rules that are concerned with how jurors respond to evidence, and where the rulemakers are employing their beliefs about both cognitive and social psychology.

---

**Rule 404(a). Character Evidence**

(1) Prohibited Uses. Evidence of a person's character or character trait is not admissible to prove that on a particular occasion the person acted in accordance with the character or trait.

(2) Exceptions for a Defendant or Victim in a Criminal Case. The following exceptions apply in a criminal case:

(A) a defendant may offer evidence of the defendant's pertinent trait, and if the evidence is admitted, the prosecutor may offer evidence to rebut it;

(B) subject to the limitations in Rule 412, a defendant may offer evidence of an alleged victim's pertinent trait, and if the evidence is admitted, the prosecutor may:

(i) offer evidence to rebut it; and

(ii) offer evidence of the defendant's same trait; and

(C) in a homicide case, the prosecutor may offer evidence of the alleged victim's trait of peacefulness to rebut evidence that the victim was the first aggressor.

(3) Exceptions for a Witness. Evidence of a witness's character may be admitted under Rules 607, 608, and 609.

---

The doctrine of privileges (embodied in Rule 501), which protects communications between people in certain types of relationships from being disclosed in trials. The variety of privileges reflects beliefs about the importance of certain roles and relationships, coupled with the normative views of rulemakers concerning which relationships should be granted protection from intrusion by the legal process—and which should not. The decision to grant a privilege rather than to require evidence to be disclosed reflects a complex judgment about the nature of those relationships, the likely harm such relationships would suffer if their communications were subject to disclosure at trial, and the value society places on preserving those kinds of relationship notwithstanding the cost of foregoing evidence. Familiar privileged relationships are lawyer-client, doctor-patient, and spousal. More contested relationships are journalist-source and parent-child. In setting out the rule on privileges, a set of rules that contemplates the nature and functioning of relationships and organizations, the rulemakers are acting as sociologists and social psychologists.

---

**Rule 501. Privilege in General**

The common law—as interpreted by United States courts in the light of reason and experience—governs a claim of privilege unless any of the following provides otherwise:

- the United States Constitution;
- a federal statute; or
- rules prescribed by the Supreme Court.

But in a civil case, state law governs privilege regarding a claim or defense for which state law supplies the rule of decision.

*Authors' note: Rule 502 defines the attorney-client privilege applicable in federal courts. As indicated by Rule 501, all other recognized privileges are borrowed from common law or state law.*

---

These examples illustrate how the rules of evidence are in part, some in large part, a product of the beliefs that rulemakers have about human psychology.

### *The Psychology of the Evidence Rulemakers*

Often, when rulemakers adopt a general rule of evidence,[12] they do so by trying to compare the optimal or ideal or proper inferences to be drawn from a class of evidence to how they imagine average jurors will interpret the evidence. If no discrepancy were expected between perfect decision making and the decision making of human factfinders, few rules of evidence would be needed. In concluding that a gap exists, rulemakers share the company of psychologists who have found whole classes of erroneous inferences and judgments that humans routinely make.[13]

The figures in this section will deepen and expand one's appreciation of the challenge that rulemakers face, and the multifaceted roles that psychological issues play, in thinking about evidence rules.

This gap between the ideal inference and the inference a jury is likely to make is depicted in Figure I.1. Box A represents ideal inferences, Box B represents the actual inferences jurors draw, and the arrow between them represents the gap between those two sets of inferences. When that gap is perceived as too large, a rule is likely to be developed to try to avoid or reduce the error, usually by excluding evidence.

The actual situation is much more complicated because the rulemakers are acting not only as amateur psychologists, but also as amateur

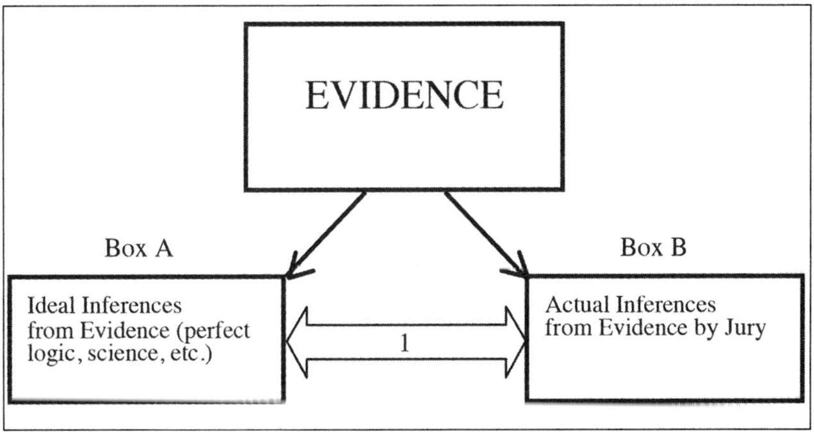


Figure I.1. Factfinders' Imperfect Beliefs about the Inferences to Be Drawn from Evidence

logicians, statisticians, and scientists of various kinds. Figure I.2 illuminates this problem.

The rulemakers cannot measure either the reality of perfect inferences or the reality of average jurors' inferences or, of course, the gap between them. The rulemakers are actually comparing their estimate of the ideal inferences (Box A*) against their estimate of what the jurors' inferences might be (Box B*). Their estimate of what the correct inference is from any given type of evidence is the product of their human, usually intuitive, judgment, and is not necessarily correct. Their estimation of what inferences jurors likely will draw from the evidence is a largely intuitive prediction about the decision making of other people—an exercise in predictive mind reading (or "metacognition"). In other words, the rulemakers behave as though they are assessing the gap between Box A and Box B (Gap 1), but all they have access to is their own reasoning and intuition, which has them assessing the gap between Box A* and Box B* (Gap 4).

The greater the gap between Box A and Box A* (Gap 2), the greater the error rulemakers are making about what the correct inference is from the evidence. The greater the gap (Gap 3) between what rulemakers think jurors think (Box B*) and what jurors actually think (Box B), the greater the error that rulemakers are making about the factfinders. Rulemakers (and judges) might be no better than jurors at drawing such inferences, so that the rulemakers are overestimating jurors' misunderstanding of the evidence, and therefore have created a rule where one is not needed. Or jurors might be far worse at processing the evidence than the rulemakers realize, so that the rulemakers are underestimating the gap between correct inferences and the jurors' inferences, and therefore have not created a rule where one would be useful.

Trying to evaluate the gap between Box A and Box A* for any given rule or any given item of evidence is beyond the scope of this book. This book examines instead the gap between the actual inferences that average people draw from evidence (Box B) and what rulemakers believe the inferences are that average people draw (Box B*), that is, Gap 3. To some extent we can also examine the gap between what judges think is the correct inference from evidence (Box A*) and the inferences actually drawn by average people (jurors) (Box B).[14] In short, in this book we

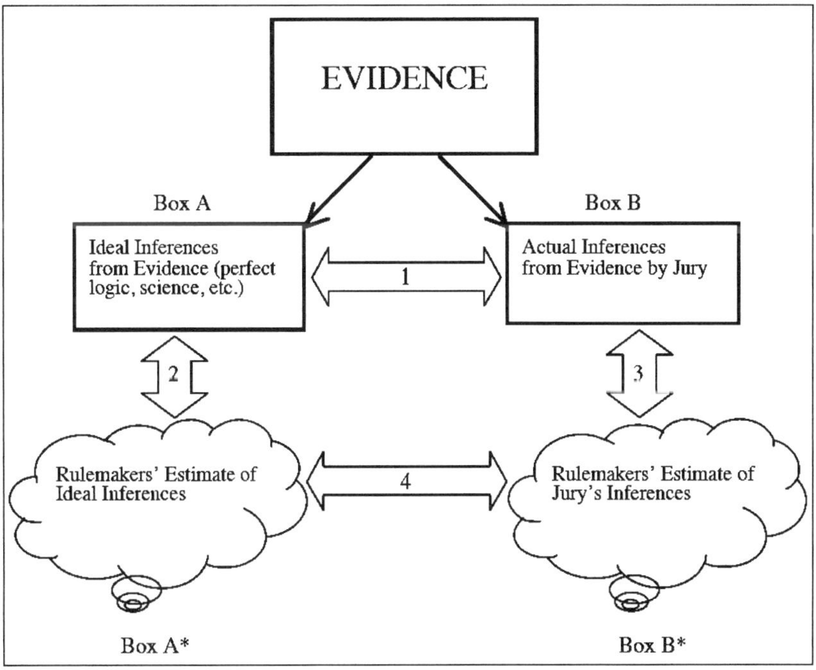


Figure I.2. Rulemakers' Imperfect Beliefs about the Proper Inferences and Jurors' Inferences

will be learning about the psychology of rulemakers and judges as well as the psychology of witnesses and jurors.

## The History and Purpose of Evidence Rules

This section provides some background on what the rules of evidence do and how they came into being and evolved. As you might already know—or can figure out by skimming the rules of evidence (which are provided in Appendix B at the back of this book)—after addressing a number of preliminary issues, the rules of evidence define relevant evidence (Rule 401) and declare evidence that is relevant to be admissible (Rule 402) and evidence that is not relevant to be inadmissible. Most of the remaining rules can be characterized as rules of exclusion, defining types of evidence that are inadmissible despite their relevance, along with rules that specify exceptions to those general rules of exclusion (i.e., types of evidence to be admitted despite a more general rule that would make them inadmissible).

---

**Rule 401. Test for Relevant Evidence**

Evidence is relevant if:

(a) it has any tendency to make a fact more or less probable than it would be without the evidence; and

(b) the fact is of consequence in determining the action.

---

**Rule 402. General Admissibility of Relevant Evidence**

Relevant evidence is admissible unless any of the following provides otherwise:

- the United States Constitution;
- a federal statute;
- these rules; or
- other rules prescribed by the Supreme Court.

Irrelevant evidence is not admissible.

---

### *Why Do We Have Rules of Evidence?*

Why does our trial system have rules of evidence? And why are our rules of evidence so extensive and detailed?

A century ago, lawyers and legal scholars theorized that juries were the reason that rules of evidence had evolved in Anglo-American law.[15] They noted that continental European countries, which used the "inquisitorial" system of trials (in which judges both investigate the facts of the case instead of lawyers and serve as factfinders instead of juries), had and have very brief evidence codes. On the other hand, English common law countries, which used the "adversarial" system of trials (in which opposing lawyers develop and present the evidence to third-party factfinders, typically lay jurors) had developed extensive rules regulating what evidence was to be admitted to and what excluded from trial. Prominent legal scholars, led by James Thayer,[16] inferred from this situation that juries must be the reason why we have extensive rules of evidence. Where judges alone were factfinders, few rules existed. But where laypersons were factfinders, many specific rules were needed to filter and shape the evidence to help those amateur factfinders reach correct verdicts. Simeon Baldwin—a law professor at Yale as well as a justice of the Connecticut Supreme Court and a member of Congress—put the matter bluntly, writing that, "for the most part, English Judges centuries ago" created rules of evidence "because they had to deal with juries composed of illiterate men of untrained minds, incapable of making nice discriminations as to the weight of testimony."[17]

But a more careful look at history has led to a different conclusion.[18] By looking at *when* our rules of evidence grew into their voluminous form, scholars saw that the pivotal distinction was not whether judges or juries were deciding the cases, but whether evidence was presented through an adversarial or inquisitorial system of trial. Soon after lawyers in adversarial systems acquired their central role in investigating, developing, and presenting evidence in court, rules of evidence rapidly evolved to place more, and more detailed, constraints on what those lawyers could offer at trial. Because lawyers in an adversarial system are highly motivated to try to find evidence that supports their client's position, to think about how best to present that evidence, and to argue as persuasively as possible in support of the desired evidence and the desired conclusions, limits had to be placed on what those lawyers would be permitted to do. The rules came into being to rein in the inevitable excesses of lawyers in an adversarial system. Juries were a constant—they existed before and after the advent of rules of evidence. Determinedly adversarial lawyering was the innovation that impelled further change, and extensive rules of evidence were that change.

The rules of evidence apply to bench trials (that is, when a judge tries a case without a jury) as well as to jury trials; so, in theory at least, judges are also being protected from the excesses of advocates. But it is less practical for judges to screen evidence from themselves than from jurors, and judges doubtless believe that they are not in great need of protection. Typically, they previously were trial lawyers and they understand advocacy. So perhaps it is more complete and accurate to suggest that adversarial processes without juries, or juries without adversarial processes, do not need extensive rules of evidence. But put the adversary process together with juries, and evidence rules become a necessary device for restraining lawyers, thereby protecting jurors from being deceived or misled.

As we will see in more detail in the next chapter, common law judges and their successors, rules drafting committees, have done a remarkably good job of reining in lawyers. In tandem with the rules of procedure, the rules of evidence place limits on the persuasive efforts of lawyers, making it quite difficult for them to use what psychological research has found to be the most powerful tools of influence and persuasion. At the same time, it should be noted that the rules of evidence also empower lawyers in certain ways. The rules can be used to control an opponent and, sometimes, even the judge. Like it or not, a judge must, for example, grant a lawyer's request to exclude a witness from the courtroom until the witness's turn comes to testify (unless limited exceptions apply), or exclude hearsay evidence, and certain other evidence, unless that evidence falls within an exception.

## Evolution of the Rules

Our legal ancestors seem to have been more acutely aware of the contested nature of the assumptions underlying evidence doctrine than their modern descendants are. The declining awareness of the assumptions underpinning evidence doctrines is partly a consequence of the increasing crystallization and the eventual codification of the rules—into the Federal Rules of Evidence which, as noted above, are the law in both the federal courts, and most state courts of the United States.[19] One of the purposes of this book is to bring those assumptions—those hypotheses about human beings and society—closer to the surface again for examination. Knowing the assumptions helps deepen one's understanding of the policies behind a rule and, therefore, when exceptions to a rule might sensibly be sought and permitted.[20]

Judge-made rules of evidence are law, of course, but in that form they tend to be more debatable. Once a rule is codified into a statute by a legislature, however, its fundamental assumptions seem less vulnerable, and attention shifts to other matters: interpreting the rule's command, determining how different parts of the evidence code interact with each other, and navigating difficulties of application in concrete cases. Declining awareness of a rule's behavioral assumptions does not mean the assumptions have gone away, or that they are necessarily correct, but only that they have become less visible in discussions of the doctrine.

For example, at common law—when laws, including evidence rules, were made by judges, which was the situation at the time of the founding of the United States—anyone who stood to gain or lose from the outcome of a case was barred from testifying, and that included plaintiffs and defendants.[21] Judges (the common law rulemakers) reasoned that parties were unavoidably biased in their own favor, would therefore be incapable of testifying to the unvarnished truth, and therefore a rule barring the testimony of parties was a sound one. The reasoning behind such rules, and therefore their limits, were discussed openly.[22] By the latter half of the nineteenth century, the rule disqualifying interested parties from testifying had changed. The rule changed because the beliefs underlying the rule changed—beliefs about the power of the temptations of interested witnesses to lie, about the ability of the evolving adversary trial system to expose those biases to the jury, and about the ability of jurors to discount the testimony once they learn of a witness's biases and interest in the outcome. Today, what was once prohibited is now routinely permitted, and concern that it would lead to inevitable deception of factfinders has evaporated.

Thus the rules of evidence as we know them today are the result of centuries of work by judges, lawyers, and eventually legislators.[23] They are the product, over generations, of efforts by countless lawyers to insert or exclude various items of evidence and the rulings of countless judges concerning such efforts. They continue to change, however slowly, and those changes rest in part on changes in beliefs about the behavior of parties, witnesses, lawyers, and factfinders.[24]

### *Debating the Nature of Evidence Rules*

Simon Greenleaf's three-volume *Treatise on the Law of Evidence* (1842–1853), which was a standard textbook in American law throughout the latter half of the nineteenth century, asserted that "[t]he student will not fail to observe the symmetry and beauty of this branch of the law . . . and will rise from the study of its principles convinced, with Lord Erskine, that 'they are founded in the charities of religion, in the philosophy of nature, in the truths of history, and in the experience of common life.'" Half a century later, James Bradley Thayer, who succeeded Greenleaf in his Harvard professorship, responded to Greenleaf, writing, "[I]t would be juster and more exact to say that our law of evidence is a piece of illogical, but by no means irrational, patchwork, not at all to be admired, nor easily to be found intelligible."[25] Edward Cleary, an eminent mid-twentieth-century evidence scholar observed: "the rules of evidence largely have been constructed out of anecdotes and unsystematic observation, plus what hopefully passes for reason but could more honestly be labeled conjecture about human behavior."[26]

Beautiful or chaotic, most evidence scholars recognized that evidence rules had gone through many changes over time, and were in continuing need of change. Thayer argued for a more experimental view of evidence rules, one that would continually test their ability to meet contemporary needs and question their underlying assumptions. Today's social and behavioral scientists would be entirely in agreement with that view. Indeed, among many legal commentators, "[t]here is no real debate over whether legal scholarship should make use of insights and methods from other disciplines."[27]

That evidence doctrine and trial procedures reflect the rulemakers' beliefs about human cognitive abilities, decision making, and organization of the trial and society, leads to the corollary that improved foundational knowledge could lead to more effective rules and more satisfactory trials. Cleary, who was one of the drafters of the Federal Rules of Evidence, called for more use of the scientific method to help strengthen that foundation. In 1952, he wrote:

> In the realm of honest searching after facts, nothing could be further removed from scientific method than the rules governing procedures used in courts. . . . In science a theory possesses a recognized provisional and tool-like character. If the empirical data collected do not support the theory, the theory is discarded. Since the law never collects any [systematic] empirical data, it is spared the embarrassment of having ever to discard a theory on that basis.[28]

Cleary thought that evidence law was unusually well suited to a partnership with empirical social science:

> Most substantive law is . . . filled with oughts and value judgments. . . . Evidence is almost unique in being primarily concerned with the is.

> Other than some minor value judgments . . . the rules of evidence are constructed upon certain assumptions as to how people do in fact act under particular circumstances, rather than how they ought to act.[29]

The customary approach of research psychologists seems entirely compatible with the approaches to evidence law suggested by the legal scholars just described.

## How Psychologists Approach Problems Like Those Faced by Evidence Rulemakers

An empirical question is one that has to do with the nature of the material world—what is the actual nature of some thing or phenomenon, what are the causal interconnections, what works and what doesn't, how accurate is a test?

Empirical questions need to be distinguished from various kinds of legal questions (e.g., are baby carriages forbidden by a rule that prohibits "vehicles" from entering the park on weekends?), or questions about logic (if the law has not yet declared the constitutionally required minimum number of jurors, but has held six to be above the minimum, does it follow that five cannot be below the minimum?), or morality (is it right to enrich oneself while some fellow citizens are too poor to feed their children?). Those are questions for which empirical inquiry cannot provide the answers.

### *Answering an Empirical Question: Example of Disregarding Evidence*

When the answer to an empirical question is sought, how does one find it? How does one go about obtaining sound answers to questions such as the following: Does bleeding a patient through the application of leeches cure disease? Do astrological signs predict one's future? Is each person's handwriting (or fingerprint) unique? Do vaccines cause autism? Does it harm a witness's credibility for the weaknesses in her testimony to be brought out on direct examination (by the very lawyer who called the witness to the stand)? When instructed to disregard inadmissible evidence, can jurors put that information out of their minds and decide the case as if they had never heard it?

Whereas rulemakers typically proceed by reaching a consensus on their assumptions, impressions, anecdotes, and reasoning about human behavior, psychologists proceed by trying to empirically test assumptions and theories. In other words, the approach generally taken by psychologists is the application of the scientific method. At bottom, the scientific method is an effort to obtain answers to questions about the nature and workings of the material world by designing ways to draw out an answer about the phenomena of interest from the world itself.[30]

Suppose we want to know whether instructing jurors to disregard inadmissible evidence that nevertheless had been blurted out in a trial is an effective way to remove the impact of that evidence from the jurors' decisions. One research possibility would be to design a study in which mock jurors hear testimony about a case. One randomly created group of mock jurors does not hear the damaging inadmissible evidence (the "not-hear" condition). Two other groups do hear the damaging inadmissible evidence: some jurors hear it with no objection; others hear an attorney objecting and the judge giving a standard instruction to disregard the evidence.

The subsequent decisions of jurors in the three different conditions could be compared to each other. How much impact did the inadmissible evidence have? We can find out by comparing the not-hear condition to the no-objection condition. If the evidence were inculpatory in a criminal case, we would expect to find more guilty verdicts in the no-objection condition. How much impact did the instruction to disregard have? We can find out by comparing the disregard condition to the other conditions. Did jurors' decisions in the disregard condition look the same as in the no-objection condition, suggesting the instruction had no effect? Or did the objection lead to even more guilty verdicts, suggesting that the instruction underscored the inadmissible evidence and made a bad situation worse? Or did the instruction to disregard "work" and reduce the impact of the inadmissible evidence? If so, how much? Was the harm completely undone, so that decisions in the disregard condition looked just like those in the not-hear condition, indicating the instruction was completely effective? Or was it somewhere in between, indicating that the instruction was only partially successful?

You can imagine variations on such an experiment. If the standard instruction did not undo the damage of the inadmissible evidence, perhaps a more innovative instruction would—built, perhaps, on other research knowledge from psychology.[31] Are you concerned that these are mock trials and mock jurors? With additional effort, one could design similar studies to take place in the setting of actual trials.

Many different questions about what happens when evidence is admitted or withheld could be asked through such empirical studies, and many different research designs are possible to test those questions. The results of such studies could inform rulemakers about the extent of success or failure of existing rules, or suggest new and better rules.

### *Drawing on Basic Empirical Psychology Research*

Another approach to using psychology in legal settings would be to borrow from the findings of more basic empirical research, or from theoretical knowledge[32] about human perception, memory, and information processing. That is, rather than conducting new experiments on a specific legal-context question, knowledge can be borrowed from other studies asking similar kinds of questions in different contexts.

To illustrate, let's consider some general properties of the human mind. One characteristic of our mental processing is that we seek coherence—patterns, explanations, causes—and we sometimes find them when they are not there. We are tricked by visual illusions and sometimes still see them even though one part of our mind seems to be telling the other part: "No, you know the two lines are the same length; stop interpreting them as different." We humans take little bits of information and put them together with other little bits and from them we generalize: we make inductions, form categories, and even create stereotypes. Sometimes the bits of information in the world (bottom-up knowledge) and things we already believe (top-down knowledge) clash, and one gives way to the other. We quickly see disparate events or objects or people as similar, but we are also good at distinguishing instances—especially when context, knowledge, cognitive resources, or motivation propel us to do so. These are very general processes and are at work in many of our cognitive functions, including perception, memory, judgment, reasoning, and language.[33]

Among several large areas of basic psychology research discussed in this book that have many applications to the legal world, two are mental contamination and the dual systems theory of higher-order cognition. The first, mental contamination, is an umbrella term for some of the research about how knowledge or memory can affect reasoning—even when you don't want it to. The second, the dual systems theory of higher-order cognition, is a theoretical account of judgment and thinking processes that has emerged after decades of debate about human reasoning competencies.

### *Mental Contamination*

"Mental contamination"[34] is not a commonly used term in psychology, but we use it here to label a category of basic research findings about how prior knowledge can bias future judgments in an unwanted manner. Normally, prior knowledge about what you are judging is a good thing. For example, you can better evaluate an athlete's performance the more you know about the sport. However, sometimes even useful knowledge can lead us astray.

Mental contamination takes different forms in the legal system. Some of them have already been mentioned, and they come up in various rules of evidence. "Metacognition" is the ability to think about one's own and others' reasoning processes.[35] As mentioned in conjunction with Figure I.2, judges often have to engage in metacognition when trying to figure out what inferences a jury will make from certain evidence. A major problem with this type of reasoning is that judges suffer from "the curse of knowledge"—that is, because they have been through many trials but jurors have not, they might be unable to evaluate the jury's (lack of) understanding of complex testimony, arcane jury instructions, or other content or procedures that are much more familiar to the judge. These problems are particularly obvious when making balancing decisions under Rule 403, which permits judges to exclude all sorts of evidence when certain conditions are met, and when evaluating the usefulness of expert testimony.

---

**Rule 403. Excluding Relevant Evidence for Prejudice, Confusion, Waste of Time, or Other Reasons**

The court may exclude relevant evidence if its probative value is substantially outweighed by a danger of one or more of the following: unfair prejudice, confusing the issues, misleading the jury, undue delay, wasting time, or needlessly presenting cumulative evidence.

---

Another type of mental contamination is when you learn something that you shouldn't know, and might even try not to use, but it affects your judgments anyway. One example, as described above, is that of trying to disregard inadmissible information. It turns out that jurors are not good at doing so, although there are factors that will make them better or worse at it. Judges apparently have the same problems as jurors do in disregarding inadmissible information,[36] which has interesting implications for bench trials, in which judges in their role as triers of *law* will learn information that they should not be considering in their role as triers of *fact*.[37] That is, when judges are deciding how to rule on various legal issues in a case—which they must do prior to trial as well as during trials—they inevitably learn facts that have a bearing on decisions they will need to make if they are serving also as a factfinder, without a jury. Another example is when evidence is admissible for one purpose but not for another purpose. In that case jurors may be instructed to use the evidence in some ways but not in others (i.e., to both remember and forget it). Such limiting instructions are often invoked with categorical exclusion rules and character evidence.

Knowing information in the present affects your judgments about what people knew or should have known in the past. The effect of this type of knowledge is called the "hindsight bias."[38] The most common legal example of this bias occurs when judging foreseeability (for example, in a negligence case). Imagine that some people try to iron their clothes while wearing them (and suffer serious burns). Once the manufacturer becomes aware of such misuse, it looks negligent for not realizing that a warning was necessary against that "foreseeable" misuse.[39] Hindsight bias is a likely rationale for Rule 407, which excludes evidence of subsequent remedial measures. Hindsight bias can also create errors in appellate rulings of "harmless error" in which a court, knowing about pieces of evidence and what a jury decided after hearing that evidence, attempts to figure out what the jury would have decided had it not been exposed to the evidence in the first place.

### *Heuristics, Rationality, and Two Systems of Reasoning*

The previous section talked about how different kinds of knowledge, which should be irrelevant to a particular legal reasoning task, might nevertheless affect that reasoning. This section is about how people reason more generally. In the 1950s, much psychology research focused on aspects of human reasoning processes that appeared logical, objective, and scientific. That view was shattered by the groundbreaking research of Kahneman and Tversky (beginning in the 1970s) showing that humans often come to conclusions that are inconsistent with the rules of logic and statistics.[40] The 1980s and early 1990s created a cottage industry of "heuristics and biases" research—every cognitive and social psychologist wanted to discover a heuristic or bias of their very own. But the late 1990s and afterward saw researchers struggling to explain the reasons for these cognitive errors. As shown in countless demonstrations, people are not random in their thinking errors; rather, the errors are quite systematic. For that reason, much could be learned from the patterns of errors.[41]

One theory that emerged from this research is that humans have two "systems" for reasoning. Many researchers had tried to explain unusual findings in disparate areas of psychology and had come to the conclusion that two different "types" of reasoning had been at work.[42] Across the different areas, each of the two distinct types of reasoning seemed to have parallel commonalities with the two types proposed by other researchers.[43] Table I.1 shows what emerged—the idea of two systems that have a set of correlated reasoning characteristics. The basic idea is that System 1 responds to information quickly, unconsciously, and by using heuristics. System 2 is slower, conscious, and reflective. Sometimes the two systems respond differently to stimuli. Then for someone to produce an answer generated from System 2, she would have to "override" the initial answer generated by the faster System 1.[44] Analogous tables delineating the two systems vary a bit in content across authors, and some people argue that the systems have a biological and evolutionary basis whereas others think that is unnecessary for the distinction. There is still a lively debate about whether there really are two systems and what they encompass,[45] but in this book we embrace the explanatory value of the theory. Some examples follow.

One might be tempted to summarize the heuristic and biases research by saying: people typically make quick intuitive judgments that lead them to the wrong answer. But that summary would be wrong in several important and applicable ways.[46]

TABLE I.1. Characteristics of the Two Systems of Reasoning

| System 1 | System 2 |
|---|---|
| Nonconscious | Conscious |
| Implicit | Explicit |
| Intuitive | Reflective |
| Emotional | Rational |
| Heuristic | Reasoned |
| Peripheral | Central |
| Fast | Slow |
| Automatic | Controlled |
| Effortless | Effortful |
| Does not require working memory/ attention | Does require working memory/attention |
| "Old Mind" | "New Mind" |
| Evolved early | Evolved late |
| Similar to animal cognition | Distinctively human |

First, it's not true that System 1 always leads to the wrong answer and System 2 always leads to the correct one. As we will see, there are potential bad consequences of using heuristics, but as Tversky and Kahneman noted early on, heuristics usually work; that is, System 1 often gets you to the right answer. And research has found that sometimes letting System 2 "overthink" a problem can lead to the wrong answer.

One type of System 1 reasoning that has been "rehabilitated" in recent years is emotion. Although, for millennia, philosophers and then psychologists characterized emotion as obstructing good reasoning, some current research demonstrates that emotion, itself, may provide reliable information as to what our responses should be and emotion may cause us to do "appropriate" processing of external information.[47]

Moreover, even under the same circumstances, different people come up with different answers; that is, not all people will respond with decisions made by the same system. People differ with respect to how deeply and critically they want to think about a problem before they respond to it. Thus, people who are high in "need for cognition" are more likely to use System 2 solutions than are people low in need for cognition. People also differ on how expert they are in the domains that they are reasoning about. The intuition of experts, if honed under certain conditions (e.g., use it frequently, get reliable feedback, etc.) is better than the intuition of novices.[48]

Finally, there are circumstances in which System 2 reasoning is more likely to be "consulted"; for example, when there is motivation, time, and available cognitive resources. One of those circumstances is during the jury's deliberation. Deliberating ideally includes taking time to reflect on the entire trial and to articulate rational reasons for one's views. Thus, after deliberation the response of the jury as a whole will sometimes differ from the pre-deliberation responses of individual jurors.

### *Psychological Foundations*

Subsequent chapters in this book draw on knowledge that comes largely from the two lines of information described above—specific empirical studies seeking to answer a specific question that arises in a legal context (e.g., the example of disregarding evidence described above in the section "Answering an Empirical Question"), and more basic research knowledge amassed by psychologists who did not have legal trials in mind when they designed their studies (e.g., the examples of metacognition and two systems of reasoning). Although the approaches of law and scientific psychology are different, the questions the fields are interested in sometimes have considerable overlap.

## Confluences, Collisions, and Collaborations

The findings of psychological research were first introduced to the law early in the twentieth century, but that initial introduction soon fizzled owing to forces coming from within as well as outside of the fields. Psychological research on legal questions began flourishing again in the 1970s and 1980s, as cognitive and social psychologists began to study the types of mental processes that had been ignored when behaviorism (an approach to accounting for behavior that eschewed appeals to mental processes such as cognition and emotion) had been the dominant strategy in psychological research. Concern with psychological aspects of weaknesses in the trial process blossomed further in the 1990s, when new ways of analyzing DNA evidence left at crime scenes led to the exonerations of scores, and then hundreds, of prisoners who had been erroneously convicted of crimes they did not commit.[49] Much of what was going wrong had important psychological dimensions, involving various kinds of evidence: eyewitness identifications and testimony, confessions, false testimony, pattern-matching types of forensic identification evidence. Psychology research has lit the way to some improvements in police and trial procedures, and is being turned to for help in improving crime laboratories.

The first scholar to apply psychological findings and principles to legal problems was Hugo Münsterberg, a German American professor who had been recruited to Harvard in the late 1890s by the philosopher-psychologist William James. Münsterberg had been a student of Wilhelm Wundt, the father of experimental psychology, who founded the first formal psychological research laboratory at the University of Leipzig in 1879. In addition to his Ph.D. from Leipzig, Münsterberg also earned a medical degree from the University of Heidelberg. Münsterberg was quite interested in the application of psychological principles to practical problems, and he invented one field of applied psychology after another: applications of psychology to industry, to education, to medicine, to psychotherapy, to business, and to law.

Münsterberg conducted numerous experiments using his students, through which he uncovered problems that should be of great interest to the law, such as wide-ranging differences in the recall of people who had been observers of the same event. His 1908 book, *On the Witness Stand*,[50] was a collection of a series of popular magazine articles that dealt with such topics as eyewitness perception and memory, influences on witness testimony, factors that produce false confessions, hypnotism and crime, jury decision making, and suggestions for testing the observations claimed by witnesses. Some of his suggestions were sound, others premature, and still others speculative. Nevertheless, many of these topics remain core research areas for psychologists interested in the law and Münsterberg's efforts presaged an entire interdisciplinary movement.

Unfortunately for the development of a law and psychology collaboration, the great evidence scholar John Henry Wigmore took a strong dislike to Münsterberg's book, and published a peculiar and hostile critique of it.[51] Some evidence scholars today believe that Wigmore frightened off many potential interdisciplinary teams; Roger C. Park and Saks, for instance, wonder "what [might] the body of psychology and evidence law scholarship . . . have developed into, and how much sooner, if the initial encounter had not been hobbled by the overreaching of its first important contributor and the overreaction of its first important critic?"[52]

Despite Wigmore's efforts to keep the law of evidence and scientific psychology apart, one noteworthy collaboration did nevertheless emerge, led by a young Yale law professor, Robert Hutchins, who in 1926 had just begun to teach evidence. Again, Wigmore tried to scuttle the effort, not only by warning Hutchins off directly, but also writing to Yale's president to caution him about Hutchins.[53] Undeterred, Hutchins formed a collaboration with Yale psychologist Donald Slesinger, and together they wrote prolifically on psychology and evidence law.[54]

Their collaboration generated a series of law review articles in which they leveraged what was then known from psychological research to scrutinize evidence doctrine, identify weaknesses, and suggest improvements. Their articles addressed a number of evidence topics: spontaneous exclamations,[55] memory,[56] family relations,[57] witness competency,[58] state of mind to prove an act,[59] state of mind in issue,[60] and consciousness of guilt.[61] They explained: "In this series, preliminary to experimental attack, the law of evidence is being analyzed in order to make explicit its psychological assumptions, and criticise them in light of those of modern psychology."[62] Their work grew out of a wider vision of law as a kind of applied psychology:

> For centuries the law has been fumbling with what has only recently become the subject matter of psychology. Lawyers, judges, juries, legislators, and governmental officers have always vaguely known that their task was the prediction and control of human conduct. In performing this task they built up an empirical technique of regulation called the law, in every branch of which, from contracts to crimes, appear assumptions as to why and how people act in given situations. . . . Out of this technique of regulation has grown a rough and ready science of behavior which crystallized before the dawn of modern psychology.[63]

Hutchins and Slesinger were not alone in their effort to analyze the law with help from empirical social science research. Other legal scholars of the 1920s and 1930s were energized by the advent of legal realism.[64] Legal realism takes the view that law does not evolve in isolation from society but is influenced by the social, historical, political, economic, and other forces in society; and that it seeks to influence the society within which it is embedded—as well as to develop improved "legal technology" (legal rules that are more effective in achieving their goals). This description of law will strike many students today as obvious, but that is because the realists "won" the debate. When it emerged on the legal scene to challenge legal formalism—the largely nineteenth-century jurisprudential notion that the correct solutions to cases could be worked out purely by the careful application of a closed system of logic—realism was intensely controversial. The methods of the realists often involved undertaking empirical projects or borrowing knowledge from the social-behavioral-economic sciences. The early realists researched and reformed banking law,[65] procedure,[66] contracts,[67] traffic regulation, and other areas of law. The book you are now reading fits right into the heart of legal realism.

Legal realism's major projects waned during the Great Depression and World War II, although numerous realist lawyers played roles in the administration of President Franklin Roosevelt. Interdisciplinary projects have bloomed again in recent decades and some have substantially affected police and trial procedures. For example, the Arizona Supreme Court appointed a committee to determine ways to equip jurors to do their job better. The committee, which included not only lawyers but also behavioral scientists, looked into the literature of human decision making. Using research findings along with hunches, the committee developed a long list of reforms, many of which were adopted into law.[68] Among these were providing jurors with trial notebooks containing key information; allowing jurors to take notes, ask witnesses questions, and discuss the case among themselves during the trial; and giving jurors instructions at times other than at the very end of a trial. Some of these practices, the impacts of which were controversial or remained in doubt, were tested in subsequent empirical studies. Among those studies were experiments on juries in the course of actual trials in Arizona, where judicial authorities permitted researchers to observe the jurors' discussions and deliberations.[69]

Relating to erroneous convictions, one of the most interesting findings has been that forensic scientists appear to be influenced by information that is extraneous to the examination they are conducting, and sometimes reach conclusions driven by that extraneous information. One of the studies, conducted by research psychologist Itiel Dror and colleagues, presented fingerprint examiners with pairs of prints they had examined years earlier and had concluded were a positive match. On the occasion of the study, those prints were presented as a new case, and examiners were given extraneous information suggesting that the prints *did not* match. Three of five examiners switched their opinions from identification to exclusion. Findings of this kind, part of a substantial research literature on *observer effects,* has led to proposals for protocols requiring crime laboratory personnel to be shielded from extraneous information when conducting their examinations.[70]

One of the most successful recent illustrations of behavioral science research that has improved the capacity of trials to yield more accurate decisions[71] is found in the psychology of perception and memory and specific research on eyewitness identification procedures. Several decades of research have produced thousands of studies on nearly every imaginable aspect of the problem of eyewitness accuracy.[72] The insights from those studies have led to the development of a number of specific improvements in eyewitness identification procedures,[73] such as preventing witnesses from influencing each others' beliefs or officers from communicating information about the suspect's appearance to the witness, conducting sequential lineups (presenting the suspect and foils one at a time rather than all at once) to prevent errors due to people's tendency to make comparisons among those in the lineup and choose whoever comes closest to looking like the perpetrator, obtaining a statement of the witness's degree of certainty of an identification when a witness believes s/he has identified the perpetrator, among others. These improvements generally have the effect of reducing the incidence of erroneous identifications while only minimally reducing the probability of obtaining correct identifications.[74] The adoption of these and other procedures has been recommended to law enforcement agencies by the U.S. Department of Justice.[75]

## Conclusion

The rules of evidence are designed to facilitate trial factfinding by controlling what evidence may or may not be presented to the factfinder. Those rules came into existence, and evolved over time, as a result of changes in trial process and structure—most notably by the rise of adversarial procedure in the trial system, whereby the power to control the marshaling and presentation of case facts shifted from judges to lawyers. Today, various refinements and reforms are undertaken to try to improve the job that the rules do. Trial judges must not only apply the rules, but in many instances they have the discretion to make rulings in light of their expectations of the impact they think the evidence will have on jurors. This is a dicey metacognitive task: one human trying to estimate the thought processes of other humans.

In all of this, evidence rulemakers have been and are, in effect, acting as applied psychologists. The rules of evidence reflect their understanding—right or wrong—of the psychological processes affecting witnesses, key participants in the legal transaction at issue, and the capabilities and limitations of lawyers and factfinders. If the rulemakers had different beliefs about those things, the rules would be other than what they are. Psychological research and methods provide an additional source of insight and assistance in that endeavor. Several rules—the excited utterance exception to the rule against hearsay (Rule 803(2)), the rules concerning character evidence (Rule 404(a)), and the rules governing privileged communications (Rule 501)—illustrate how principles of cognitive and social psychology underlie evidence doctrine more generally.

Psychologists and other social and behavioral scientists typically employ some version of the scientific method—empirically testing assumptions, theories, and hypotheses in an effort to evaluate which are the valid understandings of how people perceive, store, and retrieve information, and how information is transformed during those processes. To assess evidence rules, one could conduct experiments directly on a given rule, or borrow from existing knowledge developed in basic psychological research and see how well that knowledge supports existing or proposed evidence rules.

Fashioning evidence rules that "work"—that succeed in what the law hopes to accomplish—requires understanding the psychology of evidence law. And to understand the psychology of evidence law, we need to learn more about jurors—their role in trials and how they reason about the information they receive.

## Overview of What Is to Come

For an overview of core concepts relating to evidence law discussed in this book and which chapters contain discussions of them, please see Appendix A.

In Chapter 1, "Judges versus Juries," we compare the factfinding abilities of judges and juries, and try to understand their similarities and differences in light of psychological principles such as the two-systems theory. Interestingly, judges and juries tend to reach very similar decisions and, perhaps not surprisingly, they are susceptible to the same systematic cognitive errors.

Chapter 2, "Balancing Acts," looks at the general rule for balancing the probative value of evidence against its prejudicial effects, as well as a number of categorical rules in which rulemakers have decided that the problem of the jury being misled is so great that judges must exclude all evidence that is defined as fitting within the rule's ambit. The great psychological challenge for rulemakers and judges is that of metacognition: trying to conceive of what others (jurors) are thinking and feeling and how they will respond to evidence if it is presented to them.

Chapter 3, "Instructions to Disregard and to Limit Use," deals with two different problems: that of undoing the damage of evidence that should not have reached the jury but did, and that of getting jurors to confine their consideration of evidence to permitted uses while at the same time refraining from employing evidence in forbidden uses. We examine psychological research on motivation, memory, and reasoning that might affect people's desire and ability to perform such feats of cognitive skill when instructed to by judges, and ways the law could be more successful in achieving the aforementioned goals.

Chapter 4, "Witness the Witness," examines the psychology of various tools the law uses to try to ensure that the information provided to the jury by witnesses can be correctly assessed as true, false, or somewhere in between. Among these tools are the oath, exposure of witness demeanor (so jurors can assess witnesses' nonverbal and noncontent verbal behavior), and cross-examination (so jurors can evaluate statements as they are tested by the opponent's challenges to the testimony). We also describe the evolution of rules about who may testify and who may assert a privilege not to testify.

In Chapter 5, "Character Evidence," we consider the psychological reasoning behind the complex of rules that govern when evidence of a person's "character" may be admitted and when it must be excluded. This body of law has been said to be "archaic, paradoxical, and full of compromises and compensations. . . . But somehow it has proved a workable, even if clumsy, system."[76] In addition, psychological findings suggest that the rulemakers had latched onto some notions that are even more sound than they ever realized.

Chapter 6, "Hearsay and Exceptions," focuses on the rationale for excluding some kinds of second-hand statements while allowing many others. A slowly growing body of psychological research suggests that jurors are better at assessing the weaknesses of out-of-court statements not subject to cross examination than centuries of rulemakers have supposed. Most important, perhaps, psychology can help identify situations that are better or worse for reliability, for finding the truth, and for jurors' understanding of the dangers of different types of hearsay evidence.

In Chapter 7, "Scientific and Other Expert Evidence," we look at the steadily growing problem the law has in managing expert testimony. Expert evidence is potentially one of the most helpful sources of information factfinders might receive; yet, at the very same time, it presents a great risk of being incomprehensible, confusing, or misleading to both judges and juries. Rules of admission or exclusion have been of little help. When junky science is passed through to jurors, they are in a very weak position to separate the good from the bad. Cognitive psychology might guide the way to new and more helpful tools. But it is also possible that the problems presented by expert evidence cannot be solved without making radical—and unacceptable—changes to our system of trials.

# PART I

# Minding the Jury

# 1

# Judges versus Juries

## *Trying the Facts*

To get a sense of what a typical American juror's experience is like, imagine taking a college course in which there is no textbook or other background reading. Where most of the information you need to learn is delivered orally, by different lecturers, whose facts and perspectives often conflict. Where you are not permitted to take notes or ask questions, and not allowed to discuss the unfolding information with anyone, including the people with whom you will have to work collaboratively on the "final exam."[1]

No doubt you are beginning to appreciate that jurors have a challenging job. They must draw conclusions from evidence that often is scanty, missing, conflicting, and only semi-organized. They must attempt to reconstruct the facts of a disputed transaction and draw inferences not only about observables but also about unobservable occurrences (e.g., intentions, knowledge, and other mental states). Traditionally, and still typically, the jury is required to listen passively to evidence (direct and cross-examination), arguments, and instructions, view exhibits, and then try to sort it all out—without taking notes, without reviewing relevant evidence presented yesterday or last week, and without asking questions or discussing the evidence with the witnesses or (until the close of evidence) with each other.

Occasionally during the trial the judge will instruct the jurors to perform feats of mental virtuosity (e.g., to use a piece of evidence for one purpose but not another). And to make it even more difficult, most of what the jury will learn about the law and the ultimate decision-making task that it has been recruited to perform will be deferred until the end of the trial, delivered by the judge in one final lecture, likely to be given in language that is at best stilted and at worst opaque. Each juror's goal, by the end of the trial, is to take the messy and disputed facts learned during the trial and create a more or less coherent narrative for his or her own use; infer necessary mental states and relationships (e.g., causation); figure out what the applicable law wants done with those facts; debate their thoughts with the other jury members; reach a collective verdict; and, in appropriate cases, award damages or impose punishment.

Judges apply the rules of evidence to regulate what the jury can hear, how they may hear it, and how they may use what they hear. In general, the rules are designed to increase the likelihood that the jurors' efforts will produce a correct and proper outcome. (See Rule 102.) But the rules express other values in addition to getting to the right decision—such as efficiency, public policy (e.g., encouraging settlements and plea agreements), protecting the privacy of victims (e.g., in rape trials), and safeguarding the confidentiality of some relationships (e.g., spouses; lawyers and clients). The various rules guarding these other values sometimes make the jurors' job even more difficult.

---

**Rule 102. Purpose**

These rules should be construed so as to administer every proceeding fairly, eliminate unjustifiable expense and delay, and promote the development of evidence law, to the end of ascertaining the truth and securing a just determination.

---

The jury's task, the judge's management of it, and the part played by the rules of evidence raise numerous questions. Why does the law think rules of evidence are needed? How do the rules of evidence affect the relationship between the judge and jury and the role each plays in trials? How important is evidence, as compared to other factors—such as the backgrounds, beliefs, and biases of the people who make up the jury? How do individual jurors, and the jury as a group, make decisions using evidence? How (and why) do the decisions of juries differ from those of judges?

## Division of Labor: How the Roles of Judge and Jury Interact

Having both a judge and a jury at trials allows for a division of labor: the judge is the "trier of law" and the jury is the "trier of fact" or "fact-finder." When there is a jury, the judge can screen evidence in ways that would not be possible for a judge sitting alone. Although in principle the rules of evidence apply regardless of whether the factfinder in a case is a judge or a jury, the practical reality is that the rules cannot be applied well in a bench trial (that is, when the presiding judge is also the factfinder). Applying the rules requires that someone (the judge) first decide whether evidence that is objected to ought to be admitted, limited in some way, or excluded altogether, and then someone else (the jury) can work their way to a verdict based only on that admitted evidence. The judge cannot do both, because in performing the first task the judge is learning the sometimes toxic facts that are supposed to be excluded from consideration. (That is, the judge is suffering from a type of mental contamination, discussed in the Introduction.) Although judges and legal theorists have long thought that judges can hear the excludable evidence and then "give it appropriate weight" (including zero weight when the rules require exclusion), empirical studies, as we shall see below, have not borne out that expectation. The jury, on the other hand, gets to focus exclusively on evidence that has passed through the judicial filter.

However, judges sitting with juries do have some judicial factual determinations to make *in the course of deciding what evidence to admit and what to exclude.*[2] Some examples are rulings on motions asking that evidence be suppressed as being in violation of the Fourth Amendment's prohibition on unreasonable search and seizure, or whether the circumstances exist that require the admission of what otherwise would be inadmissible hearsay, or whether scientific evidence achieves the degree of reliability required for it to be admissible as expert testimony. For all of these determinations, when the judge rules that exclusion is proper, the judge will be aware of the excluded evidence, but the jury will have been protected from learning it.

That said, "blindfolding" the jury to certain kinds of evidence is not always the best way to minimize the impact of inappropriate evidence.[3] When evidence can be kept from the jury without the jury being aware of the exclusion, or without the jury wondering about that issue on its own with no prompting, blindfolding should do its job effectively. But some issues will come to jurors' attention regardless of whether or not they are addressed by witnesses or the court. For example, in determining damages in a tort case, the jury will often wonder about insurance or whether to reduce damages for a plaintiff who was partly responsible for an accident. For such issues, it usually is better to explain the situation to the jurors and appeal to their duty and good sense to endeavor to reach their decision as the law has determined it should be made.[4] In other situations, where the jury becomes aware that it has been deprived of evidence that it senses would be informative in reaching their verdict, they might place a higher value on the excluded evidence than it deserves. If the jury guesses incorrectly at the content of excluded evidence, and relies on its guess, the situation is made even worse.

What at first glance might seem to be inefficient and redundant use of multiple decision makers, could instead be an ingenious use of two different decision makers—judges and juries—in ways that obtain the best service of each, and who together enable trials to be more fair than they otherwise could be.

## How Jurors and Juries Decide

In assessing the research on jury decision making, the bottom line is that despite many worries about many factors that might influence jurors in undesirable ways, the major factor affecting a jury's decision seems to be the evidence presented at trial. The most important thing for lawyers and judges and rulemakers to worry about, therefore, is the evidence.

### *Jurors versus the Evidence They Receive*

A common belief about trials is that the verdicts of juries are driven by "who they are"; that is, by the biases jurors bring with them to court. If that were so, an attorney who could shape the jury's composition to consist of more favorable jurors would have the case nearly won before the opening statements were presented. However, a substantial body of empirical research has found that, for the great majority of cases, the characteristics of the jurors make only a modest difference to the verdict, whereas the evidence and arguments presented at trial have the greatest impact.[5]

The research that has produced these findings ranges from post-trial interviews with and surveys of jurors, to studies of jury-eligible citizens sometimes conducted by parties in preparation for jury selection in trials, to experiments using mock trials that systematically vary case facts. Each type of study, in its own way, examines the relation between the characteristics of the jurors and the decisions they make about key trial issues or their verdict preferences. Those juror characteristics have included beliefs about and attitudes toward numerous background issues (e.g., attitudes toward corporations) as well as trial-specific issues, personality attributes, and demographic characteristics (e.g., age, sex, education, political affiliation, income).

Predictive power is typically calculated by measuring how much of the variation in what is to be predicted (e.g., verdicts) can be accounted for by the predictors (e.g., juror attitudes, demographics). Even by combining the best predictors together, juror characteristics have been found on average to account for only 10–15% of the variation in verdicts.[6] That leaves about 85–90% of the variance to be explained by other things, and those other things are largely the evidence and arguments presented in the case.[7]

Why would this be? Why would our impressions and intuitions about what leads people—our friends, our family, our co-workers, our classmates—to make the decisions they make not be reflected in these studies of juries? When we pause to consider the nature and circumstances of jury trials, the findings look far less surprising.

The process of assembling a jury includes eliminating those who have personal connections to, or too much familiarity with, any of the participants in the trial ("challenges for cause"). By insuring that jurors have no relationship with any of the trial participants, and therefore little probability of future interaction with those persons, the law eliminates some of the most powerful sources of influence. Typically, lawyers can also reject a number of prospective jurors whom they suspect have views contrary to the interests of their clients ("peremptory challenges"). To the extent that lawyers succeed in removing persons with the most extreme views, the jurors who remain are a more moderate mix (compared to whatever pool the selection began with). The selected jurors are then immersed in a social setting (the courtroom trial) that they have learned about from prior experience on juries or the wider culture (e.g., movies, books, news reports), which is reinforced by the judge's specific admonitions. This particular social setting emphasizes norms of neutrality, fairness, and the duty to set aside bias and to focus on evidence. That is not what life outside the courtroom is like.

Moreover, the jury is a group. Jurors have to defend and justify their views to the other jurors in light of the evidence that has been presented at the trial. Engaging in these processes can cause jurors to change their own minds as well as other jurors' minds.

But even studies of individual jurors, not just juries, suggest that the evidence carries the most weight, not the juror's initial biases. That is, different jurors tend to reach the same decisions when presented with the same evidence and arguments about the evidence. In part, this occurs because the juror's task is to solve the problem presented, to reach the correct answers based on the evidence at hand. In part, it is because many of the beliefs and biases relevant to deciding most cases are widely shared by members of a community. Thus, the research findings do not mean that people do not have attitudes and beliefs, or that their minds are blank slates before they come to the courtroom; rather, the findings suggest that people tend to have similar beliefs and biases about the issues they are assembled to resolve. Whether or not one believes in global climate change or evolution or Keynesian economics is of no relevance when deciding whether trial evidence supports the conclusion that the traffic light was red when the crash occurred or whether the defendant's firing of the gun was done negligently or purposefully.

Though the above discussion applies to the great majority of cases, it does not extend to all cases, and there are some important exceptions to the generalization that jurors are largely interchangeable. Individual factors are most likely to matter if cases are close, if they involve non-common knowledge, or if personal attributes are an issue.

If the evidence is close, then juror characteristics and predispositions become more important to the trial's outcome. When people make decisions, and a factor that would normally have a lot of influence (such as evidence) is, in effect, missing (because evidence is either lacking or is closely in balance), then weaker variables are more able to make themselves felt.[8] In some kinds of cases the evidence is inherently close. For example, in cases of rape where the defense is consent, jurors often have little to go on other than the testimony of the defendant and the complaining witness—what he says versus what she says. In such cases, a set of beliefs referred to as *rape myths* are rather good at predicting how a juror will vote, and questions about those have been assembled into a questionnaire that (sometimes) can be asked of prospective jurors.[9]

If the evidence involves technical subjects, or requires more subtle reasoning, better-educated jurors tend to make more accurate decisions than jurors with less education, and jurors with specific training in the subject matter at issue will tend to make more accurate decisions than equally well educated jurors trained in other subject matters.[10] In other words, and not surprisingly, those who understand medicine make better sense of medical evidence, whereas those who understand statistics make better sense of statistical evidence.

Still another exception to jurors being interchangeable is when personal attributes are made an issue in the case. The most familiar and most troubling example is when race or ethnicity becomes an issue: Did the police go after the defendant because of his race? Did the defendant attack the victim out of prejudice related to the victim's nationality? A case that does not otherwise raise such issues can be turned into a racially divisive case by counsel—sometimes referred to as "playing the race card"—or by the news media. Jurors do not generally align into racial, ethnic, and other groupings. In a case involving police misconduct where race was heavily discussed by media, when reporters interviewed jurors afterward, the journalists were surprised to learn that the jurors had split not by race, but by age—older jurors trusted the police more than younger jurors did.[11] But when circumstances render jurors' own group identities salient by making those identities an important part of the controversy, people find it hard to resist the invitation to associate themselves with the side that shares their own group identity.

For the most part, however, evidence is what drives most jurors most of the time to make the decisions they do. This is true despite the attempts of lawyers to use various persuasion techniques.

### *How Lawyers Convince Jurors: The Psychology of Influence and Persuasion*

Though litigators are rightly thought of as dedicated professional persuaders, often overlooked is how effectively the rules of evidence and procedure limit the lawyer's options in trials. Lawyers are forced to employ the least powerful—and most informative—means of persuasion. Perhaps the best way to understand this is to appreciate what techniques of influence have been found to be *most* persuasive.

Robert Cialdini, a social psychologist specializing in persuasion, has studied people whose jobs are to persuade others to believe something, to buy something, or to otherwise behave in certain ways. He examined the strategies and tactics of people engaged in such activities as sales, politics, and religious proselytizing, as well as psychological research and theory, to better understand and explain the most effective persuasion techniques. In his best-selling book, *Influence*, Cialdini crystallized the techniques into six "weapons of influence."[12] Most of these principles of persuasion require direct back-and-forth interaction with the target of persuasion. That kind of contact is available to many people trying to influence others: parents, religious leaders, politicians, salespeople, teachers, and others. But not to lawyers in trials.

The most potent weapon of influence is *reciprocation*: people more readily comply with requests (for favors, information, contributions, concessions, etc.) from those who have previously provided something to them. Attorneys cannot do favors for or give gifts to jurors, or treat them to lunch. The second most potent weapon is *commitment and consistency*: people more readily change their opinion in a particular direction if they see it as consistent with an existing recent commitment. The challenge, therefore, is first to get people to make a small commitment in the desired direction; they will then be more willing to take the larger step that you want them to take. Attorneys certainly cannot obtain from jurors public behavioral commitments that are favorable to one side.

The next two weapons rely on the status of the person who uses them. The principle of *authority* is that people are more willing to follow the directions or recommendations of a communicator whom they perceive as having relevant authority or expertise. Jurors might believe that attorneys are authorities—but there are attorneys on both sides. Issues of following authority are more likely to come up with judges—who are the real authorities in the room—or experts who are viewed as the most knowledgeable people regarding specific subjects. *Social proof* is the concept that people are more willing to take a requested or suggested course of action if they see others, especially others similar to themselves, doing so. Lawyers cannot deploy people to share their favorable views with the jurors. Indeed, jurors typically are instructed to avoid learning what anyone else thinks about the case they are in the process of deciding. Lawyers themselves might be torn over whether to appear to jurors as authorities or as people "just like them." But social validation is more likely to come into play among jury members, as they look to each other to try to decide what the truth is.

*Scarcity* is another weapon of influence: people find objects, activities, and information more attractive to the extent that those things are seen as scarce or declining in availability. A salesman might say, "There are only two of this product left" or "The sale lasts only until tomorrow." How to apply this tactic in a trial is not apparent. However, a notion similar to scarcity might come into play when jurors are asked to ignore some evidence. Finally, there is *liking*: people are more inclined to comply with the wishes of those they know and like than to strangers or people they know but dislike. Lawyers can't directly employ this weapon because jurors who are friends of one (or more) of the lawyers will be dismissed from the jury panel. But they might try in subtle ways to get jurors to like them.

If you think about each of the most effective principles of influence and how you might employ them as a litigator, you will discover that it is not easy to find ways to use them in trials. Thus, at best, a clever lawyer can find a way to employ only weak versions of Cialdini's weapons of influence. This situation might strike litigators as a regrettable state of affairs, but it serves the purposes of trials rather well. The "weapons" that are blocked by the rules of evidence and procedure employ psychological forces that are irrelevant to the factual issues of the trial. Whether a juror owes a reciprocal obligation to someone, or has been maneuvered into committing herself to a prior stance with which she feels she must remain consistent, or is led to believe that numerous other people have adopted a certain belief—all are irrelevant to the rational resolution of the various disputed facts. In other words, the rules that govern the trial have the effect of blocking or dampening the use of influence techniques that do not contribute to the (relatively) rational resolution of the disputed issues. In their effort to make trials more information-based and more rational, the rulemakers have done quite well by limiting the possibilities for using the most powerful tools of persuasion and influence.

What, then, can a lawyer do to persuade the jury? The answer is that a lawyer can present evidence. Or attack evidence. Or present counter-evidence. And can do so using more or less effective presentation methods. But the focus is on factual information, not on deploying social influences that are not relevant to the truth of the disputed issues. The contest for the hearts and minds of the jury is fought on a more constrained battlefield, where relevant evidence has been made paramount.

### *The Psychology of Juror Decision Making*

How do jurors hear and use evidence? Consider the flow of information to jurors as well as the content of the information. Jurors receive a lot of disparate facts and quite often evidence comes to them in bundles that are not well organized for comprehension as a chronological narrative would be, or a straightforward theory of how X caused Y. The question-and-answer format used in trials is more difficult to follow than a narrative description. But trials are conducted in that format for compelling reasons. The examining lawyer needs to maintain control over the evidence that is emerging, the opposing side needs an opportunity to object before the testimony comes pouring out, and the judge needs an opportunity to rule on objections as required by the rules of evidence. Thus, the pattern and the process by which testimony is elicited is an accommodation to the evidence rules. Moreover, attorneys might call witnesses in an order that is less than logical for telling the story—sometimes as a result of strategic choices (for example, putting the witness who observed the terrifying events first, or saving an articulate expert witness for last) or simply because of the vicissitudes of scheduling. Furthermore, one witness might have a number of different facts to relate, which bear on several different aspects of the case. These practical constraints on the flow of information in the trial add to the difficulty of the jury's task.[13]

The great majority of research on human decision makers is focused on individuals who are given information about which they are asked to form judgments, draw inferences, or reach conclusions. The question is: how do people's perceptions, inferences, and decisions change in response to differing information? The decisions that people make in response to different information can be compared to each other: do some kinds of information, from certain sources, expressed in certain ways, produce more judgments of "guilt" or larger damage awards than other types?

### HEURISTICS IN DECISION MAKING

A large body of research has shown that because even a small amount of information presents cognitive challenges to decision makers, we all take cognitive shortcuts. These help us get near a correct solution most of the time, but also can lead us far astray. This research—important enough to earn a Nobel Prize for one of the psychologists who launched the work—generally referred to as *heuristics*, has involved studies of many of these cognitive shortcuts, or biases (meaning tendencies toward certain kinds of cognitive processing).[14] Heuristics reveal that people's judgments and inferences about a person or an event are systematically affected by a number of aspects of the way the information is delivered or obtained from memory. These include: the way the event is framed (e.g., presented as a gain or a loss); the ease with which information is retrieved from memory; the similarity of an individual instance to a larger category of which it is assumed to be representative; and reliance on anchoring to a particular piece of information (such as an amount of money requested by a party in a case), before adjusting from that anchor to form estimates. These phenomena will be discussed in more detail later in the chapter.

### INTEGRATING INFORMATION

But deciding a case involves more than evaluating individual pieces of information; the numerous and discombobulated arrays of facts presented at trial need to be integrated into a more or less coherent whole by the jurors. There are two main ways to think about how juries integrate information: updating the believability of a story by adding the weight of individual pieces of evidence, or as a more holistic process of fitting pieces into a story.

A variety of different lines of psychological research are concerned with the first of those processes—how people combine bits of information into a final judgment. Studies have found, for example, that a single list of items of information will result in different final judgments depending upon the order of the items. Other studies have found that the attributes used to describe people are not separate and independent psychologically—the presence of one influences the meaning of another, and some of them spread their influence more widely than others (these are termed "central traits"). Put most generally, the meaning of information shifts when it is in the company of other information. For example, the statement that "the tree of liberty must be watered from time to time with the blood of patriots and tyrants" is interpreted and evaluated very differently depending upon whether its author is said to be Thomas Jefferson or Vladimir Lenin.

Sometimes it is possible for researchers to calculate what the mathematically correct inference is from certain items of evidence, such as probabilities based on DNA profiles, and what impact that should have on verdicts. Because of the heavy use of heuristics, among other reasons, people often do not conform their decision making to models of ideal rational decision making. The most prominent theory bearing on ideal inferences from evidence is Bayes' Theorem.[15] Named after Thomas Bayes, a minister and mathematician who developed the concept in the seventeenth century, the theorem deals with the situation in which decision makers update, perhaps repeatedly, their initial estimation of the probability that a certain conclusion is true. That should sound something like the task of a factfinder in a trial, presented with unfolding evidence. At any given point in the trial, a decision maker has an estimation of the likelihood that a certain conclusion, such as the guilt of the defendant, is true (called the *prior probability*); the decision maker is provided with additional evidence (reflected in the theorem as a *likelihood ratio*), which enables a revision of that estimation, increasing or decreasing the estimate of the probability of guilt (called the *posterior probability*). Bayes' Theorem has been used to model the concept of relevance in Rule 401—which, in part, states that a fact is relevant if "it has any tendency to make a fact more or less probable than it would be without the evidence"—and to argue for solutions to evidentiary problems facing trial factfinders.[16] Humans are not, however, intuitive Bayesians, and the extent to which conclusions that emerge from Bayesian models should be explicitly presented to juries is controversial.

Although lawyers and judges sometimes talk in terms of discrete items of evidence having weights or probabilities that must be integrated, they also think of trials as presentations of more or less complete and competing stories. Similarly, psychological studies dating back quite a few decades find that information presented "in context," with semantic meaning, as parts of stories, is much easier to remember and has greater impact on inferences and judgments. Think about how much easier it is to recall a coherent story, or even a coherent sentence, than a license plate number or a collection of random letters or words. As noted earlier, our minds seek patterns and coherence; that tells us something about how best to communicate in trials.

As obvious as the storytelling aspect of a trial is, the first systematic effort by psychological researchers to study the trial as a setting in which lawyers offer competing narratives of disputed events and where jurors try to make sense of the evidence in terms of stories is relatively recent. The "story model" of jury decision making suggests that jurors try to understand the evidence by constructing a story with it, and evaluating competing stories by testing which holds the evidence most coherently.[17] If the lawyers do not propose explicit stories, jurors will invent their own. Here is how one psychologist described the process:

> [The juror] organizes individual facts (or things that the juror believes to be facts) and the relations among facts into a causal structure that explains how the events in question came about. . . . In the simplest version of the story model a fact or a relationship is either in the structure or not in the structure; in other words, the individual elements are discrete. These structures are built by the juror and at some point (or several points in time) compared with "verdict structures" that represent the alternative verdicts in the choice set, and the fit of the two structures (story and verdict) to one another is assessed. The judgment of guilt or innocence is therefore a pattern-matching process.[18]

As the quotation suggests, the story also is fitted to the array of possible legal outcomes. For example, which verdict (first degree murder, manslaughter, self-defense, no conviction at all) has the best fit to the story that is best supported by the evidence?

Although defendants (criminal or civil) are best off providing an alternative story of their own,[19] sometimes the defendant can win by destroying the coherence of the other side's story, rather than needing to put forward an alternative story of their own. For example, a criminal defense attorney could win an acquittal by giving the factfinders reason to disbelieve one vital fact of a case, such as that the perpetrator in the prosecution's otherwise coherent story could not be the defendant (he was in a different geographic location when the crime occurred), or that the supposed murder victim was not murdered (the victim died from a cause that precludes homicide). That a major disruption of the coherence of a story can destroy its persuasiveness fits well with the legal burdens of the parties because the defense in both civil and criminal cases need only successfully challenge the plaintiff's or prosecution's version of the facts in order to avoid a verdict against their client.

## The Psychology of Jury Decision Making: From Individuals to Groups

Understanding how individuals use the evidence of a trial to reach decisions, and the psychology of judgment and decision making, is important. But we must also be aware that in addition to the cognitive processes of individuals perceiving evidence, evaluating it, and deciding the case, jury decision making involves the social processes of people interacting to combine their individual beliefs and preferences into a group decision. The processes by which a group, like a jury, works suggest some of its actual and potential advantages.

A deliberating jury might come to a different—and better—decision than a single juror (or even an individual judge) for a number of different reasons, including the averaging of information, the aggregation of information, the suppression of individual jurors' biases, and the necessity of engaging in System 2 deliberative reasoning.

Twelve people are better than one for the same reason that 12 thermometers are better than one—if they did nothing other than average their individual best estimates of the correct answer, erroneous extremes would be diluted and something closer to a correct answer would be reached.

But people bring psychological as well as statistical advantages to the task. Twelve (or 8 or 6) heads are better than one because they possess more knowledge, experiences, and information processing resources. They can aggregate their memory—if 11 forget an important fact but one remembers, that can become part of the group's pool of knowledge about the evidence in the case. Group members can correct each other's errors. Groups seem to produce more accurate recollections of the evidence than individuals do.[20] On the other hand, this improved performance on facts does not seem to apply so well to comprehension of the judge's instructions. Judicial instructions frequently are incomprehensible to non-lawyers, and the jury's discussion of them does not seem to improve matters—indeed, some studies have found that deliberation worsens the jury's understanding of the law.[21] The process of deliberating as a group also has the effect of attenuating, though not eliminating, biases held by individual jurors (a form of *debiasing*).

One important difference between group and individual decision making is that in a group people need to express their beliefs and reasoning to others, which subjects them to scrutiny and the possibility of correction of errors. Any one of us, keeping our beliefs and reasons in the privacy of our own head, might arrive at a conclusion too quickly, too easily and perhaps incorrectly. If I must explain my thinking to the group, I will need to think harder and more clearly (thus being compelled to employ System 2 cognitive processing)[22] in order to convince the others. And vice versa. In the process, I might recognize some errors in my own thinking.

There are, of course, limits to the generalization that groups make more accurate decisions than individuals (and that larger groups make better decisions than smaller groups). Eventually, the process of working as a group requires so much more time, attention, and interaction, and introduces noise and confusion, that the burdens of the process exceed the benefits, and poorer decisions result. But there is no evidence that groups as large as 12 suffer from such deficits when engaged in typical factfinding.[23]

Jury deliberations have been found to follow one of two different strategies.[24] Some juries begin by taking a vote to see how the members divide on the central questions of the trial. They then coalesce into factions based on that vote, and discuss and debate which side is correct. These have been termed *verdict-driven* deliberations. Most juries, however, adopt an *evidence-driven* deliberation style. These juries proceed by first trying to systematically review the evidence to try to reach agreement about who did what to whom, how, and perhaps why.

Because verdict-driven deliberations focus on points of disagreement, they tend not to review and consider as many of the facts of the case as evidence-driven deliberations. Also, because individuals have announced their positions, formed factions of believers, and defended their positions against the opposing faction, they have a harder time letting go of their positions and therefore a harder time reaching the necessary consensus. These findings suggest that it would be desirable for judges to give instructions encouraging jurors to delay taking their first vote until after they review the evidence.

In any event, by the close of the trial, individual members of the jury have arrived at their own beliefs about the facts and their own notions about what the correct verdict should be. Their differences will have to be reconciled if the group is to reach sufficient agreement to deliver a verdict. If they've taken votes, and there is substantial disagreement, some votes will have to change or no verdict will be possible. The jurors exchange information, reason about the facts, and offer arguments.

Though the group decision process generates more information sharing, more emotion, and more disagreement than goes on when individuals decide alone, the eventual outcome is largely predictable from the distribution of individual preferences that exists before the start of deliberation.[25] In their landmark research on juries, the eminent legal scholar Harry Kalven and Hans Zeisel, a lawyer, statistician, and social scientist, offered this graphic, if now dated, metaphor: jury decision making is like developing a photograph—though the process must unfold to achieve the result, the result is in considerable part determined by what occurred before the process began.

Numerous studies have found fairly strong majority effects—once a majority favoring a position exceeds a certain size, their preference is likely to become the group decision.[26] This finding is at least in part an illustration of *social validation*: as noted earlier, we are persuaded that something is true because other people believe it.[27] The greater the tilt toward the majority's position, the more likely that view will become the group's verdict.[28] Studies suggest that in criminal trials the critical threshold for conviction is a proportion of between .75 and .83 favoring conviction, whereas the critical threshold for acquittal is between .67 and .50. In other words, if 7 or fewer jurors out of 12 favor conviction at the beginning of deliberation, the jury will probably acquit. If 10 or more jurors believe the defendant is guilty, the jury will probably convict. When 8 or 9 jurors initially favor conviction, the final verdict can go either way.[29] An even better predictor of the final outcome is the distribution of individual preferences that exists after the first shift in votes.

As one faction begins to gain members and the other loses members, the pace with which jurors desert the minority faction increases.

While recognizing that "[w]e know that the distribution of individual jurors' predeliberation verdict preferences is a strong predictor of the jury's final verdict," social psychologists Jessica Salerno and Shari Diamond point out that a lot more could usefully be learned about how the jury gets from the individual views of jurors to a collective decision. Majorities do not always prevail; sometimes dissenters turn the majority around or prevent the group from reaching a verdict (resulting in a hung jury in nearly 10% of cases). Why are majorities influential—because the minority yields to the majority or because of a meaningful discussion that persuades the minority that the majority's facts and interpretations and assessments are correct? What are the cognitive processes through which the group deliberation produces (or fails to produce) those changes? Put simply: during deliberation, what happens to the thinking of the various jurors, and when does what happens make a difference to the outcome?[30]

Sometimes sheer social pressure is brought to bear on a holdout to join the majority so a verdict can be reached. That is to say, once rational persuasion has failed to do the job, one or two remaining holdouts are urged to go along with the group for reasons that are less than rationally based on the evidence—because a large majority must be correct, or just for the sake of getting it over with. It is not unusual for post-deliberation questionnaires or interviews to find that one or a few jurors did not agree with the verdict, but went along. Overt pressure usually is not needed because, as research on conformity has found, people find it quite difficult to stand up to the majority when they have little support. A single individual has little chance of holding out against an otherwise unanimous majority.

By the end, the deliberation usually has not only produced a verdict, but has also changed jurors' opinions and perspectives. The collective view of the central issues in the trial will have become more extreme than the average of the views held before deliberation. This is the *group polarization phenomenon*. At the same time that the group exerts a moderating force, influencing outliers to change their views to be more like the rest of the group, the entire group shifts further in the direction preferred by the majority of the group.[31]

## Comparing Judge and Jury Decision Making

Americans, including American law students, are often astonished to learn that the majority of litigated disputes are not decided by juries. When considering trials throughout the world, the United States is an outlier—it is the only country that grants jury trials for nearly all civil cases, and one of only a handful of countries that grants jury trials for all criminal cases. The great majority of criminal cases filed in state and federal courts, about 96%, are disposed of other than through a trial.[32] Similarly, 99% of civil cases filed in the U.S. are resolved through motions and negotiated settlements rather than by trial.[33] Of the cases that go to trial, 32% of civil cases[34] and 23% of (federal) criminal cases[35] are decided by judges sitting alone rather than by juries. Thus, it is important to ask about differences between judges and juries as factfinders. Let's consider how juries and judges differ in ways that *could* affect their factfinding, and what differences actually have been revealed in practice.

### *Why Judges and Juries Might Differ*

What might be expected to lead to differences in factfinding? An analysis by one of the authors of this book identified three categories of differences:

> First, there might be relevant "individual differences": judges might differ from jurors a priori in relevant ways such as being smarter or less emotional. Second, institutional roles may matter: judges are elected or appointed whereas jurors are drafted; plus judges are "repeat players" and have more accountability for their decisions. Finally, expertise may play a role: judges may differ from jurors due to their training in law, to their previous experience of judging, or both.[36]

The average judge generally is smarter than the average juror. But the judge is not necessarily smarter than the smartest juror, especially in a jurisdiction that has adopted jury selection procedures that require virtually everyone in the community to serve. Moreover, juries will have a wider pool of knowledge and experience than any one person—even a judge—has to draw upon.

Are judges less subject to the heuristics and biases that plague ordinary reasoners like jurors? Jeffrey Rachlinski, Chris Guthrie, and Andrew Wistrich—respectively, a law professor with a Ph.D. in psychology, a legal scholar, and a federal magistrate judge—have conducted a series of studies specifically testing the susceptibility of judges to the same heuristics that have been found among lay decision makers.[37] The researchers cleverly embedded their tests in legal tasks that a judge normally would perform. For example, in an exercise where judges were asked to advise parties on settlement, as part of a motion by one of the parties, some were presented with a number irrelevant to the settlement amount—which served as an anchor—while others received no anchor. (*Anchoring* is the phenomenon whereby any number, even an irrelevant number, draws a decision maker's judgment toward that number—so that high anchors produce higher judgments and low anchors produce lower judgments.) In another study, susceptibility to gain-loss framing was tested by having judges suggest a settlement amount after viewing a problem from either the plaintiff's perspective (thus looking at a potential gain) or from the defendant's perspective (thus looking at a potential loss). Suffice it to say that the results of these studies provided evidence that judges are human decision makers, too.

Are judges better able to discern the truthfulness of witnesses than jurors are? Assessing credibility is considered to be a major task of a factfinder during trial, and the law entrusts that to the jury (in a jury trial). Judges might be thought superior because they frequently get to listen to testimony. If it is possible to learn which witnesses are telling the truth and which are lying simply by listening to and observing them during their testimony, judges have more opportunity to do so. On the other hand, a dozen jurors bring a lot of varied experience in dealing with numerous kinds of people in many different situations. Studies of judges' accuracy in assessing credibility are hard to come by, but one of the few tested the accuracy of judges (along with police officers and other kinds of professionals) in assessing the credibility of video-recorded speakers who were either telling the truth or lying. All of the tested groups performed approximately at chance levels (that is, they might as well have made their decisions by tossing a coin).[38] One problem shared by judges, jurors, and the rest of us is that no one gets much feedback on our judgments about whether someone is telling the truth or not, so it is difficult to learn when we are right and when we are wrong, which is necessary if our lie-detection skills are to improve.

The most obvious difference between judges and jurors is that judges are trained in the law while jurors rarely are. But it is hard to see why knowledge of substantive law would enhance one's skill in understanding the facts of a situation. On the other hand, we should not be surprised if judges prove better at applying the law to a set of facts. Moreover, knowing the rules of evidence, and what they are designed to achieve, might cause a judge to be more *willing* to follow a rule, such as disregarding inadmissible evidence.[39] Of course, that assumes judges are *able* to mentally exclude evidence they recognize as inadmissible.

Might there be something about legal training, or legal practice, or sitting as a judge that enhances one's factfinding skills? Legal education does little that trains people in factfinding of the kind encountered at trials, or even in fact gathering. Most cases in most law classes consist of predigested case facts, which serve as a point of departure for discussing the legal doctrine that is the main point of the great majority of law school classes. Law practice and judicial practice bring one much closer to engagement with facts.

On the other hand, a judge's training in law typically means that the judge lacks formal training in other subjects. Depending on the factual issues involved in a case, factfinding might benefit from having knowledge of economics or health care or auto repair or mathematics or retail sales or science. The chances of a jury having members with relevant factual expertise are much greater than the chances of one judge being an expert on everything. Moreover, members of the jury likely are collectively more familiar with the wider community, its people, its customs, and its practices, than a judge is. Such knowledge could be useful in assessing the credibility of various different kinds of witnesses, in understanding general circumstances on the ground in a community, and so on.

In short, one can think of reasons to expect juries to be less able factfinders than judges, to be approximately equal, or even to better than judges. It might be that for some kinds of cases, involving some kinds of factual disputes and some kinds of evidence, judges will be better, while in other kinds, juries will be better. Empirical research is necessary to answer such questions.

### *Empirical Studies Comparing Decisions by Judges and Juries*

Unfortunately, not many studies have been carried out directly comparing judges and jurors on the same trial-type factfinding tasks where they are reacting to the same evidence in the same cases. Based on the studies that have been done, the short answer thus far is that judges and juries are most noteworthy for the similarities—not the differences—between their factfinding and decision making. Much like jurors, judges have difficulty setting aside information they are supposed to disregard,[40] falling prey to the same cognitive errors.[41] Moreover, judges and juries usually reach the same verdicts.[42]

The best-known empirical research on juries is the work of Kalven and Zeisel, sometimes referred to as the Chicago Jury Project.[43] Conducted in the 1950s, the research compared the verdicts rendered by juries in actual cases to the decisions that the trial judges in those same cases said they would have made if the cases had been adjudicated in bench trials. Their study sent questionnaires to thousands of judges throughout the United States who were presiding over criminal and civil trials. The judges were asked to complete their questionnaires before the jury verdicts came in—describing the evidence, evaluating the case, and stating what verdict the judge would render if the case were being tried to the judge alone.

Their findings for criminal cases, omitting the 5% of juries that deadlocked, are presented in Table 1.1. The most noteworthy result is that judges and juries agreed on the verdict in 78% of the cases (14% both acquitted; 64% both convicted). Kalven and Zeisel characterized these findings as showing enough agreement to give us confidence in the jury system, and enough disagreement to make things interesting. As the table shows, both judges and juries were much more likely to convict than to acquit (judges convicted in 83% of cases, juries in 67% of cases). When they disagreed, juries were more likely than judges to acquit (19% to 3%). This is, incidentally, a higher rate of agreement than has been found in numerous other decision-making tasks on which society depends.[44]

Several replications in later decades have tested whether Kalven and Zeisel's findings are reflected in the decisions of contemporary judges and juries. All of the replications obtained results that approximated those of Kalven and Zeisel, some more closely than others. One of those studies, carried out 50 years after Kalven and Zeisel's landmark project,

TABLE 1.1. Judge-Jury Agreement (%) in Criminal Cases

| | | Juries | |
|---|---|---|---|
| | | Acquit | Convict |
| Judges | Acquit | 14 | 3 |
| | Convict | 19 | 64 |

Based on Kalven and Zeisel (1966)

obtained results that duplicated the percentages in the table above almost exactly.[45]

Kalven and Zeisel were interested in accounting for the 22% of cases in which the judge and jury reached different verdicts. One factor that explained very little of the disagreement was the possibility that the jury had not understood the evidence. That conclusion of general jury competence—even when they and the judge disagreed on the verdict—is based in part on judges' assessments of the reasonableness of the juries' verdicts in light of the evidence. It was further supported by the finding that when the cases were divided into those with the most complex evidence and those with the least complex evidence, the agree-disagree rates did not change. This finding implies that juries understood the more complex cases as well as the judges did; had comprehension been the problem, the disagreement rate would have increased as complexity increased.

However, just because judges and juries disagree does not mean that it is the judges who "got it right." After conducting a variety of analyses with the data they received from the judges' questionnaires, Kalven and Zeisel concluded that the principal causes of judge-jury disagreement were that judges sometimes knew facts that the law required to be withheld from the jury, different evaluations of the evidence, juror sentiments about the defendant, juror disagreement with the law, and differing thresholds of reasonable doubt (jurors tended to demand more of prosecution evidence than judges did).

Let's not overlook what is on the other side of the coin from judge-jury disagreement about verdict. What is the reason for so much *agreement*? The most obvious answer is that the judge and the jury were watching, hearing, and responding to the same case. In other words, where the evidence was the same, these two very different decision makers usually found the same facts and reached the same verdicts.

This conclusion is further supported by another analysis done by Kalven and Zeisel. When they divided the cases into those evaluated by the judges as clear versus those that were close, the rate of disagreement was higher when the evidence was close. Think about what would happen if the evidence in a case was so close that it sat right on the line dividing proof beyond a reasonable doubt and proof not beyond a reasonable doubt—like a tennis ball balancing momentarily on the net, ready to fall in either direction. Under such circumstances, we would expect any set of decision makers—judges versus other judges as well as judges versus juries—to disagree more often. Put simply: the closer the evidence, the less agreement among decision makers; the clearer the evidence, the more agreement.

Civil cases in Kalven and Zeisel's research showed a similar level of overall agreement between judges and juries. In 78% of the cases the judge and jury agreed on the verdict (47% of the time both found for the plaintiff; 31% of the time both found for the defendant). When they disagreed, there was little tendency for juries or judges to be more favorable to plaintiffs or defendants.[46]

## Conclusion

Having both a judge and a jury creates a valuable division of labor—the former to decide what evidence should be considered by the factfinder and the latter to be that factfinder. This partnership enables evidence to be put to its best use, which a single decision maker would not be capable of.

The origins and purpose of the rules of evidence are found in the interconnected roles played by judge, jury, and especially lawyers. The rules of evidence came into being when control of the development and presentation of cases passed from judges to the lawyers on either side of a dispute—that is, when our trial process became truly adversarial. Common law judges then apparently thought that adversarial lawyers needed to be reined in, and the rules of evidence were the reins. That is an insight of legal historians.

A related insight from psychology suggests that the rules of evidence (and other rules of procedure) have been quite successful in accomplishing that purpose. That insight comes from comparing the kinds of persuasion and influence that research has found to be the most powerful in life more generally to the kinds of persuasion and influence legal rules permit adversarial lawyers to exercise in trials. What that comparison reveals is that the rules of trials have deprived lawyers of the most powerful tools of persuasion, and designed the trial process to make information the center of the decision making that is to occur. Thus, the rules have evolved to prevent lawyers from using the most socially influential yet informationally empty techniques of influence, thereby compelling lawyers to present to juries nothing but *evidence*. Whatever strategies and tactics lawyers employ to sway the jury, those are narrowly confined compared to what social psychology has found to be possible. And that is a good thing if we want jurors to make rational decisions based on relevant evidence.

In responding to that evidence, judges and jurors reach the same verdicts in four-fifths of the cases that are concluded by a trial—suggesting that, despite their considerable differences, judges and jurors mostly evaluate evidence the same way. Relatedly, studies of individual differences among jurors, often with jury selection in mind, have found that in the great majority of cases, differences among jurors make little difference to the outcomes. What makes a far greater difference in their decisions is the evidence with which they are presented.

None of which is to say the task is easy. Jurors face challenges to understanding, remembering, evaluating, inferring from, and using the evidence (in conjunction with the law) to reach conclusions about vigorously disputed issues. And then jurors must argue with each other about their competing views in order to combine their individual attitudes and beliefs into a collective decision. Decision making as a group has certain advantages over working as an individual—groups possess more cognitive and social resources such as wider background knowledge and experience, the ability of multiple minds to remember, to correct each other's errors, to think about the meaning of the evidence, and so on.

In all of this, evidence (information) is of supreme importance. That being the case, what evidence comes in and what evidence is kept out, and how jurors process, evaluate, and use that information, will be primarily responsible for the verdicts reached. The rest of this book takes a closer look at the major evidence rules, the psychology behind them, and the psychology of how they affect jurors' (and judges') thinking and deciding about the evidence.

2

# Balancing Acts

"Your Honor, we would like to introduce Exhibit 1—pictures of the crime scene after the shooting." "Objection! More prejudicial than probative."

For evidence to be allowed in, it must first pass the threshold test of relevance: will it tell the factfinder something useful about the case? But even evidence that is obviously relevant is almost always subject to a balancing test. The most common and general balancing test is found in Rule 403, illustrated in the dialogue above. In using Rule 403, the judge must evaluate the "probative value" of the evidence, which weighs in favor of admission, against the sum of other factors that weigh against admission. For those latter factors, the judge must guess how the jury would be affected by the information. Because experienced judges are likely to consider evidence differently from inexperienced jurors, judges must use their metacognitive skills to guess what jurors would infer from the evidence.

---

**Rule 403. Excluding Relevant Evidence for Prejudice, Confusion, Waste of Time, or Other Reasons**

The court may exclude relevant evidence if its probative value is substantially outweighed by a danger of one or more of the following: unfair prejudice, confusing the issues, misleading the jury, undue delay, wasting time, or needlessly presenting cumulative evidence.

The most important factor weighing against admission is unfair prejudice. In one sense, all relevant evidence is intended to prejudice jurors toward one side or the other. But unfair prejudice takes into account the risk that jurors will weigh the evidence improperly and then, perhaps, end up making a decision on improper grounds. The law has a special concern that highly emotional evidence will lead jurors astray, resulting in verdicts that are based on emotion rather than reason; however, recent psychology research suggests that emotion is not always incompatible with good reasoning, a view that contrasts starkly with the philosophy behind Rule 403.

Although Rule 403 applies to most evidence, the rules also include other balancing tests that pose different requirements for how much one side of the balance must outweigh the other in order for the evidence to be admitted. Rule 609 sets out several distinct balancing tests for the admissibility of a witness's prior convictions as evidence of current veracity. The "categorical exclusion rules" (Rules 407–411) reveal the rulemakers' concerns that (for psychological or policy reasons) the probative value of some evidence will always be outweighed by its prejudicial effect—at least for some purposes. In such cases, the judge need only decide whether the proffered evidence fits the excluded category and is offered for the excluded purpose. If so, the evidence is automatically excluded. But lawyers may to try to get such evidence admitted for other, allowed purposes, drawing the judge back into the balancing game.

## The General Rule of 403

Many evidence rules we discuss in this book are psychologically interesting because they raise the questions:

(a) What is the *actual* probative value of the evidence (e.g., do people really behave in accordance with evidence of their character; is a statement "made while under the stress of excitement"[1] more likely to be true)?
(b) How probative will the jury *think* the evidence is (i.e., will the jury give it the appropriate weight given its actual probative value)?
(c) Did the rulemakers, whether courts or legislatures, "get it right" when creating the rule?

For most of those rules, the judge's task is simply to decide whether the evidence fits a particular category under the rule (e.g., Is this evidence character evidence? Does this relationship meet the requirements for a privilege?). Then the rule prescribes whether the evidence is admissible.

But balancing tests are especially psychologically interesting because they also involve judgments by judges who must, in the midst of a trial, consider the actual value of a particular piece of evidence as well as how that evidence *might* affect jurors. That is, the judge needs to determine the probative value of this specific evidence and how likely it would be to cause jurors to reason badly if it were admitted. Hence, in addition to the three questions above, we would also like to know:

(d) Can judges, or anyone, accurately and objectively assess these reasoning processes in others? (Recall Figure I.2.)
(e) Even more tenuously, can judges evaluate whether the evidence would actually cause the jury—with deliberation—to reason well or badly?

### *For Admission: Probative Value*

To get a piece of evidence into a trial at all, it must pass the minimum threshold of relevance. Rule 402 states, with no qualifications, "Irrelevant evidence is not admissible." Rule 401 states that, to be relevant, evidence must make a consequential fact more or less probable. The facts can be more or less distant from the events in question as long as they might affect the factfinder's belief in the probability of the fact. As examples: Was the defendant at the crime scene? Did the victim know the accountant? Is this witness telling the truth? Note that testimony about whether a witness is likely to be telling the truth is not testimony directly about the events in question; instead, because evidence is presented by witnesses rather than directly perceived by jurors, evidence that helps jurors to evaluate whether a witness is telling the truth or lying is evidence that also makes a fact more or less probable.

---

**Rule 401. Test for Relevant Evidence**

Evidence is relevant if:

(a) it has any tendency to make a fact more or less probable than it would be without the evidence; and
(b) the fact is of consequence in determining the action.

---

**Rule 402. General Admissibility of Relevant Evidence**

Relevant evidence is admissible unless any of the following provides otherwise:

the United States Constitution;

a federal statute;

other rules prescribed by the Supreme Court.

Irrelevant evidence is not admissible.

Once evidence is determined to be relevant, it is then subject to various other rules, including balancing tests. In all of the balancing rules, the probative value of the evidence weighs toward admission. Probative value is a quantification of relevance—it asks (a) if the evidence is what it claims to be, then (b) *how* useful is the evidence in making a consequential fact more or less probable. Is it just a tiny bit probative (because the evidence is sketchy, or only distantly related to the case through a long chain of inference, or there are many competing explanations for it) or is it very probative?

So, for example, consider a simple bank robbery in which there was one robber and one getaway-car driver. The robber-defendant has been identified by several witnesses, but for the driver-defendant less inculpatory evidence is available. One witness will testify that the driver-defendant owned the model of car caught on videotape speeding from the crime. A second witness will testify that the driver-defendant is a good friend of the robber-defendant. Finally, a third witness will testify that the second witness has been in a longtime feud with the driver-defendant.

One way of quantifying probative value is by considering the probability of the fact given the piece of evidence (the "conditional probability") and subtracting the probability of the fact when the evidence is unknown. Suppose the fact we want to know is whether the driver-defendant was driving the getaway car. Before the first witness's testimony that the driver-defendant owns that type of car, we have little reason to believe that he was the driver. The witness's testimony that he owns such a car makes us somewhat more likely to believe he was the driver; that difference between our before and after beliefs in his guilt is the probative value of that evidence. Now we have some belief that he was the driver and next we learn from the second witness that the two defendants are good friends. Our belief in his guilt rises once again. Finally, we learn that the second witness might have reason to lie, so we devalue the testimony of the second witness, and our belief in the robber-defendant's guilt decreases. Thus, relevant evidence can make a fact more or *less* probable, and it is the size of that difference in the probability of the fact with and without the evidence that represents its probative value.[2]

Note that the probative value of a piece of evidence depends on what other evidence exists in the case. So, for example, when a first witness identifies the robber-defendant as the bank robber, that evidence has a lot of probative value. When a second witness testifies to the same thing, that testimony has less probative value. And so, too with the next witness who has the same thing to say. The same testimony from a tenth witness almost certainly adds nothing to any juror's belief in the likelihood that the defendant committed the robbery; thus, it has no probative value even if, had the tenth witness been the first to testify, his testimony would have been quite probative. This method of "adding" the value of evidence is an application of Bayes' Theorem, which was described in the previous chapter. Although we find the holistic-story model more plausible than this type of evidence "adding," it might be the way jurors reason when there is a lot of evidence about a particular fact and they are trying to assess its believability. This feature, that additional similar testimony decreases in probative value, is related to some of the factors on the "negative" side of the balancing scale regarding trial efficiency, described below.

### *Against Admission: Burdens and Dangers*

In Rule 403, the factors weighing against admission, which get summed together when put on that side of the scale, are varied and express different values of the legal system. Below we first discuss the last three factors—undue delay, wasting time, and needlessly presenting cumulative evidence—which all concern trial efficiency. At least one textbook writer has wondered whether those three items express some redundancy themselves.[3] But in addition to efficiency, these factors might be related to the quality of a jury's decision. Jurors possess limited capacities for attention, and might be more likely to make poor decisions when they are bored or annoyed. Then we discuss the first three factors weighing against admission, with particular emphasis on the notion of unfair prejudice.

## METACOGNITION AND THE "CURSE OF KNOWLEDGE" IN EVALUATING TRIAL EFFICIENCY

Can judges really tell whether jurors who are staring into space are bored by repetitive information or have given up due to a lack of understanding? Judges need to discern the difference when deciding whether to sustain an objection for undue delay, wasting time, or needlessly presenting cumulative evidence.

When trying to decide whether a jury understands a particular point and, thus, whether presenting more evidence is desirable, judges might be victims of the "curse of knowledge"[4]—a type of mental contamination in which someone who already has particular knowledge is unable to judge the competence of someone who does not. (See Figure I.2 and recall the discussion of mental contamination in the Introduction.) A classic case of this phenomenon is that of the college professor explaining things too quickly to a class of students; the professor knows the information so well that it is difficult for her to estimate how well students will be able to absorb it (until they deluge her with e-mail). Judges have likely heard various types of evidence (e.g., that offered by police or forensic examiners) many times, so that it becomes easy for them to process the information and more difficult for them to evaluate whether a naïve juror will understand it. Thus, a judge cannot use her own subjective experience about what might be wasting time or needlessly cumulative.

A potential source of information for judges trying to estimate juror understanding is the questions that jurors wish to ask the witnesses.[5] In some jurisdictions, jurors may submit questions for the witnesses to the judge who, in consultation with the lawyers, rules on their admissibility. For example, in the 2013 case *Arizona v. Jodi Ann Arias* jurors submitted over 100 questions for the defendant.[6] Arias admitted to killing her ex-boyfriend, but asserted that it was done in self-defense. After the usual form of testimony, the jurors gave their written questions to the judge, who ruled on their admissibility and then read the admissible questions to Arias. Many of the questions asked about specific details of her story.

Many other questions concerned discrepancies in Arias's story, specifically asking why her memory was complete regarding events outside the murder, but so hazy about the actual criminal events. A judge, having previously heard many criminal cases in which a defendant claims a hazy memory for traumatic disputed events, might cut short questioning on the hazy memory because it seems a waste of time—redundant or unproductive—to her.

### METACOGNITION FOR MISLEADING AND CONFUSING EVIDENCE

The first three factors weighing against admission in Rule 403—unfair prejudice, confusing the issues, and misleading the jury—all concern the ability of jurors to use the evidence in making a reasoned and fair judgment. These factors sound exactly like the sort of things that could lead a jury to get to the wrong answer for the wrong reasons. But how can that happen and, more importantly, how can a judge know when it is likely to occur?

Judges can probably easily evaluate whether lawyers are *attempting* to confuse issues or mislead the jury. Indeed, such attempts often use the types of persuasion tactics that we described as giving rise to the rules of evidence in the Introduction. But can judges tell whether these tactics are actually *succeeding* with the jury? We doubt it, but it turns out that the question does not matter very much; the "confusing" and "misleading" aspects of Rule 403 are not often invoked—except for expert testimony (see Chapter 7). Rather, the major application of Rule 403 is the appeal to unfair prejudice.

## *What Is Unfair Prejudice?*

By some definitions, all relevant evidence is prejudicial in that it supports an argument for one side's interpretation of the facts. So what does it mean for evidence to evoke *unfair* prejudice? The Advisory Committee on Rules states in the notes to Rule 403: "'Unfair prejudice' within its context means an undue tendency to suggest decision on an improper basis, commonly, though not necessarily, an emotional one"—that is, suggesting a decision on grounds different from the one at issue.

Below we consider three of the many possible ways to evoke a decision on an *improper basis*. Each describes how a defendant (in either a criminal or civil case) might be found guilty or responsible for some harm for reasons other than that the relevant evidence in the case points specifically to him. Note that, once again, it is up to the judge to try to figure out what and how the jury will respond to the presentation of evidence. The judge might also need to evaluate whether alternative evidence could be presented that would make the same evidentiary point with a less prejudicial effect on the jury.

### *Inflaming the Jury: Something Terrible Happened, So Someone Must Pay*

One argument about unfair prejudice assumes that when jurors learn information that is very emotional and inflammatory, they will want to punish someone—and they might be less than rational in whom they pick and how much evidence they need. Because the defendant is the suggested perpetrator, is right in front of them, and is an easy target for punishment, the jury will go after him.

#### EXAMPLE: PICTURES AS EVIDENCE[7]

A classic example of evidence presumed to be inflammatory is gruesome pictures of victims. The prosecution might want to show a victim's wounds or how a decedent's body was disposed of in order to prove certain actions or mental states on the part of the defendant. An objection that the evidence is "more prejudicial than probative" is an appeal to the ideas that (a) these pictures might make the jurors so agitated that they will make a decision on (unreliable) emotional grounds rather than (permitted) logical grounds and (b) there might be better ways to present the same evidentiary content without the inflammatory aspect. So, for example, a police officer might testify to the victim's eight gunshot wounds rather than offering photographs of the victim's wrecked body lying in a pool of blood.

Several interesting psychological questions underlie these issues. First, do gruesome photos have the effect that rulemakers have assumed? There are jury simulation studies showing that gruesome pictures can increase damage awards, raise conviction rates, and produce harsher punishment recommendations.[8] One study showed that the level of anger the mock jurors reported feeling toward the defendant (in a hypothetical trial transcript) was related to their likelihood of convicting him.[9] But there are also simulation studies that do not find an effect of grisly pictures, and we suspect that there might be many unpublished studies with similar findings of no effect. And, although we are, for the most part, believers that research from the laboratory translates well to the courtroom, we have our doubts about how well the existing research on emotion does so. Such research does not capture some of the qualities of real trials that might be relevant to the effects of emotion on jury decision making; in particular, experimental delays between the emotion-evoking stimulus in the mock trial and the mock jurors' decisions is typically much shorter (e.g., typically less than two hours) than it would be in a real trial and, perhaps most important, the current studies do not include jury deliberation.[10]

A second important question, although tangential to our discussion here, is whether visual evidence adds something to a jury's understanding that verbal-description testimony itself could not. That is, beyond being more likely to engage their emotions, is visual evidence more helpful in creating an accurate understanding of important facts of the case, or might it have extra probative value? The answer to this question is likely to be very case specific, but pictures, by virtue of the amount of information they contain, are likely to evoke more case-related thoughts and knowledge in the minds of jurors than verbal descriptions.

Third, most generally and pervasively, is the question of whether and how jurors' reasoning is adversely affected when jurors see or hear emotional evidence.

## EMOTION

Psychology's view about the effect of emotion on reasoning has changed drastically over the last few decades.[11] The early view was that emotion was the foil of good reasoning—that in states of heightened emotion, rational thought disappears and judgments tend to be shortsighted and wrong. The law, too, has long valued reason over emotion, while lamenting the "unfortunate consequences" of emotion. For example, there are heat-of-passion claims—the argument that someone reacted so strongly to the exigencies of the moment that he should be held less responsible than normal for taking some violent action.[12]

It almost seems as if the law was protecting against the emotion of the lynch mob—worrying that jurors might become so emotionally distraught by a trial that they might want to quickly act as judge, jury, and executioner. But suggesting that emotion will inevitably lead to bad decision making in the courtroom embraces a one-dimensional view of emotion and its effects. A number of recent reviews of the burgeoning research into law and emotion illuminate how emotion functions in law in many different capacities.[13] In the paragraphs below, we describe seven factors relevant to whether emotion is likely to have an "undue tendency to suggest decision on an improper basis," or whether it might serve beneficial purposes.

The first three factors involve various qualities of emotions. First, as described in the Introduction, it is not the case that the fast, automatic, and emotional System 1 always leads to the wrong answer, whereas the slow, controlled, rational System 2 always leads to the correct one. Indeed, System 1 might be correct when System 2 is not (e.g., see the discussion in Chapter 4 on detecting deception), or the two systems might arrive at the same conclusion. Emotion and reason need not be at odds. Second, emotion could provide important information about a situation. Emotions can give fast reliable clues as to whether a situation is safe or dangerous. People pay more attention to emotion-bearing information because it signals that something important is happening. Third, it is wrong to apply the effects of emotion, generally, to the broad spectrum of particular emotions that people experience. Research has shown that different emotions have different consequences for reasoning. For example, people in a happy mood are more likely to process information at a more abstract level than people in a sad mood, who are more inclined to see specifics and focus on detail.[14] The emotions evoked at trial are more likely to be those of anger or, in the case of gruesome pictures, disgust. When people feel disgust, they might increase the severity of their moral judgments.[15] And, yes, angry people tend to make decisions quickly (heuristically) and they want to blame others.[16] Disgust and anger can work together to increase moral outrage and mock-jurors' guilty verdicts.[17] These three factors suggest that in evaluating the impact of emotion on juror decision making, we should question longstanding beliefs about the accuracy of System1 versus System 2 reasoning, the inaccurate characterization of emotion generally, and the impact of each emotion individually.

The next four factors deal with how even the strongest of biasing emotions might be mitigated by the courtroom environment. Such strong emotions do not necessarily lead to bad decisions because delay, deliberation, awareness of the emotions, and people's own conceptions of themselves as rational beings will limit the effect of the emotions on their decision making. Therefore, the fourth factor is that people[18] generally prefer to think of themselves as coherent, rational, and logical. If they recognize a conflict between their emotional and their rational selves, and they are forced to explain their position, they tend to make a more reasoned argument. People also tend to be quick to acknowledge the emotional/rational conflict in the judgments other people express.

Fifth, a long delay usually separates the moment when a juror experiences the emotion from when the juror must make a judgment. There is more testimony, breaks for rest or meals, closing arguments, jury instructions, and sometimes nights of sleep or out-of-court experiences. So, even if evidence puts jurors in a highly emotional state when it is presented and, even if at the time it is presented, they are likely to view the defendant with the resulting unfair prejudice, we should be skeptical about how long that prejudicial emotional state persists. Emotions tend to lose strength over time, as does their effect on decision making. Of course, emotions might be reinvoked during the decision-making process.

This complication leads to our sixth factor—deliberation. There aren't enough good studies of real juries or of complex mock cases to know exactly what jury deliberation does to the potential biasing effects of emotion in trials. On the one hand, asking people to explain their reasons for a decision should lessen the effects of naked emotion in themselves—because System 2 reasoning is necessary for deliberation, including the evaluation of other jurors' arguments—if jurors exhibit the usual tendency to question the emotional/rational conflicts of others' expressed judgments. On the other hand, research on "group emotional contagion" shows that emotion experienced by one group member can spread to others. Further, research on "group polarization" shows that deliberating groups, including real juries, sometimes come to more extreme decisions than the average of individual opinions (e.g., mock juries post-deliberation award larger dollar verdicts than the individual jurors' median pre-deliberation award).[19] The effect of deliberation is likely to be contingent on many features of both the evidence in a case and how the deliberation is conducted,[20] and more research on the relation between emotion and deliberation is certainly warranted.[21]

The seventh factor reminds us that a lawyer's appeal to emotions can backfire. Emotions are likely to have their greatest impact when people are not conscious of exactly what is causing them.[22] If you feel angry, you might lash out at anyone; when you know that you are angry, and who or what has made you angry, you are more likely to localize the emotion and its effect. If lawyers are heavy-handed in trying to appeal to jurors' emotions, and the jurors feel as if they are being manipulated, then they might overcompensate for the "fake" emotions and react against the side they perceive as manipulative.

Can a judge foresee all of this when making a quick balancing judgment? There is an ironic twist here. Consider the juror. People show some typical biases when asked to make affective forecasting judgments—that is, when asked to state how much emotional effect some event will have in the future (e.g., winning the lottery). People can identify which emotions they will feel, but they overestimate the amount and duration of the feeling.[23] Thus, if you asked a juror how long he would feel angry about the defendant's actions, he might answer "years." However, the judge, who has seen many such cases and so is less enraged herself, and who has seen many jurors' anger cool over time, is likely in a better position to assess the long term effect of evidence on jurors than they would be themselves.

### *Inflaming the Jury: This Guy Is Terrible; He Should Pay*

A second and related type of unfair prejudice also relies on the jury becoming emotionally inflamed and irrational. Here, however, it is more specific to the defendant in that the jury has learned something about him, believes that he is a bad person, worse than the current evidence warrants, and therefore will want to punish him.

For example, in order to show that the knife the defendant used in a crime was particularly menacing, the prosecution offers a picture of the defendant in front of his collection of frightening weapons such as axes and maces, including the knife.[24] Yes, the jury gets to see evidence relevant to the important issue of whether the defendant owned the menacing knife, but by viewing the other weapons, the jury might decide that the defendant is more likely to commit future crimes than they might otherwise have imagined. Thus, they might conclude that the defendant is a bad or dangerous person who deserves to be locked up, even though they do not believe that he committed this particular crime. Learning about a defendant's prior felony convictions could also have this effect, although the issue arises only if the defendant takes the witness stand.[25] Note that this reasoning need not be conscious on the part of the jurors; in fact, the System 1 use of emotion in reasoning is automatic—neither intentional nor conscious—but if the influence remained unconscious, it might be particularly invidious.

### *Improper Basis: The (Inadmissible) Evidence Suggests He Did It*

A third type of unfair prejudice arises from the possibility that juries might draw (sensible) impermissible inferences from the evidence. Evidence might be offered and admissible to prove something, but its admission might carry along information that is relevant to some other aspect of the case—for which its use should be prohibited. In other words, the jury might learn things that they should not know (i.e., mental contamination), and infer things from such evidence that might affect their judgment.

The rules described in the rest of this chapter all address this problem in different ways. For example, Rule 609 sometimes lets in evidence of a defendant-witness's prior convictions for the limited purpose of evaluating his truthfulness, but jurors might still use that evidence to make assumptions about his likely guilt in the current case. Under Rule 407 (Subsequent Remedial Measures), evidence might be admitted to show that someone paid for the repair of a fence and so was the likely owner of the fence, but evidence of repair is not admissible to prove negligence—an inference that would be readily drawn by the jury. Our discussion of hearsay also contains many examples of evidence that could be useful to prove one thing but would be inadmissible if offered to prove something else (i.e., the truth of what was asserted).

Should such evidence—useful for some purposes but wildly prejudicial and therefore inadmissible for others—be totally excluded from trial? There is middle ground between full admissibility and total exclusion: judges can allow evidence to be admitted but do so along with limiting instructions. The Advisory Committee's note to Rule 105 states: "In reaching a decision whether to exclude on grounds of unfair prejudice, consideration should be given to the probable effectiveness or lack of effectiveness of a limiting instruction." That is, the judge should consider whether telling the jury to use the evidence for one purpose (e.g., that the defendant had committed a prior felony) but not another (e.g., that he was prone to violence) would be effective. The language of the categorical exclusion rules shows confidence that jurors can use evidence for one purpose but not for another, as discussed later in this chapter. The psychological (non)plausibility of limiting instructions is described in the next chapter.

## Thumb-on-the-Scale Balancing Tests of Rule 609

Rule 403 is different from other balancing test rules in two ways. First, Rule 403 is a *general* balancing test—it is content-free because it applies to all evidence regardless of type, unless another more specific rule overrides it. Second, Rule 403 itself has a bias—it doesn't simply balance probativeness against the other concerns. Rather, it rejects the introduction of evidence only if "its probative value is *substantially outweighed*" by one or more of the other concerns. This thumb-on-the-scale balancing test favors admission and the offset is different from those of the other balancing rules.

In contrast to Rule 403, Rule 609 is very specific and its content is controversial—it regulates the use of prior criminal convictions for impeaching a witness, most often the defendant in a criminal case. We discuss Rule 609 and the psychology behind it more extensively later. Here, we simply wish to draw attention to how the rulemakers' views about the usefulness of different types of evidence affects the balancing that judges must do at trial. The basic justification for Rule 609 is this: the witness committed a prior crime, therefore the witness is a dishonest person, so the jury should know about the witness's past crime to help them evaluate whether the witness is telling the truth now.

But Rule 609 recognizes that the relevance of a prior crime depends on what the crime was and when it was committed, and that the danger of unfair prejudice might also depend on these, among other, factors.[26] Thus, at one extreme of Rule 609 there is no judicial discretion—a prior conviction for a crime that involved proving a dishonest act or false statement *must be admitted*. Perjury is, of course, the paradigmatic crime here, and is viewed as "particularly probative of credibility."[27] Rule 609(a)(2) seems to reflect the warning, "once a liar, always a liar"—and the jury should know about it.

For other prior convictions, however, the relative importance of probative value and prejudicial weight fluctuate and may depend on factors like who the witness is and when the crime was committed. So, compared to the ease of getting in evidence under the standard balancing test of Rule 403, where the evidence will be admitted unless its probative value is *substantially outweighed* by the burdens and dangers, admission becomes more difficult in several respects.

*Who* matters: compared to felonies committed by a non-defendant witness subject to Rule 403, if the defendant is the witness, the evidence is more difficult to get in (i.e., probative value must outweigh prejudicial effect). The legislative history of the rule notes that this difference is to protect the defendant and his ability to effectively testify on his own behalf.

*When* matters: if the conviction is over 10 years old, the evidence is even more difficult to get in (i.e., the probative value must *substantially outweigh* its prejudicial effect). The rule's commentary notes that after 10 years the probative value of the evidence is diminished; however, the commentary does not provide a psychological justification for the belief that convictions over 10 years old are not predictive of a witness's truthfulness in a trial today.

And the *combination of who and when* matters: if the conviction/adjudication was of a juvenile, the evidence is nearly impossible to get in for a *non-defendant* witness (i.e., it must be "necessary to fairly determining guilt or innocence"); and, if the conviction/adjudication was of the *defendant* as a juvenile, it is not admissible at all. There are psychological justifications for these more stringent tests based on their limited predictiveness (especially over the years a person matures), but the dominant explanations are policy based.

---

**Rule 609. Impeachment by Evidence of a Criminal Conviction**

(a) In General. The following rules apply to attacking a witness's character for truthfulness by evidence of a criminal conviction:

(1) for a crime that, in the convicting jurisdiction, was punishable by death or by imprisonment for more than one year, the evidence:

(A) must be admitted, *subject to Rule 403*, in a civil case or in a criminal case in which the witness is not a defendant; and

(B) must be admitted in a criminal case in which the witness is a defendant, *if the probative value of the evidence outweighs its prejudicial effect* to that defendant; and

(2) for any crime regardless of the punishment, the evidence must be admitted if the court can readily determine that establishing the elements of the crime required proving—or the witness's admitting—a dishonest act or false statement.

(b) Limit on Using the Evidence after 10 Years. This subdivision (b) applies if more than 10 years have passed since the witness's conviction or release from confinement for it, whichever is later. Evidence of the conviction is admissible only if:

(1) its probative value, supported by specific facts and circumstances, substantially outweighs its prejudicial effect....

---

## Categorical Exclusion Rules

In contrast to the balancing of probativeness and prejudice that judges are called upon to perform during trials under Rule 403, several relevance rules purport to have done the balancing in advance, and treat whole categories of evidence as excludable if offered for certain prohibited purposes. If the categorically excluded evidence is offered for a non-prohibited purpose, however, then Rule 403 comes back into play. Most of these rules evolved through common law rulemaking, and later were codified into the current rules of evidence. These rules generally focus on substantive evidence that would, if admissible, be offered to support a claim of negligence or other wrongdoing. Under these rules, judges are called upon to determine whether proffered evidence falls within the prohibited category and, if so, to exclude it. Because these rules deal with categories of evidence, they are referred to as rules of "categorical exclusion" or "categorical balancing."

Specifically, the categorical exclusion rules refer to subsequent remedial measures (Rule 407), compromises and offers to compromise (Rule 408), payment of medical expenses (Rule 409), withdrawn pleas and statements made during plea negotiations (Rule 410), and liability insurance (Rule 411).

### *Why Exclude This Evidence?*

The categorical exclusion rules are all addressed to evidence that has two dimensions that, in the broad run of cases, are believed to cut in favor of exclusion of that evidence: a cognitive dimension and a behavioral dimension. (But there indeed might be other, hidden dimensions.) Immediately below, we illustrate these dimensions using Rule 407, which excludes evidence of repairs or other changes made after an accident that, if made before the accident, would have reduced the likelihood of its occurrence—but only if offered to prove the defendant's negligence (or another culpable state in the list; we use "negligence" as a shorthand to cover all of them). We more fully describe Rule 407 and the other rules in the next section.

---

**Rule 407. Subsequent Remedial Measures**

When measures are taken that would have made an earlier injury or harm less likely to occur, evidence of the subsequent measures is not admissible to prove:

negligence;

culpable conduct;

a defect in a product or its design; or

a need for a warning or instruction.

But the court may admit this evidence for another purpose, such as impeachment or—if disputed—proving ownership, control, or the feasibility of precautionary measures.

---

#### COGNITIVE DIMENSION: CONCERN WITH THE JURY

The cognitive dimension has to do with rulemakers' concern with jurors' ability (or lack of ability) to make proper use of certain evidence. The actual probative value of the evidence covered by these rules is thought in most cases to be low, yet the rulemakers fear that juries are likely to overestimate its value as proof of an element of the action being tried.

For example, consider the manufacturer of a slicing machine who adds a protective bar to the machine after a user slices off a finger. Or consider a sale on Black Friday (the day after Thanksgiving) during which shoppers injured each other while stampeding into a store. The following year the store erected barricades to prevent similar injuries from happening. Are these subsequent measures evidence of negligence at all? And, whether or not they actually are, are juries likely to think they are? Normally, of course, such evidence would be admissible because it is relevant—that is, it has at least some minimal "tendency to make the existence of [a] fact that is of consequence to the determination of the action more probable"—*unless*, of course, that relevance is "substantially outweighed by the danger of unfair prejudice."

You should recognize this logic as the familiar probative-prejudice balancing test discussed earlier. Why not leave it to a judge to use Rule 403 on a case-by-case basis to decide whether the evidence should come in or not? Perhaps the gain is efficiency—this way, a judge doesn't have to think about balancing the evidence, only about categorizing it. That is, the judge only has to answer two questions in the affirmative: would the measure have made the earlier injury less likely to occur and is the evidence being offered to prove negligence? Of course, some of the time saved by not having to balance may be offset by disputes over the categorization. The categorical exclusions could produce more consistently correct rulings if the rulemakers' one-size-fits-all rule is more accurate than judges' ability to balance prejudice and probativeness in specific cases. Of course a predetermined decision to exclude certain types of relevant evidence would necessarily lead to 403-type errors; that is, sometimes, given the particular facts of a case, evidence that is strongly probative and only minimally prejudicial will nevertheless have to be excluded. But the rulemakers have decided that the tradeoff is worth it. Note that assessment of the value of the rule would depend not only on the amount of time saved and the number of cases correctly resolved by the exclusion, but also on the desirability of making one type of error over another.

### BEHAVIORAL DIMENSION: CONCERN WITH PUBLIC BEHAVIOR

A second and "more impressive" (at least according to the Advisory Committee Notes to Rule 407) justification for categorical exclusion is the behavioral dimension. On this view, each rule is thought to play a part in facilitating socially desirable behavior. Thus, Rule 407 is believed to encourage people to undertake post-accident repairs in order to prevent potential future harm regardless of whether their initial behavior was legally negligent.

If this is the better reason, or the true reason, for the rules of categorical exclusion, then they are not really (or totally) about the balancing of relevance and probativeness. They are a means to promote desirable behavior outside of the trial, and are only masquerading as rules of relevance.

These social benefits could not be achieved through case-by-case balancing by a judge under Rule 403, because that rule is squarely focused on the cognitive processing of the evidence at issue. The behavioral aspect of these rules arises from the rulemakers' views on public policy, not relevance. And the rules are concerned with behavior that might be performed before any litigation is initiated, or during the process of negotiation before trial—thus, it could be important for people to know whether such behavior would be admissible in advance of a trial ruling. On this front, the questions that might be asked include whether the law is correct in its suppositions about how parties (or prospective parties) behave, to what extent it is possible to influence out-of-court behavior through rules of evidence, and what the consequences are for being mistaken on either of these counts.[28]

## OTHER DIMENSIONS

Our psychological story of the cognitive and behavioral dimensions is an appealing one and it reflects the public worries of the rulemakers (as expressed, for example, in the Advisory Committee Notes to most of these rules when proposed). But the real reasons for the rules need not be the expressed reasons for the rules. One might believe that Rule 407 is more about the desire to limit product liability litigation than about either of the psychological dimensions. And one might believe that the existence of Rule 411, which prohibits using the possession of liability insurance to prove negligence, owes more to the strength of the insurance lobby than to insights about how such evidence would affect cognition or behavior. Many commentators believe exactly these things, but reference to such justifications is, of course, not found in the rules' legislative history.

## *Specific Rules (407–411)*

Just as in Rule 407 described above, most of the categorical exclusion rules (except 410) use the same format: directing that a certain type of evidence is not admissible for a certain purpose—typically to prove negligence or liability. The evidence is admissible for other purposes, and the rules list some examples of the many potential legitimate purposes.

### RULE 407: SUBSEQUENT REMEDIAL MEASURES

As described above, Rule 407 excludes evidence of repairs or other changes made after an accident that, if made before the accident, would have reduced the likelihood of its occurrence—but only if the evidence is offered to prove the defendant's negligence or a product's defectiveness.

The rule characterizes the remedial measure as one that would have "reduced the likelihood" of the accident's occurrence. Although that might suggest that the condition was not reasonably safe at the time of the accident, that inference is precisely what the rule seeks to thwart. A situation might have been reasonably safe (at the store), or a product non-defective (the slicing machine), at the time someone was injured by it, even though a remedial measure augmented its safety. The rule-makers suspect that it is difficult for factfinders to evaluate a situation ex ante (before the accident) once they learn of events following the accident, namely the remedial measures (and, indeed, from the fact of the accident itself).

Some well-known psychological research about a type of mental contamination called the "hindsight bias" supports those concerns.[29] In a legally oriented version of that research, some experiment subjects were asked to imagine themselves as members of a city council who were required to decide in advance whether a municipality should take a precaution to prevent damage from flooding. Only 24% of those in this foresight condition thought the risk merited the investment in the precaution. Other participants were asked to judge in hindsight (after some flood damage had occurred), whether the decision not to take that precaution was negligent.[30] For this group, 57% thought the decision not to take the precaution was negligent. This is a classic demonstration of the hindsight bias—that awareness of an outcome makes the outcome seem more inevitable. When people estimate the probability of an outcome, their estimates are higher when they are aware that the outcome actually occurred, as compared to people who are not aware of that fact. Now, imagine if in a third condition the municipality undertook the precaution after a flood, to protect against future floods. That would give us the situation that Rule 407 attempts to deal with: jurors know what the outcome is and that the defendant took precautions to prevent it from happening again. That situation creates the perfect mix to deem the outcome as foreseeable and the defendant as negligent. Dozens of studies have confirmed the phenomenon of hindsight bias, as well as the difficulty of preventing it from happening.[31]

One indication that cognitive aspects of the rule are not the real reason for its existence is that repairs made by non-parties are not barred by the rule, even though such evidence will cause the same estimation errors as described above: non-party remedial measures are just as lacking in probativeness and just as likely to arouse hindsight bias as the same repairs made by the defendant. All of this suggests that the policy reason—the behavioral dimension—is the real reason for Rule 407.

The policy rationale is that the law wants to encourage defendants to make repairs, or redesign products, so that more people are not injured in the future by dangerous situations. In addition, the law believes that by removing the risk that the remedial measure will be used as evidence of negligence or defect in an accident trial, the repairs are more likely to be made.

Criticisms of the policy rationale are not hard to find. Ordinary citizens are unlikely to be aware of Rule 407, and if they are not aware of it, it is unlikely to affect their behavior. If they are aware of the rule, then they are likely to also be aware that the evidence likely will come in anyway for a non-forbidden purpose, so they will remain fearful of making repairs. But they might be even more fearful of additional injuries, which now will come with demands for punitive damages because the defendant was already on notice of a dangerous situation and did nothing to remedy it. For manufacturers, who typically make many units of a product, leaving an unsafe condition unrepaired and exposing large numbers of users to it is financially riskier than what any one jury might do if it learns of the remedial steps the company took following the initial injury. For such defendants, it is argued, an evidence rule will play a vanishingly small part in the calculus of whether to repair or not to repair. Such criticisms conclude that, as far as the behavioral rationale is concerned, Rule 407 could be dispensed with.[32]

We are aware of no empirical research testing whether the rulemakers or the critics have the stronger behavioral argument. One psychologically well-informed critique of Rule 407—which closely examines the cognitive as well as the behavioral aspects—concludes that the central purposes of evidence law would be best served by abolishing Rule 407 and allowing judges to decide the admissibility of subsequent remedial measures evidence under Rule 403 on a case-by-case basis.[33] And that is, in fact, what (only) Rhode Island dares to do.[34]

### RULE 408: COMPROMISES AND OFFERS TO COMPROMISE

Rule 408 excludes settlement offers made or sought in negotiations undertaken to try to resolve a dispute, as well as any conduct or statements made in the negotiations, if offered as evidence to prove liability or the invalidity of a claim.

---

**Rule 408. Compromise Offers and Negotiations**

(a) Prohibited Uses. Evidence of the following is not admissible on behalf of any party either to prove or disprove the validity or amount of a disputed claim or to impeach by a prior inconsistent statement or a contradiction:

(1) furnishing, promising, or offering or accepting, promising to accept, or offering to accept a valuable consideration in order to compromise the claim; and

(2) conduct or a statement made during compromise negotiations about the claim except when offered in a criminal case and when the negotiations related to a claim by a public office in the exercise of its regulatory, investigative, or enforcement authority.

(b) Exceptions. The court may admit this evidence for another purpose, such as proving a witness's bias or prejudice, negating a contention of undue delay, or proving an effort to obstruct a criminal investigation or prosecution.

---

The cognitive aspect of the rule is that such offers and demands have little relevance to the underlying liability in dispute, but might be wrongly interpreted by factfinders as indicating the defendant's consciousness of liability or the plaintiff's estimation of the claim's invalidity. Defendants who are at fault often are eager to settle, but so are some or many defendants who are not at fault (just to make the case go away). Plaintiffs might be willing to settle for something well below the value of their losses because they are in need of money, and especially if they need it quickly, not because they think their claims are unsound. Efforts to support, undermine, and argue those interpretations at trial could lead to protracted collateral inquiries.

On the other hand, is there *nothing* of relevance in such negotiations that would be useful to a factfinder? One or the other party might say something about the facts of the incident that is revealing about liability. Suppose a defendant profusely apologizes for the plaintiff's injuries? Or says, "I was not as careful as I ought to have been"?

An area of psychological research known as *attribution theory* has studied the inferences people draw from behavior and circumstances in order to make sense of the causes of observed behavior.[35] For example, a large offer by a defendant is more likely to lead a jury to infer that the defendant regards himself as liable than if the defendant made only a token settlement offer. But research has shown that the attribution would change if other facts about the defendant and his circumstances became known. For example, if the defendant has a huge business deal waiting to be completed and must get to London immediately or miss the opportunity, the jurors' perception of his reason for making a large settlement offer will change. Attribution theory is concerned not with the objective truth of why a person behaves as he does, but with how observers (e.g., jurors) draw inferences about the causes of the behavior. One important general finding is that people tend to attribute behavior to an actor's intentions or personality, and are less sensitive to external circumstances that often motivate behavior.[36]

The common law rule protected only the offers and demands exchanged by the parties. The modern rule has been greatly expanded to protect all statements, even extremely probative ones. The expansion of this rule suggests that, as we have seen before, probativeness and inferences are not really the core of this rule. As the Advisory Committee has noted, the "more consistently impressive ground" is the behavioral aspect of the rule: "promotion of the public policy favoring the compromise and settlement of disputes."

Unlike the rule on remedial measures, Rule 408 seems plainly capable of affecting the behavior it is aimed at: getting parties to talk openly about how they might resolve their dispute without having to take it to trial.

## RULE 410: INADMISSIBILITY OF PLEAS, PLEA DISCUSSIONS, AND RELATED STATEMENTS

Rule 410 has much the same purpose for criminal cases as Rule 408 does for civil cases: to facilitate a negotiated resolution of charges without necessitating a trial. Were the contents of such discussions and withdrawn pleas admissible against a defendant in a subsequent trial, such candid plea discussions would, one strongly suspects, be far less prevalent.

---

**Rule 410. Pleas, Plea Discussions, and Related Statements**

(a) Prohibited Uses. In a civil or criminal case, evidence of the following is not admissible against the defendant who made the plea or participated in the plea discussions:

(1) a guilty plea that was later withdrawn;

(2) a nolo contendere plea . . .

(b) Exceptions. The court may admit a statement described in Rule 410(a)(3) or (4):

(1) in any proceeding in which another statement made during the same plea or plea discussions has been introduced, if in fairness the statements ought to be considered together; or

(2) in a criminal proceeding for perjury or false statement, if the defendant made the statement under oath, on the record, and with counsel present.

---

## RULE 409: PAYMENT OF MEDICAL EXPENSES

Paying or offering to pay for an injury victim's post-accident medical expenses is not admissible as evidence of liability for the injury. The justifications for this rule scarcely attempt to appeal to the suspected cognitive inadequacies of factfinders (see Advisory Committee Note to Rule 409). They focus instead on the "humane impulses" that lead a person to pay for an accident victim's medical care and the law's reluctance to discourage such socially beneficial conduct or to penalize a person who has indulged such an impulse.

Unlike Rule 408, this rule does not protect statements made in conjunction with the payment. This rule is narrowly focused on the payments or offers of payment. Accompanying statements (e.g., "I'm so sorry that I ran you over while texting that I insist on paying for your ambulance") *are* admissible to prove liability.

Although the rule is plainly aimed at keeping the path open to such generous acts, is there evidence that it has any such effect? None that we know of. But it would be interesting to consider what a study to investigate the question might look like, what kind of findings could emerge from such a study, and which of them would justify a change in the rule.

---

**Rule 409. Offers to Pay Medical and Similar Expenses**

Evidence of furnishing, promising to pay, or offering to pay medical, hospital, or similar expenses resulting from an injury is not admissible to prove liability for the injury.

---

RULE 411: LIABILITY INSURANCE

Having or not having liability insurance is not admissible on the issue of negligence or other wrongful conduct. No policy (behavioral) reasons are offered in justification of this rule. What would that policy purpose be? Would people refrain from buying liability insurance coverage because they feared that in a future accident case, in which they were a defendant, a jury learning of that insurance policy would be inclined to believe that the insured defendant was careless? Far more likely, people would prefer to have insurance so that if they were accused of causing an accident their insurer would pay for a lawyer to defend against the claim and pay the award if that became necessary.

---

**Rule 411. Liability Insurance**

Evidence that a person was or was not insured against liability is not admissible to prove whether the person acted negligently or otherwise wrongfully. But the court may admit this evidence for another purpose, such as proving a witness's bias or prejudice or proving agency, ownership, or control.

---

This is the one rule of categorical exclusion that truly is concerned with cognitive issues: the balancing of relevance and prejudice. The concern usually expressed has to do with damages as much as with liability, namely, the rulemakers' suspicion that upon learning that a defendant is insured, the factfinder becomes more willing to make the defendant pay for the plaintiff's losses. That would be an improper basis for finding liability or, more likely, awarding higher damages.

But is that concern about juror decision making warranted and, if so, is blindfolding jurors to the existence of insurance an effective solution? At the time the common law rule developed, most defendants were not insured and had to pay damages from their own pockets. But today, most defendants are insured, most jurors correctly assume they are, and juries discuss the matter of insurance coverage whether it comes up during the trial or not.[37] Thus, blindfolding juries under Rule 411 does not successfully eliminate the matter of insurance—jurors already believe most defendants are insured. The real problem might be that those beliefs and their effects need to be tamed by the court or by the parties, and blindfolding does not accomplish that.

A closely related important question is whether jurors award more "correct" damage amounts when they believe that the defendant is insured or when they believe the defendant is not insured. The law assumes that juries will reach an unspoiled estimate of damages if they do not consider insurance. But suppose that what jurors have always done when they think a defendant is not insured is to *reduce* (out of improper sympathy for the plight of the poor defendant) the amount they award to something less than what they have determined to be the correct amount of damages? Then, if they come to believe that insurance will pay the damages for the defendant, they are willing to award the proper amount of damages. Thus, the traditional rule might have prevented, rather than facilitated, the making of more correct and unbiased awards. Today, when jurors assume the existence of liability insurance, they might actually be arriving at more nearly correct damage amounts.

Another issue worth considering is whether jurors' self-interest might influence their use of insurance information in damage awards. Given that most jurors will have liability insurance of some kind, perhaps jurors are motivated to protect their own insurance rates, and on this improper basis *reduce* the amount of damages they are willing to award to something less than the proper amount.

The law does not know the answers to these questions, which makes the task of fashioning a sensible and workable rule difficult. As with some other rules of evidence,[38] the best way to get jurors to set aside the biasing effects of suspicions or knowledge of insurance might be to explain the source of the bias, rather than blindfolding them to its potential. As the results of one study of these issues revealed: "We find, consistent with a picture of the jury as active rather than passive, that jurors are more likely to follow judicial instructions when they are given explanations rather than bald admonitions."[39] But even giving judicial instructions with explanations is no guarantee that the jurors will follow them—which is the focus of the next chapter.

## Conclusion

Evidence law is about keeping information away from jurors. Rulemakers—that is, legislatures and courts acting at a distance—can establish general rules to keep out specific categories of evidence (e.g., plea discussions, hearsay). Judges, acting as up-close gatekeepers at individual trials, have to decide whether evidence fits those particular categories. But judges also, on the fly, must decide whether particular evidence will pass a particular balancing text, typically evaluating its probative value versus its possible prejudicial effect.

When legislatures or courts create categorical rules for prohibiting certain types of evidence, they know that, as for all legal rules, the implementation of the rule will not always lead to the legally preferred result. But they might create such rules for various different reasons. They might believe a rule is constitutionally required. They might believe that it protects important relationships (e.g., attorney-client privilege) or serves public policy (e.g., Rules 408 and 410 on negotiations and plea bargaining) so that it is important for everyone to know these rules will apply in advance of a trial. Or they might believe that jurors would not be able to give the evidence the proper weight. These rules all usurp something judges could do at trial but, overall, for evaluating whether jurors can give something its proper weight, judges are usually in charge. Most evidence is subject to a balancing test, so judges get to consider whether particular evidence in particular cases will be appropriately weighed by the jury.

Whether designed by rulemakers or applied by judges, decisions about jurors' use of evidence involves metacognition—beliefs about how one's own, and others', cognitive processes work. For some categories of evidence, the rulemakers have stolen the metacognitive balancing task from the judge, and categorically conclude that (despite the potential for errors) it is best for the jury not to hear those types of evidence at all. A well-established body of research on the hindsight bias supports this procedure when evidence of what happened later is introduced to prove what someone should have known or believed earlier. For other types of evidence, particularly those that judges have much more experience with than juries, the judge needs to try to avoid the "curse of knowledge" when trying to guess what jurors will understand and be influenced by.

Balancing tests tend to be messy because they involve multiple types and layers of psychology. Most of the reasons for the rules make psychological sense in theory. However, there is still much to be learned about whether they work (e.g., are efficient, lead to the best result, encourage socially desirable behavior) in actual practice.

This chapter addressed the issue of how judges decide what jurors should hear. But what if jurors, perhaps accidentally, hear some evidence that they are not supposed to use when making their judgments? That is the question to which we now turn.

3

# Instructions to Disregard and to Limit Use

If you want to make psychology researchers laugh, tell them about a case (real or fictional) in which the judge says, "The jury will disregard that evidence." When you ask them why they are laughing, the answer will be something like, "Memory doesn't work that way; it can't just be erased." In one way, the psychologists are right—except in odd circumstances, memories can't be erased on command. But that is not what the judge is asking jurors to do. To disregard does not require forgetting; it requires behaving *as if* the evidence had not been heard. This chapter addresses the question of whether the legal system can get jurors, and judges, to behave that way.

The problem of disregarding information comes up in several different guises. One is before a trial even begins, and that is the problem of a juror hearing "pre-trial publicity." Before seating jurors, courts try to assess whether the potential jurors have heard or read something about the trial that might influence their later judgments; if knowledge of trial evidence is ubiquitous in the geographic area, a lawyer may attempt to move the trial to a venue in which there has been less publicity.[1]

During a trial, such to-be-disregarded information might arise as evidence that has accidentally slipped into the proceedings (e.g., a witness answering an improper question before a lawyer can object, or giving an impermissible answer to a proper question) or as evidence that should be considered for one purpose but not for another (e.g., as in the categorical exclusion rules described in Chapter 2). For the former, jurors may be given instructions to "disregard" the evidence; for the latter, jurors may be given "limiting instructions," telling them to use the evidence for one purpose but not another. It is ironic that psychology researchers have done hundreds of studies of disregarding, whereas limiting use, which has been studied much less, is much more relevant to the rules of evidence.

The myriad studies reveal some obvious conclusions about what happens. We know that people are often influenced by what they have heard despite being told to disregard it but, importantly, there are factors that make them better or worse at that task. Yet to explain jurors' behavior it is important to ask: are jurors *unable* to disregard evidence or *unwilling* to disregard evidence? Both mental contamination and the dual-systems theory are relevant to understanding this behavior. The latter is particularly important for understanding how deliberation might make the effect that the information has on the jury different from what it has on individual jurors.

Not only jurors, but also sometimes judges, are expected to disregard certain types of evidence. Judges acting as factfinders in bench trials often know information relevant to a verdict that the rules of evidence say should not be taken into account in the decision (e.g., pre-trial motions to admit the defendant's prior criminal record if he takes the stand; knowledge about evidence suppressed as a result of an unlawful search and seizure; expert testimony from a *Daubert* hearing when the judge rules that the expert may not testify). In appellate courts, judges might have to disregard the decisions of juries or lower courts when evaluating, in hindsight, whether evidence that should have been inadmissible at trial was, in fact, important to the trial verdict (i.e., deciding whether its admission was harmless or reversible error). Of course, judges are different from jurors in many ways—they are experts and repeat players and, on average, smarter than most jurors. But those differences do not mean that they would necessarily differ in the basic human (in)ability to disregard inadmissible evidence.

## Instructions to Disregard

Evidence that jurors may be instructed to disregard can slip into the proceedings either intentionally or unintentionally, either explicitly or implicitly. Such evidence can be in the form of a witness's answer to a question or in the content or implications of a lawyer's question. It could even arise in the content of an objection. Rule 103(d) addresses the goal—that the jury should be prevented from hearing inadmissible evidence—but it neither describes the processes for insuring that it does not happen nor the remedies if it does.

**Rule 103(d). Preventing the Jury from Hearing Inadmissible Evidence**

To the extent practicable, the court must conduct a jury trial so that inadmissible evidence is not suggested to the jury by any means.

If an opposing lawyer's question asks about inadmissible evidence, counsel may object to the question, and the objection will be sustained. The jury may be instructed to draw no inferences from the question. But what happens if a witness responds quickly or, in an answer to an admissible question, wades into inadmissible waters? Then counsel may "move to strike." If the motion is sustained, the jury is supposed to ignore what was said, and counsel may ask the judge to instruct the jury about their duty to disregard it. But can and will they do so? And how do we know?

### *Measuring Whether Jurors Disregard*

People's inability to disregard relevant but inadmissible evidence has been shown in dozens of psychology experiments.[2] How do psychologists study this (in)ability? In a typical study on disregarding, experimental subjects acting as "mock jurors" (who typically are potential jurors after they are dismissed from their jury service, members of the jury-eligible public, or college students) read a mock trial transcript or are shown a video clip of a mock or real trial. In the best basic version of the experiment, there are three groups of mock jurors, two of which provide baseline data. One group ("No Testimony") sees a version of the trial in which no reference is made to the inadmissible evidence. A second group ("No Objection") sees a version of the trial in which the inadmissible evidence is presented but no objection is made to it. When the mock jurors later make decisions about the defendant's guilt (or civil liability, but typically the studies are done using criminal cases), comparing those two conditions reveals what difference, if any, the (typically incriminating) evidence made to the verdicts. These two conditions are illustrated by the two leftmost bars in Figure 3.1.

In the "Objection Inadmissible" condition, which is the main condition of interest, mock jurors hear the evidence as in the regular No Objection condition, but this time an objection is made and the evi-

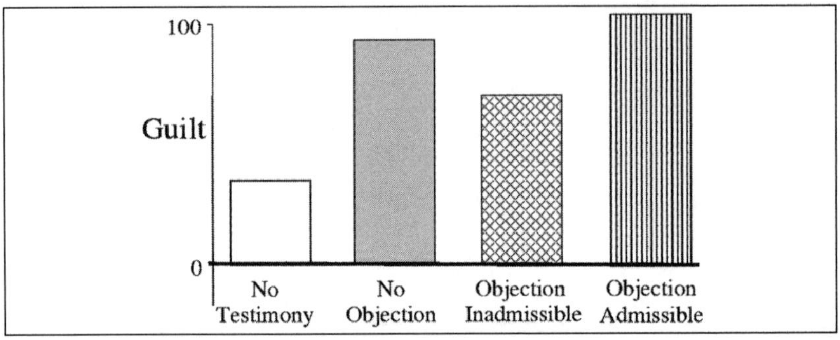


Figure 3.1. Conditions in Experiments about Disregarding Evidence. In this study, the inadmissible evidence would support a guilty verdict. The y-axis could represent the percentage of subjects voting guilty or a measure of likely guilt on a 0–100 scale. All studies on disregarding should use at least the three leftmost conditions.

dence is ruled inadmissible. In theory, if jurors could fully disregard the inadmissible evidence, then their judgments of guilt would be the same as in the No Testimony condition, in which jurors did not hear it. If jurors could not disregard at all, then their judgments would be the same as in the No Objection condition. The third bar of Figure 3.1 shows the typical finding: when jurors hear the evidence and are told to disregard it, they are, on average, somewhat, but not fully, affected by the inadmissible evidence. (The fourth bar is discussed later in this chapter.) The jurors who hear pro-prosecution evidence and are told to disregard it are more likely to convict than jurors who did not hear the evidence but they are less likely to convict than jurors who heard the evidence with no instruction to disregard. In other words, the average results from the studies show that jurors disregard the evidence to some extent.[3]

Although the finding described above is typical, it is far from universal. In some studies mock jurors do not disregard at all; in others that they do so fully. Below we describe several theories of why mock, and real, jurors would or would not disregard and several factors that might affect their ability or willingness to do so. The theories predict which factors should make jurors better or worse at the task. Running the studies and seeing which strategies work to ameliorate the effects of inadmissible evidence can then inform us about which theories are likely to be true. Together, the studies and theories suggest ways to better deal with the problem.

### *Theories about Failures and Successes in Disregarding*

There are many psychological theories about why jurors typically don't disregard evidence. These theories can be broken down along two important dimensions. See Table 3.1. One dimension is whether people are *unable* to disregard or instead are *unwilling* to disregard. Perhaps people are unable to disregard because human cognition is just not capable of doing that task—either people can't forget on demand or they can't help being affected by what they have learned when making their decision (even if they don't want to be). On the other hand, perhaps people are able to disregard but, despite that, are unwilling to disregard either because of some resistance they have to being told what information to use or on account of their desire to deliver substantive justice. The other important dimension is whether the inability or unwillingness is internal to the jurors themselves or whether there is something about the situation of being a juror that creates the inability or unwillingness (i.e., whether it is a cognitive or social phenomenon). We illustrate with some examples below. Note that both dimensions play out differently when it is a judge, rather than a juror, who is supposed to disregard evidence; we discuss those differences near the end of this chapter.

TABLE 3.1. Proposed Reasons Why Jurors Do Not Disregard Evidence When Instructed to Do So

| | Unable to Disregard | | Unwilling to Disregard |
|---|---|---|---|
| | Can't forget | Can't adjust decision | Don't want to disregard |
| Individual Cognition | Ironic Processes<br>Story Construction | Belief Perseverance<br>Hindsight Bias<br>Mental Contamination | Justice |
| Social Environment | It's a Secret | | Reactance<br>It's a Secret |

#### WHEN INFORMATION GETS INTO MEMORY

Memory researchers are fond of noting that "memory is not like a videotape" (or a DVD or whatever the current technology for high-fidelity recording is). They say this not only because memory is fragile and forgetting is easy, spotty, and frequent, but also because information is changed once it gets into memory and because what is remembered depends on what you already know. For example, suppose you see a license plate that you want to remember: 212718646. That's a lot of digits to remember unless you can think, "New York City area codes"; having that prior knowledge lets you remember the new information more easily. However, that prior knowledge might also lead you to misremember and believe that 917 (another New York City area code) was also on the license plate—a mistake that someone without that prior knowledge would not make. The way prior knowledge can affect whether you remember new information is another example of mental contamination (as we have discussed in previous chapters).

Sometimes people actually can "forget" things on demand—but the mechanism at work is more likely to be that it never got into long-term memory in the first place rather than that it was forgotten. In experimental studies on the "item-method of directed forgetting," subjects see words, presented one at a time, and after each word get an instruction to remember or forget the word. So, they might see: TABLE—*remember*; LLAMA—*forget*. At the end of the list, when asked to recall *all* of the items from the list, people remember fewer of the "forget" items. But such directed forgetting works only for quick presentations, with instructions to forget that are simultaneous with or given soon after the presentation, and for items that are not related to each other. The explanation is that once you are told to forget, you spend time thinking more about the to-be-remembered items than the to-be-forgotten items, so that the latter never go from short-term to long-term memory and therefore cannot be remembered later.[4] But courtroom conditions are not like these experiments—even though the instruction to forget (i.e., to disregard) comes right away, the information is relevant to the case and thus related to other information; therefore, it will get incorporated quickly into a juror's story of the case.

Information in memory frequently gets reorganized into sensible causal stories. (Recall the previous discussion of the story model.) For example, if you heard that a friend was in a car crash and, independently, you also heard that she had a broken leg, you would likely infer (and then believe you had actually learned) that the car crash caused the broken leg—even though that causal connection was not told to you. The fact that memory creates such links is beneficial in many circumstances but can be detrimental when people are asked to remember *ex-*

*actly* what happened (as a witness might be) or when asked to forget something that they have already heard (as a juror might be). When information is closely linked to other information, or creates causal links between other information, it is more difficult to "unremember" it—not just to forget it happened (was someone in a crash?), and not just to remember that it did not happen (oh, right, Susan was not in that crash), but also to disconnect the causal connections it had made (but I'm sure Susan's leg was broken in some crash). This research suggests that the most "connected" information, which might also be the most important information for deciding a case, might be the most difficult to "unremember" once learned.[5]

### INABILITY TO DISREGARD

When jurors are *unable* to disregard testimony, explanations tend to be about their cognitive abilities. Some explanations are more concerned with jurors' inability to forget information and others with their inability to adjust their judgments.

Two things that make forgetting information difficult are calling attention to it and integrating it with other information. (It turns out that both are good strategies to help you remember where you parked your car.) The ironic processes theory proposes that when you are trying not to remember something, ironically you have to remind yourself of what not to remember. Suppose you have been told to disregard the question of whether the defendant had insurance. Part of your mind is focused on the trial, but part is worrying: "Have I thought about insurance? I must stop thinking about it." This need to remember what you are supposed to forget while monitoring your memory increases the memorability of that information. And the harder you try to forget, the more likely it is that the thought will surface.[6] Thus, according to this theory, judicial instructions might not simply be ineffective, they might also backfire. Jurors will concern themselves more, not less, with what they are told to disregard precisely because they are told to disregard it.

The story model,[7] described in Chapter 1, suggests that people automatically take information and try to create patterns or causal stories out if it. The information presented at trial is typically linked, and jurors try to organize evidence in order to create a coherent representation of events. To be able to disregard testimony, jurors must deconstruct the story they have already constructed using it—which is more difficult with evidence that is more central to the story.

Other explanations of the inability to disregard focus not on the inability to forget but on the inability to adjust a decision to reflect what the decision would have been if the information had not been learned in the first place. These theories invoke different types of mental contamination.

Two different theories make claims about how people consider the truth of information that they have learned and the difficulty of "unlearning" it. One theory[8] proposes that in order to comprehend information people must believe it—at least at the initial stage of making sense of it. Given time and mental effort, they can then "correct" their view, but renunciation of information is difficult after the fact. So, for example, if a witness says, "Jack was at the scene of the crime," jurors cannot just keep the sentence in mind waiting to judge its truth or falsity. Rather, in understanding the sentence, they must first accept it as true and then later decide whether to "unbelieve" it or not. This process could be particularly damaging when jurors hear a statement like "the defendant committed the crime."

Another theory related to the truth-value of information, and often cited in papers about disregarding information, is belief perseverance. This theory proposes that when people learn some information, and then generate explanations for the information, they are likely to maintain their belief in the original information even after they have been told that it is false.[9] This effect might especially be true with respect to information suggesting the character or personality of human beings. For example, if people learn that Bob hit Ted, they will quickly infer and believe that Bob is violent, making it difficult to later unbelieve that Bob hit Ted. Thus, if jurors have already begun to generate some explanatory structure for certain testimony, which they are likely to be doing for more central, critical and causal testimony, subsequent instructions to disregard the testimony likely would fail.[10]

The hindsight bias, mentioned in earlier chapters, also has something to say about the ability to adjust a decision when people try to ignore information. Even if testimony about particular facts could be disregarded, research on the hindsight bias suggests that inferences that jurors had drawn from those facts probably could not be. Hindsight bias occurs when individuals overestimate the importance or likelihood of an event because of a known outcome.[11] For example, as we describe in the Chapter 2 discussion of Rule 407 (Subsequent Remedial Measures), only 24% of experiment subjects said that a city should take certain precautions to prevent future damage from flooding, whereas 57% of those in a group who learned that such damage had occurred said that the decision in the past not to take the precautions was negligent.[12] According to Fischhoff, when individuals are attempting to reconstruct events, they create a coherent causal story (and seem to forget other causal stories that might have seemed possible in the past). The result is that the actual outcome appears to be inevitable. Of particular relevance is Fischhoff's finding that even when individuals are successful in suppressing specific knowledge leading to an insight or inference, they are unable to suppress insights gleaned from having that specific (outcome-related) information. This research suggests that even if jurors were able to suppress thoughts about specific evidence, their verdicts might still be affected by the inferences created as a result of having heard the information.

Now, suppose that someone was aware that she had heard information that should not influence her decision and, in fact, did not want the information to influence her decision. So, the person decides to try to adjust her decision making to be what it would be if she didn't know the information. Can she do so? Even with this knowledge and motivation, it would be quite tricky. She would have to be aware of the direction and magnitude of the bias and also be able to compensate by adjusting her response exactly the right amount.[13]

### (UN)WILLINGNESS TO DISREGARD

Two theories suggest why jurors, although able to disregard evidence, might nonetheless be unwilling to disregard evidence when instructed to do so: one is because they want to come to the right conclusion (a just result), and the other is because they don't want authorities telling them what they can or cannot think about.

That jurors might be unwilling (rather than unable) to follow instructions to disregard is strongly supported by an experiment in which there were four groups of mock jurors in a modified disregard study.[14] The evidence at issue was statements that the defendant had made to a friend on a phone that had been wiretapped. One group did not learn the evidence that was ruled inadmissible (the No Testimony condition). Two groups did learn the evidence and were instructed to disregard it. One disregard group was told to disregard because the quality of the tape was too poor to be sure what was said (i.e., it was unreliable). The other disregard group was told to disregard because the evidence was illegally obtained. Mock jurors in the bad-quality condition voted guilty only as often as the jurors in the No Testimony condition, meaning that they behaved as if they had fully disregarded the evidence. Mock jurors in the illegally obtained condition voted guilty more often than those in the No Testimony condition, but not as often as those in the fourth condition—which was an "Objection Admissible" baseline condition (rather than a usual No Objection baseline condition). So jurors were more likely to disregard when the evidence was said to be unreliable than when it was illegally obtained—suggesting that jurors can disregard if they want to. But the exact moral of the story here is far from clear.

Does giving a reason for disregarding help? In this study, giving the jurors a reason did help them disregard—at least in the bad-quality condition but maybe not in the illegally obtained condition. So, although these results encourage giving jurors an explanation, this study and a number of others have suggested that merely providing an explanation for disregarding does not always work.[15] What about giving a reason that goes to the reliability of the evidence? In this study, jurors disregarded the unreliable bad-tape evidence, but perhaps they didn't want to disregard the reliable illegally obtained evidence because they could use it to get to the correct verdict.[16] Although giving reasons why unreliable information should be disregarded often works, in other studies mock jurors have disregarded even reliable information when given a convincing reason to do so.[17] So the reliable versus unreliable distinction cannot explain all of the results.

Another theory supporting the unwillingness to disregard is reactance theory—the idea that when someone orders people to do something ("you *must* disregard this information"), they feel as if their freedom to choose is threatened, and then, like any three-year-old, will want to ignore the order, and perhaps do the opposite. A few studies have shown that the more insistent judges' instructions are about not using the testimony, the more likely jurors will be to want to use it. For example, mock jurors who were instructed, "You have no choice but to disregard it," were less likely to disregard than jurors who were simply told that the objection was sustained.[18] But, again, stronger admonitions are not always less likely to be followed.[19]

## IT'S A SECRET

An often-overlooked explanation for many of these effects is the "secrecy" explanation.[20] When people believe that someone is trying to hide information from them, they start to believe that the information is more important and of higher quality, and thus weight it more heavily, than if the same information is not kept secret.[21]

An attorney's objection signals the jury that the objected-to testimony is an important secret: something one side does not want them to know about or use. The testimony must be important because the lawyer is spending the time (and is willing to annoy the judge) to make sure that they do not learn it. This effect seems similar to the effect of scarcity, which was one of the "weapons of influence" described in Chapter 1; it claims that people are attracted to things they believe are scarce or declining in availability. Jurors might also show reactance against the objecting attorney's attempt to limit their use of the evidence. Reactance might be even stronger against lawyers than against judges because lawyers represent one side of the case. Jurors might therefore become more suspicious of the lawyer's motives in hiding information than they would of the (supposedly) unbiased judge.

The rightmost bar in Figure 3.1 shows how data can support this hypothesis. A few experiments on instructions to disregard include a condition in which the evidence is objected to but the judge rules that it is admissible. This evidence often turns out to have a greater impact on decisions than the same evidence does when presented but not objected to.[22] Why do jurors give it more weight when objected to? The it's-a-secret hypothesis suggests that jurors won't easily forget it and won't try to disregard it because they believe it is particularly valuable for their determination.

Note that an important strategic conundrum for a litigator arises from this finding: objecting to the introduction of inadmissible evidence might lead to jurors relying on it more heavily if the objection is overruled; however, failing to object will cause the aggrieved party to lose its right to challenge the introduction of the evidence on appeal.

### GENERALIZING FROM THIS RESEARCH

The results of this body of research on instructions to disregard seem quite messy. There is no clear rule for which types of instructions are guaranteed to work or for what kind of evidence they are going to work.[23] But there are also several caveats. First, the many existing studies have so many different variables that it is difficult to put enough similar studies together to draw firm conclusions. Not only do the studies vary in which baseline conditions are used, what type of evidence is inadmissible and for what reason, and the specificity and strength of the judge's instructions, but they also vary in other factors like whether the trial is civil or criminal, which side the inadmissible evidence favors, how believable the witness was, and when and how often the instructions to disregard are given. Second, the major problem with the generalizability of this research to real courtroom cases is probably *not* that it does not use real cases with real jurors in real courtrooms per se. Rather, the three biggest problems are that (1) the number of objections in these mock trials tends to be rather small, thereby likely increasing the jurors' attention to them; (2) the length of time between the trial and the mock jurors' decision is relatively short;[24] and (3) a large majority of these studies involve individuals making decisions (verdict, sentencing, damages) alone and not after deliberation. We do know that in both mock and real deliberations jurors sometimes mention "forbidden information" and that other jurors often remind them that they were told to disregard it.[25] However, we do not yet have enough data to draw firm conclusions about the effects of deliberation on the use of evidence that jurors are instructed to disregard.

## *Alternative Remedies*

If jurors typically do not follow instructions to disregard, and the evidence is critical to the verdict, what else can be done? Psychologists are quick to say, "Call a mistrial," ignoring the time and expense (and potential for manipulation) that such a solution entails. Such consequences cause judges to be loath to declare a mistrial, and treat it as a last resort. Another dramatic solution offered by psychologists is that all trials be videotaped (or otherwise recorded) and presented to jurors in that form after actual or suggested inadmissible evidence has been excised.[26]

This, too, creates logistical problems (e.g., who might have heard the testimony before the jury does and what might they do with that information; what problems will arise when the lawyers and judges can't use the jury's reactions to inform their arguments or rulings; will the jury be able to see the parties' and the witnesses' reactions simultaneously?). For criminal cases, this procedure would be likely to raise a constitutional challenge on Confrontation Clause grounds.[27]

Thus, for simplicity and efficiency, instructions to disregard seem here to stay. How can they be made better and more likely to serve their purpose? A recent paper by Linda Demaine on exactly this question considers the various theories and findings described above. Demaine recognizes that jurors can't forget information, so the best strategy for effective instructions is to get jurors to neutralize the effect of the information.[28] One important step is to make sure that jurors understand which information they are being directed to and what they are supposed to do with it. Thus, the simple ruling, "Sustained," might not be the right way to go. Instead, a judge should remind the jurors that "sustained" means that they are supposed to disregard and then make it clear exactly which information they are supposed to disregard—including, if necessary, restating the information. Note that this strategy goes against previous suggestions that judges do as little as possible to draw attention to the specific evidence to be disregarded because that would make the evidence more difficult to forget. But rather than worry about memory, this strategy worries about use. It indicates that jurors should be told that the inadmissible evidence might have an "improper influence" on their judgment and it suggests ways to help them disregard it. There are, of course, worries about whether jurors will over- or undercorrect their judgments given such instructions, but the limited research so far suggests that this procedure is better than more traditional jury instructions.[29]

## Instructions to Limit Use

In some ways, asking jurors to limit the use of evidence to some purposes and not use it for others seems like a subset of asking them to disregard in that they need to ignore the information for parts of their decision. But trying to limit use is both more difficult to study and requires even more elaborate mental gymnastics. Rule 105 describes limited-use evidence and how it should be treated.

---

**Rule 105. Limiting Evidence That Is Not Admissible against Other Parties or for Other Purposes**

If the court admits evidence that is admissible against a party or for a purpose—but not against another party or for another purpose—the court, on timely request, must restrict the evidence to its proper scope and instruct the jury accordingly.

---

The situation of multiple parties is more straightforward than that of multiple purposes. Consider, for example, a civil case with two defendants, co-renters of a house, who were sued for negligent damage done to a neighbor's car when they pulled down a broken tree branch that had cracked in a storm. The defendants claimed that they were trying to secure the branch so that it wouldn't fall before the city could cut it down. But one defendant had said to a mutual friend, "I was in a rush to get to my girlfriend's house after the storm," which is admissible against him as an "opposing party's statement" (FRE 801(d)(2)).

What are the dangers to the other defendant? One is that jurors might believe that if he is a friend of a negligent person, he is more likely to be negligent himself. Another danger is that by the end of the trial, jurors might be confused when trying to remember which defendant had made that statement (i.e., they might show a type of mental contamination called "source confusion"). Evidence for this problem comes from experimental studies in which mock jurors learn about multiple charges against one defendant. In such studies, evidence relevant to charge A that is ruled inadmissible might still have the effect of making the defendant seem more guilty of charge B (compared to when jurors did not hear the irrelevant-to-B inadmissible evidence). So if mock jurors mix up which charge evidence is relevant to when there is more than one charge, they are also likely to mix up which defendant evidence is relevant to when there is more than one defendant. In the situation of two defendants the solution to the problem seems easy—have separate trials for each. But that solution leads to added time and expense (due to redundancy in testimony, etc.) and there is no constitutional protection requiring severance in civil cases, as there might be with such potentially damaging evidence in criminal cases.

A more interesting solution is to have one trial for the co-defendants but use separate juries. That was the solution in the 1993 trial of Lyle and Erik Menendez, rich young California men who were accused of murdering their parents in 1989. Some evidence would pertain to one brother and not the other but the majority of the witnesses and arguments would be relevant to both. After years of motions and appeals, the judge ruled that there would be one trial with separate juries—and that jurors would be marched out of the courtroom when evidence was presented that they should not hear. This procedure was more efficient than having two trials, although the trial continuity was sometimes awkward for the jurors; for example, there were references to previous witnesses and to testimony that some had not heard. Compared to such procedures, giving jury instructions to limit use is simple. But does it work? As with instructions to disregard, the general answer is: not very well.

### *Measuring Limited Use*

As described above, Figure 3.1 illustrates the conditions needed in a study to evaluate whether people can disregard inadmissible information. Inadmissible information should be given a weight of zero, so if subjects can completely disregard, they should make judgments just like the subjects who didn't learn the evidence (i.e., Objection Inadmissible bar = No Testimony bar).

When the limited use pertains to one party but not another, analogous comparisons can be made to see whether the evidence has been disregarded for the appropriate party. However, limited-use information when one piece of evidence could serve two purposes—one admissible, one not—regarding one party creates more difficulty. If the forbidden use of the evidence does have probative value, and jurors can limit, the judgments of jurors who were instructed to limit use should be less punitive than those who were not so instructed. But we have no idea what the right amount of that decrement should be. Because the admissible use (presumably) has probative value, jurors given limiting instructions should not be in the same position as jurors who had not heard the evidence at all.

How do dual-use evidence problems arise? They can arise when a piece of evidence is admissible under one rule but not under another. They can also arise when a rule allows only a limited set of uses for a piece of evidence.

### *Instantiated across Rules: Impeachment Using Prior Convictions*

An important piece of potentially dual-purpose evidence is the prior crimes or bad acts of a defendant who chooses to testify. Rule 404(b) (1) prohibits evidence of other acts to be used to prove a person's character (or "propensity") to have committed the current crime. However, Rule 609 sometimes permits the use of prior felony convictions for purposes of impeachment. Exactly when that use is allowed is dealt with in Chapter 2 (Balancing). The question here is: when a prior conviction is allowed for purposes of impeachment, but not for purposes of character evidence, what happens? Judges may issue limiting instructions under Rule 105, however, research suggests that jurors will not or cannot limit the use of the evidence to its proper purpose, veracity. Rather, mock jurors who learn of a prior conviction are more likely to convict in the current case, especially when the prior crime and current crime are similar (i.e., jurors are using the prior conviction as character propensity evidence, even though that use was expressly prohibited in the instructions).[30] The fear of having prior convictions revealed often makes defense lawyers reluctant to have their clients testify.

---

**Rule 404(b). Character Evidence; Crimes or Other Acts**

(b) Crimes, Wrongs, or Other Acts.

(1) Prohibited Uses.

Evidence of a crime, wrong, or other act is not admissible to prove a person's character in order to show that on a particular occasion the person acted in accordance with the character.

(2) Permitted Uses; Notice in a Criminal Case.

This evidence may be admissible for another purpose, such as proving motive, opportunity, intent, preparation, plan, knowledge, identity, absence of mistake, or lack of accident.

---

### *Instantiated within Rules: Categorical Exclusion Rules*

Most categorical exclusion rules, discussed in Chapter 2, take the form of forbidding the use of some type of evidence for some purposes but then allowing it for other purposes (and giving a non-comprehensive list of potential other purposes). A good example is Rule 407 regarding subsequent remedial measures.

---

**Rule 407. Subsequent Remedial Measures**

When measures are taken that would have made an earlier injury or harm less likely to occur, evidence of the subsequent measures is not admissible to prove:

negligence;

culpable conduct;

a defect in a product or its design; or

a need for a warning or instruction.

But the court may admit this evidence for another purpose, such as impeachment or—if disputed—proving ownership, control, or the feasibility of precautionary measures.

---

In the previous chapter, we addressed the question of whether jurors are indeed likely to infer from a subsequent remedial measure that the party was negligent (and concluded that jurors would be likely to overweight such evidence). For that reason, as well as the policy reason of encouraging repairs or other remedial measures, the rule bans the use of subsequent remedial measure evidence for the purpose of proving negligence.

Suppose a plaintiff was injured by dangling wires while walking alongside an allegedly negligently maintained wire fence between two properties. In the case, the issue of ownership of the fence is contested. After the injury, but before the trial, the defendant had called the fence company to repair the fence and had paid the bill. Rule 407 makes clear that such evidence of subsequent repair is admissible if it is relevant to the question of whether the defendant owned the fence. However, jurors are supposed to use the evidence only for the issue of ownership and not for the issue of negligence.

Similar allowances for alternative uses apply to Rule 408 (compromise offers and negotiations), Rule 409 (offers to pay medical and similar expenses—although no specific permissible uses are enumerated), and Rule 411 (possession of liability insurance). In contrast, Rule 410 (pleas, plea discussions, and related statements) does not allow for similar alternative uses.

Far less research has been done on instructions to limit use in these kinds of civil cases compared to Rule 609 in criminal cases. That might be because, in addition to the problems in interpreting experimental results, the danger of misusing evidence for the prohibited purpose might be less dramatic in civil cases than in criminal cases. In civil cases, the danger is that the inference from behavior to prohibited inference—for example, from repair to negligence, from offer to pay medical expense to liability—is about possible legal responsibility in the current case (and, as described in Chapter 2, is likely to be a weak inference). In criminal cases involving prior crime evidence, the forbidden inference is typically about the evil nature of the defendant. As we will see in Chapter 5, inferences about character (e.g., "once a thief always a thief") are particularly frequent and strong.

The overwhelming conclusion from empirical research on the ability (or willingness) of jurors to follow instructions to use evidence for a limited purpose is like that for disregarding evidence—instructions fail to accomplish their purpose and can even backfire, making the forbidden use more influential than had no instruction been given. A review of research on limiting instructions and instructions to disregard such matters as pre-trial publicity, inadmissible confessions, inadmissible hearsay, illegally obtained evidence, and information that a defendant was covered by insurance or attempted to settle the case, as well as previous convictions, concluded that "admonitions to disregard evidence may not only be ineffective in many situations but may serve to focus jurors' attention on inadmissible evidence and increase their reliance on it in their decision making."[31]

These findings present no surprise to many judges and lawyers. Lawyers know that they may benefit if they can cleverly get the jury to hear excludable material through this route. As one judge commented: "To tell a jury to ignore the defendant's prior convictions in determining whether he or she committed the offense being tried is to ask human beings to act well beyond mortal capacities."[32] Courts are not required to issue limiting instructions to juries without a request by counsel, and courts recognize that "[c]ounsel may refrain from requesting an instruction in order not to emphasize potentially damaging evidence."[33] If such beliefs are widely held, they suggest that a limiting instruction is little more than a fig leaf, hiding something the law is embarrassed about, yet for which it has given up the search for a real solution.

## What about Judges: Can They Do It and Does It Matter?

Any judge would be happy to tell you that the rules of evidence are to control what information gets to the jury, not to the judge, even when there is a bench trial. And, indeed, as described in previous chapters, some of the rules are designed to keep evidence away from the jury particularly because, when exposed to lawyers' persuasive tricks, delicate inexperienced laypeople might find the evidence inflammatory, or overweight it, or use it in some other prejudicial manner. Judges, however, will claim that they can "give it the proper weight."[34] And that is why judges in non-jury trials will often, and openly, ignore many of the rules of evidence. Some rules, however, are designed to keep out information entirely, purely for policy reasons (e.g., the exclusionary rules for illegally obtained evidence; privilege rules). For these rules, the "proper weight" of the evidence is supposed to be zero. We have seen how experiments can reveal when people have successfully disregarded information—in effect, giving the evidence a weight of zero—as would be indicated by the No Testimony and Objection Inadmissible bars being equal in Figure 3.1. But there is no way to experimentally reveal whether limited-use evidence has been given the proper non-zero weight, except, perhaps, if the evidence is all statistical.

The legal question regarding judges is: in what situations are they required to totally disregard evidence? The parallel psychological question is: can judges disregard relevant but inadmissible evidence when they are supposed to do so? This question arises in two settings: when trial judges are the factfinders in bench trials and when appellate judges must decide whether an error was harmless or reversible after ruling that some evidence was incorrectly admitted at trial.

### *Trial Judges and Factfinding*

Chapter 1 describes similarities and differences between judges and jurors with respect to personal characteristics and trial verdicts. In studies comparing judge and jury criminal verdicts, judges are typically more likely to convict than juries, at least in state courts.[35] (Of course, as we noted, because the ground truth is unknown, we do not know who is correct.) When the study compares a jury with the judge who presided over the case, an information inequality arises: the judge usually has heard, and ruled on, evidence that never reached the jury. When stating what her decision would have been in the case had there been a bench trial, perhaps the judge could not, or would not, or did not even try to disregard that inadmissible evidence. Or, perhaps the judge heard the evidence, which would have been forbidden to the jury for fear of overweighting, and gave it the "appropriate weight"—which was appropriately greater than zero. Regardless of whether judges are treating evidence appropriately, one of the explanations given by Kalven and Zeisel for the fact that for the same criminal cases judges would convict more often than juries is that judges know facts about the cases that the juries did not know.[36]

But judges differ from juries not only in what they hear, but also on average in education, intelligence, status, motivation, the fact that they are repeat players, and that they can be, but (allegedly) don't like to be, overruled. Are any of those likely to make judges differ from juries in whether they will disregard evidence? Theoretically, yes. Consider motivation. The fact that judges are embedded in the legal system suggests that they should be more motivated to "do the right thing." And, in law, "doing the right thing," meaning following the law, is not always the same as reaching a just outcome. But when these values conflict, both legally trained and non–legally trained people often prefer doing the just thing to doing the legally correct thing.[37] On the other hand, there is research suggesting that jurors might be even more motivated than judges to try to "do a good job"; after all, a trial is an important novelty for them.[38] Thus, jurors might be paying more attention to the evidence whereas sometimes judges, who have "heard it all before," might be doing less deep System 2 processing and relying more on general prior knowledge in drawing conclusions. The short of it is that which way the motivation question cuts, and what implications that has for the use of forbidden evidence, is still a mystery given current knowledge.

Motivation aside, are judges more likely to be able to intentionally forget evidence or adjust judgments better than jurors? The fact that judges are human, and have the same human memory and cognitive failings as others (see Chapter 1), suggests otherwise. It used to be notoriously difficult to round up judges for experimental research. However, two experiments (one small, one large) that examined judges' ability to disregard revealed that judges were not perfect at disregarding either.

In a study comparing 88 judges attending a judges' conference with 104 members of a jury pool waiting for voir dire, everyone read one of three versions of a products liability case in which the defendant took a subsequent remedial measure. In one version there was no exposure to potentially biasing material about that remedial measure, in two versions there was exposure, one with a judicial ruling to exclude and one with a ruling to admit. (The jurors were told that the decision was a judge's ruling on the defendant's objection at trial; the judges were told that it was a pre-trial motion to exclude.) Did learning about the remedial measure affect verdicts? Yes, learning about the inadmissible evidence made both judges and jurors much more likely to find liability than when the evidence was not present; in fact, there was no difference between the inadmissible and admissible conditions. This pattern was the same for judges and jurors.[39]

And in a study of judges using seven different vignettes[40] (no judge read all of them), in five of those vignettes judges' decisions were influenced by information that they were supposed to disregard. The five included vignettes with excludable information from a pre-trial settlement conference, about the sexual history of a victim in a criminal assault case, and regarding the criminal record of a party in a civil case. Judges did disregard in a vignette in which they learned of the outcome of a search before deciding whether they would have granted a search warrant and a vignette involving an illegally obtained confession. No one has come up with a coherent explanation for why those two vignettes should produce results different from the other five, and no one has yet tried to replicate the study. It is especially interesting to speculate why judges might be better at disregarding the exact information that jurors find particularly difficult to disregard.

As a result of data such as these, several legal scholars have suggested (more or less seriously) bifurcation of judicial responsibility in bench trials analogous to that of judge and jury in jury trials. That is, in a bench trial, a judge who, for example, supervises settlement negotiations or makes evidentiary rulings or is otherwise exposed to information that a jury would not have heard should not also be the factfinder in the case.[41] Practically speaking, what that would likely mean is that exclusions resulting from pre-trial rulings (be they by a magistrate or a separate motions judge) would be kept from the trial judge as factfinder. But exclusion issues that arise on the fly mid-trial would have to be ruled on by the trial judge (even if sitting without a jury). Anything else would be too unwieldy and disruptive.

A more nuanced argument is that judges should not be allowed to hear evidence that is prohibited from jurors for policy reasons, but they should be allowed to hear evidence that is prohibited from jurors for fear that jurors will give it the wrong weight. This practice is what judges typically claim they do when they disregard the rules of evidence in non-jury trials.[42]

### *Appellate Judges: Harmless Error as Disregarding Evidence*

Appellate judges might also have to do the equivalent of disregarding evidence. For example, in a criminal case, when a jury hears inadmissible evidence (either by accident or because of an incorrect ruling by the trial judge), and it finds the defendant guilty, the defendant may appeal regarding the introduction of the evidence. (Of course, as mentioned earlier, the defense lawyer must have reserved the right to appeal by objecting—thus triggering problems with the jury having to disregard.)

If an appellate court hears the case, and decides that the evidence was wrongly allowed, it will then conduct a harmless-error analysis.[43] The analysis revolves around the question: if the jury had *not* heard this evidence, would it still have come to the same conclusion? In a criminal case involving a constitutional question, the prosecution has the burden of showing beyond a reasonable doubt that the error did not contribute to the verdict.[44] Doing such an analysis involves confronting two sources of mental contamination.

One source is the evidence that the appellate court itself has just ruled should not have been admitted. The court is then supposed to figure out what a jury would have done if it had not known of the inadmissible evidence. We know that people, jurors or not, have trouble figuring out what they would have decided if they hadn't known something; that is the standard situation leading to hindsight bias—the ubiquitous problem that knowing how something turned out will affect a person's ability to judge what should have, would have, or could have happened and the judgment would not be the same as someone who did not know the outcome information. Here we have a seemingly more difficult trick involving metacognition: figure out what someone else would have decided had they not known something.

The other source of mental contamination is the verdict: the jury has found the defendant guilty and the appellate court knows that. The question raised is whether the appellate judges' knowledge of the verdict will influence their decisions in harmless-error analysis. Again there is a problem of hindsight bias. Knowing that the lower court convicted would be likely to make the total evidence seem stronger; thus, mentally removing one piece of evidence after the fact might not have as much power to change a judgment as not having heard the evidence in the first place. As for so many other instances of mental contamination, psychology research strongly suggests that the effects of knowledge on judgments cannot be accurately undone.

## Conclusion

The problem of being exposed to information that shouldn't be considered when making a legal decision occurs in many guises for both jurors and judges. That such exposure will (or in cases of appellate review *must*) inevitably happen, argues for more investment in devising better ways to accomplish what the rules of evidence seek, or even changing the rules themselves (e.g., see below regarding insurance).[45]

The research findings show that jurors and judges cannot be made to forget things that they have heard. Furthermore, there is good reason to believe that people automatically make inferences from information, weaving it into explanations and stories, and that those inferences can neither be forgotten nor easily extracted. The fact that jurors and judges cannot forget information does not, by itself, mean that they cannot behave as if they had never heard it in the first place—which is what the law really wants—but to get them there takes some tricky maneuvers. To promote disregarding it might be best to point out what information needs to be disregarded, make jurors and judges aware that from that information they have made inferences, and remind them that they should not be considering either the facts or the inferences made from them. General strategies on how to adjust their decisions accordingly might be given to jurors before trials. For non-admissible information that jurors are likely to speculate about regardless of whether it was mentioned at trial (e.g., insurance),[46] it might, in fact, be best to let in the evidence, or address it in an instruction even if it has not come up during the trial, and then instruct juries about why it should be given no weight. Acting as if a court is trying to hide (obviously important) information might be the worst thing to do to get people to avoid using it.

Even more challenging is how to help factfinders limit their use of evidence to certain purposes and to refrain from using it for other, forbidden, purposes. And perhaps more challenging still is how to endow judges with the ability to perform these same and even more breathtaking (e.g., harmless-error analysis) cognitive feats themselves. The solutions to these problems, if there are solutions, remain to be discovered. More, better research is needed.

In these first few chapters, we have described some of the basic requirements for allowing evidence into a trial (e.g., that it is relevant and not unfairly prejudicial) and techniques for restricting the improper use of evidence after it has slipped in. The next chapter addresses the who and how of trial testimony and speculates on why we would expect such a cumbersome system of rules and procedures to produce justice.

# PART II

# Judging the Witness

# 4

# Witness the Witness

Countless television shows, movies, and plays depict trials. From the fictionalization of famous historical trials (e.g., *Inherit the Wind*, based on the famous Scopes "monkey" trial) to pure flights of fancy (e.g., *Miracle on 34th Street*, in which a court must determine whether Santa Claus is real), from portrayals that occur almost entirely in the courtroom to those that merely use it as backdrop—trials make for gripping drama and biting social commentary. For observers, it is great theater. There might be well-developed characters that we love or hate; plot lines of passion, greed, lust, loyalty, and betrayal; and a well-worn plot order that is also open to surprise twists.

Trial as theater is a common analogy but one that is likely more useful from the outside than the inside. From the inside a better analogy might be trial as game, and perhaps even better: a real-life role-playing game. There are characters with opposing goals, with various competencies and resources, who each may take specific actions according to the rules. There are adversaries and allies, skill and luck, devotion and deception, and there is the ever-present consideration of strategy—considering the actions others take before choosing your own. And, in the end, there are winners and losers.

Regardless of the analogy, the major goal of the production is to give factfinders the information and the tools that they need to determine the facts of the case so that truth may be ascertained and justice done. At the same time, there are also the goals of having trials be efficient, fair (or at least appearing so), and respectful of other legal and societal values (see Rule 611(a)). Some of those other societal values at times prevent people with the most probative information from being allowed to testify; these privileged relations include those with a spouse, clergyperson, psychotherapist, and, of course, lawyer.

To determine the facts, jurors rely largely on the testimony of witnesses who have information relevant to the case. When supplying that information, witnesses are typically relying on their own memories. In evaluating the testimony, jurors not only need to listen to the questions and answers of the testimony, but they also need to evaluate whether the witness's memory is sound and whether the witness is telling the truth. Thus, jurors are evaluating both the testimony and the witness.

---

**Rule 611. Mode and Order of Examining Witnesses and Presenting Evidence**

(a) Control by the Court; Purposes. The court should exercise reasonable control over the mode and order of examining witnesses and presenting evidence so as to:
  (1) make those procedures effective for determining the truth;
  (2) avoid wasting time; and
  (3) protect witnesses from harassment or undue embarrassment.

(b) Scope of Cross-Examination. Cross-examination should not go beyond the subject matter of the direct examination and matters affecting the witness's credibility. The court may allow inquiry into additional matters as if on direct examination.

(c) Leading Questions. Leading questions should not be used on direct examination except as necessary to develop the witness's testimony. Ordinarily, the court should allow leading questions:
  (1) on cross-examination; and
  (2) when a party calls a hostile witness, an adverse party, or a witness identified with an adverse party.

---

It would certainly make the factfinders' job easier if they knew when witnesses were telling the truth. The trial process attempts to pressure witnesses to tell the truth by having them take an oath to do so. But jurors are provided with other tools to evaluate witnesses' truthfulness. They can watch witnesses as they testify, and they can hear the lawyer's attempt to impeach the witnesses' credibility and get them to contradict themselves on cross-examination. Table 4.1 shows these various tools and some of their uses.

Factfinders can be misled not only when witnesses are lying, but also when witnesses are mistaken in good faith. Gary Wells, a psychologist who has been instrumental in reforming lineup procedures, has said, "The legal system is set up to sort between liars and truth tellers and it's actually pretty good at that. But when someone is genuinely mistaken, the legal system doesn't really know how to deal with that."[1]

In this chapter we first describe factors that can lead to memory errors of witnesses and jurors. Then we describe the psychological view of various courtroom procedures that are designed to help factfinders get to the truth including limiting who can testify and what they can testify to, requiring an oath, observing witnesses' demeanor, and cross-examination. Finally, we discuss the psychological justifications for some of the testimonial privileges.

TABLE 4.1. Tools for Evaluating Testimony (Seeking Accuracy and Truthfulness) and What They Are Good at Evaluating

| | Oath | Demeanor | Impeachment | Cross-Exam |
|---|---|---|---|---|
| Perception | | | | X |
| Memory | | | | X |
| Ambiguity | | | | X |
| Sincerity | X | X | X | X |
| Confidence | | X | | X |
| Judgment | | | | X |

## The Malleability of Witness and Juror Memory

In previous chapters we discussed many issues of memory and of mental contamination—that is, the problems that arise from learning or knowing information that might adversely affect memory or judgments. When giving or listening to testimony, some of the same issues come up for both witnesses and jurors, especially about contamination by leading questions and hearing other people's views. These are examples of *source confusion*: having a real memory but not remembering who or what or where it is from and then using it in the wrong situation.

Years of research have led psychologists to conclude that human memory is not like an accurate recording device. There are no accessible high-fidelity images and sounds just waiting to be called up. Rather, human memory is reconstructive—meaning that it relies on bits of different pieces of information, rejoined, to create a different-from-fact memory. Those bits include not only things we learned at the time that the memory was encoded (i.e., first stored) but also other information we have encountered at other times in our lives. Thus, what we remember can be affected by what we already know, what we are exposed to, and the circumstances under which we are asked to retrieve our memories.

That memory is malleable, and that leading questions may change memory, is beautifully illustrated in a number of studies by Elizabeth Loftus, a modern pioneer of legally relevant memory research.[2] The studies are variations on this procedure: subjects view a video presentation of an event—for example, a red car not slowing down at a yield sign and then hitting a blue car. Some subjects in the study were asked, "How fast was the car going when it *hit* the blue car?" Their average answer was 34 mph. Others were asked, "How fast was the car going when it *smashed into* the blue car?" Their average answer was 41 mph. A week later all subjects were asked, "Was there broken glass?" Of those who had been in the "hit" condition, 14% said yes, but in the "smashed" condition, 32% said yes. Thus, because of the way the initial question was asked, people reported different memories not only at the time of responding to that question but also a week later. The difference at the time of asking might be due to what is called *demand characteristics*—factors of the situation that push a subject to act a certain way (e.g., "smashed" asks for a larger number than "hit"). However, the subjects in the two groups also gave different answers a week later in response to the broken-glass question, suggesting that their memories had been altered.

The phrasing of a question, therefore, can affect how witnesses will respond to that question. Rule 611(c), as well as longstanding practice and law, prevents the use of leading questions (i.e., questions that suggest particular answers) in direct examination, that is, when witnesses are initially laying out whatever information they have. This policy seems good for several reasons. First, witnesses' answers will be less biased by the question when they tell the story in their own words rather than simply agreeing with the examining lawyer's words. (Of course, the form of the question might not matter at all for a witness who has already practiced his or her testimony.) Second, jurors will not mistakenly incorporate the information given in the question into their memories of the testimony.[3]

Memory can also be affected by hearing other people talk about events that they have experienced. To demonstrate this effect, researchers sometimes show a video or stage a live event and then ask subjects to report independently what they remember. Of course, because of differences in current attention, prior knowledge, and other factors, subjects remember things a bit differently from each other. However, as they hear each other recount the event, their reports become more consistent—and not always in the direction of becoming more accurate.[4] These results provide an important lesson for the police when interviewing eyewitnesses: keep the witnesses separate so that they cannot talk to each other or hear others talk to you. The results also suggest that, in the courtroom, parties might not want some witnesses to be able to hear the testimony of other witnesses. Rule 615 provides for this preference—it is sometimes referred to as *sequestration of witnesses*—and it is a common procedure in many state and federal trials. The most common exception is for parties to the litigation, who need to be aware of the testimony for and against them so that they can assist their attorneys in advancing their best case, and who, when defendants in a criminal case, have a constitutional right to attend the proceedings in their entirety.

These characteristics of memory are important to keep in mind as we consider various trial procedures.

---

**Rule 615. Excluding Witnesses**

At a party's request, the court must order witnesses excluded so that they cannot hear other witnesses' testimony. Or the court may do so on its own. But this rule does not authorize excluding:

(a) a party who is a natural person; . . .

---

## Limiting Who May Testify and to What

In an ideal world, witnesses would have first-hand knowledge of what they were testifying about, would remember what happened accurately, and would report it all clearly and truthfully. But witnesses sometimes cannot or do not want to do those things, so courtroom procedures are designed to eliminate what might be very unreliable information and to enhance jurors' ability to evaluate the information that they do get.

## *Limiting Who May Testify*

Courts have shifted dramatically over the years in how they deal with potentially unreliable witnesses. Within the U.S. court system, there is a clear historical progression of allowing more and more types of people to testify. Previously, entire groups of people were disqualified as witnesses, including women, African Americans, felons, atheists, and, of course, children. In addition, the parties themselves were long disqualified from testifying. The contrast between older common law rules of witness exclusion on grounds of incompetence[5] and the modern rules shows a huge social/cultural/psychological shift in beliefs not only about the competence of people as witnesses but also about the jury's ability to judge the reliability of witnesses and their testimony.

### DISQUALIFICATIONS

The two major justifications for disqualifying someone as a witness fell under the headings of lack of ability (incompetence) and lack of trustworthiness. Incompetence, itself, can take two forms. One is the inability to accurately remember or convey information. The second is the inability to distinguish truth from lies or to understand the duty to tell the truth. Both of these justifications covered people with mental disabilities (e.g., low intelligence, insanity), people under the influence of drugs or alcohol, and children. At various times these reasons were considered sufficient justification for the exclusion of Native Americans, African Americans, Chinese Americans, and women.[6]

The justifications regarding trustworthiness assume that people know what it means to tell the truth but question their willingness to do so either in general or for the specific case at hand. Some witnesses were thought to have no motivation to tell the truth. These included people who would not understand the oath (e.g., mentally disabled people and children) and people who would not take the oath (e.g., those whose religions forbid the oath, those of no religious beliefs, and atheists). Other groups of people were assumed to be untrustworthy in general, again including atheists, minority groups mentioned above, and people with prior criminal convictions. Remnants of that last belief remain in Rule 609, which sometimes allows evidence of a witness's prior convictions for purposes of judging his credibility on the witness stand.

Other witnesses were excluded because they were believed to be strongly motivated to lie in the particular case. Thus, courts formerly excluded as witnesses people who typically had the most knowledge of the case: the parties themselves and other people with interests in its outcome. However, now being a party is not at all a barrier to testifying; it is assumed that jurors will understand those witnesses' motivations and weight their testimony accordingly. The courts also previously disqualified spouses of the parties for the same reason. Presently, spouses are not disqualified by reasons of competence but might be prevented from or choose not to testify by reasons of spousal privilege (see below).

The present view is thus to presume competence. No blanket class membership disqualifications exist anymore (although children are treated delicately).[7] The opposing party is, however, allowed to challenge the competence of individual witnesses on sensible grounds (e.g., mental defect, use of psychotropic drugs). Such a challenge is heard by the judge but not the jury. If the witness is allowed to testify, then it is up to the jury to decide for themselves how much credence to give to that testimony.

---

**Rule 601. Competency to Testify in General**

Every person is competent to be a witness unless these rules provide otherwise. . . .

---

## OATH

All witnesses are required to take an oath or affirmation before testifying. In the past, the oath was thought to place a burden on witnesses, especially ones who believed that lying under oath was a particularly grave type of sin. Now the penalties of perjury—commonly threatened but rarely applied—treat lying under oath as more serious than simply not telling the truth to a public official. But even now, when few people believe that lying under oath will consign them to eternal damnation, the justification for the oath is that it will make witnesses aware of their duty to tell the truth. Although less common than previously, it is still possible to have a witness declared incompetent on grounds of not being able to understand such an oath.

---

**Rule 603. Oath or Affirmation to Testify Truthfully**

Before testifying, a witness must give an oath or affirmation to testify truthfully. It must be in a form designed to impress that duty on the witness's conscience.

---

The ritual of oath taking prompts several interesting psychological questions, some about witnesses and some about jurors. The first major question is, of course: does taking an oath not to lie, in fact, make people less likely to lie? Courts claim that "those who have been impressed with the moral, religious or legal significance of formally undertaking to tell the truth are more likely to do so,"[8] but are courts correct in reaching this essentially psychological conclusion?

The limited psychology research on swearing to tell the truth reveals that in some cases promising not to lie or cheat does in fact make people less likely to lie or cheat. Dan Ariely, a prominent behavioral economist, and his colleagues[9] have conducted a series of studies examining factors that make people act more or less honestly. In a typical study, experimental subjects are given easy but boring math tasks that they would be able to solve correctly given enough time and motivation. For example, in one task they see a set of 12 numbers between 0 and 10, each given to two decimal places (e.g., 4.62, 7.51, etc.) and have to pick out the two that sum to 10. They were given 20 sets of such numbers and had four minutes to complete them (no one finishes all of them), at the end of which they would be paid based on their performance. One important difference between groups of subjects was who was responsible for counting the number of correct answers. Half the subjects gave their answer sheet to the experimenter, who scored it. The other half scored the answers themselves and were told to take their original answer sheet with them to recycle. Not surprisingly, the subjects in the "recycle" condition claimed significantly more answers correct than those in the baseline "experimenter counts" condition. That is, the former cheated when they reported their scores. But here's the twist. In this study, before doing the math task, half the subjects were asked to spend two minutes writing down the names of 10 books that they had read in high school, while the other half were asked to write the Ten Commandments (from memory). For subjects in the "experimenter counts" condition, which list they wrote had no effect on scores. But for those in the "recycle" condition, only the subjects who wrote the 10 book names cheated; the scores of the subjects who tried to write the Ten Commandments were no different from those in the "experimenter counts" condition. In a follow-up study, college student subjects who signed the university honor pledge on the math task sheet also did not cheat. So it would seem that making the ethical obligation of honesty prominent has the effect the law thinks (and hopes) it would.

An obvious critique of the Ariely research is that the stakes are not as high either in terms of penalties to the witness (perjury) or consequences of the case. And another question of application is whether these results would extend to people who take the oath over and over. When students have to sign the honor pledge for everything, does it become automatic and meaningless? In the legal system, there are some people who testify often, such as police officers, medical examiners, and some other expert witnesses. Would the oath affect them? And what about people who are determined to lie when they take the witness stand?

The second major question about oaths is: does knowing that someone has taken an oath make jurors *think* that person would in fact be less likely to lie? A related question is whether a jury would disfavor or treat differently someone who prefers to make an affirmation rather than take an oath.[10] The majority of witnesses still take an oath, and the major reasons that people choose not to are religious ones. Religious beliefs are no longer allowed as evidence to attack a witness's credibility,[11] but jurors might nonetheless make inferences from the witness's choice to the witness's credibility. On the one hand, people who choose not to take the oath and, maybe especially, those who make a personalized declaration might be the ones who take the oath most seriously, so jurors should believe them more rather than less. On the other hand, consistent with various in-group biases, people are probably more likely to find members of their own religious group the most credible.[12]

---

**Rule 610. Religious Beliefs or Opinions**

Evidence of a witness's religious beliefs or opinions is not admissible to attack or support the witness's credibility.

---

*Limiting What They May Testify About*

In addition to providing more reliable testimony by limiting who can testify, the FRE also limit the source of the information that witnesses can testify about. Specifically, Rule 602 provides that non-expert witnesses may testify only regarding matters of which they have personal knowledge. Limiting witnesses to such information allows for the observation of witnesses as they are conveying the story and for cross-examination regarding details about which they should have knowledge. We will see, in the chapter on hearsay, that the law is quite skeptical of allowing people to testify about the truth of things for which they have no first-hand knowledge.[13]

---

**Rule 602. Lack of Personal Knowledge**

A witness may not testify to a matter unless evidence is introduced sufficient to support a finding that the witness has personal knowledge of the matter. Evidence to prove personal knowledge may, but need not, consist of the witness' own testimony. This rule is subject to the provisions of Rule 703, relating to opinion testimony by expert witnesses.

---

**Rule 701. Opinion Testimony by Lay Witnesses**

If the witness is not testifying as an expert, the witness' testimony in the form of opinions or inferences is limited to those opinions or inferences which are (a) rationally based on the perception of the witness, and (b) helpful to a clear understanding of the witness' testimony or the determination of a fact in issue, and (c) not based on scientific, technical, or other specialized knowledge within the scope of Rule 702.

---

Non-experts are also limited to recounting their perceptions and not opinions. For example, rather than say, "He was having a heart attack," a witness might be limited to saying, "He starting sweating. Then he clutched his chest and fell to the floor." The idea is that witnesses can describe the facts that they have directly perceived, but drawing conclusions from those facts is "within the province of the jury." However, courts do let witnesses testify about what might be ordinary opinions, for example, "She was tall," or "He was drunk."[14]

These limitations on what non-experts can rely on and testify to contrast with what experts are allowed to do. (See Table 4.2.) In contrast to ordinary witnesses, expert witnesses may testify about things that they were "made aware of" in addition to things they have personal knowledge of. Experts also have broad latitude to testify to their opinions. But one ground for excluding some proffered expert testimony is, as above, that it is deemed to be an invasion of the province of the jury.

For example, criminal defendants sometimes want to call in psychology experts to testify about the fallibility of lineup identifications or of eyewitness testimony. Several surveys have shown that potential jurors, and even judges, believe different things about how memory works than eyewitness experts do. Among the biggest differences between experts and potential jurors was that more experts believe that eyewitness testimony can be contaminated by information learned after an event (94% versus 60%) and that a witness's confidence is *not* a good predictor of accuracy (87% to 38%).[15] However, eyewitness experts have often been excluded from testifying by judges who believe that jurors, based on their own experiences, likely know how memory works and know how to assess a witness's accuracy and credibility. But the tide seems to be turning. The modern trend is to allow general expert testimony on the accuracy (or not) of eyewitness identification.[16] But experts are still not allowed to give an opinion about the likelihood that a particular witness was lying or telling the truth, or being accurate or inaccurate.

The rules try to draw a bright line between the testimony of experts and non-experts, but perhaps the line is not really so clear. For example, where is the line between the matters that allow lay opinion, such as whether someone was drunk, and matters that require expert testimony, such as whether someone was impaired by smoking marijuana?[17] Substantial legal consequences turn on that line, because expert testimony must meet a higher standard of reliability than lay testimony. In Chapter 7, on expert testimony, we discuss this higher standard, around whose justification some questions remain.[18] Indeed, at times it seems anomalous that lay testimony would be allowed under circumstances in which similar expert testimony might not be.

TABLE 4.2. Lay and Expert Witnesses Differ in Sources and Types of Testimony Allowed

| | Lay Testimony | Expert Testimony |
|---|---|---|
| Knowledge Basis (Foundation) | 602. The witness has personal knowledge of the matter | 703. Facts or data . . . that the expert has been made aware of or personally observed |
| Opinion | 701. Limited Based on perception, helpful, NOT based on 702-type knowledge | 702. Broad (within expertise) Helpful, based on sufficient facts, product of reliable principles and methods reliably applied |

## Lie Detectors: Human and Otherwise

The rules of evidence, whether from formal codification (e.g., the FRE) or from case law, want the jury to be able to evaluate both what the witness is saying and how he or she is saying it. Thus, the law much prefers (and often requires) that witnesses appear in person. How the witness is communicating—whether she seems truthful and confident—appropriately goes to how much credence the jury should put in her statements. But how good are jurors at reading those cues coming from witnesses? And might they also be influenced by cues coming from the lawyers asking the questions? Might non-human lie detectors be preferable?

### *Demeanor (and Other Cues to Deception)*

The setup of the courtroom—with the jurors typically quite close to the witness stand—encourages jurors not only to listen to what witnesses say but also to pay attention to how they say it. The legal system believes that "how they say it" yields important clues to whether the witness is telling the truth and how strongly he or she should be believed. Courts are adamant that assessing the veracity (i.e., the truthfulness) and credibility (i.e., the overall believability) of witnesses is the exclusive purview of the jury.[19] And that is why, as we discuss below, courts have been traditionally hostile to polygraphs, to expert testimony on witness truthfulness, and the like. Moreover, one reason appellate courts practice restraint in "retrying" a case is that the appellate judges were not present at trial to assess the non-verbal behavior of witnesses. And among the reasons for excluding hearsay is the inability of the jury to evaluate the demeanor of the out-of-court declarant whose statement is being offered for its truth.

Hundreds of empirical studies have tested thousands of research participants as they try to discern lies from truth.[20] The results overwhelmingly suggest that people are not very good at making these assessments on the basis of the speaker's demeanor. Across all of these studies, accuracy in distinguishing lies from truths is only a bit above 50%—scarcely better than chance. More surprising, reliance on visual cues does not improve accuracy; it makes it worse.

Many of these studies, in particular the 206 studies in the Bond and DePaulo (2006) meta-analysis, work in the following way:[21] the researchers arrange for one set of people (the "senders") to lie or tell the truth about something and another set of people (the "receivers"), who don't know the sender, to decide whether the sender is lying or telling the truth. In one common setup, the sender is shown a picture that is not visible to the receiver and is told to either lie or tell the truth when describing the picture. Typically the senders have been videotaped making the statements so that the same videos can be shown to a large number of receivers. And, analyzed in many different ways, the receivers' average accuracy rate is just over 50%.

The big question then is: why? People believe that they are good at detecting lies and courts assume that judges and jurors can detect lies. Why are people barely better than chance?

One issue with many studies is that the senders are instructed to tell the truth half the time and to lie half the time. The receivers, regardless of whether they are told about that distribution, typically guess that more statements are truths than lies. This "truth bias" shows up often but not in all studies or all populations. (For example, when deciding whether a criminal defendant is telling the truth or lying, receivers show a "lie bias.")[22] Having a truth bias means that receivers could not be correct on 100% of their guesses. But it does not explain why the accuracy rates are so close to 50%.

A common explanation of the poor performance is that people use the wrong cues when trying to figure out when someone is telling the truth or lying. When you ask people to reveal what cues they look for to detect a lie, they will say things like gaze aversion and fidgeting. But although that is what they *say* they use, that is not what they *do* use. It turns out that people's judgments of veracity are more dependent on a different set of cues than the ones that they state they use—they rely more on the sender's competence and engagement and the realism of the story. Even more interesting, it turns out that the cues that people do use are better predictors of veracity than the cues they say they use.

But given all that—which suggests that people are judging veracity more sensibly than was suspected—again, why are the accuracy rates so close to 50%? The underlying reason might be that the cues to veracity just aren't that strong. Liars and truth tellers do not behave much differently. Liars are more tense (e.g., show more voice stress), less forthcoming (e.g., give fewer details), and tell less coherent stories than truth tellers. But the cues are all more strongly related to perceived than to actual deception and are not reliable enough to make easy and frequent distinctions. [23]

The analysis showing that people use better cues to detect deception unconsciously than consciously (that is, System 1 is better at it than System 2) explains some of the confusing previous data. For example, studies have shown that people are better at detecting deception when they listen to audio without watching the video. Many of the real cues to deception come through verbal channels and many of the cues people think are good but are not come through visual channels. Also, some older as well as newer studies have shown that receivers are better at detecting deception when they are not asked directly whether the sender is telling the truth or lying but, rather, when they do tasks that measure beliefs in veracity indirectly. For example, receivers will rate liars as more ambivalent than truth tellers and rate true stories as more coherent than lies.[24]

These findings suggest two ways to improve lie detection—get receivers to rely on better cues or get senders to provide better cues. Attempts have been made to train people to focus on diagnostic cues rather than non-helpful cues, but such efforts have met with little success. If it is true that there aren't many good diagnostic cues, then there is a limit on what such training could do. But another approach is to enhance the diagnosticity of cues. The argument is that telling lies is difficult and takes more cognitive resources than telling the truth. If more pressure can be put on senders to make it even more difficult to lie (e.g., push harder in questioning, ask more surprise questions, ask for more systematic details, have them tell events backward), then lies will look more lie-like as the cues to deception become amplified.[25]

Of course, there are also characteristics of the experiments that could be critiqued: the stakes are low, the subjects don't know each other, the senders have been told to lie—which sort of makes it not a lie at all. There are studies that address most of those variables—making the interaction longer, the stakes higher, etc. And still, overall, the conclusion is:

> Despite decades of research effort to maximize the accuracy of deception judgments, detection rates rarely budge. Professionals' judgments, interactants' judgments, judgments of high-stakes lies, judgments of unsanctioned lies, judgments made by long-term acquaintances—all reveal detection rates within a few points of 50%. [Are we ready to] accept the conclusion implied by the first 384 research samples—that to people who must judge deception in real time with no special aids, many lies are undetectable.[26]

## *Non-Human Lie Detectors*

Because jurors and judges are not proficient at it, the legal system has long searched for better ways to determine who is telling the truth. The first lie-detecting machines were created in the early twentieth century, and efforts to use them in litigation followed not long thereafter. In 1923, however, in *Frye v. United States*, the United States Court of Appeals for the District of Columbia rejected the use of a lie detector at trial because the methodology employed was not yet "generally accepted" within the relevant scientific community.[27]

In addition to, and related to, the general issues of the admissibility of scientific evidence, admitting non-human lie-detection evidence raises many concerns. Below we briefly discuss two concerns with presenting such evidence to a jury—the same two concerns we have with many types of evidence. First is the actual accuracy of the lie-detection techniques. Second is the potential influence of the evidence on a jury.

## ACCURACY

The crude polygraphs of 1923 have been replaced by more sophisticated and accurate ones that measure heart rate, respiration (breathing) rate, systolic blood pressure, perspiration, and occasionally bodily movements. Other lie-detection technologies and techniques have also been developed, including the measurement of blood flow and body temperature around the eyes, the analysis of facial micro-expressions, and the examination of voice stress patterns. And not only have the physiological measures become more sophisticated over the years, but also so have the questioning techniques. But none of these methods have fared much better than the basic polygraph in being accepted for courtroom use. Although some state and federal courts have become more open to a flexible and case-specific approach to the admissibility of polygraph evidence,[28] and although New Mexico generally permits it,[29] the traditional blanket exclusion of polygraphs and related lie-detection techniques is still the prevailing rule.[30]

Within the last decade, however, the issue has become even more prominent because of claims that modern neuroscience can, in essence, produce a better lie detector: fMRI (functional magnetic resonance imaging), often referred to as "brain scans." Proponents say that the patterns of brain activation identified by brain scans will be able to distinguish lies from truth.

It is important to recognize that nothing about fMRI lie detection is different in kind from the various methods of which it is a successor. First, it is still an indirect measurement of lying. fMRI measures changes in blood flow in different parts of the brain as a result of different mental activities. But that is far from seeing a little red flag appear that says, "Lie." Rather, just as for the polygraph, inferring that a physiological pattern means that someone was lying is a leap. Second, it involves interpretation, human interpretation. Just as with polygraphs, someone (or something) has to determine that the response to a question has passed some physiological threshold for calling it a "lie." The same biases (and others) can arise during that decision process. (See the discussion of fingerprint examiners in Chapter 7.)

Perhaps, however, fMRI is just better than other types of lie detection. It turns out that both polygraphs and fMRI are better than humans, but they are far from perfect. The existing studies claim an accuracy rate for fMRI methods in sorting honesty from deception as somewhere between 70% and slightly over 90%, depending on the study and its interpretation.[31] These rates are similar to those of the traditional polygraph and other non-fMRI methods, which range from 70% to 87%.[32] However, the promise of fMRI approaches is that they might, if not now then in the foreseeable future, secure a degree of reliability higher than currently appears to be possible by the use of more traditional methods.

Many prominent neuroscientists and others have been insisting that the current level of reliability and validity of the research allegedly supporting it are not nearly sufficient to justify actual courtroom use,[33] while commercial proponents of the technology,[34] some lawyers,[35] and some scientists[36] are more sympathetic.[37] And the most prominent of the very few judicial decisions on the question has refused to allow its use, even when, as is most common, it is offered by a defendant in an attempt to support the defendant's account and thus the defendant's innocence.[38]

### EFFECT ON JURY

The other traditional exclusion of lie-detection technology is based on a fear that jurors and judges will overvalue it—that they will give it disproportionate weight, and believe it to be even more reliable than it is. These fears of overvaluation surface with particular frequency in the context of brain scan evidence. Some early studies did, indeed, suggest that mock jurors would give the information provided by fMRI scans substantially more weight than they would give the exact same information when presented in verbal or less vivid graphic form.[39] But a later set of studies concluded that the inflated value produced by fMRI evidence is no greater than the inflated value produced by other visual or expert evidence that the legal system routinely admits.[40] A short recent review concurs, critiquing the initial studies based on informational disparities between conditions and noting recent failures to replicate the earlier results.[41]

### WHY NOT USE NON-HUMAN LIE DETECTORS

So if fMRI is better than humans at detecting lies, and if mock jurors do not overweight the evidence, then why not use it (or polygraphs, for that matter) in court? There are several different forms of answer. One is that whether or not it is actually "good enough," rulemakers might not believe it is good enough, relying on arguments that the research does not reflect what happens in real situations. For example, most studies used to produce accuracy rates for both non-human and human lie detection typically have the flaw that the subjects were instructed to lie (although in some recent fMRI research, subjects have been given real incentives to tell real lies).[42] In addition, non-human detectors deal with yes-no questions and do not, thus far, deal with witnesses giving narrative answers to questions; perhaps jurors are better at detecting lies from the big picture. But that fact would not argue against keeping out reports of lie-detection test results. Perhaps that lie-detection tests are done outside the courtroom draws suspicion. Yes, other scientific tests are done outside the courtroom, and those who administer the tests can be called as witnesses, but perhaps there is something special about lie detection. And, indeed, it has long been noted that evaluating witness credibility is (also) within the province of the jury. It is debatable whether that means that jurors could not be given information, like the report from a lie-detection test, to help them judge credibility (as they are sometimes allowed to hear expert evidence on, for example, circumstances that evoke false confessions) without that invading the province of the jury.[43] But even then we suspect that there might be some sense that the moral legitimacy of trials requires that people be evaluated by other people. If so, then no threshold of non-human lie-detection accuracy nor the correct human weighting of it would change the rules.

## Cross-Examination: The Greatest Engine for Truth-Seeking Ever Devised

Cross-examination holds a prominent place in the tools of evidence doctrine. It was claimed by the great evidence scholar John Henry Wigmore to be the "greatest engine" of truth seeking ever devised.[44] The Sixth Amendment right to be confronted by the witnesses against one reflects a commitment to the importance of cross-examination; in addition, a key motivation behind the exclusion of hearsay evidence is the inability to cross-examine an out-of-court declarant. Cross-examination brings to light the source of the evidence against an accused and seems imperative for procedural fairness. But what substantive effects does cross-examination have?

---

**Sixth Amendment**

In all criminal prosecutions, the accused shall enjoy the right . . . to be confronted with the witnesses against him. . . .

---

In a well-known article about hearsay evidence, Harvard Law professor Laurence Tribe analyzed the four "testimonial infirmities" of hearsay evidence. These infirmities—"ambiguity, insincerity, faulty perception, and erroneous memory"—are potential problems in testimony that a factfinder must consider when trying to infer what actually happened from mere hearsay evidence.[45] Tribe notes that factfinders must make similar inferences from all witness testimony, not just hearsay testimony, and adds:

> But the process has long been regarded as particularly suspect when the act or utterance is not one made in court, under oath, by a person whose demeanor at the time is witnessed by the trier, and under circumstances permitting immediate cross-examination by counsel in order to probe possible inaccuracies in the inferential chain.[46]

Can cross-examination help cure the testimonial infirmities of regular witness testimony? There are cross-examination procedures that can be used to cast doubt on a witness's sincerity (which we will sometimes refer to as truthfulness or veracity). These techniques are often known as "modes of impeachment." Technically, however, the set of procedures that cast doubt on a witness's accuracy (including their perception, memory, judgment, and confidence) might be called impeachment as well because they also call credibility into question. Plus, the manner in which cross-examinations are conducted can additionally influence a jury's decision.

### *Casting Doubt on Truthfulness*

Given how bad people generally are in determining truthfulness from simply listening to someone answer a few questions, it is probably a good thing that the rules provide other ways for lawyers to impeach the testimony of opposing (and, under Rule 607, even their own) witnesses. As usual, however, there are questions regarding whether the techniques are effective.

---

**Rule 607. Who May Impeach a Witness**

Any party, including the party that called the witness, may attack the witness's credibility.

---

There are techniques to make witnesses look as if they are liars in general (e.g., by their character) and techniques to make them look as if they are likely to lie in the particular case at trial. Note how these characteristics are the same two as were used to justify excluding entire classes of people as witnesses before the competency rules became less restrictive.

### CHARACTER FOR TRUTHFULNESS

The ways to impeach witnesses in general are discussed in the next chapter, on character evidence, because they involve attacking a witness's overall character for truthfulness. But briefly: We have already mentioned some of the problems with using Rule 609—which (sometimes) allows evidence of prior crimes only for the purpose of impeaching a witness. These prior crimes are likely to be revealed in cross-examination, although sometimes the lawyer calling the witness might ask the witness about the prior crimes in an attempt to defuse the power of the information (and demonstrate that there is nothing to hide). In addition, Rule 608 allows lawyers to call character witnesses to attack other witnesses' credibility using only reputation and opinion evidence but not by using specific instances of conduct, although those may be used on cross-examination. Research on the use of character testimony for truthfulness (of a defendant, not of another witness) shows that giving vague general testimony (e.g., reputation or opinion) is not nearly as effective as giving evidence of specific acts. Jurors do not get a good impression of a character witness who testifies in generalities, and the impression of the witness affects their opinion of the defendant. By analogy, we suspect that the same happens with character evidence about witnesses:[47] reputation and opinion evidence are not worth much, but specific-act testimony may be effective.

**Rule 608. A Witness**

(a) Reputation or Opinion Evidence. A witness's credibility may be attacked or supported by testimony about the witness's reputation for having a character for truthfulness or untruthfulness, or by testimony in the form of an opinion about that character. But evidence of truthful character is admissible only after the witness's character for truthfulness has been attacked.

(b) Specific Instances of Conduct. Except for a criminal conviction under Rule 609, extrinsic evidence is not admissible to prove specific instances of a witness's conduct in order to attack or support the witness's character for truthfulness. But the court may, on cross-examination, allow them to be inquired into if they are probative of the character for truthfulness or untruthfulness of:

(1) the witness; or

(2) another witness whose character the witness being cross-examined has testified about.

By testifying on another matter, a witness does not waive any privilege against self-incrimination for testimony that relates only to the witness's character for truthfulness.

## LYING IN THIS CASE

Unlike for impeachment in general, cross-examination is particularly good at revealing whether jurors should believe that a witness might be lying in a particular case. One motivation for lying is that he might have some interest in the process or outcome of the case. Such interests typically involve personal or financial relationships. We suspect that jurors use such information to discount the credibility of a witness's testimony. However, the problem with doing research on this credibility question is that "the correct answer" for whether and how much the testimony should be discounted would be very case specific.

Other evidence that a witness might be lying in a particular case comes from the presentation of contradictory evidence from other witnesses, from other statements the witness has made on the witness stand, or from statements the witness made at an earlier time. These are all types of evidence that an opposing attorney would likely be very happy to reveal during cross-examination because they could attack both a witness's accuracy and credibility. Rule 613 describes how witnesses may be questioned about earlier statements. Note the distinction—there are criteria for letting in an earlier conflicting statement for the issue of impeachment ("he's changing his mind, he's probably lying") versus stricter criteria for letting in an earlier conflicting statement as going to the truth of the matter ("what he said earlier is correct"). Using earlier statements as evidence for their content is a matter dealt with by an exception to the rule against hearsay. A summary of the research on contradictions concludes that a witness's inconsistency certainly will decrease mock jurors' credibility ratings of the witness, but it does not always have an effect on mock jurors' verdicts.[48]

In our discussion of lie detection earlier, we referred to research showing that putting people ("senders") under pressure makes lies easier to discern because lying takes more cognitive resources than truth telling. Keeping witnesses under pressure can thus be a useful technique on cross-examination.[49]

### *Casting Doubt on Accuracy*

Table 4.1 illustrates how the various tools for seeking truth and evaluating testimony can be used. Oath and demeanor and impeachment (as the term is commonly used) might cast doubt on the *veracity* of a witness. Cross-examination is the major force in potentially casting doubt on the *accuracy* of a witness. As mentioned above, doubt may be cast by statements that conflict with statements that the witness had made earlier or with statements of other witnesses. It may also be cast by having a witness fill in some missing evidence that creates doubt about what she previously said.

The law is concerned with making sure that jurors get from witnesses an accurate portrayal of what they know. Through cross-examination, witnesses may be tested on their perception of events. For example, a witness who testified that she got a good look at a defendant might be asked about the lighting conditions or the distance or whether she was wearing her glasses; many answers would cast doubt on how good that look really was. Witnesses may be asked about the bases for their judgments and for their confidence. For example, if they report that something was large, or a car was speeding, or someone was drunk, they can be asked about the bases for those judgments. If they say something that does not fit into their story, for example, identifying someone by what seems to be the wrong name, they may be asked about their own testimony, and so fix errors of or ambiguities in narration. And often they will be asked, in many ways, questions about their memory of the events at issue.

### ASSERTIONS OF CONFIDENCE AND CREDIBILITY

Note that in comparison to questions on direct exam, the content of which are limited by relevance and admissibility, the content of questions on cross-examination are even more limited. In addition to relevance and admissibility, Rule 611(b) limits the scope of cross-examination to the subject matter of the direct examination and to "matters affecting the witness's credibility" (although sometimes cross-examiners are given latitude to ask questions "as on direct"). However, research suggests that because any testimony might help jurors assess a witness's calibration, any testimony can be relevant to evaluating whether a witness is likely to have made other mistakes (or, at least, misreported their confidence).

In addition to demeanor, jurors rely on (and, in fact, are sometimes encouraged to rely on),[50] witnesses' expression of confidence in assessing credibility. Confidence may be expressed by bodily movements, tone of voice, use of filler words like "um," or words themselves (e.g., "I'm sure that . . ."). Studies show that mock jurors believe witnesses who express a lot of confidence—through actions or language—more than they believe those who express less confidence.[51]

When it comes to direct assertions of confidence (e.g., "I'm sure"), however, the research shows that witness accuracy and witness confidence are generally not highly correlated. Jurors, however, place great stock in such assertions of confidence. Thus, this is an example of where the actual value of the evidence and how jurors perceive the value of the evidence are far apart—that is, an area begging for a rule. But why are confidence and accuracy not highly correlated?

It turns out that, often, the cues to memory that make us more or less accurate are different from the cues that make us more or less confident. For example, suppose you were a witness to a crime on a dark and stormy night. You did not get a good view of the perpetrator and you know that you did not. In this case, the conditions would lead both to low accuracy and to low confidence. Now, suppose you tell the events over and over—to family, to friends, and to the police. As you repeat the story, your confidence in your memory of it grows even though your accuracy does not. Then, maybe some friends ask you the equivalent of the misleading information questions from the car crash study. Your accuracy might decrease as your confidence remains unchanged. Next, suppose you go to the police station and pick someone out of a lineup and afterwards the officer in charge says, "Good job." Again, your confidence grows but your accuracy does not.[52]

The fact that jurors believe witnesses who are confident more than witnesses who are not suggests that lawyers should always tell their witnesses to be as confident as (justifiably) possible on the witness stand. However, some research shows that this strategy could backfire. Mock jurors were instructed to read competing depositions about a car accident from a confident and a cautious witness. The confident witness said that she was sure about two things she had done earlier the day of the accident and was certain about who caused the accident. The cautious witness said that she was sure about one thing she had done that day, was uncertain about a second, but was certain about who caused the accident. After learning this information, mock jurors were more likely to believe the confident witness's version of the accident. But then the mock jurors were told that each witness was wrong about one of the things they said they had done that day. The confident witness was wrong about something she had been sure about; the cautious witness was wrong about the thing that she had been uncertain about. In light of this information, jurors were asked whose version of the accident they believed, and they were more likely to believe the cautious witness's version. The cautious witness had shown that she was better calibrated—that is, that she knew the relation between her confidence and her accuracy. Thus, if there is the potential to be shown to be wrong about events, a well-calibrated witness is likely to be a more potent witness than someone who is confident about everything but then is shown to be wrong about even an unimportant detail.[53]

Calibration information about a witness is useful for evaluating the witness's testimony on important matters, but it might take a lot of testimony to determine her calibration. This difficulty argues for a larger scope of cross-examination (see FRE 611(b) and below).

CONTRADICTION

Studies have also been done that involve mock jurors learning about the testimony of witnesses who contradict themselves or who are contradicted by others. In a study in which mock jurors read brief (mock) trial transcripts that included zero, one, or two eyewitnesses for the prosecution and either zero, one, or two eyewitnesses for the defense, unsurprisingly the witnesses were most effective when unopposed by conflicting witnesses. In the same article, a different study showed that inconsistent testimony by one witness did not decrease jurors' belief in his testimony.[54] However, in these (and some other) studies,[55] the measure for the effectiveness of the testimony was a change in guilty votes. Other research has shown that contradictions might change mock jurors' evaluations of a witness's credibility without changing their verdicts. A methodological reason for that divided result could be that measures of credibility (usually on a scale) are more sensitive than the measure of verdict (guilty or not). But a theoretical reason could be source confusion. At the time of cross-examination, jurors note that the witness has contradicted himself and so is unreliable. However, later, when considering how the facts of the case fit together, jurors have source confusion—they have heard various information and don't remember who said what (a credible or non-credible witness). Problems of "overwriting" previously learned information from now-discredited witnesses are similar to those that we discussed in the chapter on disregarding information.

## *Other Effects of Cross-Examination*

Cross-examination can help in the assessment of a witness's truthfulness, accuracy, confidence, and judgment. (See Table 4.1.) But aside from gathering more informational content that can (and should) affect a juror's decision, the style of cross-examination may affect jurors in non–legally relevant ways.

Leading questions are allowed on cross-examination, ostensibly to get the witness to be very specific in the answers, but they are not allowed on direct examination. The worry on direct is that a leading question will influence what the witness says. Of course, as we know from the

Loftus "misinformation effect" studies, leading questions may also create source confusion, at least at a delay, for the witness or the jury or both. And not only what is asked, but also how it is asked, might influence a jury.

For example, mock jurors read a simulated trial transcript in which the lawyer asked two presumptuous questions of an expert witness (e.g., "Isn't it true that your work is poorly regarded by your colleagues?") or of the rape-victim witness on cross-examination. The witness reacted by either denying or admitting to the accusation or the defense lawyer objected to the question and it was withdrawn before an answer was given. Compared to conditions in which these questions were never asked, the expert's credibility ratings went way down, regardless of whether he admitted to, denied, or never answered the question. (The victim's credibility ratings were not significantly affected by the questions.)[56] Thus, again, as for the misinformation effect, it seems as though the information in the leading question has gotten mixed up with the facts.

## Saving the Best for Never: Privilege

As we mentioned at the beginning of the chapter, some of the rules of evidence incorporate societal values that prevent people who have the most useful or detailed information from testifying at all. The privilege rules regulate when people who are otherwise competent to testify may be excused or prohibited from testifying, typically because of their relationship with any of the parties to the dispute in a civil case or their relationship to the defendant in a criminal case. Depending on the type of privilege and the jurisdiction, the potential witnesses' testimony may be barred by the witness or by the related party. Because people with privileges are often those who know extremely probative information, allowing such privileges is costly to the search for truth. Thus, the justification for privileges must involve strong claims—and those claims are about psychology and public policy. However, there is little research on the claims made about the psychological justifications for the rules and, thus, this is an area that is ripe for study.

*Privileges and Rationales*

The Federal Rules contain only one privilege: Rule 502—the attorney-client privilege. However, Rule 501 defers to the federal common law for governance and, in civil actions, to state law when it provides the legal decision rules. Thus, federal courts also recognize the psychotherapist-patient privilege[57] and a variation of the spousal privilege.[58] And, of course, there is the privilege that protects the most knowledgeable witness of all—the privilege against self-incrimination provided by the Fifth Amendment to the U.S. Constitution.

---

**Rule 501. Privilege in General**

The common law—as interpreted by United States courts in the light of reason and experience—governs a claim of privilege unless any of the following provides otherwise:

- the United States Constitution;
- a federal statute; or
- rules prescribed by the Supreme Court.

But in a civil case, state law governs privilege regarding a claim or defense for which state law supplies the rule of decision.

---

**Fifth Amendment**

No person shall be . . . compelled in any criminal case to be a witness against himself.

---

Privileges that are recognized by most or all states (but not contained in the FRE) include those for: spouses (two types of privilege), doctor-patient, clergy-petitioner, and journalist-source.[59] There is a rare privilege for parent–minor child.[60] The privileges mostly fall into three different domains.

LEGAL PROTECTION

Anecdotal evidence suggests that most Americans think that the most important privileges are the constitutional privilege against self-incrimination and the attorney-client privilege—the only one codified in the rules. It seems imperative, at least to Americans, that parties to a case should be able to present the best possible arguments for their side, and to do that their lawyers must know the truth. And, they argue, parties who have been involved in wrongdoing will only tell their lawyers the truth if they believe that their discussions are privileged. It has long been noted, however, that many clients lie to their own lawyers for reasons such as not knowing of the privilege, not believing that the lawyer will keep the information confidential, or believing that the lawyer will fight harder if she believes that the client is not responsible or not guilty. Sophisticated litigants might also refrain from telling their lawyer the truth if they intend to commit perjury because the lawyer has an ethical obligation not to offer false evidence and may take actions that the client does not want (including withdrawing from the case). The privilege is for past actions and not for future crimes.

### MEDICAL, THERAPEUTIC, AND COUNSELING RELATIONSHIPS

Another set of privileges lets witnesses seek treatment or counsel from, and have confidential communications with, professionals who may be able to help them preserve their own physical, mental, or spiritual health. Naysayers sometimes ask why someone who has done something wrong should be entitled to keep such care and related communications confidential.

Most states have a physician-patient privilege that covers a patient's confidential communications to a physician regarding treatment. But federal courts, and all states, recognize some variation of the psychotherapist-patient privilege for confidential communications in the course of treatment.[61] The Supreme Court asserted that, unlike treatment by a physician, effective psychotherapy "depends upon an atmosphere of confidence and trust in which the patient is willing to make a frank and complete disclosure of facts, emotions, memories, and fears." In his inimitable fashion, Justice Scalia wrote in dissent:

> When is it, one must wonder, that the psychotherapist came to play such an indispensable role in the maintenance of the citizenry's mental health? For most of history, men and women have worked out their difficulties by talking to, inter alios, parents, siblings, best friends and bartenders—none of whom was awarded a privilege against testifying in court. Ask the average citizen: Would your mental health be more significantly impaired

by preventing you from seeing a psychotherapist, or by preventing you from getting advice from your mom?[62]

Psychotherapists, like attorneys, are required to try to prevent clients/patients from taking certain illegal actions. In *Tarasoff v. Regents of the University of California* (1976), the California Supreme Court held that psychotherapists (in California) must violate confidentiality and warn law enforcement personnel or the potential victims about a patient's serious threats to harm them.[63] But do such "exceptions" stop people from seeking help or put a chill on open communication?

Most states also have a clergy-penitent privilege that covers the penitent's confidential communications to a member of the clergy who provides spiritual counseling. This privilege originated not for the benefit of the penitent but, rather, for the benefit of Catholic priests. Priests are not allowed to disclose what they have learned in confession. Calling on a priest to testify in court, therefore, gives him an ugly choice—defy the Church and suffer the punishment or defy the legal system and suffer the punishment. Over the years, the privilege expanded to include other religions and ownership of the privilege shifted from the clergyperson to the penitent.

## FAMILY PRIVILEGES

A third set of privileges protects communications between spouses, the rationale being that marriage is an important relationship, good for both the individuals and society, and should be protected. Forcing spouses to testify against each other could tear apart that relationship. There are two types of spousal privilege; some states have the former and almost all have the latter. The spousal testimonial privilege is about having one spouse testify against the other during the marriage. The privilege allows (either or both) one spouse to *prevent* the other from testifying or the witness-spouse to *refuse* to testify. The marital confidences privilege covers all confidential communications made during the marriage and persists even after a marriage is dissolved.

A few states have partial privileges that allow parents not to testify against their minor children, relying on similar justifications about the importance of the relationship, and the potential damage that could be done, plus the existence of other ways that parents are involved with legal problems of their children.[64] Another justification for broad family privileges is that people often want to provide special protections to members of their family. We suspect that, if forced to testify, a person's desire to protect a family member (spouse or child) would frequently create a considerable temptation to lie on the witness stand.

## *Research on Privileges*

The privileges and their justifications raise many empirical questions. What kinds of behavioral consequences do these privileges have? Do people even know what the privilege rules are where they live? If not, then the privilege is not affecting behavior. Would marriages (and medical and psychiatric care) suffer if there were no relevant privileges? Would people choose not to seek treatment, or to withhold communications, if they believed that there was no privilege? If so, then the privilege is not keeping any information from the court that it would have been able to obtain if there were no privilege. Would the disclosure of confidential communications destroy the relationship?

Psychologists have not done much research on privileges, most likely because they are not amenable to experimental research, but there is some survey research that tries to answer some of those questions. In 1979, Texas introduced a psychotherapist-patient privilege. A study soon after asked questions of therapists, lay patients, lay non-patients, and judges about the privilege. The study has some flaws but the questions and answers are suggestive. For example, most of the laypeople were unaware of the privilege; thus, it could not affect their decision to seek therapy. A few patients answered that they might have gone into therapy sooner had they known about the privilege, but there was not a big increase in the number of people starting therapy in the year after the privilege was enacted. Forty percent of the patients said that they had withheld some information from their therapists. The authors believe that those failures had more to do with fear of the therapist's judgment than fear of disclosure. The therapists, who also were largely unaware of the (new) privilege, believed that their patients had not been psychologically harmed when therapists had previously revealed what would have been privileged testimony.[65]

Other surveys have been conducted regarding *Tarasoff* and the corporate attorney-client privilege.[66] The absence of behavioral science researchers as authors of these surveys is noticeable, but it is doubtful that a survey methodology could provide good reliable answers to most of the important questions about privileges.

## Conclusion

A goal of trials is to find the truth, but to find the truth by questioning witnesses can be a long and torturous road. The law provides many tools to help insure and assess the veracity and accuracy of witnesses. However, the effects of some of them (e.g., the oath) are unknown and people (in general) are bad at using others (e.g., demeanor cues in assessing veracity).

Cross-examination does provide methods to get at both veracity and accuracy. But for something so important, there is surprisingly little psychology research on it. There is, however, growing research on cross-examining expert witnesses. One thing to worry about with cross-examination is exactly one of the worries that psychologists have about leading questions—source confusion. It is possible that jurors sometimes don't remember which witness said what, and so don't remember which testimony was discredited during cross-examination. The mechanisms at work here might also be similar to those involved with the problems in disregarding evidence: for many reasons it can be difficult or impossible to erase what has already been learned.

Evidence law used to preclude people from testifying whom the law assumed would be likely to lie or make mistakes. The rules then became more lenient, allowing nearly everyone to testify, with the assumption that lawyers could expose, or jurors could recognize, when witnesses were lying. But some privileges remain from the past and some new ones have been created. It is perhaps ironic that the privileges, which preclude some potential witnesses from testifying for various psychological and policy reasons, end up precluding many of the potential witnesses who would have the most incentive to lie on the witness stand.

# 5

# Character Evidence

## *Propensity and Impeachment*

If you watch actual criminal trials, you might be struck by the prosecutor's efforts to paint the defendant as a "bad person"—not merely trying to show that the defendant performed certain prohibited acts with a particular intent, and therefore should be found guilty as charged, but as a bad person through and through. Comparable, though often more subtle, efforts occur in civil trials. Why do litigators attack in this fashion? How far would they take their efforts if evidence rules did not draw some lines that they may not cross? And why does the law place limits on this tactic, anyway? Doesn't knowing something about the "kind of person" someone is tell us a lot about how he or she has behaved or will behave?

Many of us (at least us North Americans and Europeans) tend to instantly perceive behavior as springing from something inside the person doing the behaving, rather than having been triggered by the circumstances in which the person is embedded. The implicit theory of human behavior that we have without even trying to have one has several familiar manifestations. In addition to attributing the causes of behavior internally to the behaver, we perceive that internal something to be a stable set of traits (e.g.: warm v. cold, shy v. outgoing, conscientious v. careless, honest v. dishonest, etc., etc., etc.) that are consistent over time and across situations, and that knowing what traits people have enables us to both explain and predict their behavior. The familiar assumption is that one's personality (or what the law calls "character") has a strong bearing on one's propensity to behave in certain ways rather than in others. As one legal commentator summed it up: "[W]e all believe that people act predictably according to character."[1] And that is exactly why it is of interest to the law: if behavior can be predicted from someone's personality, then such evidence would help the factfinder determine whether the witness is being truthful, whether a victim started a fight, or whether a criminal defendant committed the crime charged.

Quite a few rules of evidence concern themselves with what the law refers to as the "character" of a witness or an accused or a victim. The law does not invest much effort in defining what it means by "character,"[2] but for most purposes it is safe to regard "character" as roughly equivalent to what people think of as "the kind of person" someone is, the set of a person's traits, one's personality characteristics or psychological attributes. The great evidence scholar John Henry Wigmore equated "character or disposition" with "a fixed trait or the sum of traits."[3] A later well-known definition by another evidence scholar is that "character" is "a generalized description of one's disposition, or of one's disposition in respect to a general trait, such as honesty, temperance, or peacefulness."[4]

Some elements of "character" have come up so often in common law cases that judges and lawyers readily view them as character traits. Leading examples are one's "character for" truthfulness, honesty, temperance, violence, or peacefulness. In years past, chastity (or its opposite) would have been on this list, but now a victim's sexual history is generally inadmissible under Rule 412(a).[5]

But the law also apparently believes that people do not dependably behave in accord with their personalities, that the lines connecting these elements are fuzzy and incomplete, and that errors in prediction are therefore likely to occur. Exceptions are made, however, for some kinds of character information used by legal decision makers for certain kinds of purposes.

By now you might realize that the character evidence rules are troubling to some and troublesome for all. As one famous Supreme Court opinion summed up the views of the common law form of these rules:

> We concur in the general opinion of courts, text writers, and the profession that much of this law is archaic, paradoxical, and full of compromises and compensations by which an irrational advantage to one side is

> offset by a poorly reasoned counter-privilege to the other. But somehow it has proved a workable, even if clumsy, system when moderated by discretionary controls in the hands of a wise and strong trial court. To pull one misshapen stone out of the grotesque structure is more likely simply to upset its present balance between adverse interests than to establish a rational edifice.[6]

The Federal Rules preserve most of these unadmired attributes.

## Overview of the Character Evidence Rules

Rules about character evidence appear in two different articles of the Federal Rules of Evidence. Article IV contains the more general rules that apply to everyone plus some specific provisions that apply only to victims and defendants. Article VI contains rules specific to the character of witnesses and evidence of their credibility. Although these rules are often treated separately in evidence casebooks and classes, we treat them together here because they can be informed by the same psychology research.

### *Article IV: General Character Rules*

Rule 404 states the most important rule concerning evidence of character: "Evidence of a person's character or character trait is not admissible to prove that on a particular occasion the person acted in accordance with the character or trait" (Rule 404(a)(1)). This is often referred to as the "propensity" rule because what it prohibits is the use of character evidence to infer a *propensity* to behave in a particular way. Although this basic rule states the important way in which character evidence is *not* allowed, there are many ways in which character evidence *is* allowed.

---

**Rule 404(a). Character Evidence**

(1) Prohibited Uses. Evidence of a person's character or character trait is not admissible to prove that on a particular occasion the person acted in accordance with the character or trait.

(2) Exceptions for a Defendant or Victim in a Criminal Case. The following exceptions apply in a criminal case:
  (A) a defendant may offer evidence of the defendant's pertinent trait, and if the evidence is admitted, the prosecutor may offer evidence to rebut it;
  (B) subject to the limitations in Rule 412, a defendant may offer evidence of an alleged victim's pertinent trait, and if the evidence is admitted, the prosecutor may:
    (i) offer evidence to rebut it; and
    (ii) offer evidence of the defendant's same trait; and
  (C) in a homicide case, the prosecutor may offer evidence of the alleged victim's trait of peacefulness to rebut evidence that the victim was the first aggressor.

(3) Exceptions for a Witness. Evidence of a witness's character may be admitted under Rules 607, 608, and 609.

---

Sometimes character is made relevant by the substantive law of a case, a situation referred to as "character in issue." All other uses are "circumstantial" in that they require inferences from character to the fact sought to be proved. But in the relatively rare instances in which character is in issue—in which a person's character is an element of a claim or defense—character evidence not only is not barred, but the party with the burden of persuasion on the matter is required to prove its existence. For example, consider a defamation case in which a person was publicly called dishonest. In suing for damages to compensate for his besmirched reputation, the plaintiff will seek to prove that he is actually an honest person while the defendant will try to prove that the plaintiff is a crooked, double-dealing, sticky-fingered scoundrel. Character is also "in issue" in disputes over child custody (regarding the parents' character) and in an employer's alleged negligence in failing to properly supervise an employee with dangerous character traits. Numerous laws call upon courts and other decision makers to consider a person's character when making decisions about bail setting, sentencing (including execution), parole, and civil commitment.

When character is admissible, Rule 405 regulates the methods by which it may be proved. In all circumstances where character evidence is admissible, proof may be made by a witness's opinion or by testimony about the person's reputation in the community. Only when character is in issue may proof also be made by evidence of specific instances of conduct.

---

**Rule 405. Methods of Proving Character**

(a) By Reputation or Opinion. When evidence of a person's character or character trait is admissible, it may be proved by testimony about the person's reputation or by testimony in the form of an opinion. On cross-examination of the character witness, the court may allow an inquiry into relevant specific instances of the person's conduct.

(b) By Specific Instances of Conduct. When a person's character or character trait is an essential element of a charge, claim, or defense, the character or trait may also be proved by relevant specific instances of the person's conduct.

---

These procedures imply some interesting things about the law's view of character evidence. Specific instances of conduct are going to produce a more complex and contradictory mosaic of behavior—leading to a more accurate, but a more-difficult-to-form, picture of the character that is at issue. And, of course, it will take more time to present instances of behavior than the more summary kinds of statements that constitute opinion or reputation testimony. The law allows this more extensive kind of evidence only when character is a material fact relevant to the substantive law of the dispute. The distinction of methods is broadly consistent with the law's attitude toward character evidence. That pairing of methods and purposes suggests that the law does not regard opinion and reputation evidence as being as valuable as specific instances of behavior. When the kind of person someone is really matters (when it is relevant to the substantive law of the case), then the better evidence and the time needed to debate it are considered worthwhile. Otherwise, fuzzier disputes over opinion and reputation will suffice.

Character evidence also is admissible to prove propensity if initiated by the defense in a criminal case. Rule 404 contains a number of these exceptions. An accused may offer character evidence on his own behalf, such as through a witness who will testify that a person charged with theft has the character trait of honesty or that a person charged with battery has a proclivity for peacefulness (Rule 404(a)(2)(A)). An accused also may offer evidence of a victim's character, such as that the person the defendant killed, arguably in self-defense, was a violent person, which would support an inference that the victim made an unprovoked attack on the defendant (Rule 404(a)(2)(B)). Whenever a defendant exercises his right to offer character evidence, the prosecution gains the right to offer rebuttal evidence related to character.

Rule 404 also permits the admission of character evidence, or something closely akin to character evidence, when the evidence goes to a purpose other than propensity, "such as proving motive, opportunity, intent, preparation, plan, knowledge, identity, absence of mistake, or lack of accident" (Rule 404(b)(2)). Not surprisingly, attorneys blocked from presenting evidence for the forbidden propensity purpose will try to find reasons why the evidence satisfies one of these other purposes—and perhaps hope that the factfinder will use it to infer propensity and then from propensity to infer conduct.

Two cousins of character evidence are addressed by Rule 406, which allows "[e]vidence of a person's habit or an organization's routine practice" to be admitted, regardless of whether or not it has been witnessed or corroborated, "to prove that on a particular occasion the person or organization acted in accordance with the habit or routine practice." Because character evidence is barred and habit evidence is admissible, you will not be surprised that, when arguable, attorneys will argue about whether a given kind of behavior is the product of character or habit. As we will see, though, the psychology of character and habit suggest that the common law rulemakers drew a psychologically sensible distinction.

We noted before that a victim's sexual history is generally barred. Somewhat ironically, however, three rules were added in the mid-1990s that fundamentally changed the law in regard to alleged sexual propensities of *those accused of sexual assault*. Evidence of commission of any past sexual assault (Rule 413) or child molestation (Rule 414) may be offered against a defendant charged with sexual assault or child molestation, respectively, and such evidence "may be considered on any matter to which it is relevant." Rule 415 makes the provisions of Rules 413 and 414 applicable in civil cases as well. These rules invite jurors to draw the very kinds of inferences that the propensity rule (Rule 404(a)) prohibits.[7]

## *Article VI: Character Rules Regarding Witnesses and Credibility*

Other uses of character evidence bear on the credibility of witnesses. Rule 608(a) provides that if a witness's character for truthfulness has been attacked, evidence of that witness's truthfulness can be offered by other witnesses in the form of opinion or reputation evidence. Specific instances of conduct reflecting on a witness's truthfulness or untruthfulness may, under conditions specified in Rule 608(b), be inquired into on cross-examination. Of course, not all impeachment of a witness, or rehabilitation of that witness, involves character evidence, and elsewhere in this book we discuss impeachment by other means.[8]

Rule 609 governs impeachment of a witness's credibility by means of bringing to the factfinder's attention that witness's prior criminal convictions. If the prior crime involved dishonesty or false statement, it is admissible regardless of its seriousness. Examples of crimes involving dishonesty or false statement include fraud, embezzlement, bribery, forgery, filing false reports, counterfeiting, and (the one most relevant in the present context) perjury. Other crimes involve various weighted balancing tests as described in Chapter 2. Prior crimes punishable as felonies are admissible, subject to probativeness-prejudice balancing, in civil or in criminal cases, including when the witness is a defendant. The more time that separates the offense or punishment from the present trial, the less relevant the prior crime is thought to be. Thus, prior crimes a decade old, or when committed as a juvenile, are generally not admissible.

Another bar to character evidence is Rule 610, which makes inadmissible evidence of a witness's religious beliefs or opinions when offered to suggest that, because of those beliefs, the witness is deserving of less or more credibility. At one time the common law's rules of witness competency excluded persons suffering a "defect of religious beliefs," which meant that only Christians were assured of the right to testify.[9] When non-Christians were eventually allowed to testify, cross-examiners were permitted to attack their credibility by inquiring into their religious beliefs, and relying on the biases of the time and place to do their work on jurors. This line of attack was not clearly barred until the adoption of Rule 610, in 1975.[10]

**Rule 610. Religious Belief or Opinions**
Evidence of a witness's religious beliefs or opinions is not admissible to attack or support the witness's credibility.

## The Psychology of "Character" and the Policies of Evidence Law

Like so many of the evidence rules we consider in this book, we need to consider two types of issues that psychology can speak to. First is the question of how useful the evidence actually is. Here, that translates to whether evidence of character is sound and relevant to proving someone engaged in particular conduct on a particular occasion. Second is the question of how the evidence is treated by factfinders: will jurors or judges use the evidence appropriately?

With respect to the basic prohibition on propensity inferences, it is worth reflecting on the intuitive psychology of common law judges, stretching back several centuries. They almost certainly shared our implicit personality theory that the source of behavior resides fairly coherently within each individual, expressing itself more or less consistently across different times, places, and circumstances. Further, however, they apparently believed that character is not a highly dependable predictor of behavior. (Which itself is a remarkable achievement: to rise above one's own intuitions to realize that those intuitions overstate cross-situational, personality-behavior consistency.) And, although *they* recognized that limitation, their intuition or reasoning also suggested to them that jurors would not share the same appreciation for the uncertainties of the character/behavior relationship, and would give excessive weight to the inference from character to the behavior at issue.

Similarly, today's courts, commentators, and rulemakers generally state that character evidence is *relevant* to determining whether on a particular occasion the person acted in a particular way—but such evidence nevertheless is inadmissible. Wigmore tells us that courts have long assumed that character evidence "is essentially relevant."[11] An English court in 1865 stated that, "logically speaking, it is quite clear that an antecedent bad character would form . . . [a] reasonable . . . ground for the presumption and probability of guilt."[12] In 1948, the Supreme Court noted that "[t]he inquiry [into what guidance character evidence might afford] is not rejected because character is irrelevant."[13] Legal scholars agree: "we all believe that people act predictably according to character."[14] Therefore, "[b]y excluding such evidence, the propensity rule contradicts everyday experience."[15] Thus, acting as applied psychologists, judges and lawyers have concluded that people possess some stable mental traits (which the law calls character), and that character has some kind of causal impact on behavior. That is the propensity inference.

Courts, commentators, and rulemakers also routinely explain why, despite widely shared intuitions of character, its causal connection to behavior, and the judgment that it is relevant, judges and rulemakers also believe that such propensity inferences should be forbidden. Their reasons come down to two essential concerns. The first is that jurors are likely to give the character evidence more weight than it deserves. Despite its relevance, for centuries[16] common law judges have thought that factfinders will treat such evidence as being substantially more probative than it actually is. To prevent jurors from overvaluing character evidence, they concluded that it should be excluded altogether. Their second concern is that, upon learning some unfavorable facts about the sort of person the defendant is, jurors will want to punish him regardless of the evidence of guilt on the specific charges at bar, or will require less evidence of guilt than they should demand of the government before deciding to convict a person of a crime. To prevent jurors from effectively lowering the threshold of reasonable doubt on which they are willing to convict, or nullifying the criminal law, jurors should be denied the evidence. Note that, again, acting as amateur psychologists, common law judges estimated how factfinders would use certain information, and concluded that admitting this kind of evidence would lead to more error than withholding it would.

Thus, the common law and the Federal Rules drafters have conducted a generalized probativeness-prejudice balancing, and concluded that prejudice is so likely to exceed probativeness so often and by so much that they adopted a categorical exclusion of character evidence when it is offered to prove charged conduct. (Much of the previous discussion should sound a lot like the discussion of the categorical relevance rules in Chapter 2.)

Psychological research on the predictive connection between personality and behavior, plus how people perceive character and its relationship to behavior, lends considerable support to the conclusions of the common law rulemakers. Indeed, it is possible that the rulemakers are standing on firmer ground than they realized. That is, the research suggests that the probative value generally might be less, and the risk of prejudice more, than the common law judges and modern rulemakers thought.

### *Predictive Power of Character*

At this point, for the legal notion of character let's substitute the psychological concept of personality traits—embracing the same idea that traits have a persistent causal connection to behavior across diverse situations. A century of empirical research searching for and studying personality traits led psychologists to conclude that they were looking for the wrong thing, in the wrong place, or in the wrong way. Put simply, the power of personality measures to predict (or postdict) behavior turned out to be surprisingly weak. (We say "postdict" because in a trial the question is whether a defendant did something in the past, though the tools the factfinders are being invited to use are those of [intuitive] prediction.)

In a number of research programs, various "individual differences" (personality traits and demographics) of experiment participants were measured. Such traits included Machiavellianism, anomie, religiosity, authoritarianism, social desirability, social responsibility, conscientiousness, ego strength, defenses, repression, dependency, and sociability, to name a few. The question studied was whether behavior could be predicted from such measures.

One large and seminal research program, launched in the 1960s by social psychologists Bibb Latané and John Darley and flowering into the subfield of helping behavior (or altruism), focused on the problem of bystander intervention in emergencies: trying to understand what leads people to intervene and take action when they might help others or avoid harm to themselves.[17] The researchers created various kinds of simulated emergencies (e.g., smoke seeping under the door of the room the participants were in, or a person nearby having a seizure) with differing situational contexts in order to test different hypotheses about what led to more versus less bystander intervention. From their hundreds of research participants the researchers also collected data on well over a dozen different individual difference measures, among them some of the best validated personality tests. What they found was that *none* of the personality measures was able to predict who helped and who ignored a crisis. The most potent predictor to emerge was a seemingly trivial situational factor: how many people were present at the time of the incident. The smaller the group, the more likely someone would investigate the problem, or come to the rescue, or call the police. The larger the group, the less likely anyone was to do anything.[18]

In an especially revealing study of bystander intervention, ministry students were conscripted to tape a video extolling the virtues of joining the ministry. The video, they were told, was going to be used to recruit more students to the ministry. Each speaker was to give a brief unscripted talk; they could think about what they wanted to say as they walked across campus to the recording studio. Half were assigned to talk about the material well-being enjoyed by members of the clergy; the other half were assigned the theme of ministry as service to those in need. Thus, half of the ministry students would walk to their appointment at the film studio with thoughts of personal comfort coursing through their minds, while the other half were primed to be thinking about a very different norm: helping those in need. In addition, half of each group were told they were already late for their appointment with the cameras and needed to hurry across campus, while the other half were told that they had plenty of time before the taping and could take their time. Along the route to the studio was an actor, slumped in a doorway, moaning and coughing. Which of the ministry students stopped to help and which stepped around the sufferer? The only thing that predicted whether the participant stopped to help was whether he was in a hurry or not. Those whose minds were working on a message of a career as a Good Samaritan were no more likely to offer help than those who were musing about the comforts and security of a clerical career. The participants in the study also had completed questionnaires containing several personality scales, as well as measures of the nature and depth of their religious commitments. None of these trait measures predicted help-giving.[19] That is, neither personality measures, nor salience of norms for helping those in need, nor depth of religious views were at all related to whether help was offered to a sick or injured person lying on a campus sidewalk. But whether one was in a hurry or not was a significant predictor of help-giving.

A famous series of studies that inquired into the opposite kind of behavior is Milgram's research on obedience.[20] Yale social psychology professor Stanley Milgram used newspaper ads to recruit ordinary adult citizens to come to a nondescript address to participate in a study of "learning." The real purpose, however, was to study the willingness of people to inflict serious, possibly fatal, harm on an innocent fellow participant. Which of two participants was chosen to be the "learner" and which the "teacher" was determined by a coin toss (or so it was made to appear), so that from the "teacher's" perspective, their roles could as easily have been reversed. In actuality, the actual research participant was always assigned the role of teacher and the learner (the victim) was always the other person, who was an actor. As part of the learning "study," the "teacher" had the job of inflicting increasingly severe electric shocks on the "learner" every time the learner made an error or failed to answer. Even after the learner demanded to be released, and later fell silent (perhaps having suffered a heart attack), the teacher continued to inflict the shocks—so long as the experimenter (the authority figure) instructed that it be done and "took responsibility" for the teacher's acts and any harm to the learner. Most of us think only sadists would do such things. But these were normal adults who, when placed in the right situation, were willing to inflict what they believed (no actual shocks were administered) was terrible harm. Most of us think that we would not behave as those people did—it's not in our "character." But under some conditions, Milgram was getting virtually 100% compliance.[21]

Milgram's, and other studies of dangerous, harmful, or violent behavior, are of special interest because few studies of personality involve harmful conduct, and those that do tend to involve minor aggressions by young people, even children. By contrast, criminal trials typically involve people who have committed serious crimes, some of them violent. Perhaps people who are charged with (we cannot yet say "commit") serious crimes might be different from all of the normal or not so normal people who participate in much of the research. But in studies like Milgram's, the participants are normal adults from various walks of life, and with chilling ease the right situation leads them to inflict painful injuries, possibly death, on a person who seems just like themselves—merely because someone in authority says to do it and agrees to "accept responsibility" for whatever happens. We might ponder the many of life's circumstances that can turn a "good" person bad or a "bad" person good. This is not, of course, an argument for excusing those who engage in legally proscribed harm. This is about the problem of using previous bad behavior to decide whether a person has committed a currently charged crime, while attributing the past behavior to an internal state, a character trait, and overlooking the situational variables that might have driven the earlier behavior.

The most prominent effort to summarize the ability of measures of personality to predict behavior found in study after study after study that trait-behavior correlations[22] rarely exceeded r=.30. Though certainly not nothing, this means that most of the time less than 10% of the variation in relevant behavior was being accounted for by the personality measure.[23] This discipline-shaking review by Walter Mischel, a distinguished clinical psychologist, showed that in myriad studies, looking at manifold kinds of behavior, the results did little to support the theory that people behave in accord with their personality traits.[24] In addition, Mischel noted that, while the correlations between personality and behavior were low to begin with, "[e]ven seemingly trivial situational differences can reduce correlations to zero."[25] These findings caused a major reevaluation of the psychology of individual differences because they strongly suggested that the notion that people behave consistently across different situations, reflecting stable underlying personality traits, fell disappointingly short of capturing the reality of whatever was actually going on.[26]

### *Behavior as a Function of Person-Situation Interaction*

From such findings as described in the previous section, some researchers began to wonder if the more productive question was not "what kinds of people" behave in this or that way, but "under what conditions" do people do so. For most psychologists, however, the research led to something more complicated than the conclusion that individual differences in personality should be discarded as useless. Most researchers and theorists suspected that consistency of some kind existed in some form, but that the search had been too simplistic. Although numerous alternative approaches were explored, describing them all is beyond the scope of this book. We will mention just one especially prominent alternative.

The idea that behavior is a function of the person *and* the situation was one of the axiomatic principles of social psychology.[27] It has come to be referred to as person-situation interaction, or *interactionism*.[28] The basic idea is that people are not automatons who act out some internal program regardless of circumstances. People are responsive to the situations they are in, and those responses are determined jointly by the many psychological attributes of the person (cognitive, emotional, etc.) and the context, the situation, within which the person is functioning. You probably are aware that you yourself act different ways in different circumstances: more generous when you've just been paid, more patient with children than with adults, more competitive on the tennis court, and so on.[29] By analyzing the behavior of different persons in different situations, person-by-situation consistencies might be revealed for each individual. In light of such interactionist thinking, some evidence law commentators have suggested that character evidence could be more informative and less misleading if the evidence included the extent of similarity between surrounding circumstances in prior and current conduct, the number of prior instances, proximity in time, and other factors suggested by interactionist research findings.[30] Consistency could be found in patterns of if-then, situation-behavior relationships for each person.[31] Doing this well, in order to be able to say something meaningful for various different idiosyncratic individuals, is quite a large challenge, but one that might some day be achieved.

Currently, past behavior can be used to predict future behavior better than internal hypothetical constructs like personality or character—especially when the behavior has a high frequency of occurrence, tends toward the habitual, is not highly variable from one occasion to the next, occurs in a social/environmental context that is the same or quite similar to the one in which the behavior occurred in the past, the prediction is made over a brief interval of time, and no interventions have occurred to change the person or his behavior.

Such conditions often are met when our friends, family, and coworkers encounter us. Your teachers see you in one set of situations, your parents in another set, your buddies in another set, your romantic other in still another set. They each think they are seeing "you," but each "you" differs—perhaps a little, perhaps a lot—from one set of situations to another as you navigate through them. And their perception of consistency gets help from their own cognitive tendencies.

### *Why Does the Perception That Character/Personality Causes Behavior Seem So Compelling?*

We all sense that we see in others what appears to be consistent character, or personality, and we tend to view these as predictive of cross-situational consistency in their behavior. We are thereby informed about "the kind of person" we are dealing with, and it helps us in trying to make sense of how they behave. Forming such impressions is a fundamental part of what we humans do when we interact with each other. A raft of research has been conducted to try to understand the numerous cognitive processes at work in us as we engage in these efforts. Each discovery of how this "person perception" works also reveals its imperfections, usually born of trade-offs. Speed and efficiency come at a price, and the price paid is lack of completeness and less accuracy.

Metaphorically, human social cognition is like a large and complex computer program that evolved to help us achieve our goals and keep us happy. Marvelous as this program is, its capacity to process information is quite limited. So it does the best it can with what it has, tries to efficiently and rapidly produce answers, and though many of them might be wrong answers, those wrong answers are the safer errors to make. That our cognitive system would evolve to work in this fashion makes sense if you think of our ancestors needing to avoid becoming a predator's dinner, and to work efficiently with other humans in a collective effort to be successful predators themselves. The result is a social-cognitive system that has been variously described by different theorists to be "fast and frugal,"[32] or "miserly,"[33] or to consist of two major systems, the first of which to kick in is fast and intuitive.[34] Such machinery might have served quite well in the world of our evolutionary history that created it—among small tribes of hunter-gatherers, who knew each other well enough to know what behavior to expect of each other in what situations. There were few enough people and few enough situations for them to know everything they needed to know about everybody they dealt with. In that respect, at least, we today are not so fortunate.

In modern, urban life, our social-cognitive system faces challenges it is not designed for. A cognitive system that has limited capacity but must work quickly is selective in the information taken in, interprets that limited information in ways that serve our current most pressing goals, and leads to judgments and decisions that are best guesses. Under some circumstances we will store the information gained in memory for future use, but the storage will be simplified, incomplete, and subject to systematic distortion when we later retrieve it. In a multitude of ways, our social-cognitive machinery serves us by seeking simplicity and consistency. Consequently, we typically form and maintain impressions of traits that seem more solid, consistent, and connected to behavior than actually exist.

As discussed earlier, people evolved to see patterns in the world and we look for explanations for those patterns[35]—thus, we tend to perceive the world as filled with causal linkages. We believe that things do not just happen, they are caused. That includes human behavior. And the cause of human behavior is typically seen as something inside the behaver—her intentions, motivations, personality—something dispositional. When we see a person behave in any way that catches our attention, we instantaneously "explain" the behavior in terms of the person's inferred (not observed) characteristics. We do not merely observe a stranger who does not speak much in a group; from just seeing that one bit of behavior, we infer that the person is shy. (This psychological phenomenon has a name: *spontaneous trait inference.*) If we are asked to describe the person, we will say that she is shy. If asked how we know that, we say it is because she did not speak much. All of this circularity derives from observing a bit of behavior. Judge (later Supreme Court Justice) Benjamin Cardozo, when sitting on the New York Court of Appeals, once wrote that "there may be cogency in the argument that a quarrelsome defendant is more likely [than the average person] to start a quarrel."[36] And we are more likely to describe people in terms of those inferred traits and states than to describe what we actually observed. It is easier to remember one trait summary than a lot of observations—observations which from person to person will vary to a greater or lesser degree in their consistency.

But in making sense of the world, we also like our knowledge to be consistent. When thinking of others, we view them as having constant personalities and we attribute their behavior to personality or other traits or states of the behaver (a *dispositional attribution*). We tend to overlook the situational forces that might be at work. This preference for dispositional attributions is so strong that it has been termed the *fundamental attribution error*.[37] We do not, however, perceive our own behavior as being driven relentlessly by those internal forces. We believe that we ourselves are consistent in our values and our (typically good) behavior, and when we behave otherwise it is because we see ourselves responding to demands of the situation, including the behavior of other people (a phenomenon termed the *actor-observer effect*.[38])

What do we do with the disparate information we inevitably receive about another person? Our cognitive apparatus combines the information into a summary judgment that pushes toward consistency. To accomplish this, we interpret the conflicting information in a way to make it less conflicting, or we give some pieces less weight, or we disregard discordant pieces altogether. This is far more efficient, though less accurate, than trying to hold on to a more complex mosaic of an impression of a person.[39]

All else equal, the trait-relevant information we learn first exerts more influence than later items of information. As soon as we form an impression, later information tends to be assimilated to the existing impression, rather than changing it. This is not to say that a lot of subsequent information that refutes the initial information will not change one's impression of a target person, but much more cognitive effort is required to change an impression once it is formed than it took to form it in the first place.[40] Additionally, certain bits of information heavily influence other information. If a speaker is introduced to an audience as being a "warm" person, almost all other trait judgments the audience members make about the person will shift in a direction to be more consistent with being a warm person. If the same speaker is, instead, introduced to the same audience as being a "cold" person, the other trait judgments will shift in the opposite direction.

The example just given is a specific instance of *expectation*. When we happen to expect or desire to reach a certain conclusion, we tend to *assimilate* the information we acquire in the direction of the expectation. Sometimes we have preformed impressions of certain groups or types (*stereotyping*).[41] A few bits of information about a person who is a member of a stereotyped group tends to trigger a lot of beliefs about the group. We might think we know quite a lot about the target person while we actually are simply drawing on preexisting beliefs about a group the individual belongs to. Moreover, our expectations lead us to act toward a person in a manner that tends to produce more behaviors that tend to confirm the initial perceptions (a type of *self-fulfilling prophecy*).[42] An example of this is police interrogations: when a person is thought to be guilty, the questions posed to, statements made to, and other treatment of the person evoke responses that cause the person to respond in ways that make him appear more guilty.[43]

On occasions when we have come to be motivated to reach a particular conclusion, we draw on information selectively and interpret it in ways that bring us to the conclusions we desire to reach.[44] This process occurs automatically and without awareness; we feel we are just thinking about the matter and arriving at the correct conclusion (*motivated reasoning*).[45]

As an example of some of the thought processes we have described, think about a politician you especially love or hate. Isn't it interesting that just about everything that person says or does confirms your prior impression of and feelings about the person, ossifying your judgment still further.

### *What Is Consistent?*

Before we leave the subject of why the perception of character or personality seems so real and correct, let's not overlook this: something real exists in the person that is related, even if in complex ways, to behavior over time and situations. We all have differences in our neuropsychological structure and functioning, differences due both to genetics and learning.[46] In dealing with people in our everyday lives,[47] we are sensing and responding to actual patterns, even as those patterns must be processed through our person perception machinery. We might not see those stable differences in all their person-situation complexity, but we are reacting to something that exists and persists. Some "traits" are more consistent in some people than other traits; for other people, other traits are the more consistent ones.[48]

Beyond traits, other constructs of mind have much more stability and predictive power than character does. One of the most potent of these is *temperament*. Temperament refers to such things as energy level, biological rhythmicity, reactivity to new stimuli, mood, and distractibility. Temperament is believed to be in large measure the product of a person's biology and neurology. Studies have found correlations between measures of these temperaments taken in infancy and young adulthood. Here is evidence of consistency over considerable time periods. These are things that people perceive about each other, whether clearly or dimly. But, at best, these are connected only indirectly to the sorts of behavior that the law has long regarded as reflecting a person's character.

In addition, some of the people who come into contact with the law suffer from psychiatric or neurological conditions that cause them to be consistently more dangerous or untrustworthy or to display some other troublesome behavior pattern more than most other people. That is a whole other category of predictability. Valid research about the predictability of ordinary behavior does not necessarily generalize to the prediction of extreme behavior of some or many of those who come to the law's attention. Ironically, one of the major types of such abnormality, psychopathy, is characterized not only by amorality but also by the ability to be charming and manipulative. These latter characteristics can create favorable impressions, at least in the early stages of contact with others.

### *Legal Policy Implications*

The findings we have reviewed concerning the weakness of person variables, standing alone, as predictors of particular conduct, and the advantages gained by adding consideration of situational variables suggest some lessons for the law of character evidence.

In most cases it is not likely that personality, or character, by itself, causes or predicts behavior with enough consistency to allow factfinders to accurately account for conduct from evidence of character—even assuming factfinders were provided with accurate evidence of a person's character. Errors of overprediction will be common. Consequently, the prohibition on propensity appears to be a sensible legal policy. Given how misleading propensity evidence can be, and the excessive confidence that people have in such information, the prohibition probably makes even more sense than the common law judges who invented and preserved the rule over the past three centuries fully appreciated.

On the other hand, we have noted that past behavior is a better predictor of future behavior than personality variables are. This phenomenon would be especially true if the circumstances under which the behavior occurred were known and they paralleled those of the current case being tried. Why, then, not allow such evidence even if character evidence remains forbidden? Interestingly, the rules governing the manner of presentation of character evidence bar exactly such specific-instances-of-conduct testimony. That, obviously, could be changed if specific instances of behavior came to be recognized as more probative and the barrier to admission removed. One explanation for nonadmission might be the finding that people make spontaneous trait inferences from descriptions of behavior to personality. Thus, the step from behavior to character is a very short one—and from there we are back to the problem of overconfident and inflated postdictions about the disputed behavior at issue in the case.

Thoughtful commentators have pointed out that low base rates of a behavior (e.g., only a tiny percentage of the population commits homicide)—which go hand in hand with poor accuracy and high overprediction errors—might still be quite relevant and might nevertheless help factfinders reach correct verdicts.[49]

For example, if the question is whether a murdered woman was killed by her husband/boyfriend, is it useful to know that the man physically abused the woman during their years together? Suppose we know that of every 100,000 battered women, 45 end up being murdered (by anyone) and 99,955 are never murdered. This information would not help you predict that a battered woman will end up being a murdered woman, since it so rarely happens. But the question before a jury is different: given that a woman *has been* murdered, is it helpful to know that she had been a battered woman and that her partner was the batterer? Suppose the data show that of the 45 out of 100,000 battered women who are murdered, 40 are murdered by their partners and 5 by someone else. Now we know that battered women who are murdered are eight times more likely to have been murdered by their partners than by someone else. This clearly is relevant information by the law's definition.

But we still have not reached the question a court or a rulemaker has to decide. The vital question is whether factfinders make more accurate decisions with the information (that the partner was a batterer) or without it. The information provided above (known as a likelihood ratio) would be quite useful if our minds ran naturally along Bayesian paths. We refer here to Bayes' Theorem, an analytic strategy that facilitates adjustments in the probability of an event as information of known probabilities is added to a prior estimation of the event's probability of occurrence. The trouble is that we humans are notoriously non-Bayesian in our ability to use quantitative information. We will not use the information accurately. If factfinders underincorporate the information, the defendant can have little complaint. But if factfinders overweight the information (for example, if they take the evidence of prior battering to suggest that it makes the defendant 800 times as likely to have committed the murder, rather than only 8 times as likely), then the risk of erroneous conviction of a wife-batterer for his wife's murder will be quite considerable. (And we have not even mentioned the risk that a jury is thought likely to feel that someone who battered the poor woman over years needs to be punished [now, and by this jury] whether or not he is the one who killed her.)

The problem of a jury not using the relevant statistical evidence properly could (perhaps) be solved by allowing expert witnesses to show the jury where a Bayesian analysis of the battering evidence should lead their thinking in light of all of the other evidence they've learned in the case. But, so far, courts have been loath to allow such mathematical instruction of juries.

Perhaps in the future, research will show how to find stable person-situation patterns so that reasonably accurate links can be made to current (or recent) behavior. Assuming factfinders can temper their use of such evidence—refraining from focusing on the character component and giving the patterns appropriate, not excessive, weight—the time might arrive when the law could justifiably relax the rule to allow some person-situation evidence that is especially predictive, and build from there, over time, as growing knowledge permitted.[50]

## Evidence about Individuals That Is Admissible

Some rules do allow the admission of information about the background of a witness or defendant. Some of these rules relate to what the law clearly means by "character" evidence. Other rules pertain to evidence about a person that consists of prior crimes, wrongs, and acts, as well as habits.

### *Other Acts Evidence—Rule 404(b)*

After reiterating the prohibition on admitting "evidence of a crime, wrong, or other act . . . to prove a person's character in order to show that on a particular occasion the person acted in accordance with the character," Rule 404(b) offers a non-exclusive list of purposes for which such evidence *is* admissible: "This evidence may be admissible for another purpose, such as proving motive, opportunity, intent, preparation, plan, knowledge, identity, absence of mistake, or lack of accident." As with so much of evidence law, the list developed as the common law encountered fact patterns in cases. And as with many other rules (e.g., the categorical exclusion rules), we need to worry whether jurors allowed to use evidence in a given case for one purpose are able to limit its use to that one purpose or whether they will also use it to make the forbidden propensity inference.

---

**Rule 404(b). Crimes or Other Acts**

(1) Prohibited Uses. Evidence of a crime, wrong, or other act is not admissible to prove a person's character in order to show that on a particular occasion the person acted in accordance with the character.

(2) Permitted Uses; Notice in a Criminal Case. This evidence may be admissible for another purpose, such as proving motive, opportunity, intent, preparation, plan, knowledge, identity, absence of mistake, or lack of accident.

---

Three purposes account for the bulk of what the rule lets in as evidence: identification, state of mind, and circumstances attending the charged crime (termed the "res gestae" of the incident). Several examples illustrate the kinds of evidence dealt with under the rule:

- A tool or weapon acquired in an earlier crime and used to commit the currently charged crime is offered to identify the defendant as the person who committed the current crime—but cannot be offered to support the inference that a person who committed a prior crime therefore also committed the current crime.
- A defendant is charged with a burglary during which furniture was rearranged in an odd way. Evidence of a prior burglary known to

have been committed by the defendant, during which furniture had been rearranged in a similarly odd way is offered in order to identify the defendant as the person who committed the currently charged burglary. But the evidence cannot be offered to suggest that once a burglar, always a burglar.

- A person is charged with a murder that involved biting the victim. The prosecution offers evidence that the defendant was previously convicted of an assault that involved biting the victim—offered to identify the defendant as the person who committed the murder.
- A person is sued for damages caused by a car crash. The plaintiff offers evidence that at the time of the crash the defendant was making his getaway from a bank he had robbed—offered to support an argument that the defendant had reason to be, and therefore was, driving recklessly.
- A defendant is charged with murder. The prosecution offers evidence that the defendant was engaged in a bank robbery at the time of the murder—to provide a more complete picture of the circumstances and to suggest a motive for the killing.
- In a charge for drunk driving, the prosecutor wishes to offer evidence that the defendant had an illegal weapon hidden in the car—arguably part of the res gestae of the drunk driving incident (but to what genuine issue is it relevant?).

A vast assortment of fact patterns has led to many arguments for and against admission of such other-acts evidence, which has led to a bewildering assortment of inconsistent judicial rulings. The examples above should make it apparent that there is ample opportunity for drawing forbidden propensity inferences from such evidence at the same time that the evidence provides information that is probative of genuine factual issues. If a court thinks that the evidence is being offered for a proper purpose in a case, the evidence is not excludable under 404(b). But the court also is likely to be asked to evaluate the evidence under Rule 403 for its impact on prohibited propensity inferences. As discussed in an earlier chapter, Rule 403 is concerned with the dangers of unfair prejudice, confusion of issues, and misleading the jury. Other-acts evidence often is fraught with all three of those risks. If the risks substantially outweigh the probative value of the evidence, courts will (or should) exclude it. Sometimes courts let the jury hear the other-acts evidence but try to reduce the risk of prejudicial effects by giving a limiting instruction, telling the jury to use the evidence for the permissible purpose but not to use it to draw any impermissible inferences. Although studies have not specifically evaluated limiting instructions involving other-acts evidence, much research has found, and judges have in candid moments opined, that following such an instruction is all but impossible for jurors. Note, not incidentally, that in performing this balancing, the judge must again act as an applied psychologist—trying to predict the impact of the evidence on jurors for the two different purposes and assessing whether the balance tilts too far in the unacceptable direction.

### *Habit—Rule 406*

Rule 406 says that a judge "may" (but need not) admit evidence of a person's "habit" or an organization's "routine practice" to prove that the "person or organization acted in accordance with the habit or routine practice" on a particular occasion related to the litigation. An important part of the work that Rule 406 does is in the final sentence: evidence of habit or routine practice is admissible "regardless of whether it is corroborated or whether there was an eyewitness." That nullifies an older view that habit evidence was not admissible if other, supposedly more dependable, evidence was available.

---

**Rule 406. Habit; Routine Practice**

Evidence of a person's habit or an organization's routine practice may be admitted to prove that on a particular occasion the person or organization acted in accordance with the habit or routine practice. The court may admit this evidence regardless of whether it is corroborated or whether there was an eyewitness.

---

Another part of the work the rule does is through the Advisory Committee Note, which defines "habit," and quotes a statement from Prof. McCormick's evidence treatise:

> Character and habit are close akin. Character is a generalized description of one's disposition, or of one's disposition in respect to a general trait,

> such as honesty, temperance, or peacefulness. "Habit," in modern usage, both lay and psychological, is more specific. It describes one's regular response to a repeated specific situation. If we speak of character for care, we think of the person's tendency to act prudently in all the varying situations of life, in business, family life, in handling automobiles and in walking across the street. A habit, on the other hand, is the person's regular practice of meeting a particular kind of situation with a specific type of conduct, such as the habit of going down a particular stairway two stairs at a time, or of giving the hand-signal for a left turn, or of alighting from railway cars while they are moving. The doing of the habitual acts may become semi-automatic.

Character evidence is generally inadmissible; habit evidence is generally admissible. Were counsel to proffer character evidence in the guise of habit evidence, the Advisory Committee Note to the rule is ready to guide judges to block the effort.

Habits, or "automatic behavior" (a synonym often used when referring to humans in contrast to animals), "are learned dispositions to repeat past responses. They are triggered by features of the context that have covaried frequently with past performance, including performance locations, preceding actions in a sequence, and particular people. Contexts activate habitual responses directly, without the mediation of goal states."[51] Habits have a complicated relationship with goals. Goals influence habit formation; once formed, the habit is performed in response to the eliciting context whether or not it achieves the original goal. If a new goal is in conflict with the habit, the habit is not as easily suppressed as we might wish it would be. Behavior is considered automatic if (1) the triggering sensory events almost always elicit the behavior, and (2) the behavior can be executed successfully while the person is simultaneously engaged in some other secondary task.[52]

All of this should sound highly consistent with the law's notion of habit, especially the idea that it is concretely situation-specific and focused on behavior that is repeatedly tied to specific circumstances. Since contextual cues are the elicitors of habit, evidence establishing that an individual was acting according to habit should rest upon whether or not the situation was the one in which the habit occurs and the cues to the habit were present. As emphasized earlier, the law's doubts about the usefulness of the concepts of character and personality are on the correct track psychologically. As to habit, from the perspective of psychological research and theory, the law is even more on target.

### *Witness Credibility: Prior Convictions—Rule 609*

Federal Rule of Evidence 609 allows the jury to learn of certain kinds of prior convictions for one, and only one, purpose: impeaching the credibility of the witness by seeking to establish that the witness lacks a "character for truthfulness." Because a prior criminal conviction is expected to have a potent impact on the jury, the kinds of admissible convictions are limited to felonies and any crime that involved a "dishonest act or false statement," regardless of its seriousness.

---

**Rule 609. Impeachment by Evidence of a Criminal Conviction**

(a) In General. The following rules apply to attacking a witness's character for truthfulness by evidence of a criminal conviction:

(1) for a crime that, in the convicting jurisdiction, was punishable by death or by imprisonment for more than one year, the evidence:

(A) must be admitted, subject to Rule 403, in a civil case or in a criminal case in which the witness is not a defendant; and

(B) must be admitted in a criminal case in which the witness is a defendant, if the probative value of the evidence outweighs its prejudicial effect to that defendant; and

(2) for any crime regardless of the punishment, the evidence must be admitted if the court can readily determine that establishing the elements of the crime required proving or the witness's admitting a dishonest act or false statement.

(b) Limit on Using the Evidence After 10 Years. . . .

(c) Effect of a Pardon, Annulment, or Certificate of Rehabilitation. . . .

(d) Juvenile Adjudications. . . .

(e) Pendency of an Appeal. . . .

---

The law's theory is that a person who has been convicted of a crime involving dishonesty or false statement, or any serious crime, can be inferred to have a character for untruthfulness, and the factfinder is welcome to infer that such a person might be lying on the witness stand right now. But does a forthright murder or assault or robbery imply a propensity to lie? Wouldn't burglary imply a greater inclination to deceive? Or fraud? Certainly. But the law makes no distinction. It assumes that, whatever else law breaking tells us about a person, it tells us that the person has a substantially increased likelihood of telling lies (or "being" a liar).

The law also realizes that prior conviction evidence presents a great risk of disadvantaging those charged with crimes who wish to take the stand in their own defense. Instead of using the prior conviction exclusively to assist them in assessing credibility, factfinders might draw the inference that a person who commits a crime has a criminal character and therefore is more likely to be guilty of the crime charged. Or worse, if the prior crime is the same sort of crime as the one currently charged, factfinders might assume something on the order of "once a thief, always a thief."[53] To try to prevent improper use of prior crimes evidence, courts will instruct jurors to use that evidence solely to evaluate credibility.[54]

The available empirical research is unanimous in finding that, notwithstanding judicial instructions to the contrary, most people travel the forbidden path of using prior crimes evidence to make substantive inferences about the likelihood that the testifying defendant committed the current crime charged.[55]

In one of those experiments,[56] mock jurors comprising non-student adults in Boston read one of several trial summaries in which the fictional defendant was charged with either murder or auto theft. Because the defendant took the witness stand (in order to give evidence supporting his claim that he was innocent), the prosecution was permitted to introduce evidence of his prior crimes. The defendant had one of several prior convictions—for homicide, for auto theft, for perjury—or had no prior conviction at all. Note that in some versions of the case, the prior crime was the same as the current charge (e.g., auto theft + auto theft), and in some they were different (e.g., auto theft + murder). The jurors who learned of a prior conviction also received a judicial instruction that this evidence was to be used solely for the purpose of assessing the credibility of the defendant's testimony.

If jurors analyzed the evidence as the law instructs, the highest rate of convictions would occur where the prior crime was perjury. After all, what prior crime could be more illuminating about the defendant's propensity for not telling the truth in court than a prior conviction for lying under oath in court? But that is not what the results showed the mock jurors to be doing. The highest conviction rates occurred when the prior crime was the same as the crime currently charged. Those findings suggest that jurors drew a character inference something like this: the defendant previously committed crime X, so he is the kind of person who has a propensity to commit crime X, and therefore he probably committed crime X this time, too. Thus, contrary to the law's instructions and expectations, the jurors were unable or unwilling to use prior convictions exclusively for the purpose of evaluating credibility.

Interestingly, the law is mistaken for a second reason. The study also asked the jurors to rate the credibility of each witness in the trial. In each version of the case, the defendant received the lowest credibility rating of any of the witnesses, even when he had no prior convictions.[57] Jurors were, apparently, skeptical of any defendant charged with any crime. And why not? Who has a greater motive to lie than the defendant (in an effort to obtain an acquittal)? Importantly, the ratings of the defendants' credibility did not differ from one case condition to another—that is, credibility ratings were not lower if there was a prior conviction for perjury or another violation, and not higher if there was no prior conviction. Credibility that is near the floor to begin with cannot be pushed much lower, even if jurors were following the instruction to use prior convictions to help them assess witness credibility. The research suggests, then, that prior conviction evidence contributes little or nothing to credibility assessment of defendants who take the witness stand, while at the same time creating the risk that jurors will draw improper propensity inferences.[58]

### *Witness Credibility: Character and Conduct—Rule 608*

Rule 608 focuses on credibility generally. Few matters are more central to the task of a trial factfinder than deciding what testimony to believe and what to doubt. If the judge or jurors know which witnesses are liars, they can discount the testimony of those witnesses and rely more heavily on the witnesses they know to be truth tellers. And Rule 608 helpfully permits a witness's character for truthfulness to be inquired into.[59] How simple. But, as you doubtless have grown to suspect, matters of personality and behavior are rarely so simple.

**Rule 608. A Witness's Character for Truthfulness or Untruthfulness**

(a) Reputation or Opinion Evidence. A witness's credibility may be attacked or supported by testimony about the witness's reputation for having a character for truthfulness or untruthfulness, or by testimony in the form of an opinion about that character. But evidence of truthful character is admissible only after the witness's character for truthfulness has been attacked.

(b) Specific Instances of Conduct. Except for a criminal conviction under Rule 609, extrinsic evidence is not admissible to prove specific instances of a witness's conduct in order to attack or support the witness's character for truthfulness. But the court may, on cross-examination, allow them to be inquired into if they are probative of the character for truthfulness or untruthfulness of:

(1) the witness; or

(2) another witness whose character the witness being cross-examined has testified about. By testifying on another matter, a witness does not waive any privilege against self-incrimination for testimony that relates only to the witness's character for truthfulness.

First of all, the rule itself is somewhat complex. It specifies the circumstances under which character for truthfulness may be inquired into in the form of opinion or reputation, and when the inquiry may go to specific instances of conduct. Moreover, a witness's character for truthfulness may be inquired into only after the other side has attacked the witness on cross-examination as being untruthful.

How do people come to the opinion that a person is a prevaricator? Presumably they have caught the person in what they believe to be a lie, or several lies, or been told by one or more third parties that the person is a dissembler. Upon reaching the inference that a person who has lied *has a character trait* for telling lies, the witness informs the factfinder of that "fact." Then the factfinder has to decide how to use that information to evaluate the testimony given by the person whose honesty is in question. After all, does being "a liar" mean you lie with every breath, or only that you have a greater tendency for prevaricating than the rest of us do? Surely, the latter. So factfinders still have a difficult judgment to make about credibility, whether or not they realize it.

The reality of human honesty and dishonesty makes the challenge faced by factfinders even more challenging. Psychological research has found that lying and cheating are familiar occurrences in society. Most of us do it—not all of the time and not to a great extent, but sometimes, somewhat, to some extent. Most of us lie and cheat, more often than we seem to realize. Here is how the magnitude was described by Dan Ariely, whose research on lying with respect to oaths was described in the previous chapter: "Across all of our experiments, we've tested maybe 30,000 people, and we had a dozen or so bad apples and they stole about $150 from us. And we had about 18,000 little rotten apples, each of them just stole a couple of dollars, but together it was $36,000. [That's] actually a good reflection of what happens in society."[60]

In one experiment, people were given 20 fairly simple math problems on a sheet of paper and five minutes to solve as many as they could. They were to be paid $1 for each correct answer. The participants self-graded their quiz, shredded the quiz, and reported the number they got correct to the experimenter. Unknown to the participant, the shredder was designed to shred only the margins of the paper, so the number they actually got right could later be compared to how many they claimed to have gotten right. On average, people reported getting six correct, though they actually got only four correct.

As you will by now suspect, the situation plays an important role in whether people lie, cheat, or steal. If we are in an environment where others are known to be cheating (making it socially acceptable), more people cheat and cheat more. But some seemingly minor elements of a situation can have a major effect. In a variation on the experiment described above, instead of telling the experimenter how many they got right and being handed dollars, they were given plastic tokens, which could be exchanged (moments later and only 12 feet away) for dollars. Doing it that way doubled the amount of dishonest reporting.

Should such findings really surprise us? Have you never told an untruth to your family, friends, or colleagues? Have they always been completely honest with you? Do businesspeople and public officials always share the unvarnished truth with their clients and the public? Are there not circumstances that lead them to edit, trim, fudge what they say to make themselves or their product or their policies or their performance appear better than they actually are?

The research findings do suggest, however, that among all of us little liars is a relatively small number of really big liars. What the judge and jury need to learn is not whether the witness has told numerous lies during his or her life (that is true of all witnesses), but whether this is someone who tells really big lies under really serious circumstances. It is not apparent that any of us are any good at making that distinction when we are told by a third party that in the third party's opinion the person in question is a liar, or has told lies on specified occasions (and therefore has a character trait of being a liar). The risk is great that we ordinary liars will be too easily lumped in with the big, bad liars.

As discussed in an earlier chapter, our legal system at one time sensed that the role a person occupied (a situational variable) could be more powerful than character. Two hundred years ago, common law evidence rules prohibited parties from testifying in their own cases. The theory was that in one's own case the temptation to lie in an effort to win is too great, so the best course was to dispense with the parties' testimony altogether. On the other hand, it might be that the trappings of the courtroom—the formality, the judge on high in a black robe, the oath, an awareness that a lie here could be punished as a crime, a suspicious audience watching every word and movement—are situational factors that tend to induce people to tell the truth, even people who in less high-pressured situations might lie. This latter course is the one to which the rules of evidence obviously have moved. But who had the better rule: our legal ancestors or their descendants?

### *Sexual Conduct Exceptions to the Rule against Character Evidence—Rules 413, 414, 415*

As mentioned earlier in this chapter, Rules 413, 414, and 415 were added to the federal evidence code in the mid-1990s and allow evidence concerning prior criminal sexual conduct to be admitted and for inferences to be drawn concerning "any matter to which it is relevant." Such "matters" would certainly include the inference that the defendant has a propensity to commit sexual assaults and acted in accordance with that trait on the now-relevant occasion. Such an inference is, of course, precisely what Rule 404(a) prohibits, and what the common law has prohibited for centuries and continues to prohibit for other purported propensities.

The logic of this exception has to be that sex crimes are different.[61] If we had sound evidence that persons who committed a sex crime in the past had a substantial likelihood of committing a similar crime in the future, and that the probability exceeded that for all other crimes (because if perpetrators of assault or kidnapping or reckless endangerment or robbery or drunk driving had higher propensities to reoffend, then surely *those* too would be crimes that should be the subject of an exception to the rule against propensity evidence), and if we knew that factfinders could give the evidence its approximately appropriate weight, then we would have a foundation from which to argue that sound policy would be to admit a past sex offense as proof that the defendant committed the current crime charged. The proponents of Rules 413, 414, and 415 asserted as much, but had no empirical evidence to support the claim.[62]

---

**Rule 413. Similar Crimes in Sexual-Assault Cases**

(a) Permitted Uses. In a criminal case in which a defendant is accused of a sexual assault, the court may admit evidence that the defendant committed any other sexual assault. The evidence may be considered on any matter to which it is relevant.

(b) Disclosure to the Defendant. If the prosecutor intends to offer this evidence, the prosecutor must disclose it to the defendant, including witnesses' statements or a summary of the expected testimony. The prosecutor must do so at least 15 days before trial or at a later time that the court allows for good cause.

(c) Effect on Other Rules. This rule does not limit the admission or consideration of evidence under any other rule.

(d) Definition of "Sexual Assault." In this rule and Rule 415, "sexual assault" means a crime under federal law or under state law (as "state" is defined in 18 U.S.C. § 513) involving:

(1) any conduct prohibited by 18 U.S.C. chapter 109 A;

(2) contact, without consent, between any part of the defendant's body—or an object and another person's genitals or anus;

(3) contact, without consent, between the defendant's genitals or anus and any part of another person's body;

(4) deriving sexual pleasure or gratification from inflicting death, bodily injury, or physical pain on another person; or

(5) an attempt or conspiracy to engage in conduct described in subparagraphs (1)-(4).

---

As discussed earlier in this chapter, even if the frequency of such behavior is quite low, predictive relevance could still exist. But, as we also discussed, for such evidence to lead closer to a correct conclusion would require a kind of statistical-mindedness that we humans are, without the assistance of explicit computation to guide us, terrible at. Some of the better studies of the predictive utility of past instances of sexual misconduct make such predictions even dicier than the predictive utility of other, non-sexual criminal behavior.

Studies of persons who have committed sexual offenses suggest that they are more variable and less predictable than persons who commit other kinds of criminal offenses.[63] A longitudinal study of over 6,000 individuals, followed for 20–30 years, found that the best predictor for adult sex offending was frequency of offending as a juvenile—but it did not matter what those juvenile offenses were.[64] Males who had been adjudicated as having committed juvenile sexual offenses were no more likely to have future sexual offenses charged to them than males who committed juvenile non-sexual offenses.[65] Moreover, those who had been charged with a juvenile sex offense were unlikely to have any type of adult criminal record. That suggests that "sex crimes are different" in a way quite unlike that which has been assumed by many judges and legislators, at least for juveniles. The overall findings of the research led to the conclusion that law enforcement efforts aimed at deterring recidivism in juvenile sex offenders will fail to detect 90% of individuals who eventually grow up to commit sex crimes as adults, and will erroneously label 90% of juvenile sex offenders as being at heightened risk of becoming future adult sexual predators.[66]

---

**Rule 414. Similar Crimes in Child-Molestation Cases**

Authors' note: This rule is very similar to Rule 413, except that it applies to cases charging child molestation.

---

**Rule 415. Similar Acts in Civil Cases Involving Sexual Assault or Child Molestation**

Authors' note: This rule is very similar to Rules 413 and 414, except that it applies to civil cases involving a claim for relief based on a party's alleged sexual assault or child molestation.

---

As to adult offenders, a recent study of adult males convicted of sexual offenses, aimed at predicting future sex crimes, also found prediction to be difficult. The study concluded that its "[f]indings suggest that a sex crime is more reflective of a transitory phase of the criminal career rather than evidence of a 'sexual criminal career' in the making."[67]

Inquiries into recidivism rates for various crimes regularly find that "the highest . . . correlation between previous crimes and commission of the same crime in the future exists for property crimes and drug crimes. . . . One of the lowest statistical correlations exists between prior sexual crimes and future sexual misconduct."[68] To put specific numbers on these data from reports of the U.S. Sentencing Commission and the U.S. Department of Justice, the recidivism rates, as a percentage of prior offenders who are charged with a reoffense of the same category of crime, are: sex crimes: 2.5–7.7%; violent crimes: 27.5–30.4%; drug crimes: 24.8–41.2%; property crimes: 46.3–49.8%.[69]

The irony is apparent: the rules do not admit propensity evidence for high-recidivism crimes, but now routinely allow for the admission of propensity evidence regarding prior sexual misconduct, whether or not the alleged sexual misconduct resulted in a conviction.[70]

## Conclusion

The chief psychological lesson of this chapter is that rules limiting character evidence are more sensible than even the rulemakers themselves fully appreciated. Personality traits are less predictive than most people realize. On the other hand, social situations and the interaction of situations and personality seem to be the more potent drivers of behavior. Yet most people tend to perceive others through lenses of personality, traits, and propensity, and as a consequence they tend to overattribute and overpredict consistency between character and conduct. Put simply, we attribute to persons more consistency than actually exists. So the law of character evidence has diagnosed a complex problem that is supported by psychological research, and the law has taken some sensible steps to temper those tendencies in order to prevent unfair and inaccurate verdicts. The basic propensity rule—"Evidence of a person's character or character trait is not admissible to prove that on a particular occasion the person acted in accordance with the character or trait" (Rule 404(a)(1))—combats the tendency to mislead ourselves.

A great deal of psychological research conducted over the past century casts doubt on the assumption that traits of character are a useful concept for understanding how personality is organized or for predicting behavior. Correlations between personality measures and behavior are low. Situational factors can overwhelm personality factors and drive much behavior. And complex interactions between personality traits and situations can boost predictive power even more—though putting that information to practical use is far from easy. Perhaps equally interesting are all of the processes of social cognition that help explain why we perceive the hypothetical construct of personality, attribute behavior to it, and perceive it as driving behavior across time and situations.

The rules allow for numerous exceptions—opening the door to admission of some character evidence out of fairness or aiming to admit potentially helpful evidence while still prohibiting its more misleading aspects. Thus, for example, defendants in criminal cases are permitted to offer evidence of their own character or the character of a victim, and character evidence may be offered by any party for a non-forbidden purpose (to prove "motive, opportunity, intent," etc.) And, of course, sometimes character is unavoidably relevant under the substantive law implicated in a case (e.g., defamation).

Close relatives of character evidence are evidence of an individual's habit or an organization's routine practice. Psychological research findings suggest that the law has drawn quite a sensible distinction between habit and character. Since habit and routine practice *are* admissible, a key issue is determining where the line is that separates forbidden character evidence from permissible habit evidence.

Other exceptions are made to assist factfinders in their task of evaluating the credibility of witnesses. The rules carefully restrict attacks on a witness's character so that the evidence may "refer only to character for truthfulness or untruthfulness." A special case is evidence of a witness's conviction of prior crimes, whereby a somewhat complex maze of rules specifies when a prior crime is or is not admissible—though, of course, only on the issue of truthfulness or untruthfulness. Research has consistently found that (people in the role of) jurors are much more likely to rely on that evidence for its improper propensity purpose, despite stern instructions from judges about the limited use to which it may be put.

In recent years, a controversial set of rules has been added that permit evidence of a defendant's prior criminal sexual conduct to be admitted and allow the factfinder to draw inferences from that evidence about "any matter to which it is relevant." These rules are controversial because they fly in the face of centuries of Anglo-American legal thinking about character evidence and actually invite jurors to make what had for so long been forbidden inferences. Moreover, the new rules were advanced and adopted without any empirical evidence showing that prior criminal sexual behavior was more predictive than any other kind of prior criminal behavior. (And most research suggests that other kinds of criminal behavior are considerably more predictive.)

# PART III

# Other Types of Evidence

6

# Hearsay and Exceptions

In the children's game of "telephone," one child thinks up something to say, maybe something true about herself, for example, "I like to sing and dance." She whispers it to the next child, who whispers it to the next child, and so on down the line. Finally, the last child announces the sentence: "I hike and bike in France." The results of the game can be funny and surprising. But they belong at a party, not in the courtroom.[1]

The problem of hearsay evidence is the problem illustrated in the telephone example. The first child, who is the analog of the "declarant" for purposes of the hearsay rule, knows what she has said and knows whether it is true or false. But we haven't heard from her, we have only heard from the last child, the analog of the in-court witness in the hearsay rule. We can check the last child's perception and veracity, etc., but that's a far cry from being sure about the first child's statement.

## Rule against Hearsay

Normally witnesses may testify only to things about which they have personal knowledge. They can testify to what they saw and heard and experienced. In Chapter 4, we described "Tribe's Testimonial Triangle"[2]—an analysis of the potential SPAM (sincerity, perception, ambiguity, memory) infirmities in testimony illustrated at the top of Figure 6.1. We described the various techniques that can be used to help assess whether a witness is mistaken or lying: she would have taken an oath, the jury can watch her demeanor, a lawyer can impeach her credibility and cross-examine her. Each of those techniques addresses one or more of the infirmities (as shown in Table 4.1).

Witnesses are not permitted to testify to the truth of what other people claim they saw or heard or experienced. That is, if Jake told Fred that Jake saw a lion nearby, we might let Fred testify that he heard Jake say, "I saw a lion," because Fred does have first-hand knowledge that Jake

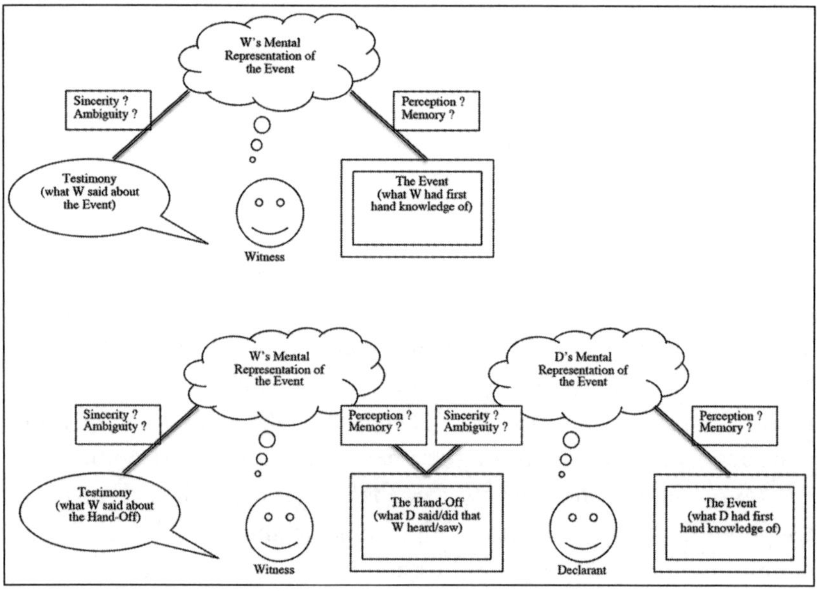


FIGURE 6.1. A Witness Testifies Regarding Personal Knowledge (top); A Witness Testifies Based on Hearsay (bottom)

uttered that sentence. But we do not want Fred's testimony to be offered as proof that there actually *was* a lion because Fred did not see it and has no personal knowledge of it. The bottom of Figure 6.1 illustrates these points. This is the essence of the rule against hearsay: people (other than experts) can testify about things only when they have personal knowledge of them.

### *Hearsay Depends on the Source and Use of the Evidence*

What type of evidence might be counted as hearsay? In the examples above it was something spoken by someone who was not the witness giving testimony. In fact, hearsay is much broader than that. First, hearsay does not have to be heard-and-said. Hearsay includes any "statement" made by someone—which means in writing, orally, or nonverbally (e.g., by gesture or conduct)—as long as it was intended as an assertion; that is, as long it is was intended to communicate a fact or belief. Thus, it includes Jake's statement about the lion, a company's ledger indicating its daily sales for the last 10 years, a road repairer's wave signaling that it is your turn to proceed, and a report from the laboratory saying that your blood alcohol level was over the legal limit. Second, the statement must have been made outside of the current trial but could have been made by anyone, including the testifying witness himself on some other occasion. Thus, it includes all types of transmitted information outside of the trial regardless of whether the transmitter might end up as a witness at the trial.

Although any of those example "statements" *could* be hearsay, they need to meet one more requirement before they *will* be hearsay—and that concerns how the statement is to be used in court. Hearsay is a statement offered "to prove the truth of the matter asserted." In the Fred and Jake example, that means that Fred's testimony about what Jake said is being used as evidence that there actually was a lion—something about which Fred has no independent personal knowledge. So for that use, it is hearsay. But Fred's testimony could be used as evidence that Jake was (still) alive: Jake spoke; the truth of what he said is irrelevant. Or suppose that Jessica also heard what Jake said and she got scared, found Jake's gun, and accidentally injured someone with it. Now, Fred's testimony about what Jake said might be relevant to Jessica's state of mind. Fred has personal knowledge that Jake made the statement and, again, whether the statement is true or not is irrelevant—what matters is whether Jessica heard and believed it. Thus, for this purpose, Fred's testimony would not be hearsay because it is not being used to prove the truth of the matter.

Such non-hearsay uses of what would otherwise be hearsay evidence should bring to mind the same issues as with other limited uses of evidence. For example, Rule 407 does not allow evidence regarding a subsequent remedial repair to prove negligence or liability, but it might be allowed to prove ownership or feasibility. Similarly, Rule 609 allows evidence of prior crimes for impeachment but not for propensity. Thus, Jake's statement about the lion might be allowed in only to prove Jessica's state of mind and not that there actually was a lion—thereby necessitating limiting instructions (i.e., that the jury could use the evidence for only one purpose but not another). As we have seen for the analogous rules, in which information to be disregarded still affects jurors' beliefs and judgments, jurors typically have difficulty with that mental feat. But note the difference: maybe jurors believe that hearsay evidence is less reliable than other evidence so they might be better at disregarding it.

---

**Rule 801. Definitions**

The following definitions apply . . .

(a) Statement. "Statement" means a person's oral assertion, written assertion, or nonverbal conduct, if the person intended it as an assertion.

(b) Declarant. "Declarant" means the person who made the statement.

(c) Hearsay. "Hearsay" means a statement that:

(1) the declarant does not make while testifying at the current trial or hearing; and

(2) a party offers in evidence to prove the truth of the matter asserted in the statement.

---

*Problems and Values in Hearsay Exceptions*

Evidence that meets the definition in Rule 801 is hearsay and Rule 802 is very clear about hearsay: it is not admissible. Except, of course, when there is an exception. And for hearsay there are over two dozen exceptions.[3]

---

**Rule 802. The Rule against Hearsay**

Hearsay is not admissible unless any of the following provides otherwise:

- a federal statute;
- these rules; or
- other rules prescribed by the Supreme Court.

---

What is wrong with hearsay evidence? As illustrated above, the witness is testifying to something the declarant asserted out of court. Because the declarant is typically not the one testifying,[4] the truth-seeking tools are mostly not available. Thus, there are no direct ways to evaluate whether the declarant is mistaken or lying, although, as described below, impeachment is still available.

In addition to not being able to easily assess the declarant's mistakes (of perception and memory) and veracity, hearsay also makes it impossible to assess the declarant's judgment, narration, and confidence. If the witness reports that the declarant said, "The knife was large," no amount of questioning can tell us how large it was; whereas if the declarant was on the stand we could ask for a more specific size description. If the declarant makes a slip of the tongue, and the witness reports the declarant's words verbatim, we cannot merely ask the witness whether that was what she really meant to say. Plus, how sure could we be sure that the witness was correctly assessing the declarant's confidence in his assertion? There might also be ambiguity in what the declarant said. Due to lack of context and lack of redundancy, small amounts of communication have more ambiguity than larger amounts—and often the allowable hearsay is short. When people hear an ambiguous communication, they often fill in the missing information in accordance with their own prior knowledge or beliefs,[5] so it could be impossible to disentangle what the declarant actually said from what the witness understood by it on the witness stand. And even more complicated, how could we know if the witness appropriately picked up the declarant's sarcasm, or other tone of voice information, which could change the meaning of the assertion entirely?

Despite all those difficulties, courts and legislatures have created dozens of exceptions to the rule against hearsay, allowing various types of assertions into evidence. What is special about those types of assertions? Some provide information that would be very useful at trial. Some provide information that could come from no other source—and the source is unavailable for testifying. Some arise from circumstances where it seems that there would be no chance for the declarant to be mistaken or lying, so that the tools for seeking truth and evaluating testimony would not be needed. Rule 807 describes the "residual exception," which allows a judge to admit hearsay testimony that is not covered by one of the specific rules. Rule 807 sets out the requirements for admissibility: trustworthiness, necessity (i.e., there is no other easily available probative evidence), and the interests of justice. Often trustworthiness and necessity seem to trade off against each other such that the most necessary hearsay evidence is often the least trustworthy and vice versa.[6]

**Rule 807. Residual Exception**

(a) In General. Under the following circumstances, a hearsay statement is not excluded by the rule against hearsay even if the statement is not specifically covered by a hearsay exception in Rule 803 or 804:

(1) the statement has equivalent circumstantial guarantees of trustworthiness;

(2) it is offered as evidence of a material fact;

(3) it is more probative on the point for which it is offered than any other evidence that the proponent can obtain through reasonable efforts; and

(4) admitting it will best serve the purposes of these rules and the interests of justice.

## Overview of Research on Hearsay

In contrast to eyewitness testimony and instructions to disregard, there is relatively little psychology research focused on hearsay broadly speaking and very little focused on specific hearsay rules. We believe that might change soon, however, given some new experiments on testimonial infirmities plus the existing general psychology research that is relevant to various hearsay exceptions.

### *Problems Trying to Research Specific Hearsay Exceptions*

We suspect that there are three reasons for the dearth of research about specific hearsay exceptions. First, the exceptions are technical and often complicated. Empirical research on hearsay is therefore best done by collaborations between lawyers and psychologists, or by someone trained in both fields, rather than by researchers trained in only one field. Second, there is no way to know whether people are treating hearsay evidence correctly—that is, giving it the appropriate weight. Remember that when mock jurors are told to disregard evidence, researchers can evaluate whether they have done so by comparing their responses to mock jurors who have not heard the to-be-disregarded evidence at all. There, the disregarded evidence should have no effect. In contrast, admissible hearsay should probably, in many cases, be given some weight—more than zero, but less than if the same evidence were provided by non-hearsay means.

However, what counts as the "right" amount is likely unknowable. And third, because hearsay exceptions were created from a patchwork of situations and justifications, it is unlikely that studying one or two would help reveal much about the specific inner workings of many others.

The research that does exist regarding hearsay evidence more generally mostly focuses on the questions of whether hearsay evidence is given less weight than other types of evidence and on whether the same evidence is given less weight when offered as hearsay testimony than when offered by a witness who has personal knowledge.

### *Disregarding Hearsay Evidence*

Hearsay evidence shows up in the instructions-to-disregard research (described in Chapter 3). In a few of those studies, the evidence that mock jurors were instructed to disregard was hearsay. Sometimes the mock jurors were given an explanation, sometimes not. Sometimes the instructions to disregard were mild, sometimes severe. Overall, in the studies considered by the big meta-analysis described in Chapter 3,[7] hearsay evidence was not entirely disregarded but it had a relatively small effect on verdicts compared to other types of to-be-disregarded evidence. This finding is suggestive—perhaps people are more skeptical of, and hence more willing to disregard, hearsay evidence than other evidence. (Recall that they are more willing to disregard evidence for being unreliable than for being illegally obtained.) However, there are not enough studies varying the types of hearsay to draw conclusions about specific hearsay exceptions.

### *Investigator's Testimony on Child's Behalf*

Perhaps the biggest strand of the existing hearsay research concerns how people treat the testimony of an adult who is testifying on behalf of a child who was the actual witness. The child may have suffered abuse or other trauma and, to protect the child, some courts allow adult forensic investigators who have interviewed a child to provide a description of the child's statements. As we have asked about earlier evidence, we can also ask here: (1) how good is the actual evidence provided and (2) how good do jurors think it is? Studies show that the veridicality of the testimony provided by actual investigators is questionable; for example, when compared to the audiotapes of actual interviews with children, the investigators' notes are often missing important details.[8] In laboratory studies, mock jurors believed testimony from an adult investigator—that is, a hearsay witness—more than the same testimony when it came from the child witness.[9] Thus, the mock jurors overweighted the hearsay evidence. Such findings have led to requests that jurors in trials containing such testimony be able to hear from experts regarding the failings of this type of hearsay evidence.[10]

### *General Hearsay versus Direct Testimony*

As a more general variant of the child-witness studies described above, there are studies that compare mock jurors' reactions to testimony given by an adult witness with personal knowledge (the declarant) against testimony given by an adult witness who has merely heard the declarant. The studies differ greatly in both methods and findings. Many, but not all, of the studies find that the mock jurors give less weight to the same testimony when presented as hearsay than when presented by the witness with personal knowledge. Those results should give us some confidence in the good sense of jurors (or at least mock jurors). The studies vary on the hearsay exception that the information falls under, the instructions of the judge to the mock jurors, whether there was deliberation by the mock jurors, whether an expert testified on the problems of hearsay evidence, etc. With so many variables and so few studies, the research is not rich or systematic enough to draw conclusions about specific hearsay exceptions.

### *Testing Tribe's Infirmities and Hearsay within Hearsay*[11]

In two recent experiments focusing on Tribe's SPAM (sincerity, perception, ambiguity, or memory) infirmities, legal scholar and social psychologist Justin Sevier found that (mock) jurors are sensitive to those infirmities of hearsay evidence and appear to appropriately discount out-of-court statements.

The first experiment addressed the effect of the different infirmities on the believability of in-court versus hearsay testimony. The mock jurors read about a trial involving a theft from a music store. In addition to reading the testimony of the police officer who arrested the teenagers accused of the crime, they also read the prosecutor's direct examination of a bystander who had been outside the store at the time of the theft. The bystander testified that he heard the store manager yell, "I saw the one in the red hat steal the CDs!" That testimony is obviously hearsay.

In the baseline condition of the study, there was no more testimony offered from either side, but then there were closing arguments, jury instructions, and the jurors were asked to rate the likelihood that the defendant committed the crime and the strength of the evidence against him. This condition provides the data for when there was no cross-examination to reveal SPAM infirmities.

In the other 12 conditions of the study, cross-examination revealed one of the testimonial infirmities of the in-court witness, the hearsay declarant, or both. For example, for sincerity, cross-examination of the bystander revealed that (a) the bystander had disliked the defendant and had argued with him, or (b) the manager had also yelled that he hated the kid in the red hat. Some jurors read about one infirmity of the bystander/witness, some about one infirmity of the manager/declarant, and some read about both (e.g., as in [a] and [b] above—the same infirmity for both the witness and the declarant).

The research addresses three questions. First, were jurors sensitive to the number of infirmities revealed in the testimony? The answer is a clear yes: jurors thought that the evidence was strongest when there were no SPAM infirmities, less sure of guilt when there was one infirmity (in either the non-hearsay or the hearsay testimony), and even less sure of guilt when there were infirmities in both the witness and declarant testimony.

Second, did revealing the infirmity in cross-examination have the same effect when the infirmity was in the witness's testimony or the declarant's utterance? The experiment showed no difference; that is, the hearsay testimony was just as likely as the in-court witness's testimony to lose its power when it suffered from one of the infirmities. Third, were the types of SPAM infirmity differently or equally influential—that is, for example, do problems with sincerity decrease belief in the evidence more than problems with memory? Again, the results showed no difference: each type of infirmity caused jurors to discount the testimony about as much as any other type. (The second and third results need follow-up research as described below.)

A second experiment tested mock jurors' skepticism of hearsay evidence in a FRE 805 hearsay-within-hearsay example—which looks a lot like a game of telephone. In the baseline no-hearsay condition, a stock boy who observed a robbery testified to what he saw. In the hearsay condition, the store manager testified to what he learned from the stock boy. Now the story gets richer, as FRE 805 allows a chaining of hearsay testimony as long as each out-of-court statement meets one of the hearsay exceptions. In the double hearsay condition, the storeowner testified to what the store manager told him the manager had learned from the stock boy. And in the triple hearsay condition, the store's co-owner testified to what the storeowner told him he had learned of the incident from the store manager, who had learned his information from the stock boy. There was no cross-examination of the witness. The question is: do jurors spontaneously discount the layers of hearsay, recognizing its growing weakness, without being prompted by the experimenter? The answer again is: yes. With each new layer of hearsay, belief in the underlying observation became weaker and less influential. In this study, jurors were sensitive to the declining trustworthiness of the information as it was passed along from person to person to them, even without having specific hearsay weaknesses made known to them.

There is much to commend these experiments but also a few caveats. There are the standard concerns: having many conditions and small sample sizes makes conclusions of "no difference" suspect. In addition, the research needs to be followed up because some results (the second and third results from the first study) could be due to the particular examples of infirmities used in the vignettes. We illustrated the sincerity infirmities with the two similar revelations of bias, but the perception infirmities involved the bystander's questionable hearing and the manager's questionable vision. Different instantiations of infirmities, and different grounds for admissibility of the hearsay testimony, need to be explored. But, together, these two experiments do suggest that people evaluate hearsay more critically than evidence rulemakers have long believed they do.

**Rule 805. Hearsay within Hearsay**

Hearsay within hearsay is not excluded by the rule against hearsay if each part of the combined statements conforms with an exception to the rule.

## Some Specific Exceptions Illustrating the Interplay of Accuracy, Prevarication, and Necessity

Although there is little psychology research on specific hearsay exceptions, there is plenty of general psychology research that is applicable to some of the specific hearsay exceptions, particularly with regard to worries about the various infirmities of such testimony. Each hearsay exception is (allegedly) founded on some combination of necessity and trustworthiness, but whether the evidence is likely to be trustworthy, and to what extent jurors will consider the issue of trustworthiness, raises psychological issues.

**Rule 806. Attacking and Supporting the Declarant**

When a hearsay statement—or a statement described in Rule 801(d)(2)(C), (D), or (F)—has been admitted in evidence, the declarant's credibility may be attacked, and then supported, by any evidence that would be admissible for those purposes if the declarant had testified as a witness. The court may admit evidence of the declarant's inconsistent statement or conduct, regardless of when it occurred or whether the declarant had an opportunity to explain or deny it. If the party against whom the statement was admitted calls the declarant as a witness, the party may examine the declarant on the statement as if on cross-examination.

As mentioned, testimony given on the witness stand is subject to the various tools—oath, demeanor, impeachment, and cross-examination—that can help jurors evaluate a witness's SPAM (plus judgment and confidence) infirmities. With an out-of-court declarant, those tools cannot be brought to bear directly on the declarant—although the declarant, or the declarant's assertion, may be shown to be less than reliable by introducing contradictory testimony. Rule 806 allows the same types of evidence for impeachment of declarants as it does for impeachment of witnesses on the stand and, certainly, some types of impeachment might be effective against non-present witnesses. But which of those problems of not having the witness present were the courts most worried about? The Advisory Committee Notes to the hearsay rules are quite clear in their emphasis: the answer is prevarication (sincerity). As eminent evidence scholar Edward Imwinkelried explains: "From its inception, the Anglo-American law of Evidence has been obsessed with the prevention of perjury."[12] The hearsay exceptions were drafted with a careful eye toward whether declarants might be lying. They are far less concerned with issues of misperception and decaying memories.

However, psychologists' increasing understanding of the fallibility of memory would suggest that issues of memory reliability might be, perhaps even should be, of greater concern. This possibility has been recognized by legal scholars.

> As years passed . . . it became increasingly clear that the common law ascribed too much weight to the insincerity factor and insufficient importance to the memory factor. . . . A consensus emerged among psychologists and legal commentators that most testimonial errors are unintentional, frequently caused by misrecollection. Psychological research demonstrated that in many cases, the emotions that seemingly ensure sincerity distort the accuracy of the observer's perception and memory. The early common law had facilely equated sincerity or truthfulness with objective accuracy. However, the same stress factors that produce sincerity can cause serious error.[13]

Below we discuss a few of the many exceptions to the hearsay rule, highlighting the tension between concerns about prevarication and other concerns, especially those that lead to mistakes. These include the first three exceptions in Rule 803 and the second exception in Rule 804. See Table 6.1.

### *Present Sense Impression and Excited Utterance*

Rule 803's first two exceptions are 803(1) for present sense impressions and 803(2) for excited utterances. Although these exceptions have different histories and different underlying theories of admissibility, evidence sometimes falls under both. They are useful for admitting 911 calls and other victim statements that occur during or soon after an event. Their use for admitting statements made by victims of domestic violence who later choose not to testify has come under scrutiny because of the Sixth Amendment Confrontation Clause. The exceptions also nicely illustrate the tension between concerns with accuracy and concerns with lying.

**Rule 803(1). Present Sense Impression**
A statement describing or explaining an event or condition, made while or immediately after the declarant perceived it.

**Rule 803(2). Excited Utterance**
A statement relating to a startling event or condition, made while the declarant was under the stress of excitement that it caused.

TABLE 6.1. Description and Potential Guarantees of Veracity and Accuracy for the Hearsay Exceptions in This Chapter

| | 803(1) Present Sense Impression (PSI) | 803(2) Excited Utterance (EU) | 803(3) Then-Existing Condition | 804(2) Dying Declaration |
|---|---|---|---|---|
| When | At the time of the event or immediately after | While under the stress of the event | At the time | Belief death is imminent |
| What | Describing or explaining the event | Related to the event—so broader than 803(1) | Existing mental, emotional, or physical condition | Related to the cause of potential death |
| Necessity | Varies | Varies | High necessity | High necessity |
| Veracity | Too quick to lie | Too excited to lie | ??? | Fear to die telling a lie |
| Discover Lie | Yes; others could verify | Yes; others could verify | Not likely | Probably irrelevant |
| Accuracy | It happened right then | Excitation decreases accuracy | It happened then (but little guarantee for intent or plans) | Excitation or losing mental capacity decreases accuracy |

## PRESENT SENSE IMPRESSION

Present Sense Impression (PSI) is the newer of the two exceptions and before being codified into the FRE, it was not admissible in many jurisdictions.[14] The exception is for statements that describe or explain an event while (or immediately after) the event occurred. "I see Bonnie and Clyde walking into the bank" or "I just saw Bonnie and Clyde walk into the bank" both fit the bill. This exception was championed by Thayer, and called "an ideal exception to the hearsay rule" by Hutchins and Slesinger in 1928.[15] They listed three necessary components of such ideal exceptions: (1) emotion absent, (2) speed present, and (3) the person who heard the declaration is available for cross-examination.

Contemporaneity (or speed) was thought, correctly, to reduce the risk of inaccurate memory. It was also thought to reduce the risk of fabrication—which is an odd argument unless some other circumstances are present. Why wouldn't or couldn't someone just make up something that they were going to say, then wait for an appropriate time and place, and then recite the invented story, pretending that it was a spontaneous PSI statement? We believe that the overlooked piece here is that people are reluctant to lie when they think they might be found out. With PSIs, the witness who heard the declaration is available for cross-examination and might know some information that would discredit the declarant. In addition, other witnesses might have observed the same event and could contradict the declarant. We believe that the fear of being found out to be a liar justifies the belief that declarants are not lying in many PSI situations.

A third factor in favor of the PSI exception was the absence of emotion. In the 1920s, Hutchins and Slesinger argued, based on empirical evidence, that emotion can distort perception. Subsequent psychology research has confirmed, but also refined, those findings. In general, yes, absence of emotion is good for accurate perception and communication.

On the other hand, Wigmore was highly critical of the PSI exception. He was worried about the problem of lying; he insisted that the appropriate guarantor of trustworthiness was spontaneity caused by shock or excitement. The Advisory Committee Notes about PSI focus (oddly) solely on negating the possibility of lying: "The underlying theory . . . is that substantial contemporaneity of events and statement negative the likelihood of deliberate or conscious misrepresentation." We do not see that as a good justification against lying, although it is a fine justification against mistakes. It is an open question how reliable lay people think such PSI statements are.

### EXCITED UTTERANCE

Similar issues regarding the tension between a declarant's lying and mistakes come up with respect to the excited utterance exception (EU). EU is the older of the two exceptions and such utterances were admissible through common law in all of the states before the codification of the FRE. This exception allows witnesses to testify to what a declarant said when the declarant was under the "stress of excitement" and the statement relates to the event or condition that caused the excitement.

Like the PSI exception, this exception also limits time and content, but it allows a broader range of testimony than the PSI exception. The declarant must be under the stress of an event—which, in contrast to PSI, means that the statement need not be made so soon after the event. And the content may be something "related to the event," not merely describing or explaining it. (Hence its use for 911 calls and police interviews if they occur soon after an event while the declarant is still excited by it.)

The Advisory Committee is quite taken with Wigmore's belief that spontaneity and excitement leave no cognitive capacity for conscious fabrication. This is an interesting hypothesis about how cognition works and it is largely correct. In Chapter 4, we described how people are not good at consciously determining whether other people are lying. But lying is more cognitively taxing than truth telling, and when speakers are stressed or excited or otherwise cognitively burdened, it is more difficult for them to lie (and their lying is then easier for others to detect).[16]

The Advisory Committee does acknowledge the offsetting problem, namely, that there is research showing that as people become more excited their accuracy declines. There has long been evidence of how excitement can decrease accuracy but with that evidence came criticisms that the various laboratory experiments did not involve "real" excitement of the intensity involved in the kinds of shocking experiences that occur in real life. However, in the last decade or so there have been several studies of the accuracy of perception and memory in highly stressful real-life situations—studies that use experimental designs with manipulated variables and plenty of motivated subjects. The subjects in these experiments are military personnel enrolled in survival school. They participate in a mock POW camp in which they are exposed to stresses similar to those in real POW camps (e.g., interrogations, lack of food and sleep)—stresses much greater than those used in typical research. Results of various studies show that stress impairs short-term and long-term memory and increases susceptibility to misleading information.[17]

Despite acknowledging the greater possibility of mistakes with EU testimony, the Advisory Committee favored adoption of the rule because of the guarantees against prevarication and because so many cases had already used it. We believe that this rule evokes at least one of the types of problems we have been concerned with: that the evidence is not as reliable as the law thinks. Some studies suggest, however, that jurors are not likely to think that a statement made under stress is more reliable than it actually is (that is, they will not give it more weight than psychologists think it deserves).[18]

### *Then-Existing Mental, Emotional, or Physical Condition*

Another psychologically interesting exception is the one that allows the witness to report a declarant's statement of his then-existing state of mind or body—that is, how he feels or what he is planning. The Advisory Committee Notes state that this exception is "a specialized application of Exception 1 [PSI]." However, psychologists are much more skeptical of this exception than the law seems to be.

One problem is that statements about one's own then-existing mental, emotional, or physical condition are typically impossible to independently verify. Children learn early that claiming to feel sick might get them out of a day or two of school; adults use similar excuses to get out of their own unwanted situations. There is no reason to think that people would systematically make mistakes about such claims, but there is also no support for their veracity. At least with PSI there was (allegedly) an external triggering event that happened at a given time and place. For both PSI and EU, there could be other witnesses who could have seen the event and contradicted the declarant's claims; thus, declarants are likely to be in situations where they can be discovered to be lying. For then-existing conditions, there is no external triggering event; thus, the claims can be made at any pre-planned time, and there is no threat that someone will have external evidence to prove that the declarant was lying. Fabrication of a then-existing condition is just too easy.

A second problem arises with statements of motive—sometimes they might not be lies but might not be accurate either. People are notoriously bad at explaining their own reasons for doing things. We come up with reasons whether or not any exist, and we tend to come up with reasons that put ourselves in a better light. The former is illustrated by some oft-cited studies in which shoppers were asked to participate in a "consumer survey" to evaluate different articles of clothing (either four identical nightgowns or four identical pairs of stockings). The subjects did have preferences, most often the one on the right, but when asked about the reason for the choice, they came up with a variety of invalid reasons and never mentioned location.[19]

A third problem involves statements of intent or plan. In the well-known *Hillmon* case,[20] a man's letters to his sister and his sweetheart, saying that he intended to go on a trip "with a certain Mr. Hillmon" were later offered as evidence that he had gone on the trip and had done so with Hillmon. (The issue of Hillmon's presence was relevant to whether an unidentified body was his; if it was Hillmon's body, then his wife was entitled to life insurance benefits which the insurer did not want to pay.) Psychology research about people's statements of intent show some interesting effects. One is that if we make a public commitment that we will do something, the commitment increases the chance that we will actually do the thing we say we will do. (Getting public commitments is one of the "weapons of influence" we mentioned in Chapter 1.) Those data would argue that, in fact, such a statement would at least meet the relevance threshold. A second finding is that people tend to make more claims about what we will do in the future than we possibly could do. When asked to take on a task this week, we say no, but we will agree to do that thing, and (too) many other things, a month from now.[21]

Another finding relevant to statements of intent or plan is that we tend to overpredict our own future good behavior. For example, a university has a spring fund-raising event during which students buy flowers to support a charity. Students in a psychology class were asked to predict whether (a) they would buy at least one flower and (b) what percentage of their classmates would buy at least one flower. When the "daffodil days" were over, students reported anonymously on what they had bought. Eighty-three percent of the students had predicted that they would buy a flower but merely 43% had done so. This study and analogous ones show that people privately overestimate their likelihood of doing future good actions—which might be the content of a declarant's statement. Of course, in addition to knowing whether people are reporting true and accurate then-existing conditions, like intentions and plans, we are also interested in how jurors would weight such testimony. In the flower study, although people vastly overpredicted how likely they themselves would be to buy a flower, they were much better at predicting the behavior of their classmates (prediction for others: 56%, not far above the actual 43%).[22] Thus, it is likely that jurors give at least somewhat less weight to such self-enhancing statements.

---

**Rule 803(3). Then-Existing Mental, Emotional, or Physical Condition**

A statement of the declarant's then-existing state of mind (such as motive, intent, or plan) or emotional, sensory, or physical condition (such as mental feeling, pain, or bodily health) . . .

---

### *Dying Declarations*

One of the most entertaining hearsay exceptions, at least to modern eyes, is that for dying declarations. The exception places extreme limits on who may make such a declaration and what it may concern. The declaration must be made by someone who believes that his own death is imminent and it must be about the cause or circumstances of the (potential) death. The declarant need not actually die, but the hearsay exception is under Rule 804 not 803, meaning that it can be invoked only if the declarant is unavailable as a witness, thus indicating that it was viewed as a highly necessary exception (e.g., because a victim is likely to be the only witness).

The exception for dying declarations is a very old doctrine. Edgar Allan Poe, writing in 1833 (in the epigraph to his short story "MS Found in a Bottle") quotes Quinault, writing in French in 1676: "He who has a moment to live, no longer has anything to dissimulate." The basic rationale usually given for the dependability of dying declarations is that nobody wants to meet their maker with a lie on their lips. The Advisory Committee Note recognizes that "the original religious justification for the exception may have lost its conviction for some persons over the years," but then goes on to say, "it can scarcely be doubted that powerful psychological pressures are present." Again we see the emphasis on veracity rather than accuracy.

The recent research on the accuracy of people in extremely stressful circumstances (described in the EU section above) should raise concerns about the accuracy of statements made when death is imminent. And, of course, in addition to being under stress, someone who is in fear of imminent death is also likely to be in less-than-perfect physical shape in ways that would affect perception, memory, and reasoning (e.g., injured, drugged, losing blood). Also, some cross-cultural work finds that people from certain cultures are known to incriminate their enemies from their deathbeds. Thus, dying declarations make for good theater, and maybe even good leads for law enforcement, but not for good evidence. On the other hand, we suspect that jurors are appropriately skeptical of someone's dying words and thus weight it appropriately.

---

**Rule 804(2). Statement under the Belief of Imminent Death**

In a prosecution for homicide or in a civil case, a statement that the declarant, while believing the declarant's death to be imminent, made about its cause or circumstances.

---

## Once and Future Rules

There are, of course, plenty of other exceptions to the rule against hearsay. Many of them have to do with the introduction of various types of records: business, public, and religious. Some of the exceptions allow in evidence that we have talked about in other chapters. For example, Rule 803(22) allows in prior convictions, which may be used for impeachment under Rule 609. There are several exceptions allowing for reputation evidence, like Rule 803(21), which is needed because reputation is not the "personal knowledge" of the witness.

---

**Rule 803(21). Reputation Concerning Character**

A reputation among a person's associates or in the community concerning the person's character.

---

Reputation is an interesting concept in both the law and psychology. As previously described, reputation evidence of the sort allowed in Rule 803(21) does not hold much sway with jurors (as opposed to testimony about a person's acts). But take a look at Rule 804(3) regarding the exception for a statement against interest. The current rule lets in only statements that are against the declarant's proprietary or pecuniary interests. The drafters had wanted the rule to also contain language allowing an exception for statements against the declarant's reputation, statements that would "make him an object of hatred, ridicule, or disgrace." Congress removed that language, reasoning that such statements lack sufficient guarantees of reliability. One has to imagine that in the current instant-reporting-to-the-world state of communications, expanding this rule to include this exception could use some rethinking. Also of interest due to the current state of communications is whether e-mailed, texted, tweeted, etc. messages with appropriate content could be allowed in under the present sense impression and excited utterance exceptions.[23]

---

**Rule 804(3). Statement against Interest**

A statement that:

(A) a reasonable person in the declarant's position would have made only if the person believed it to be true because, when made, it was so contrary to the declarant's proprietary or pecuniary interest or had so great a tendency to invalidate the declarant's claim against someone else or to expose the declarant to civil or criminal liability; and . . .

---

We acknowledge that we have not addressed the interplay of the recent Sixth Amendment Confrontation Clause rulings and the hearsay exceptions. That is partly because the Confrontation Clause applies only to criminal cases and partly because the doctrine is in flux. But some of the recent rulings do raise interesting psychological questions, for example, when the Supreme Court tries to distinguish "non-testimonial" versus "testimonial" parts of what would certainly be an excited utterance (e.g., a 911 call that is partly a report of an ongoing emergency—hence, non-testimonial—and partly a description of other surrounding circumstances), does such a distinction have any justification in either the likelihood of the declarant telling the truth or the jury believing the evidence?[24] On the other hand, if the Confrontation Clause protection were entirely a constitutional procedural safeguard, then the psychological analysis of it would have no practical implications.

## Conclusion

The exceptions to the rule against hearsay allow in a great deal of evidence that would otherwise be inadmissible. The rules and its exceptions are complicated, typically taking up about one-fourth of (American) evidence casebooks, or so a survey of our own bookshelves suggests. The rulemakers seem most concerned with preventing lies from reaching the witness stand; psychologists would be much more wary of the problem of unintentional inaccuracies.

We cannot know how often people actually lie or make mistakes as declarants, nor how often witnesses misreport what a declarant might have said, nor what percentage of the time these failings are detected. But psychology can identify situations that are better or worse for reliability, for finding the truth, and for jurors' understanding of the different dangers of different types of hearsay evidence. Psychology research could do a lot more to explore these mostly neglected issues.

7

# Scientific and Other Expert Evidence

Who would have predicted that many of the most popular works of crime fiction would revolve around (purported) scientific evidence uncovered by scientific detectives: Poe's Auguste Dupin, Conan Doyle's Sherlock Holmes, Cornwell's Kay Scarpetta, and the heroes of numerous television programs like *CSI*, *NCIS*, and *Bones*.[1] Scientific expert testimony is often the centerpiece of real criminal trials as well, offering the hope of resolving vital questions with a certitude that ordinary fact witnesses cannot. Of course, the offerings of expert witnesses go far beyond fingerprints, footprints, and DNA. Expert witnesses include physicians, economists, engineers, psychologists, and a kaleidoscope of other experts in civil as well as criminal cases.

Courts wrestle with claims about the way the world works—and therefore with scientific and other technical information—in three major situations: rulemaking, gatekeeping of expert testimony, and the use jurors make of admitted expert evidence in trials. In *rulemaking*, judges often work with facts that sometimes consist of scientific information. The psychological questions are how, and how well, they make use of such knowledge, as opposed to getting tripped up by various decision-making traps. *Gatekeeping* involves evaluating the validity of proffered expert evidence. *Expert evidence* that passes through the judicial gate and is presented as testimony must then be evaluated by the jurors and incorporated into their decisions about the overall case.

## Rulemaking

Judges frequently are called upon to create legal rules, modify existing rules, or decide the extent to which an existing rule applies in the circumstances of a case. To be clear: these are not *rulings* (decisions made under existing rules applied to the facts of a case), but the creation or modification of *rules*. Of course, courts are expected to be deferential to existing rules, and especially deferential to legislation and constitutional provisions. But, under appropriate circumstances, courts must engage in rulemaking if cases are to be decided in principled ways. Sometimes, in order to resolve such legal questions, judges must resolve scientific questions, and most often those are behavioral and social science questions because so much of the law involves human behavior.[2]

Facts that are used to help determine what a rule of law should be are often called "legislative facts." The Advisory Committee Note to Federal Rule 201 makes clear the

> fundamental differences between adjudicative facts and legislative facts. Adjudicative facts are simply the facts of the particular case. Legislative facts, on the other hand, are those which have relevance to legal reasoning and the lawmaking process. . . . In determining the content or applicability of a rule of domestic law, the judge is unrestricted in his investigation and conclusion. He may reject the propositions of either party or of both parties. He may consult the sources of pertinent data to which they refer, or he may refuse to do so. He may make an independent search for persuasive data or rest content with what he has or what the parties present. . . . [T]he parties do no more than to assist; they control no part of the process.

For example, suppose two states banned billboard advertising of alcohol, to which alcoholic beverage sellers in both states responded by challenging the legislation as infringing on free speech rights. And suppose that a federal district court in one of those states—having been presented with relevant data on the effects of such advertising on highway safety—concluded that the legislation did indeed violate the First Amendment, based on its finding that alcohol advertisements on highways did not increase the incidence of drunk driving (and therefore the state lacked a compelling interest that its statute was narrowly tailored to serve). Meanwhile, the federal district court in the other state reached the opposite conclusion on the data and consequently upheld the state legislation. Facts about the effects of alcohol advertising are legislative facts being used to make a rule: how far the First Amendment's protection extends. When these two conflicting cases come to the circuit court of appeals, what is that court to do? Should the higher court defer to the factual findings of both lower courts, and uphold them both? Or should it find that one is correct and the other incorrect? And on what basis? The law's answer is that higher courts are supposed to take a fresh look at the relevant data (because appellate courts review findings of legislative facts de novo, the same standard of review that is applied to holdings of law) and, depending on what the appellate court finds, uphold one of the lower courts and reverse the other.[3]

Judges often arrive at the answers to questions of legislative fact by relying on their intuition rather than on research.[4] As one judge informally put it: judges should either be good at reading empirical research or they should be good guessers. Consider, for example, a question such as whether the death penalty provides a marginally greater deterrent effect compared to life in prison. The constitutionality of the death penalty has turned on precisely this question.[5] Though empirical research by psychologists and other social scientists casts light on such a question, all of us, including judges, have our intuitions about the answer. Our intuitions, of course, might be right or they might be wrong.

Psychological research that suggests areas of decision making in which people are prone to errors when relying on their intuition also suggests areas where judges risk making incorrect rules. As discussed in earlier chapters, research has identified a variety of psychological phenomena that tend to lead to erroneous decisions.[6]

One U.S. Supreme Court case that illustrates the problem is *Williams v. Florida* (1970). Florida employed 6-person juries to decide all felony prosecutions except capital cases. A defendant challenged the constitutionality of a jury smaller than 12. The Supreme Court reasoned that the Constitution spoke of juries without specifying any particular number, and therefore the constitutionality of any given size jury should be determined by comparing its performance to that of the conventional 12-person jury on several dimensions of the jury's behavior. The Court then undertook to assess whether juries of 6 would differ from juries of 12 in terms of their ability to vigorously deliberate, to reach correct results, to provide a representative cross-section of the community, and so on. In regard to cross-sectional representation, the court intuited that "while, in theory, the number of viewpoints represented on a randomly selected jury ought to increase as the size of the jury increases, in practice, the difference between the 12-man and the 6-man jury in terms of the cross-section of the community represented *seems likely to be negligible.*"[7] Had the Court understood the statistics of sampling, it might have discovered how far off the mark its intuition was. For example, in sampling from a population consisting of 90% subscribing to one ideology and 10% to another, 47% of random samples of size 6 would contain at least one member of the minority, while 72% of samples of size 12 would contain at least one member of the minority. Is a 25-percentage-point difference negligible?[8]

This example illustrates a major and persistent lesson of psychology for the law, which in the rulemaking context is amplified by all of the cases to which the rule will be applied: human intuition generally does a poor job making sense of statistical pictures of the world. When our reflective thinking (System 2) is not equipped to analyze the problem, our intuitive thinking (System 1) is often quite ready to lead us astray. So there is a big problem. Most people, including most judges and jurors and lawyers, have difficulty making good use of statistical pictures of the world, yet statistical pictures often provide some of the most complete and accurate depictions of reality that are available to us.

## Gatekeeping: Admissibility of Expert Evidence

Trial judges are said to be the gatekeepers of evidence, and gatekeeping is where most of the formal legal action is. It is the focus of the rules of evidence concerned with expert testimony, the focus of most of the academic and public debates about scientific evidence, and the focus of the Supreme Court's expert evidence cases.

### *Basics of Expert Testimony*

Several points about expert testimony deserve some attention at the outset. First, the main privilege an expert witness has that ordinary witnesses lack is that experts are permitted to offer opinions—that is, inferences—about what the observable evidence means. We can all look at an X-ray, but only "experts" may offer interpretations of what the X-ray shows. Second, although people usually envision experts as being scientific or professional specialists, by the law's definition anyone with knowledge that is not shared by the average person could serve as an expert. Auto mechanics, drug addicts, beekeepers, and students could all be expert witnesses on the appropriate issues. Third, the touchstone of admissibility is helpfulness. The purpose of an expert witness is to help the jury to understand factual issues in the case. The other side of that coin is the risk that an expert might mislead rather than help a factfinder. Fourth, although the law envisions expert witnesses playing the role of neutral educator, far too often the expert becomes an advocate for the positions of the party calling the expert.[9] These basic points should begin to illuminate why the law has developed rules for trying to filter expert testimony before it reaches the jury.

In the typical civil case, about four experts testify—though sometimes there are none and other times there are many more than four. About 40% of the experts in civil cases are from medical or mental health fields; about 25% from business, finance, law, or economics; about 25% from engineering or safety fields; and the rest tend to be from other scientific fields. In criminal cases, expert witnesses usually are forensic scientists of one kind or another, and the overwhelming majority are offered by the prosecution. This is because forensic scientists are employed mainly by government crime laboratories, whereas the defense usually has no money to pay for experts, even if they were available. When the defense does offer experts, they typically are from mental health fields, offered in insanity defenses or on issues related to sentencing.[10] In more recent years, criminal defense teams have started to offer scientists and statisticians to challenge claims of government expert witnesses.

Why does the law think it needs expert witnesses? Doubtless, it is in the hope of finding correct answers to factual questions important to deciding cases. But by opening their doors to the opinions and conclusions of people who usually have no personal knowledge of the facts of the case, who are offering to explain the meaning of the facts supplied by others, the courts open up a supermarket full of cans of worms. Here are some of the worms: The expert's field might lack true knowledge of the subject at hand. The expert might stretch real knowledge out of recognition to apply it to the facts of the case. The particular witness proffered might lack adequate knowledge of the field. And the expert witness is likely to be biased in favor of the calling party, and give an incomplete or skewed or even fabricated account in order to support an opinion favorable to the employing party.

To combat those dangers, the rules provide for judicial screening of expert witnesses—the law's first and major line of protection—as well as cross-examination and rebuttal witnesses. The rules of evidence also empower judges to appoint experts of their own choosing. Interestingly, the drafters of that latter rule believed its principal function was to serve as an ever-present threat that would prevent lawyers from presenting expert testimony that is too biased or misleading, knowing that the trial judge could always put on a court-appointed expert to debunk the other experts. But the drafters did not intend judges to actually appoint their own witnesses, expecting that the existence of the power to do so would be enough to keep lawyers and experts on good behavior. Although judges obligingly rarely use their power to appoint expert witnesses, there have been periodic calls to make more active use of court-appointed experts.[11]

## *Psychology of Expert Witnesses—Civil Cases*

Having "objective" expert witnesses come to a consensus about the meaning of the evidence, and sharing that consensus with the factfinder, might seem an ideal practice. But lawyers, judges, scholars of various kinds, and many scientists themselves tell us that such an appealing scenario is overly simplistic: knowledge often is not straightforward nor does it come neatly packaged.[12] Even if knowledge were created that way, and witnesses were automatons who offered nothing but the absolutely correct and unvarnished truth, a properly working adversarial system ensures that the factfinder will receive something quite different.

The parties develop and present the evidence in their cases. That is the essence of the adversarial process. The parties are motivated to find expert evidence that best advances their positions, as well as experts who seem disposed to present their opinions in ways that support the claims of the party selecting them. Moreover, the witnesses who have been engaged can be dismissed and replaced. Although fact witnesses are limited—for example, the people who observed a car crash or were present during a crime—expert witnesses exist in more generous numbers, and so there is a variety from which to choose. Once they are aligned with one or the other party, experts acquire an "allegiance bias," which leads them to see the facts, and reach judgments, in ways that are more helpful to the party with whom they are aligned. In one experiment, forensic psychologists and psychiatrists were hired and paid to evaluate the same case files using objective scoring instruments. These experts were randomly informed that the party for whom they were working was either the defense or the prosecution. That was sufficient to produce results that leaned strongly in the direction that would be favored by the party employing the expert.[13] In actual cases, one can expect the bias to be stronger still. What psychological processes produce such effects?

The views of expert witnesses can be shaped by interactions with the attorneys they work with, who provide case facts to their experts and in ways both subtle and not so subtle persuade their witnesses of the justice of the cause they have been enlisted in. Although Cialdini's "weapons of influence," discussed in an earlier chapter, are of limited use with jurors, they can be quite applicable in working with one's experts. The interactions between attorneys and experts offer opportunities for reciprocity, for developing liking for the attorney, for putting the expert in a position where she will feel compelled to maintain consistency, and for deferring to the authority of the attorney on certain matters.[14]

In many of life's situations, people are motivated to find the correct answer to a problem or question. Ideally, they gather and weigh evidence in an unbiased manner to help them reach the correct solution. Under these circumstances, people are engaging in accuracy-motivated reasoning.[15] But once an expert has been recruited to a case, selectively fed information about the case, has formed a working relationship with one side's lawyers, and so on, interesting psychological processes subtly come on line. Once people are motivated to favor one or another conclusion, they (all of us) tend to find evidence and evaluate that evidence in ways that support the preferred outcome. Thus, sometimes our *motivated reasoning*[16] steers us not toward reaching the right answer, but toward a goal, toward a conclusion, that we want to reach. Litigation is a social process that is not known for conducing accuracy-motivated reasoning.

In thinking about how the body of knowledge of the expert's field applies to the case facts, an expert who has become committed to the case will tend to engage in motivated reasoning. Once we desire to reach or hold onto a conclusion, that motivation activates a number of cognitive processes to push our reasoning in the direction of the desired conclusion. Our mind discounts contrary evidence and overweights confirmatory information, stretches or shrinks logical connections, widens or narrows categories, etc., all to help us reach the conclusion we want to be able to reach. The expert does not intentionally mislead. Indeed, when this phenomenon occurs, the witness is misleading him- or herself.[17] As the eminent physicist Richard Feynman once cautioned: "The first principle is that you must not fool yourself—and you are the easiest person to fool."[18]

### *Psychology of Expert Witnesses—Criminal Cases*

The preceding paragraphs describe some of the psychological influences on experts in (mostly) civil litigation. Much of what has been described above applies to experts in criminal cases as well, with the added problem that they are not occasional witnesses with professional identities outside of the litigation system. In criminal litigation, the processes of selection and shaping of the thinking of crime laboratory personnel have been going on for generations. If expert witnesses on the civil side are temporary hired guns, crime laboratory personnel are permanent hired guns. Their livelihoods; their everyday relations with colleagues, superiors, and sometimes police; their personal identities—all are tied up in thinking and behaving as their group expects.[19] And what is expected of them is to help complete the case against people suspected of having committed crimes. Recent research has found that, contrary to the fictional image, the role of forensic science in the criminal justice system is not so much the detective work of figuring out who committed a crime, but rather is to help build a case against a suspect selected by police using more old-fashioned detective work.[20] It might be for this reason that forensic science expert testimony is associated with more erroneous convictions than any kind of testimony other than that of eyewitnesses.[21]

Major problems with forensic science often arise when humans have to judge the similarity of two different patterns (fingerprints, bullet marks, footprints) and decide whether any differences (and there always are differences) mean they cannot be from the same source, or whether they can be declared to be indistinguishably alike.[22] Consider your own fingerprints. There they are on file—laid down, or scanned, slowly and carefully when you applied for a job or some license issued by the state (we're assuming that you haven't previously been arrested). And then there are the "latent" prints left at a crime scene: from one or two fingers, laid down hurriedly and with uneven pressure, and perhaps smeared, dirty, incomplete, or layered on top of other prints. Thus, those prints are typically far from being an "exact" match to the pristine file prints. When judging their similarity, the human perception and reasoning system might be influenced in some non-optimal ways.

Similar to motivated reasoning is the more automatic process of "context effects" (or "observer effects") on perception. Put simply, this is the tendency to see what we hope or expect to see. A fascinating example comes from a British study of fingerprint experts. Each examiner was presented with a latent print from a crime and a file print of a suspect, and asked to compare the two and determine whether or not the suspect was the source of the crime scene print. First, however, the experts were informed that what they were going to be shown was a pair of prints that the FBI had recently misidentified, linking a print from a terrorist bombing in Spain to what turned out to be an innocent American in Oregon. But put that aside, the British fingerprint experts were told, and use your own expertise to evaluate the pair of prints. Unknown to the experts, each was in actuality being shown a pair of prints that he or she had examined years before in their casework and had reported to be a positive identification. But on this occasion, looking at the prints again, only one out of five experts held to the original view. The contextual information they were supplied with changed their perception of the similarity of the prints.[23] The same process operates in routine cases, if and when experts are given other inculpatory information about a case. They tend to resolve ambiguities in favor of the outcome they are led to believe is the correct one.

Some areas of forensic science are noted for the extent to which they oversimplify and exaggerate what their fields are capable of concluding. Increasingly well-recognized examples include identification by handwriting, firearms, bite marks, and even fingerprints.[24] Over the years, experts in these fields stretched their claims and asserted them repeatedly so that in time extraordinary claims came to be widely regarded by the public as intuitively obvious and certain. (Such beliefs are termed *cultural truisms*.)

In recent years, scientific organizations have begun to revisit these claims, and have recognized that they often lack sound scientific foundations.[25] But it is sobering to keep in mind that these contortions of science are in some considerable part the product of the legal process. Had crime labs been organized differently—being made independent from police and prosecutorial agencies and answerable to leaders who were scientists rather than police, prosecutors, or politicians—the scientists likely would view and do their jobs differently. The idea that different organizational arrangements would produce different behavior on the part of those working in the organization reflects the idea that behavior is a product not only of people's internal traits and states, but of the organizational structures and situations they find themselves in.

The same adversary process that creates pressures to distort the science that is brought to court also creates pressures to expose the flaws in the expert evidence presented. One sees this corrective mechanism more readily in civil litigation. In preparing for cross-examination and rebuttal testimony, with the help of their experts, attorneys search for differences, conflicts, and uncertainties in the other side's expert evidence.[26] This adversary process is beneficial to the search for truth to the extent that it uncovers weaknesses in the evidence and prevents factfinders from accepting overly simplified or exaggerated expert claims. It makes the search for an answer harder in that, if done well, it aims to raise every possible doubt and uncertainty. And where only one side has access to the expertise, it is hard to see how the adversary process can work at all.

### *Development of Legal Filters*

In view of the kinds of concerns described, it should be no surprise that courts have for centuries felt the need to screen expert evidence—excluding what they find to be insufficiently helpful or overly misleading.

From the time experts started being proffered, at least as far back as the seventeenth century, judges had to decide whether or not to admit them. The earliest test of admissibility appears to have been to assess the "qualifications" (credentials, education, experience) of the proffered witness. Once courts realized that a field of expertise exists separate from the person offering to represent the knowledge of the field, qualifications alone no longer sufficed. The most highly qualified astrologer can offer a court no more than what the field of astrology has to offer.

In the nineteenth century, courts often employed what has been termed the *marketplace test*: if a body of expertise was valued by consumers, then a person successful in that field was acceptable to the court as an expert witness on a relevant question.

In 1923, the appellate court in *Frye v. United States*[27] was confronted by a proffered expertise that was too new to have been tested in the marketplace: an early type of polygraph. How was the court to evaluate it? The court modified the marketplace test: instead of asking what consumers thought of the asserted expertise, the court asked whether the technique had gained "general acceptance in the particular field in which it belongs"—that is, the court asked what the *producers* thought of the product.

The *Frye* test always had its drawbacks. Producers are likely to tout their products more uncritically than consumers. (For example, were a relevant issue to present itself, a literal application of *Frye* would obligate courts to admit the expert testimony of astrologers.) So, if judges are going to evaluate an alleged expertise by reliance on what others think of it, the shift from consumers to producers was not likely to be an improvement. When, for purposes of applying the *Frye* test, a court adopted a narrow definition of the relevant fields to include only the practitioners, the court would almost certainly find their wares to be generally accepted within their field. (An example would be personnel in crime labs who used voiceprint analysis to identify the person who made a threatening phone call.) But when a court adopted a broad definition of the relevant fields to include not only practitioners, but scientists from other relevant fields, then the judgment of the field under scrutiny would be more circumspect. (If, in addition to voiceprint practitioners, the relevant fields included acoustical engineering, linguistics, and statistics, then voiceprints would fare less well.)[28] This is, in fact, exactly what happened in courts. In virtually every case where a court evaluated voiceprints using a narrow-field *Frye* test, the court ended up admitting the testimony. And in virtually every case where a court evaluated voiceprints using a broad-field *Frye* test, the court ended up excluding the testimony. Courts could manipulate the outcome of a hearing by choosing a narrow *Frye* test when they were inclined to admit the expert testimony and a broad *Frye* test when they wanted to exclude the testimony.

In 1993, the U.S. Supreme Court held in *Daubert v. Merrell Dow Pharmaceuticals*[29] that the *Frye* test had been superseded by Federal Rule of Evidence 702, and that the touchstone of admissibility is proof that the expert evidence is valid: "The Rule's requirement that the testimony assist the trier of fact to understand the evidence or to determine a fact in issue goes primarily to relevance by demanding a valid scientific connection to the pertinent inquiry as a precondition to admissibility." With that, judges, not consumers or producers, were to become the arbiters of evidentiary soundness.[30]

---

**Rule 702. Testimony by Expert Witnesses**

A witness who is qualified as an expert by knowledge, skill, experience, training, or education may testify in the form of an opinion or otherwise if:

(a) the expert's scientific, technical, or other specialized knowledge will help the trier of fact to understand the evidence or to determine a fact in issue;

(b) the testimony is based on sufficient facts or data;

(c) the testimony is the product of reliable principles and methods; and

(d) the expert has reliably applied the principles and methods to the facts of the case.

---

The principal rules of admissibility for scientific evidence in the federal system, under the federal rules and the Supreme Court's decisions in *Daubert* and subsequent cases,[31] can be summed up in a nutshell:

- There are two distinct decisions to be made: the validity of the area of expertise and the qualifications of the expert witnesses (Rule 702).
- The trial court is to hear evidence and arguments on the validity of the proffered expert evidence in a proceeding at which the proponent must prove admissibility by a preponderance (and where the rules of evidence do not apply) (Rule 104(a), *Daubert*).
- This test applies to non-novel (familiar expert evidence) as well as to novel (new areas of expert evidence) proffers (*Daubert*).
- The test applies to all expert evidence—not just "science" (*Kumho Tire v. Carmichael* [1999]).

- General acceptance within the field is by itself insufficient for admission (*Kumho Tire*).
- The trial court can decide to admit, exclude, or admit with limitations.
- If the court decides that the evidence will be admitted, the opposing side may attack the expert evidence again at trial—on weight and credibility (Rule 104(e)).
- The standard of review for the trial court's decision is abuse of discretion (and therefore appellate decisions generally have no precedential effect on the question of admissibility) (*General Electric v. Joiner* [1997]).

---

**Rule 104. Preliminary Questions**

(a) In General. The court must decide any preliminary question about whether a witness is qualified, a privilege exists, or evidence is admissible. In so deciding, the court is not bound by evidence rules, except those on privilege.

...

(e) Evidence Relevant to Weight and Credibility. This rule does not limit a party's right to introduce before the jury evidence that is relevant to the weight or credibility of other evidence.

---

It has been noted that the *Frye*/*Daubert*/marketplace tests have strong parallels to what cognitive science thinks of as a dual-processing mode of responding to information and making decisions.[32] The law has invented two quite different ways of assessing the quality of expert evidence, just as our minds have two quite different ways of assessing information. As discussed earlier, System 1 is an implicit, automatic, effortless, non-conscious, inflexible, fast process, which places minimal demands on the mind's working memory. If we see people fleeing a building, we don't ponder the situation—we immediately follow them. If we learn that others think a particular expertise or technique is valid, we tend to go along with them (sounds like *Frye*). By contrast, System 2 is an explicit, controlled, conscious, flexible, slow process that requires time, effort, and working memory. In short, it requires careful thought, which is what *Daubert* requires. It seems the Supreme Court has been moving the admissibility rules from System 1 to System 2. But have lower federal courts and state courts followed?[33]

Several studies have sought to measure the changes in admissibility of expert evidence wrought by *Daubert*, if any. The studies found that in civil cases judges are more likely to exclude challenged expert testimony than they had been before *Daubert*. One study found that challenged experts were excluded about 50% of the time before *Daubert* and up to 70% of the time after *Daubert*.[34] Federal judges responded to a survey indicating that they excluded or limited challenged expert evidence 25% of the time pre-*Daubert*, compared with 41% of the time post-*Daubert*, and more often excluded the evidence of plaintiffs.[35] Other studies focused on decisions after *Daubert*. A study found that defendants challenging plaintiff experts in federal cases succeeded about two-thirds of the time. Plaintiffs challenging defense evidence succeeded less than half the time.[36] A reading of the cases confirms that courts have become more aggressive in their scrutiny and exclusion of evidence in civil cases.[37]

On the criminal side, the picture is quite different. In federal district courts, post-*Daubert* challenges by the defense to government evidence succeeded less than 10% of the time, while prosecution challenges to defense evidence succeeded two-thirds of the time.[38] The most recent such study, looking at only the post-*Daubert* period and at only four forensic sciences, but using a more expansive database than the earlier studies, found that in cases where the government's forensic science experts were challenged, courts excluded or imposed limits on the testimony in 15% of cases.[39]

None of these findings actually tells us about the validity of the evidence proffered. And we don't know to what extent different advocacy abilities of lawyers played a part, rather than the foundations of the evidence itself. But the fact that some of the scientifically weakest types of expert evidence that come to court are admitted more regularly than other more scientifically sound evidence is food for thought.[40]

At bottom, the question is how good are judges at their gatekeeping duties. Are judges capable of doing the job their supreme courts and legislatures have assigned to them?[41] After all, it is more than a little paradoxical to put non-experts in the position of assessing one body of knowledge after another, and weighing competing claims by competing experts. And yet the purpose of filtering expert evidence is to protect jurors from evidence that might be misleading or false. Jurors, as laypersons, are thought to be in a weak position to evaluate the expert evidence. The need for that protection is at its greatest when jurors have an unthinking faith in the asserted expertise, when the expertise is obscure and therefore the evaluation is especially difficult, and when the risk of exaggeration or fraud are at their greatest. How much less vulnerable are judges than jurors to being hoodwinked by the very same faith, obscurity, and exaggerations?

At least three fields of supposed forensic science knowledge, each of which was for decades welcomed into court by judges and credited by jurors, have in recent times been found by scientific review and research to be invalid, and have largely or completely disappeared from courts due to the work of scientific organizations—not by judges applying admissibility rules.[42] In commenting on the problems of unscientific forensic science in the nation's courts, a major report of the National Research Council[43] noted that "[f]orensic science professionals have yet to establish either the validity of their approach or the accuracy of their conclusions, *and the courts have been utterly ineffective in addressing this problem*."[44]

Ironically, the law's procedures have convinced the public that courts do an exceptionally rigorous job of screening evidence, including expert evidence. As a result, people relax their critical judgment and are more persuaded by expert evidence presented to them in a trial context than they are of the exact same evidence presented to them outside of the trial context.[45] Thus, if a judge does not do the skillful job of screening evidence that the law and the public expect, and unsound evidence is admitted, the jury will accord that evidence a degree of credibility that they normally would not have given it. In this way, the evidence evaluation process can fail twice. Judges do not do their job as well as they could, relying on the jury to do the more thorough evaluation. And juries do not do their job as well as they might, relying on judges to have determined what evidence is worthy of belief. This is an example of what social psychologists call *diffusion of responsibility*.[46]

## Comprehending and Using Expert Testimony at Trial

Beyond defining the filter for admitting or excluding expert evidence, the law has little to say about the use to which factfinders put the evidence. Judges usually instruct juries that it is up to them to give as much or as little weight to each item of evidence as they see fit. So, unless the jury makes a manifestly irrational decision, the law leaves factfinders on their own to make the best sense they can of the expert evidence that the parties present to them, and to make appropriate use of that evidence in reaching their verdict.

We noted earlier the paradox that the law assigns to persons not especially knowledgeable about various fields of expertise the duty to screen out false or misleading opinions offered by people who are purportedly experts in those fields. Jurors are in much the same situation. They are expected to evaluate and incorporate expert opinion into their individual thinking, their deliberations, and their verdicts.

### *Problems of Understanding Expert Evidence: Some General Principles*

Research indicates that juries are plainly competent in sorting out facts in simple cases. Their ability in more complex cases is open to question. Unsurprisingly, juries do better when there are fewer witnesses and simpler testimony. Complexity may arise due to the difficulty of the issues being considered or to the sheer volume of information presented to the jury. Both types of complexity present challenges to juries.

The benchmark against which juries must be compared will always be the judge: would a judge do better, the same, or worse? On this, recall from our earlier discussion of juries versus judges that the pattern of agreement and disagreement in verdicts between judges and juries did not differ as the complexity of the case increased—suggesting that jurors understood the case about as well (or as poorly) as judges did.[47]

People can follow one of two basic strategies for thinking about what they have been presented by a communicator. These strategies constitute two different ways that people process information, termed *central* versus *peripheral*.[48] Central, or systematic, processing involves working through the information to try to comprehend it and its implications for the case. Peripheral processing involves attending to superficial characteristics of the communicator or the message, and associating judgments and conclusions with what those characteristics suggest about the witness. Examples of superficial characteristics would be the witness's appearance or accent, or what schools the witness attended.

Studies have found that people tend toward central processing of information when they are intelligent, when they are knowledgeable about the topic, when the topic is relevant to their concerns, when they are interested in it, and when the information is comprehensible to them—in short, when they have the motivation and/or the cognitive resources to do so. They then engage in a high degree of cognitive processing of the message content. When the opposite circumstances exist, then they will engage in little cognitive work, and rely mostly on the association of superficial cues with the conclusions advocated by the communicator.

On the one hand, trials should be an excellent setting for inducing central processing. The jurors' role as decision makers in a serious and formal proceeding should arouse considerable motivation to understand the evidence in order to reach correct conclusions. The information-rich nature of trials as well as their adversarial nature ensures that jurors will have considerable resources from which to draw. And research on jurors uniformly finds that jurors take their task seriously. On the other hand, if the expert evidence is so complex or otherwise incomprehensible that it is inaccessible, jurors will not be able to centrally process it. Indeed, some research suggests that jurors do not get much below the surface of the expert and the expert's testimony. Interview studies of jurors show them assessing credentials, motives, and superficial content, rather than evaluating the underlying validity of the testimony.[49] Nor do judicial opinions seem to dig much deeper than that, especially on the criminal side. The other evidence in the case, which is more likely to be comprehended, will likely be centrally processed. But difficult expert evidence will be peripherally processed or ignored.

The dilemma is illustrated in Diamond and Casper's study of jurors' reactions to experts in an antitrust case.[50] Jurors recruited during their jury service were shown a videotaped antitrust trial. The testimony included damages estimates from opposing experts. One expert presented an estimate of damages based on the performance of a similar company that was not affected by the alleged price-fixing agreement—called a yardstick model. The opposing expert presented a statistical model that used past performance to project what would have happened in the absence of the price-fixing agreement. The jurors showed adequate comprehension of the testimony by both experts, but the statistical testimony was somewhat more difficult for them than the more concrete yardstick evidence. Although the statistical expert was perceived as more expert than the yardstick expert, the yardstick expert was better understood, so the two attributes of testimony (comprehensibility and perceived expertise) canceled each other out in terms of impact on the jurors' verdicts.[51]

Overall, such simulation research suggests that factfinders engage in some peripheral processing when assessing expert testimony, whether or not they understand the evidence, and that peripheral cues become more important to the decisions as the scientific evidence becomes more complex.

Another psychological issue is concreteness versus abstractness, or the explicitness with which expert testimony is tied to factual issues in the trial. One can think of expert testimony as a syllogism. The abstract principles in which the expert is proficient are the *major premise.* For example, it is known that if eyewitnesses are told "Good job" after picking the suspect out of a lineup, that will artificially increase their confidence that they identified the actual perpetrator. The case-specific facts are the *minor premise.* Evidence discloses that the policeman who administered the lineup said, "Good job," to the witness (who, when testifying in court, asserts confidence that he recognized the perpetrator and would never forget that face) after the witness falteringly and with obvious uncertainty picked the suspect from the lineup. Putting the major and minor premise together leads to the *conclusion*: the police officer's conduct at the lineup gave the witness an exaggerated sense of confidence in the accuracy of the identification.[52]

An expert on eyewitness evidence could testify to the major premise (the scientific findings regarding factors that affect the accuracy of eyewitness identifications) or, after hearing the adjudicative fact witnesses describe the circumstances under which the crime was witnessed, could offer an opinion (a conclusion) about the likely accuracy of the eyewitness identification. How might juries react to the two different versions of that expert testimony? It will come as no surprise to litigators that jurors are more influenced by the expert testimony when it concretely ties the abstract principles to the particulars of the case and the conclusion is explicitly asserted (rather than being limited to the realm of abstract principles).[53] That does not mean the information cannot come from several different people: a scientific expert who explains the abstract principles, other witnesses who describe the case facts, and the attorney who draws the conclusion in a closing argument. As a tactical matter, however, lawyers prefer to have their experts assert the conclusion they want the factfinder to reach, and that is what judges are accustomed to: conclusory opinions first, and the basis for them coming later.

The potential power of the expert's conclusion is illustrated in a series of studies by social psychologist Gary Wells.[54] A dog is run over by a bus. The bus belonged to either the Blue Bus Co. or the Grey Bus Co. Investigators were able to obtain a tire tread pattern from the dog's body, and compare it to tires on the buses of the two companies. An expert witness testifies that the tread pattern from the accident scene matches 80% of the buses owned by the Blue Bus Co. This statistical evidence leads about 70% of mock jurors (as well as trial judges) to make a subjective probability estimation that the Blue Bus Co.'s bus killed the dog. But only around 10% of the judges *and* the mock jurors are willing to hold the company liable on the strength of that "naked" statistical evidence.

Other groups of mock jurors and judges hear the same testimony, with one small addition. After presenting the same data, the expert states that *he believes*, on the basis of the tire tread evidence, that the bus that ran over the dog belonged to the Blue Bus Co. Now, 60% of mock jurors and nearly 70% of judges said they would find the Blue Bus Co. liable. That is a dramatic increase in factfinders who are willing to find liability, simply because the expert asserted what inference he drew from the data, even though the factfinders already knew all the facts that the expert knew.

The law at one time prohibited experts from giving such conclusory opinions when they went to an "ultimate issue" in the case, but conclusory opinions now are commonly admitted.[55] Interestingly, experts on eyewitness accuracy—the major non-mental-health area of psychology which is offered to courts—almost always refrain from asserting an opinion on the accuracy of the eyewitness in the case at bar. They describe the relevant principles and the research bearing on human perception and memory and stop there, leaving the jury to apply that major premise to the circumstances of the crime and its aftermath.[56]

## *Probability and Statistics*

The Wells research introduces us to one kind of evidence on which judges and jurors—and all of us—are prone to stumbling: statistical data, especially probability evidence. Of all commonly encountered expert evidence, this is certainly one of the most challenging.

An important illustration of the problem is found in studies of what have come to be called the *prosecutor's fallacy* and the *defense attorney's fallacy*. These errors can occur when an expert testifies that a match exists between crime scene evidence and a sample known to be taken from the defendant, and data are offered to assist the factfinders in evaluating the likelihood that the defendant was the source of the crime scene evidence. Here is an example: a blond hair is found at a crime scene and a suspect with blond hair is arrested. The significance of the blond hair depends on how common or how rare that characteristic is. The blond hair would be much more incriminating if the crime occurred in China than if it occurred in Sweden. The fallacies describe how people use data they are given relating to those probabilities.

In the prosecutor's fallacy, factfinders mistakenly think that the frequency of the trait in the population tells them more about the probability of guilt or innocence of the defendant than it really does. Jurors might think that if only 2% of the population has long blond hair, then the probability that an innocent defendant would have this trait is 2%, or that the probability that it is the defendant's hair is 98%. In the defense attorney's fallacy, factfinders might realize that a population rate of 2% would mean that in a city of, say, one million people, 20,000 would have the trait. Because 20,000 people could have been the source of the blond hair, they view the evidence as having virtually no probative value. The first error greatly overvalues the evidence and the other greatly undervalues it. These and other studies suggest that "it is easy to talk people into using inappropriate judgmental strategies to evaluate [this kind of] evidence."[57]

An example of the complications that heuristics add to making sense of probabilities is the following, illustrating effects of *framing* in probability estimations based on DNA identification. Law professor and cognitive psychologist Jay Koehler found that in presenting DNA findings at trial, the expert witness can focus on the defendant and specify the probability that a person selected at random would have the same DNA profile as the one found at the crime scene (for example, one in 10 million). Presented this way, decision makers conclude that it is extremely likely that the defendant is the perpetrator who left his DNA at the crime scene. Alternatively, relying on the very same data, the witness could focus instead on the population and report the number of people (in addition to the defendant) who would have the same genetic profile as was found at the crime scene. Presented this way, decision makers think it is much less likely that the defendant was the source of the crime scene DNA.[58]

In general, the major problem people have with probability is the underutilization of it: probability information often does not get incorporated well (or at all) into people's analysis of a problem. Moreover, emotional arousal exacerbates the tendency to ignore probability data and rely on less information than is available to solve a problem. Thus, when the story of a case shocks or angers jurors, they make less use of probability data and other statistical information than they otherwise would.[59]

### *Making Sense of Statistical Evidence of Causation*

A very important factual determination that jurors must make in a great many cases is whether one thing caused something else. Causation is something that is inferred, not observed. For that reason, many causal relationships are elusive—for example, whether or not a medication or chemical caused a plaintiff's illness. Not surprisingly, then, scientific studies often are used to assist in proving or disproving the claim that the defendant's product caused a plaintiff's injury or illness. These studies put statistics to work to illuminate causation. How well can jurors understand the kinds of evidence that come from those studies?

Mock jurors who were recruited from a county jury pool exhibited poor performance when assessing causality from data summaries that would be readily understood by almost any scientist or statistician, not only epidemiologists.[60] The jurors' performance did not improve when an epidemiologist provided a detailed explanation of how such tables are to be read, how relative risk and odds ratios are calculated, and how to properly interpret the data. A sample of undergraduate college students presented with the same data table performed far better than the jury pool members had. Additional research further demonstrates the difficulty experienced by the general public in understanding probability, statistics, and causation.[61]

But that does not mean that setting a minimum level of education for jurors would be an acceptable solution. For one thing, there are legal, ethical, and political barriers to limiting participation on juries to the educated elite. For another, the educated elite often have trouble reaching correct conclusions about statistical reasoning and causal inference. In some of the same studies described above, the researcher also tried to present the data in several innovative ways that she hoped would increase the ability of people to interpret it correctly. Although college students were much better at interpreting the epidemiological evidence than average jurors were (only 8% of whom reached correct answers), 80% of the students still made at least one error in arriving at their conclusions.[62] Other research has demonstrated similar errors in statistical reasoning among college seniors, graduate students and even university faculty members,[63] as well as doctors looking at data in their own fields.[64]

### *Clinical versus Statistical/Actuarial Experts*

From what has been described already, you might expect that expert witnesses who present data are going to be less well understood and perhaps less influential than those who present testimony that is more narrative and qualitative. And you would be correct.

In a study comparing quantitative against qualitative expert testimony,[65] a "clinical opinion expert" opined that the defendant was a severe sociopath and represented a future danger to society, based on the expert's interview with the defendant and his "years of experience." A quantitative "actuarial expert" had identical experience and training as the clinical expert. In addition, the actuarial expert used a data-based instrument called the Violence Risk Assessment Guide (VRAG) to assess future dangerousness. The expert explained the instrument and testified that, based on his interview with the defendant and the VRAG results, he believed the defendant represented a future danger to society. Who was more effective at changing mock jurors' ratings of the defendant's dangerousness? The clinical expert.

In another experiment, both types of experts were met with opposing expert testimony and an effective cross-examination, which emphasized the high error rates in predictions of dangerousness. These countermoves did reduce mock juror estimates of future dangerousness from where they had been after hearing the first expert's testimony, but "their influence was significantly less on the clinical opinion expert testimony. Adversary procedures failed to return mock jurors who received clinical opinion expert testimony to their initial dangerousness rating levels."[66]

The researchers explain the greater persuasiveness of clinical expert testimony partly in terms of the story model:[67]

> The very nature of clinical opinion expert testimony may link the testimony being offered directly to the defendant in the case, whereas actuarial expert testimony based on large samples of individuals may be more difficult for jurors to perceive as directly relevant to a defendant and the facts in the particular case before them. As a consequence, the clinical opinion expert testimony may be easier than the actuarial testimony for jurors to fit into their story of the case and, therefore, may end up being more influential in their decision making.[68]

A similar study found clinical expert opinion to be even more powerful in the sentencing phase of a capital trial.[69] The initial expert gave poorly grounded (one might even say, false) opinions, and the research question was whether the damage could be undone by cross-examination and sound counter–expert testimony. The first experimental condition, with an expert asserting a strong prediction of future dangerousness, no opposing expert, and a weak cross-examination would be expected to produce the highest percentage of verdicts favoring death. The second condition provided a strong cross-examination to challenge the expert opinion. If cross-examination is an effective tool to combat unreliable testimony, the second condition should reduce the percentage of death penalty verdicts. The third condition combined a powerful cross and an opposing expert to explain the weaknesses of the expert's prediction of future dangerousness. The law would expect this cross and rebuttal to produce still fewer death penalty verdicts. Ideally, this version would produce verdicts indistinguishable from the fourth condition, in which the prosecution's own expert acknowledged that predictions such as his were incorrect two-thirds of the time.

The findings, however, were that neither the strong cross nor the strong cross plus an opposing expert were able to reduce the proportion of votes for death or reduce juror ratings of confidence in their death penalty conclusions.[70] The only condition that produced a significant reduction in votes to execute the defendant was the fourth condition, where the prosecution expert himself testified that predictions such as his were wrong twice as often as they were correct.[71]

Courts have long suggested that expert opinion testimony can be effectively countered through cross-examination and the evidence of opposing experts. The results of these and other studies should give pause to anyone who has unfettered confidence in the traditional tools of the adversarial process. In some circumstances they are ineffective, which is one of the reasons for rules requiring expert evidence that is not demonstrably sound to be filtered out by the judge.[72]

### *Improving Understanding of Expert Evidence*

We have learned that scientific and technical evidence, especially statistical and probability data, create special difficulties for jurors (and judges as well). The underutilization of probability evidence is pronounced, and trying to understand the causes has kept cognitive psychologists quite busy. Even when factfinders understand statistical and probability evidence, they can make errors which lead them to undervalue the evidence. When expert evidence is too difficult to understand, it pushes people toward greater reliance on peripheral features of the evidence or the witness. Since causation evidence often involves statistical data, drawing correct inferences about what the data reveal is difficult. Moreover, quantitative evidence is difficult to incorporate into a story about the case and therefore tends to be undervalued when pitted against other evidence such as testimony from a clinical expert addressing the same point, especially when the clinician's testimony is focused on the specific facts and parties in the case at bar. Lawyers can increase the likelihood that expert evidence will not be put to its most rational use by making emotional appeals.

## GENERAL TRIAL PROCEDURES

We cannot change people's brains or suspend the trial while jurors (and judges) return to school to become better equipped to understand and use expert evidence. Whatever is to be done to improve comprehension has to be done here and now in court. Within the bounds of evidence rules and trial procedures, can some of the findings of psychological research help?

Several simple methods have been introduced by some courts to try to improve factfinders' ability to deal with expert evidence, while accepting as given any limitations on jurors' ability to understand statistics, causality, and the content of the evidence at issue.

Perhaps the most thorough test of the effectiveness of such innovations is found in a study led by Michael Dann, a former Arizona judge and pioneer in trial procedure reform.[73] Using hundreds of jurors recruited from a Delaware court, several innovations were tested using a videotaped mock trial. These included note taking, asking questions of the experts, a trial notebook (which included the experts' slides and a glossary of terms), and a checklist to use in thinking about the scientific evidence. The mock jurors saw a video of a criminal case in which the interpretation of mitochondrial DNA analysis was critical to the outcome. The jurors were invited to use the various innovations while observing the trial, and their subsequent understanding of the expert testimony was measured.

As you will by now expect, jurors showed a basic general comprehension of the evidence, some fell prey to the prosecutor's and defense attorney's fallacies, and better educated jurors (especially those with science or mathematics backgrounds) understood the evidence better. It is not just that those with a background in a subject understand it. Knowledge accretes knowledge—knowing something about a topic makes it easier to learn more about that and related matters.

Did the innovations help? Because deliberation provides a chance to learn from other jurors, the cleanest measure of comprehension gains is found in tests given to individuals before deliberations. By itself, note taking added nothing to understanding the science, though it did help jurors' memory and general understanding of the other evidence in the case. Question asking also conferred no benefits—though perhaps because not enough questions were asked or not enough time was given to answering them. Only trial notebooks provided evident gains in understanding. Combining innovations, the study found modest evidence of benefit for use of the notebook and checklist in combination with note taking, especially after deliberation.

One of the most interesting lessons from the study is how poorly people understand their own thinking. (This is another failure of metacognition, discussed at greater length earlier in this book.) Most jurors thought most of the innovations were helpful and supported their continued use. But the measures testing actual comprehension showed no significant improvements in understanding (prior to deliberation), except for the notebooks. This is a good illustration of why the numerous studies in which judges, lawyers, and jurors are asked what they find helpful and what they do not find helpful should be taken with a generous sprinkling of salt. What legal policy makers need to know is how much improvement *actually* is achieved by one or another innovation.

### *Better Presentation of Statistics*

Rather than giving jurors tools of the kind described above, a different strategy is to find ways to present information that makes the expert evidence intrinsically comprehensible to people with no special training.

Gerd Gigerenzer, a German psychologist who does research on heuristics in decision making, has studied this problem with a variety of colleagues, and found a number of ways to make probability evidence easier to comprehend.[74] Focusing on the problem of making medical data understandable, including to doctors, their research led to the following advice.

- Exorcise the "illusion of certainty." When thinking about probabilities, certainty almost never exists, and trying to find the one definitely correct answer will only mislead.
- Use numbers, not just words. Numbers are clearer to most people.
- Present the numbers in data tables.
- Make the numbers transparent by using forms of data that research has found are inherently clearer to people.[75]

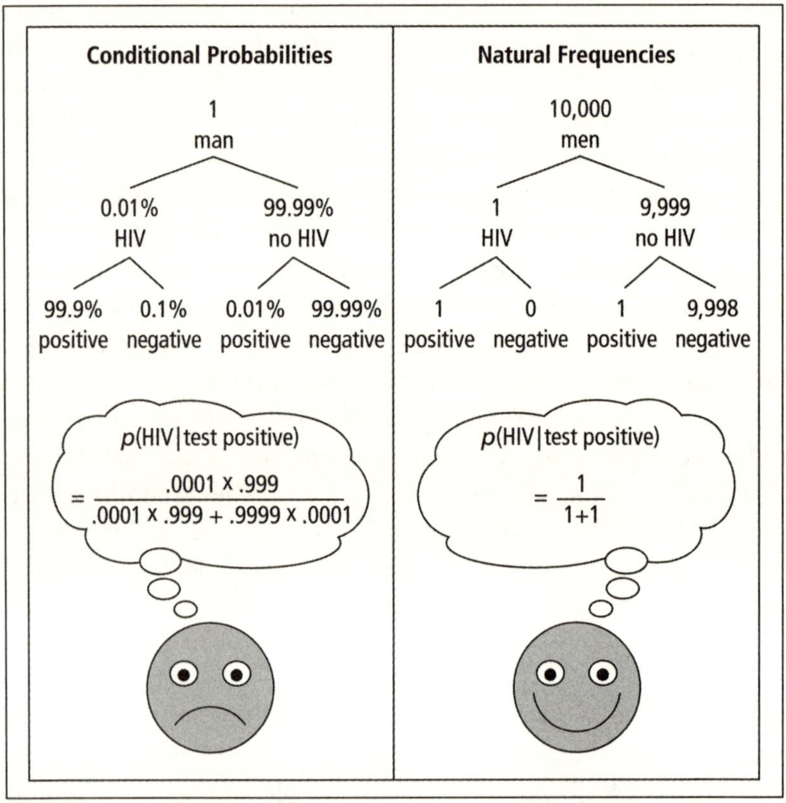


FIGURE 7.1. Two Ways of Presenting Data on the Likelihood of Breast Cancer

Here is an example. Suppose a mammogram has yielded a positive result for a patient (that is, the test raises a red flag for the possibility of cancer). What is the likelihood that the patient actually has breast cancer? What one needs to know to figure out the answer is that 1% of women in the relevant population develop breast cancer (the base rate). For those with breast cancer, the test produces a positive result 90% of the time (true positives). For those who do not have cancer, the test produces a positive result 9% of the time (false positives). Figure 7.1 offers two different ways these data can be put together to reach an answer. On the left, the data are presented as conditional probabilities, the customary way that statisticians work with such data. On the right is a way of presenting the data that follows Gigerenzer's advice for achieving greater transparency and easier understanding. Work through the two methods yourself and see which confuses you and which makes the solution obvious.[76]

These two methods were tested on gynecologists, the doctors whose job includes explaining the meaning of mammogram results to their patients. Provided with just the basic data on the base rate of the disease in the population and the probabilities of true and false positive test results, only 21% of the doctors reached the correct result. When a different group of gynecologists was shown how to think about data of this kind using natural frequencies, 87% of them reached the correct result.[77]

### *Educating the Jury*

Still another strategy for helping jurors to understand the technical information they will be presented with in the trial is straightforward education—in court. Several studies suggest that it might be possible to provide this education in a surprisingly short period of time.

One group of researchers has shown that it might be possible to give ordinary people from a variety of educational levels, including no formal higher education at all, a general education in formal principles of statistics that improves their everyday problem reasoning ability. Significant improvements in reasoning ability occur even when the training is very brief (25 minutes). Importantly, the effects of the general training in statistics can be seen even when the problem encountered is completely unrelated to the context of the training itself. That means that it might be possible to train jurors on content that does not intrude on or suggest answers to the subject matter of the case they will be asked to decide.[78]

Another research project focused on doing the same thing for the understanding of causation evidence from research studies.[79] Mock jurors, drawn from a jury-eligible population, viewed a simulated toxic tort trial, in which the factual issue was whether the defendant's product caused the plaintiff's lung disease. An expert witness presented one of four different versions of research bearing on the causal connection between the product and the disease—and on which the verdict should turn.

One version of the research presented by the expert witness was sound and valid. In three other versions, the research suffered from one of the three classic flaws of causal inference: lack of temporal precedence (causes must occur before effects), lack of covariation (causes and effects must occur together—when one is present, the other must be present, and vice versa), and spuriousness (plausible alternative explanations for an apparent relationship must be ruled out, usually by having control groups).

Half of the mock jurors received no training in causal inference, and were left to rely on their intuitions and whatever pre-existing knowledge they might have. The other half of the jurors received generalized training in the formal rules of the logic of causal inference and practice in evaluating claims of causation. The training consisted of reading a four-page magazine-style article designed to be easily readable (at the eighth-grade level), understandable, and very general that included examples of flawed claims, followed by a worksheet with three examples that the jurors were to evaluate using what they had learned. This training intervention took about 15 minutes.

The untrained jurors were completely unable to distinguish between the valid and the invalid versions of the research presented by the expert witness. The trained jurors were better able to distinguish the good research from the poor research, especially when the flaw was a lack of covariation. But the effect of the training was small.

These findings offer some promise of equipping factfinders to evaluate scientific evidence of causation, though more effective methods clearly are needed. Perhaps with twice as much training (30 minutes), especially more practice in applying what they have learned, improved effects can be obtained.

## Conclusion

Scientific and other expert evidence offer courts the potential for resolving what might otherwise be unfathomable quandaries. At the same time, however, such evidence demands much of judges and juries. Judges have the duty to filter proffered claims from varying disciplines that judges generally are ill equipped to evaluate.[80] In their turn, jurors are expected to make critical sense of and rationally use the expert testimony that is admitted. Ensuring the well-informed use of scientific and technical evidence in the course of deciding cases has been the most daunting challenge the rules of evidence have faced. To say the rules have succeeded in helping judges to screen more intelligently and juries to gain the benefits of such evidence while minimizing the risk of being misled would be quite an exaggeration.

Reviews by scientific commissions, such as the National Research Council, inform us that many of the forensic sciences "have yet to establish either the validity of their approach or the accuracy of their conclusions," but that "the courts have been utterly ineffective in addressing this problem."[81] Perhaps the most glaring illustrations of this failure are provided by once-popular but now-deceased forensic sciences. The opinions of their practitioners were being routinely admitted right up to the moment when their fields' claims of expertise were determined by scientific bodies to be either undependable or downright invalid.

A little further downstream, the rules of evidence and procedure have contributed little or nothing to the challenge faced by jurors: to better evaluate, understand, and incorporate expert testimony into their decisions. When junky science is passed through to jurors, what tools do they have to help them separate the good from the bad? Not many—only those they might remember from school or bring from their jobs, plus whatever help they might get from the lawyers on either side of the case. Empirical research by psychologists and others has done little more than to document the failings of judges and the struggles of jurors.

Work continues on methods for educating judges and jurors in how to assess basic scientific claims or to properly interpret findings presented in the form of statistical data. Glimmers of promise have appeared. But the overall problem of scientific illiteracy among judges and jurors remains to be overcome. We humans do not come well equipped to evaluate and use scientific and statistical evidence. Without special training, and often even with such training, we do not do well. On the other hand, we are, unfortunately, rather good at accepting a conclusion asserted by someone we think is an authority on a subject. Perhaps these are problems that cannot be solved without making radical—and perhaps unacceptable—changes to our system of trials.

# Conclusion

## *The Lessons of Psychology for Evidence Law*

The central lesson of our exploration of the psychological foundations of evidence law is that evidence rulemakers—be they common law judges or more modern rules committees—unavoidably operate as applied psychologists. At nearly every turn they find themselves having to devise rules based on what they think they know about the perceptions, memories, and motivations of witnesses; about the effects of trial processes on testimony and other evidence; and about the capabilities and limitations of human beings to comprehend and evaluate evidence, both as individuals (judges and jurors) and as members of groups (juries).

What knowledge do rulemakers bring to these tasks? What knowledge should they bring? When their knowledge comes from anecdotes, from unsystematic experience with cases, from introspection, or from attempts to logically puzzle out how certain phenomena work, rulemakers can mislead themselves much as doctors have often misled themselves into thinking treatments worked that actually did not. Such amateur applied psychology cannot bring the rulemakers very far in creating rules that achieve their intended purposes with any certainty. In law, as in medicine and every other field that tries to understand how the world works, the more systematic methods of science can deepen comprehension and improve the effectiveness of interventions.

Rulemakers and trial judges have the further challenge of struggling with metacognition: they must not only try to determine what correct inferences the trial evidence supports, but they must also try to imagine what inferences other people (jurors) will believe the evidence supports. (In the Introduction, see Figure I.2 and accompanying discussion.) The problem of metacognition adds considerably to the complexity of the rulemakers' task.

Evidence doctrine has changed, in some respects quite dramatically, over generations as the structure of the trial changed and as rulemakers' beliefs changed regarding the behavior of witnesses, the effectiveness of lawyers, and the capabilities of factfinders (juries).

Beginning in the twentieth century, a number of prominent evidence scholars and some psychological researchers recommended the incorporation of knowledge from systematic empirical research to improve evidence rules by improving the rulemakers' understanding of the phenomena they are dealing with. The addition of scientific psychology could contribute to the effort to come ever closer to crafting optimal rules (in the practical sense of fashioning evidence rules that do the job that the law is seeking to do). To say that the rulemakers could do better should not, however, obscure that they often have generated rules that empirical research confirms to be standing on solid psychological ground. Verification of what does not need fixing is yet another benefit of bringing scientific psychology into the conversation.

For a time, legal historians thought that the advent of the rules of evidence was a direct response to the rise of the lay jury as the chief trial factfinder. More recent historical analysis has concluded that the rules are more a product of the nineteenth century's procedural shift of power from judges to lawyers. The rules of evidence came into being centuries after juries had become a fixture in Anglo-American courts, but only decades after lawyers took on their powerful adversarial role in the development and presentation of cases. That timing suggests that the rules arose in Anglo-American courts not because jurors were thought to be inadequate decision makers but because lawyers were viewed as excessively zealous advocates. The rules appear, then, to have evolved primarily to rein in lawyers.

## *Juries and Judges*

With that historical insight in mind, we can better appreciate the centrality of evidence to trials and what the rules of evidence do to try to keep information at the heart of the decisions juries make. The rules that have evolved prevent lawyers from using the most powerful, yet the most informationally empty, techniques of persuasion—though such methods of influence can be found in wide use elsewhere in society.

Litigators are, thus, compelled to fight their battles by presenting juries with information. This makes jury trials one of the most rational exercises in self-government that our society has developed.

Studies conducted on jury decision making (using both mock trials as well as data from actual trials) indicate that evidence—factual information about the events in dispute—is the most potent force driving the verdicts of conventional American trials. One such finding is that, in responding to the evidence presented, judges and jurors reach the same verdicts in four-fifths of trials. These two very different decision makers reach essentially the same decisions because apparently they are responding to the same information. Moreover, studies of individual differences among jurors—differences in demographics, attitudes, personalities, knowledge—have found that differences among jurors usually make only a small difference to the outcomes of cases. Variation in the strength of evidence typically makes a far greater difference than who is hearing the evidence. All of that is good news if we want trials to produce rational decisions based on evidence.

The focus on evidence makes a juror's job a demanding one, presenting challenges to understanding, remembering, evaluating, drawing inferences, and using evidence (in conjunction with the law) to reach conclusions about a disputed matter. Working as a group helps. Groups have advantages over individuals: they possess more cognitive and social resources such as wider background knowledge and experience, the ability of multiple minds to remember, to correct each other's errors, to think about the proper meaning of the evidence, and so on.

### *Balancing Acts*

Many of the rules of evidence employ balancing tests, of which the best known is Rule 403, requiring a judge to compare (for example) the probative value of evidence against its prejudicial effect. Here, the problem of metacognition arises where a trial judge is making a decision during an ongoing case. Doing the required balancing involves more than just knowing a rule and the import of the evidence; it engages the judge's beliefs about how others people's cognitive and emotional processes work, predicting how someone else will respond to the evidence, and comparing that to how the judge thinks the evidence ought best be responded to. For some categories of evidence, the rulemakers have performed the metacognitive balancing for the judge, deciding that because jurors are likely to overvalue the evidence, it is best if the jury does not hear those types of evidence at all.

These categorical exclusion rules are designed, in part, to encourage socially desirable behavior. For example, to encourage repairs to potentially dangerous situations the rules bar the use of evidence of such repairs to prove negligence. A well-established body of research on the "hindsight bias" supports the law's suspicion that jurors will use evidence of an accident and its repair to answer the question of whether the risk should have been recognized ex ante, and conclude that the failure to correct the situation earlier was negligent.

The balancing tests generally make good psychological sense in theory. Much remains to be learned, however, about whether they "work" (that is, are efficient, lead to the best result, encourage socially desirable behavior) in actual practice.

### *Instructions to Disregard and Limit Use*

The problem of being exposed to information that shouldn't be considered when making a decision—"mental contamination"—comes up in many guises in the trial process for both jurors and judges. In the pursuit of justice, and the sometimes conflicting pursuit of expedience, the law asks jurors and judges to perform feats of cognitive gymnastics that usually cannot be done: to disregard relevant information that might also be important when making a decision, or to use information for one purpose but not another.

Jurors often do not follow instructions to disregard evidence or instructions to limit its use solely to its admissible purpose. Though this phenomenon is supported by plenty of research evidence, there is no dominant psychological theory for why the failure to disregard or limit use occurs. Perhaps jurors are unable to follow instructions to disregard information on command; perhaps they are unwilling to do so because, for example, the information that has been declared forbidden is nonetheless useful to solving the mystery of the trial.

This problem is also encountered by trial judges who, when trying cases without juries, hear inadmissible evidence in their role as gatekeepers. If they cannot properly disregard it or limit its use to a proper purpose (and the research suggests they cannot), they will be more likely (than a jury deciding the same case) to be influenced by that inadmissible evidence when deciding their verdict. The inability to disregard is also likely to affect appellate judges who rule on harmless error issues.

Rather than pretend that people can perform impossible feats of cognitive gymnastics merely because the law orders that such feats be performed, more investment could be made in devising other ways to accomplish what the law of evidence seeks to accomplish. It is important to note that juries need not forget inadmissible information; rather, they just have to act as if they never heard it. Some psychological research has discovered procedures that can improve the likelihood that juries will disregard evidence when instructed to do so. Among these procedures is to give an explanation that calls into question the reliability of the evidence and having the judge instruct the jury both immediately and again just before deliberating. More work might find more, and more effective, procedures.

### *Witness the Witness*

The major source of information in a trial's search for factual truth is the oral testimony of witnesses. The main worry about those witnesses is that they will be in error or will intentionally lie or mislead. Consequently, the law provides tools to help assess the veracity and accuracy of witnesses. However, we don't know the effects of some of those tools (e.g., the oath), and we do know that people in general are bad at using certain other tools (e.g., demeanor cues in assessing veracity).

Cross-examination often is praised as the law's greatest method for getting at both veracity and accuracy, but for something so important, there is surprisingly little psychology research on it. One thing to worry about with cross-examination is the same thing that psychologists worry about with leading questions: source confusion. That is, jurors sometimes don't remember which witness said what, and so don't remember which testimony was discredited during cross-examination. Like the problem of disregarding inadmissible evidence, it can be difficult or impossible to ignore what has already been learned.

Historically, evidence law precluded people from testifying when the law assumed they would be likely to lie or make mistakes. The rules then opened the courtroom doors wider, allowing nearly everyone to testify, with the assumption that lawyers could expose or jurors could recognize when witnesses were lying. Interestingly, privileges, which prevent some potential witnesses from testifying for various psychological and policy reasons, end up precluding the testimony of many potential witnesses who would have the most incentive to lie on the witness stand.

### *Character Evidence*

The basic rule limiting character evidence is even more sensible than the rulemakers appreciated. Personality traits are less predictive than most people (certainly including jurors) realize, whereas social situations, and the interaction of situations and personality, are more potent drivers of behavior. Yet, as the law suspected, most people tend to perceive the behavior of others through lenses of personality, traits, and propensity and, as a consequence, overattribute and overpredict consistency between character and conduct. Put simply, we attribute to persons more trait-behavior consistency than actually exists. So in fashioning the law of character evidence the common law judges correctly diagnosed a problem and took sensible steps to temper those attributional tendencies in order to avoid inaccurate or unfair verdicts.

The rules allow for numerous exceptions, admitting some character evidence out of fairness or with the aim of permitting helpful evidence while still barring its most misleading variants. Thus, for example, defendants in criminal cases are permitted to offer evidence of their own character or the character of a victim. For another, any party may offer character evidence for a non-propensity purpose (to prove motive, opportunity, intent, etc.).

Other exceptions are made to assist factfinders in their task of evaluating the credibility of witnesses. The rules carefully cabin attacks on a witness's character so that the evidence may "refer only to character for truthfulness or untruthfulness." A special case of that rule is evidence of a witness's conviction of a prior crime. Many characteristics of the prior crime (who, when, what) are relevant to whether it will or will not be admissible. Research, however, has found that people are much more likely to rely on prior crime evidence for its improper propensity purpose, largely ignoring instructions from judges to limit its use to evaluating credibility.

In recent decades, a controversial set of rules was added that permits prior criminal sexual conduct to be admitted and allows factfinders to draw inferences from that evidence about "any matter to which it is relevant." These rules are controversial because they invite jurors to engage in precisely the kind of propensity thinking that centuries of evidence doctrine prohibited. Moreover, the new rules were advanced and adopted on the theory that criminal sexual behavior is more predictive than other kinds of criminal behavior, while most research suggests that it is not.

### *Hearsay*

Witnesses typically may testify only regarding things about which they have personal knowledge. But the various exceptions to the rule against hearsay permit witnesses to testify about many things that they have learned from someone else outside of the courtroom, and permit that testimony to be offered to prove the truth of matters about which the witnesses have no first-hand knowledge.

Courts and commentators have noted that hearsay testimony comes with a variety of infirmities—that because the person with first-hand knowledge is not the one testifying, the tools for truthseeking (oath, demeanor, impeachment, cross-examination) cannot be employed to uncover whether the declarant is sincere, or has made an error in memory, perception, or communication. Because of those worries, and the worry that jurors will not appropriately discount the reliability of hearsay evidence, the extant hearsay exceptions are predicated on the testimony being necessary and trustworthy.

Research has found that in at least some circumstances, people are appropriately skeptical of hearsay evidence. For example, they more readily disregard hearsay testimony than other testimony when instructed to do so, they discount hearsay that has been shown to suffer from specific infirmities, and they decrease belief in hearsay evidence the further away it is in a hearsay-within-hearsay chain. But perhaps because of the complexity and variety of hearsay rules, researchers have not specifically studied particular exceptions—thus we do not know whether some exceptions really are especially trustworthy nor do we know whether jurors are appropriately skeptical about those that are not. However, basic principles of psychology suggest that the courts' and legislatures' justifications for the trustworthiness of some exceptions are not well founded. But if, as suggested above, jurors can give the evidence the appropriate weight, then admitting it creates no risk. Further research should investigate whether jurors give appropriate weight to both current exceptions to the rule and other types of hearsay evidence that have long been considered too dangerous to admit.

## *Scientific and Other Expert Evidence*

Although most evidence that comes to court is non-technical—observations of everyday events by witnesses, records of business and other routine activities—an important and growing minority of evidence is scientific or technical. Such evidence has great potential for helping to resolve what might otherwise remain unfathomable quandaries.

On the other hand, scientific and other expert evidence demands much of judges and juries. If they do not understand the evidence, they cannot evaluate it or use it effectively. Judges have the duty to screen proffered claims from various disciplines that judges generally are poorly equipped to evaluate. In their turn, jurors are expected to make sense of and rationally use the expert testimony that is admitted. In this we have a paradox. Not only does expert evidence by its very definition occupy intellectual territory beyond the competence of lay judges and jurors (else it would not qualify as expert testimony), it typically comes to court skewed, exaggerated, cherry-picked, or even fabricated ("junk science"). If nothing else, some aspect of the soundness or the meaning of the expert evidence will be contested—at least it will be if the lawyers are doing their jobs. How are judges and juries to intelligently sift for helpful truths under such conditions? That judges have sometimes failed utterly in their gatekeeping role is most clearly illustrated by those forensic sciences that have been terminated, after decades of regular admission into evidence, because they were determined to be invalid. Their departures from the courtroom were never prompted by judicial detection of their fallaciousness, but by external science agencies or belated testing in the fields themselves.

Without special training, and sometimes even with such training, humans do not come well equipped to evaluate and use scientific and other technical evidence. Statistical and probability evidence are especially perplexing to most people. Our minds evolved to more easily comprehend and be persuaded by stories, by conclusions asserted by proclaimed authorities, and by superficial characteristics of speakers (witnesses). The acceptance of social truth and the use of System 1 thinking appear to predominate. Traditionally, intelligent and skillful advocacy was the only tool for helping judges and jurors think more clearly and deeply about the data and logic underlying expert evidence. More recently, research psychologists have been looking for ways to make data more readily understandable by finding methods of presenting scientific and statistical evidence that are better adapted to what the human mind is most capable of processing. In addition, researchers have been exploring rapid teaching techniques for quickly bringing laypeople to higher levels of numeracy and inferential competence.

## Summing Up

This book has asked: what is it that evidence law is trying to do that depends upon psychology? The answers are: to facilitate trials that are fair, accurate, and efficient, and that encourage and protect important societal values and relationships. (Those goals are sometimes at war with each other.) How have the rules of evidence sought to accomplish these goals over the centuries of their development? They have tried to restrain lawyers from using the most robust weapons of influence, from using tactics that mislead, confuse, or exert undue influence. In whole categories of situations, and by directing judges to act in particular cases, the rules of evidence have sought to balance the probative value of evidence against its tendency to suggest conclusions on misleading bases—sometimes to exclude evidence, sometimes to limit it, sometimes to instruct juries on how to think about it, or in the worst instances to declare a mistrial or reverse a trial court verdict. Further, evidence law has sought to facilitate the trial's goals by regulating the form of questions lawyers may ask, by filtering expert witnesses in an effort to prevent them from misleading factfinders, by requiring witnesses to take oaths, and, in centuries past, by excluding classes of people thought to be unreliable witnesses. The rules also try to give lawyers and factfinders the tools they need to check the witnesses' reliability, encouraging the assessment of credibility (sometimes even with unreliable demeanor evidence) and the use of cross-examination.

Some of these choices have been right, some wrong. Some are headed in the right direction but are too difficult to apply, or they expect too much of the human mind, or have not yet found the right technique to engage what the mind can do. Empirical evidence about the best ways to manage and use trial evidence will continue to grow, and the law will have increasing resources to draw from regarding how best to accomplish its purposes.

# APPENDIX A

## *Table of Concepts*

Our book draws on a variety of theories and research findings across psychology. This Table of Concepts describes some of those that are generally relevant when thinking about evidence law. Other psychology terms and specific page numbers appear in the index.

| Psychology | Description | Relevant to |
|---|---|---|
| Attribution | Psychological process of inferring the cause of an outcome. *Attribution of responsibility* is inferring moral accountability for an outcome. *Attribution error* refers to systematic biases that over- or underattribute cause or responsibility. | Offers to compromise (Ch. 2); character evidence (Ch. 5); explaining causes of behavior (Ch. 5); virtually all rules pertaining to evidence leading to findings of criminal or civil liability |
| Bayes' Theorem | A way of updating knowledge that takes into account new information within the context of previous information. | Jury and judge decision making (Ch. 1); probative value (Ch. 2); justification for propensity evidence (Ch. 5) |
| Cognitive Capacity | Working memory available to an individual for conscious processing of information. | Detecting deception (Ch. 4); cross-examination (Ch. 4); present sense impressions (Ch. 6); excited utterances (Ch. 6) |
| Confirmation Bias | See Motivated Reasoning. | |
| Curse of Knowledge | A type of mental contamination in which someone who already knows something is unable to judge the competence of someone who does not. | Judge making Rule 403 rulings (Ch. 2), assessing jury comprehension (Ch. 3). |
| Debiasing | Techniques that try to remove cognitive errors (but often fail). | Effects of group deliberation on (Ch. 1); disregard instructions (Ch. 3) |

| Psychology | Description | Relevant to |
|---|---|---|
| Emotion | Feelings (affective states) that tend to be triggered by identifiable stimuli and last for a relatively short period of time. | More in group than individual decisions (Ch. 1); unfair prejudice (Ch. 2) |
| Framing | Alternative ways to present information that affect the judgments and decisions people make in response to the information. | Jury decision making (Ch. 1); expert testimony (Ch. 7) |
| Group Decision Making | Process by which individual beliefs and judgments are combined into a collective decision. Group dynamics can produce outcomes that differ from individual decision making. | Jury decision making (Ch. 1); emotion (Ch. 2); disregarding evidence (Ch. 3); relevant to all evidence that reaches a deliberating jury |
| Heuristics | Simple, efficient cognitive shortcuts by which people often make decisions and form judgments, usually focusing on one aspect of a problem and ignoring others. Examples: availability, representativeness, anchoring, attribute substitution. | Jury decision making (Ch. 1); judges vs. jurors (Ch. 1); expert testimony (Ch. 7) |
| Hindsight Bias | Tendency to unconsciously overestimate the likelihood one would have assigned to an event once the outcome is known. | Need for exclusion rules (Intro.); subsequent remedial repair (Ch. 2); inability to disregard (Ch 3); harmless error (Ch. 3) |
| Individual Differences | Measureable factors that vary across individuals (e.g., demographics, IQ, attitudes, expertise, personality traits [hypothesized stable attributes], etc.). | Jury selection (Ch. 1.); judges vs. jurors (Ch. 1); character evidence, propensity (Ch. 5) |
| Inferences | The cognitive act of deriving conclusions from information, assumptions, beliefs—whatever the nature of the process: intuitive, reflective, biased, etc. | Need for rules of evidence (Intro.); factfinder decision making (Ch. 1); story construction (Ch. 3); evaluating testimony (Ch. 4); predicting behavior (Ch. 6); causation (Ch. 7) |
| Influence and Persuasion | Phenomena, social cognitive processes, and techniques for creating or changing attitudes and/or behavior. | Justification for FRE (Intro.); import of evidence (Ch. 1); misleading the jury (Ch. 2); objecting (Ch. 3); statements of intent (Ch. 6); experts (Ch. 7) |

| Psychology | Description | Relevant to |
|---|---|---|
| Mental Contamination | Knowledge that interferes with a judgment one has to make (regardless of whether one should have that knowledge). (See also Curse of Knowledge.) | A reason for exclusionary rules (Intro.); bench trials (Ch. 1); categorical exclusions (Ch. 2); limited use (Ch. 3); instructions to disregard (Ch. 3); prior convictions (Ch. 3); fingerprint verification (Ch. 7) |
| Metacognition | Thinking about thinking (e.g., considering how you or others make decisions). | Drafting FRE (Intro.); balancing tests (Ch. 2); confidence vs. accuracy (Ch. 4); trial procedure innovations (Ch. 7) |
| Motivated Reasoning | People are motivated to seek accuracy and truth but also tend unconsciously to process information in a way that is consistent with one's pre-existing preferences or goals. | Character evidence as driver of (Ch. 5); expert testimony (Ch. 7) |
| Situation | Factors in the environment (i.e., outside the individual) that can affect an individual's behavior. | Influences on responses of witnesses (Ch. 4); explaining causes of behavior (Ch. 5); influences on expert witnesses (Ch. 7) |
| Source Confusion | Mixing up or being uncertain where information or a memory comes from | Joint trials (Ch. 3); witness commingling (Ch. 3); (mis)leading questions (Ch. 4); cross-examination (Ch. 4) |
| Story Model | Model of jury decision making that holds that jurors construct a story of what happened that fits the evidence presented and match that story to the verdict options given to them. | Jury decision making (Ch. 1); inability to disregard (Ch. 3) |
| System 1/System 2 (similar to central vs. peripheral processing) | Theory that reasoning consists of processes that work intuitively, unconsciously, and quickly, and processes that work consciously, reflectively, and slowly. | Jury deliberation (Ch. 1); emotion in unfair prejudice (Ch. 2); detecting deception (Ch. 4); evaluating experts (Ch. 7) |

## APPENDIX B

*Federal Rules of Evidence (Abridged)*

### Article I. General Provisions

*Rule 101. Scope; Definitions*

(a) Scope. These rules apply to proceedings in United States courts. The specific courts and proceedings to which the rules apply, along with exceptions, are set out in Rule 1101.
(b) Definitions. In these rules:
    (1) "civil case" means a civil action or proceeding;
    (2) "criminal case" includes a criminal proceeding;
    (3) "public office" includes a public agency;
    (4) "record" includes a memorandum, report, or data compilation;
    (5) a "rule prescribed by the Supreme Court" means a rule adopted by the Supreme Court under statutory authority; and
    (6) a reference to any kind of written material or any other medium includes electronically stored information.

*Rule 102. Purpose*

These rules should be construed so as to administer every proceeding fairly, eliminate unjustifiable expense and delay, and promote the development of evidence law, to the end of ascertaining the truth and securing a just determination.

*Rule 103. Rulings on Evidence*

(a) Preserving a Claim of Error. A party may claim error in a ruling to admit or exclude evidence only if the error affects a substantial right of the party and:

(1) if the ruling admits evidence, a party, on the record:
   (A) timely objects or moves to strike; and
   (B) states the specific ground, unless it was apparent from the context; or

(2) if the ruling excludes evidence, a party informs the court of its substance by an offer of proof, unless the substance was apparent from the context.

(b) Not Needing to Renew an Objection or Offer of Proof. Once the court rules definitively on the record—either before or at trial—a party need not renew an objection or offer of proof to preserve a claim of error for appeal.

(c) Court's Statement about the Ruling; Directing an Offer of Proof. The court may make any statement about the character or form of the evidence, the objection made, and the ruling. The court may direct that an offer of proof be made in question-and-answer form.

(d) Preventing the Jury from Hearing Inadmissible Evidence. To the extent practicable, the court must conduct a jury trial so that inadmissible evidence is not suggested to the jury by any means.

(e) Taking Notice of Plain Error. A court may take notice of a plain error affecting a substantial right, even if the claim of error was not properly preserved.

*Rule 104. Preliminary Questions*

(a) In General. The court must decide any preliminary question about whether a witness is qualified, a privilege exists, or evidence is admissible. In so deciding, the court is not bound by evidence rules, except those on privilege.

(b) Relevance That Depends on a Fact. When the relevance of evidence depends on whether a fact exists, proof must be introduced sufficient to support a finding that the fact does exist. The court may admit the proposed evidence on the condition that the proof be introduced later.

(c) Conducting a Hearing So That the Jury Cannot Hear It. The court must conduct any hearing on a preliminary question so that the jury cannot hear it if:

(1) the hearing involves the admissibility of a confession;

   (2) a defendant in a criminal case is a witness and so requests; or
   (3) justice so requires.
- (d) Cross-Examining a Defendant in a Criminal Case. By testifying on a preliminary question, a defendant in a criminal case does not become subject to cross-examination on other issues in the case.
- (e) Evidence Relevant to Weight and Credibility. This rule does not limit a party's right to introduce before the jury evidence that is relevant to the weight or credibility of other evidence.

*Rule 105. Limiting Evidence That Is Not Admissible against Other Parties or for Other Purposes*

If the court admits evidence that is admissible against a party or for a purpose—but not against another party or for another purpose—the court, on timely request, must restrict the evidence to its proper scope and instruct the jury accordingly.

*Rule 106. Remainder of or Related Writings or Recorded Statements*

If a party introduces all or part of a writing or recorded statement, an adverse party may require the introduction, at that time, of any other part—or any other writing or recorded statement—that in fairness ought to be considered at the same time.

## Article II. Judicial Notice

*Rule 201. Judicial Notice of Adjudicative Facts*

- (a) Scope. This rule governs judicial notice of an adjudicative fact only, not a legislative fact.
- (b) Kinds of Facts That May Be Judicially Noticed. The court may judicially notice a fact that is not subject to reasonable dispute because it:
   - (1) is generally known within the trial court's territorial jurisdiction; or
   - (2) can be accurately and readily determined from sources whose accuracy cannot reasonably be questioned.
- (c) Taking Notice. The court:

(1) may take judicial notice on its own; or
(2) must take judicial notice if a party requests it and the court is supplied with the necessary information.

(d) Timing. The court may take judicial notice at any stage of the proceeding.
(e) Opportunity to Be Heard. On timely request, a party is entitled to be heard on the propriety of taking judicial notice and the nature of the fact to be noticed. If the court takes judicial notice before notifying a party, the party, on request, is still entitled to be heard.
(f) Instructing the Jury. In a civil case, the court must instruct the jury to accept the noticed fact as conclusive. In a criminal case, the court must instruct the jury that it may or may not accept the noticed fact as conclusive.

## Article III. Presumptions in Civil Cases

### *Rule 301. Presumptions in Civil Cases Generally*

In a civil case, unless a federal statute or these rules provide otherwise, the party against whom a presumption is directed has the burden of producing evidence to rebut the presumption. But this rule does not shift the burden of persuasion, which remains on the party who had it originally.

## Article IV. Relevance and Its Limits

### *Rule 401. Test for Relevant Evidence*

Evidence is relevant if:

(a) it has any tendency to make a fact more or less probable than it would be without the evidence; and
(b) the fact is of consequence in determining the action.

### *Rule 402. General Admissibility of Relevant Evidence*

Relevant evidence is admissible unless any of the following provides otherwise:

- the United States Constitution;
- a federal statute;

- these rules; or
- other rules prescribed by the Supreme Court.

Irrelevant evidence is not admissible.

*Rule 403. Excluding Relevant Evidence for Prejudice, Confusion, Waste of Time, or Other Reasons*

The court may exclude relevant evidence if its probative value is substantially outweighed by a danger of one or more of the following: unfair prejudice, confusing the issues, misleading the jury, undue delay, wasting time, or needlessly presenting cumulative evidence.

*Rule 404. Character Evidence; Crimes or Other Acts*

(a) Character Evidence.
  (1) Prohibited Uses. Evidence of a person's character or character trait is not admissible to prove that on a particular occasion the person acted in accordance with the character or trait.
  (2) Exceptions for a Defendant or Victim in a Criminal Case. The following exceptions apply in a criminal case:
    (A) a defendant may offer evidence of the defendant's pertinent trait, and if the evidence is admitted, the prosecutor may offer evidence to rebut it;
    (B) subject to the limitations in Rule 412, a defendant may offer evidence of an alleged victim's pertinent trait, and if the evidence is admitted, the prosecutor may:
      (i) offer evidence to rebut it; and
      (ii) offer evidence of the defendant's same trait; and
    (C) in a homicide case, the prosecutor may offer evidence of the alleged victim's trait of peacefulness to rebut evidence that the victim was the first aggressor.
  (3) Exceptions for a Witness. Evidence of a witness's character may be admitted under Rules 607, 608, and 609.

(b) Crimes, Wrongs, or Other Acts.
  (1) Prohibited Uses. Evidence of a crime, wrong, or other act is not admissible to prove a person's character in order to show that

on a particular occasion the person acted in accordance with the character.

(2) Permitted Uses; Notice in a Criminal Case. This evidence may be admissible for another purpose, such as proving motive, opportunity, intent, preparation, plan, knowledge, identity, absence of mistake, or lack of accident. On request by a defendant in a criminal case, the prosecutor must:

(A) provide reasonable notice of the general nature of any such evidence that the prosecutor intends to offer at trial; and

(B) do so before trial—or during trial if the court, for good cause, excuses lack of pretrial notice.

*Rule 405. Methods of Proving Character*

(a) By Reputation or Opinion. When evidence of a person's character or character trait is admissible, it may be proved by testimony about the person's reputation or by testimony in the form of an opinion. On cross-examination of the character witness, the court may allow an inquiry into relevant specific instances of the person's conduct.

(b) By Specific Instances of Conduct. When a person's character or character trait is an essential element of a charge, claim, or defense, the character or trait may also be proved by relevant specific instances of the person's conduct.

*Rule 406. Habit; Routine Practice*

Evidence of a person's habit or an organization's routine practice may be admitted to prove that on a particular occasion the person or organization acted in accordance with the habit or routine practice. The court may admit this evidence regardless of whether it is corroborated or whether there was an eyewitness.

*Rule 407. Subsequent Remedial Measures*

When measures are taken that would have made an earlier injury or harm less likely to occur, evidence of the subsequent measures is not admissible to prove:

- negligence;
- culpable conduct;
- a defect in a product or its design; or
- a need for a warning or instruction.

But the court may admit this evidence for another purpose, such as impeachment or—if disputed—proving ownership, control, or the feasibility of precautionary measures.

*Rule 408. Compromise Offers and Negotiations*

(a) Prohibited Uses. Evidence of the following is not admissible—on behalf of any party—either to prove or disprove the validity or amount of a disputed claim or to impeach by a prior inconsistent statement or a contradiction:
  (1) furnishing, promising, or offering—or accepting, promising to accept, or offering to accept—a valuable consideration in compromising or attempting to compromise the claim; and
  (2) conduct or a statement made during compromise negotiations about the claim—except when offered in a criminal case and when the negotiations related to a claim by a public office in the exercise of its regulatory, investigative, or enforcement authority.

(b) Exceptions. The court may admit this evidence for another purpose, such as proving a witness's bias or prejudice, negating a contention of undue delay, or proving an effort to obstruct a criminal investigation or prosecution.

*Rule 409. Offers to Pay Medical and Similar Expenses*

Evidence of furnishing, promising to pay, or offering to pay medical, hospital, or similar expenses resulting from an injury is not admissible to prove liability for the injury.

*Rule 410. Pleas, Plea Discussions, and Related Statements*

(a) Prohibited Uses. In a civil or criminal case, evidence of the following is not admissible against the defendant who made the plea or participated in the plea discussions:
  (1) a guilty plea that was later withdrawn;
  (2) a nolo contendere plea;
  (3) a statement made during a proceeding on either of those pleas under Federal Rule of Criminal Procedure 11 or a comparable state procedure; or
  (4) a statement made during plea discussions with an attorney for the prosecuting authority if the discussions did not result in a guilty plea or they resulted in a later-withdrawn guilty plea.

(b) Exceptions. The court may admit a statement described in Rule 410(a)(3) or (4):
  (1) in any proceeding in which another statement made during the same plea or plea discussions has been introduced, if in fairness the statements ought to be considered together; or
  (2) in a criminal proceeding for perjury or false statement, if the defendant made the statement under oath, on the record, and with counsel present.

*Rule 411. Liability Insurance*

Evidence that a person was or was not insured against liability is not admissible to prove whether the person acted negligently or otherwise wrongfully. But the court may admit this evidence for another purpose, such as proving a witness's bias or prejudice or proving agency, ownership, or control.

*Rule 412. Sex-Offense Cases: The Victim's Sexual Behavior or Predisposition*

(a) Prohibited Uses. The following evidence is not admissible in a civil or criminal proceeding involving alleged sexual misconduct:
  (1) evidence offered to prove that a victim engaged in other sexual behavior; or
  (2) evidence offered to prove a victim's sexual predisposition.
(b) Exceptions.
  (1) Criminal Cases. The court may admit the following evidence in a criminal case:
    (A) evidence of specific instances of a victim's sexual behavior, if offered to prove that someone other than the defendant was the source of semen, injury, or other physical evidence;
    (B) evidence of specific instances of a victim's sexual behavior with respect to the person accused of the sexual misconduct, if offered by the defendant to prove consent or if offered by the prosecutor; and
    (C) evidence whose exclusion would violate the defendant's constitutional rights.
  (2) Civil Cases. In a civil case, the court may admit evidence offered to prove a victim's sexual behavior or sexual predisposition if its probative value substantially outweighs the danger of harm to any victim and of unfair prejudice to any party. The court may admit evidence of a victim's reputation only if the victim has placed it in controversy.
(c) Procedure to Determine Admissibility.
  (1) Motion. If a party intends to offer evidence under Rule 412(b), the party must:
    (A) file a motion that specifically describes the evidence and states the purpose for which it is to be offered;
    (B) do so at least 14 days before trial unless the court, for good cause, sets a different time;
    (C) serve the motion on all parties; and
    (D) notify the victim or, when appropriate, the victim's guardian or representative.

(2) Hearing. Before admitting evidence under this rule, the court must conduct an in camera hearing and give the victim and parties a right to attend and be heard. Unless the court orders otherwise, the motion, related materials, and the record of the hearing must be and remain sealed.

(d) Definition of "Victim." In this rule, "victim" includes an alleged victim.

### *Rule 413. Similar Crimes in Sexual-Assault Cases*

(a) Permitted Uses. In a criminal case in which a defendant is accused of a sexual assault, the court may admit evidence that the defendant committed any other sexual assault. The evidence may be considered on any matter to which it is relevant.

(b) Disclosure to the Defendant. If the prosecutor intends to offer this evidence, the prosecutor must disclose it to the defendant, including witnesses' statements or a summary of the expected testimony. The prosecutor must do so at least 15 days before trial or at a later time that the court allows for good cause.

(c) Effect on Other Rules. This rule does not limit the admission or consideration of evidence under any other rule.

(d) Definition of "Sexual Assault." In this rule and Rule 415, "sexual assault" means a crime under federal law or under state law (as "state" is defined in 18 U.S.C. § 513) involving:

(1) any conduct prohibited by 18 U.S.C. chapter 109A;

(2) contact, without consent, between any part of the defendant's body—or an object—and another person's genitals or anus;

(3) contact, without consent, between the defendant's genitals or anus and any part of another person's body;(4) deriving sexual pleasure or gratification from inflicting death, bodily injury, or physical pain on another person; or(5) an attempt or conspiracy to engage in conduct described in subparagraphs (1)-(4).

### *Rule 414. Similar Crimes in Child-Molestation Cases*

(a) Permitted Uses. In a criminal case in which a defendant is accused of child molestation, the court may admit evidence that the defendant committed any other child molestation. The evidence may be considered on any matter to which it is relevant.

(b) Disclosure to the Defendant. If the prosecutor intends to offer this evidence, the prosecutor must disclose it to the defendant, including witnesses' statements or a summary of the expected testimony. The prosecutor must do so at least 15 days before trial or at a later time that the court allows for good cause.

(c) Effect on Other Rules. This rule does not limit the admission or consideration of evidence under any other rule.

(d) Definition of "Child" and "Child Molestation."

In this rule and Rule 415:

(1) "child" means a person below the age of 14; and

(2) "child molestation" means a crime under federal law or under state law (as "state" is defined in 18 U.S.C. § 513) involving:

(A) any conduct prohibited by 18 U.S.C. chapter 109A and committed with a child;

(B) any conduct prohibited by 18 U.S.C. chapter 110;

(C) contact between any part of the defendant's body—or an object—and a child's genitals or anus;

(D) contact between the defendant's genitals or anus and any part of a child's body;

(E) deriving sexual pleasure or gratification from inflicting death, bodily injury, or physical pain on a child; or

(F) an attempt or conspiracy to engage in conduct described in subparagraphs (A)-(E).

*Rule 415. Similar Acts in Civil Cases Involving Sexual Assault or Child Molestation*

(a) Permitted Uses. In a civil case involving a claim for relief based on a party's alleged sexual assault or child molestation, the court may admit evidence that the party committed any other sexual assault or child molestation. The evidence may be considered as provided in Rules 413 and 414.

(b) Disclosure to the Opponent. If a party intends to offer this evidence, the party must disclose it to the party against whom it will be offered, including witnesses' statements or a summary of the expected testimony. The party must do so at least 15 days before trial or at a later time that the court allows for good cause.

(c) Effect on Other Rules. This rule does not limit the admission or consideration of evidence under any other rule.

## Article V. Privileges

### *Rule 501. Privilege in General*

The common law—as interpreted by United States courts in the light of reason and experience—governs a claim of privilege unless any of the following provides otherwise:

- the United States Constitution;
- a federal statute; or
- rules prescribed by the Supreme Court.

But in a civil case, state law governs privilege regarding a claim or defense for which state law supplies the rule of decision.

### *Rule 502. Attorney-Client Privilege and Work Product; Limitations on Waiver*

[Contents omitted]

## Article VI. Witnesses

### *Rule 601. Competency to Testify in General*

Every person is competent to be a witness unless these rules provide otherwise. But in a civil case, state law governs the witness's competency regarding a claim or defense for which state law supplies the rule of decision.

### *Rule 602. Need for Personal Knowledge*

A witness may testify to a matter only if evidence is introduced sufficient to support a finding that the witness has personal knowledge of the matter. Evidence to prove personal knowledge may consist of the witness's own testimony. This rule does not apply to a witness's expert testimony under Rule 703.

*Rule 603. Oath or Affirmation to Testify Truthfully*

Before testifying, a witness must give an oath or affirmation to testify truthfully. It must be in a form designed to impress that duty on the witness's conscience.

*Rule 607. Who May Impeach a Witness*

Any party, including the party that called the witness, may attack the witness's credibility.

*Rule 608. A Witness's Character for Truthfulness or Untruthfulness*

(a) Reputation or Opinion Evidence. A witness's credibility may be attacked or supported by testimony about the witness's reputation for having a character for truthfulness or untruthfulness, or by testimony in the form of an opinion about that character. But evidence of truthful character is admissible only after the witness's character for truthfulness has been attacked.
(b) Specific Instances of Conduct. Except for a criminal conviction under Rule 609, extrinsic evidence is not admissible to prove specific instances of a witness's conduct in order to attack or support the witness's character for truthfulness. But the court may, on cross-examination, allow them to be inquired into if they are probative of the character for truthfulness or untruthfulness of:
    (1) the witness; or
    (2) another witness whose character the witness being cross-examined has testified about.

By testifying on another matter, a witness does not waive any privilege against self-incrimination for testimony that relates only to the witness's character for truthfulness.

*Rule 609. Impeachment by Evidence of a Criminal Conviction*

(a) In General. The following rules apply to attacking a witness's character for truthfulness by evidence of a criminal conviction:
  (1) for a crime that, in the convicting jurisdiction, was punishable by death or by imprisonment for more than one year, the evidence:
    (A) must be admitted, subject to Rule 403, in a civil case or in a criminal case in which the witness is not a defendant; and
    (B) must be admitted in a criminal case in which the witness is a defendant, if the probative value of the evidence outweighs its prejudicial effect to that defendant; and
  (2) for any crime regardless of the punishment, the evidence must be admitted if the court can readily determine that establishing the elements of the crime required proving—or the witness's admitting—a dishonest act or false statement.

(b) Limit on Using the Evidence after 10 Years. This subdivision (b) applies if more than 10 years have passed since the witness's conviction or release from confinement for it, whichever is later. Evidence of the conviction is admissible only if:
  (1) its probative value, supported by specific facts and circumstances, substantially outweighs its prejudicial effect; and
  (2) the proponent gives an adverse party reasonable written notice of the intent to use it so that the party has a fair opportunity to contest its use.

(c) Effect of a Pardon, Annulment, or Certificate of Rehabilitation. Evidence of a conviction is not admissible if:
  (1) the conviction has been the subject of a pardon, annulment, certificate of rehabilitation, or other equivalent procedure based on a finding that the person has been rehabilitated, and the person has not been convicted of a later crime punishable by death or by imprisonment for more than one year; or
  (2) the conviction has been the subject of a pardon, annulment, or other equivalent procedure based on a finding of innocence.

(d) Juvenile Adjudications. Evidence of a juvenile adjudication is admissible under this rule only if:

(1) it is offered in a criminal case;
(2) the adjudication was of a witness other than the defendant;
(3) an adult's conviction for that offense would be admissible to attack the adult's credibility; and
(4) admitting the evidence is necessary to fairly determine guilt or innocence.

(e) Pendency of an Appeal. A conviction that satisfies this rule is admissible even if an appeal is pending. Evidence of the pendency is also admissible.

*Rule 610. Religious Beliefs or Opinions*

Evidence of a witness's religious beliefs or opinions is not admissible to attack or support the witness's credibility.

*Rule 611. Mode and Order of Examining Witnesses and Presenting Evidence*

(a) Control by the Court; Purposes. The court should exercise reasonable control over the mode and order of examining witnesses and presenting evidence so as to:
   (1) make those procedures effective for determining the truth;
   (2) avoid wasting time; and
   (3) protect witnesses from harassment or undue embarrassment.
(b) Scope of Cross-Examination. Cross-examination should not go beyond the subject matter of the direct examination and matters affecting the witness's credibility. The court may allow inquiry into additional matters as if on direct examination.
(c) Leading Questions. Leading questions should not be used on direct examination except as necessary to develop the witness's testimony. Ordinarily, the court should allow leading questions:
   (1) on cross-examination; and
   (2) when a party calls a hostile witness, an adverse party, or a witness identified with an adverse party.

*Rule 612. Writing Used to Refresh a Witness's Memory*

(a) Scope. This rule gives an adverse party certain options when a witness uses a writing to refresh memory:
  (1) while testifying; or
  (2) before testifying, if the court decides that justice requires the party to have those options.

(b) Adverse Party's Options; Deleting Unrelated Matter. Unless 18 U.S.C. § 3500 provides otherwise in a criminal case, an adverse party is entitled to have the writing produced at the hearing, to inspect it, to cross-examine the witness about it, and to introduce in evidence any portion that relates to the witness's testimony. If the producing party claims that the writing includes unrelated matter, the court must examine the writing in camera, delete any unrelated portion, and order that the rest be delivered to the adverse party. Any portion deleted over objection must be preserved for the record.

(c) Failure to Produce or Deliver the Writing. If a writing is not produced or is not delivered as ordered, the court may issue any appropriate order. But if the prosecution does not comply in a criminal case, the court must strike the witness's testimony or—if justice so requires—declare a mistrial.

*Rule 613. Witness's Prior Statement*

(a) Showing or Disclosing the Statement during Examination. When examining a witness about the witness's prior statement, a party need not show it or disclose its contents to the witness. But the party must, on request, show it or disclose its contents to an adverse party's attorney.

(b) Extrinsic Evidence of a Prior Inconsistent Statement. Extrinsic evidence of a witness's prior inconsistent statement is admissible only if the witness is given an opportunity to explain or deny the statement and an adverse party is given an opportunity to examine the witness about it, or if justice so requires. This subdivision (b) does not apply to an opposing party's statement under Rule 801(d)(2).

### *Rule 614. Court's Calling or Examining a Witness*

(a) Calling. The court may call a witness on its own or at a party's request. Each party is entitled to cross-examine the witness.
(b) Examining. The court may examine a witness regardless of who calls the witness.
(c) Objections. A party may object to the court's calling or examining a witness either at that time or at the next opportunity when the jury is not present.

### *Rule 615. Excluding Witnesses*

At a party's request, the court must order witnesses excluded so that they cannot hear other witnesses' testimony. Or the court may do so on its own. But this rule does not authorize excluding:
(a) a party who is a natural person;
(b) an officer or employee of a party that is not a natural person, after being designated as the party's representative by its attorney;
(c) a person whose presence a party shows to be essential to presenting the party's claim or defense; or
(d) a person authorized by statute to be present.

## Article VII. Opinions and Expert Testimony

### *Rule 701. Opinion Testimony by Lay Witnesses*

If a witness is not testifying as an expert, testimony in the form of an opinion is limited to one that is:
(a) rationally based on the witness's perception;
(b) helpful to clearly understanding the witness's testimony or to determining a fact in issue; and
(c) not based on scientific, technical, or other specialized knowledge within the scope of Rule 702.

*Rule 702. Testimony by Expert Witnesses*

A witness who is qualified as an expert by knowledge, skill, experience, training, or education may testify in the form of an opinion or otherwise if:

(a) the expert's scientific, technical, or other specialized knowledge will help the trier of fact to understand the evidence or to determine a fact in issue;
(b) the testimony is based on sufficient facts or data;
(c) the testimony is the product of reliable principles and methods; and
(d) the expert has reliably applied the principles and methods to the facts of the case.

*Rule 703. Bases of an Expert's Opinion Testimony*

An expert may base an opinion on facts or data in the case that the expert has been made aware of or personally observed. If experts in the particular field would reasonably rely on those kinds of facts or data in forming an opinion on the subject, they need not be admissible for the opinion to be admitted. But if the facts or data would otherwise be inadmissible, the proponent of the opinion may disclose them to the jury only if their probative value in helping the jury evaluate the opinion substantially outweighs their prejudicial effect.

*Rule 704. Opinion on an Ultimate Issue*

(a) In General—Not Automatically Objectionable. An opinion is not objectionable just because it embraces an ultimate issue.
(b) Exception. In a criminal case, an expert witness must not state an opinion about whether the defendant did or did not have a mental state or condition that constitutes an element of the crime charged or of a defense. Those matters are for the trier of fact alone.

*Rule 705. Disclosing the Facts or Data Underlying an Expert's Opinion*

Unless the court orders otherwise, an expert may state an opinion—and give the reasons for it—without first testifying to the underlying facts or data. But the expert may be required to disclose those facts or data on cross-examination.

*Rule 706. Court-Appointed Expert Witnesses*

(a) Appointment Process. On a party's motion or on its own, the court may order the parties to show cause why expert witnesses should not be appointed and may ask the parties to submit nominations. The court may appoint any expert that the parties agree on and any of its own choosing. But the court may only appoint someone who consents to act.

## Article VIII. Hearsay

*Rule 801. Definitions That Apply to This Article; Exclusions from Hearsay*

(a) Statement. "Statement" means a person's oral assertion, written assertion, or nonverbal conduct, if the person intended it as an assertion.
(b) Declarant. "Declarant" means the person who made the statement.
(c) Hearsay. "Hearsay" means a statement that:
 (1) the declarant does not make while testifying at the current trial or hearing; and
 (2) a party offers in evidence to prove the truth of the matter asserted in the statement.
(d) Statements That Are Not Hearsay. A statement that meets the following conditions is not hearsay:
 (1) A Declarant-Witness's Prior Statement. The declarant testifies and is subject to cross-examination about a prior statement, and the statement:

- (A) is inconsistent with the declarant's testimony and was given under penalty of perjury at a trial, hearing, or other proceeding or in a deposition;
- (B) is consistent with the declarant's testimony and is offered to rebut an express or implied charge that the declarant recently fabricated it or acted from a recent improper influence or motive in so testifying; or
- (C) identifies a person as someone the declarant perceived earlier.

(2) An Opposing Party's Statement. The statement is offered against an opposing party and:

- (A) was made by the party in an individual or representative capacity;
- (B) is one the party manifested that it adopted or believed to be true;
- (C) was made by a person whom the party authorized to make a statement on the subject;
- (D) was made by the party's agent or employee on a matter within the scope of that relationship and while it existed; or
- (E) was made by the party's coconspirator during and in furtherance of the conspiracy. The statement must be considered but does not by itself establish the declarant's authority under (C); the existence or scope of the relationship under (D); or the existence of the conspiracy or participation in it under (E).

*Rule 802. The Rule against Hearsay*

Hearsay is not admissible unless any of the following provides otherwise:

- a federal statute;
- these rules; or
- other rules prescribed by the Supreme Court.

*Rule 803. Exceptions to the Rule against Hearsay—Regardless of Whether the Declarant Is Available as a Witness*

The following are not excluded by the rule against hearsay, regardless of whether the declarant is available as a witness:

(1) Present Sense Impression. A statement describing or explaining an event or condition, made while or immediately after the declarant perceived it.

(2) Excited Utterance. A statement relating to a startling event or condition, made while the declarant was under the stress of excitement that it caused.

(3) Then-Existing Mental, Emotional, or Physical Condition. A statement of the declarant's then-existing state of mind (such as motive, intent, or plan) or emotional, sensory, or physical condition (such as mental feeling, pain, or bodily health), but not including a statement of memory or belief to prove the fact remembered or believed unless it relates to the validity or terms of the declarant's will.

(4) Statement Made for Medical Diagnosis or Treatment. A statement that:
   (A) is made for—and is reasonably pertinent to—medical diagnosis or treatment; and
   (B) describes medical history; past or present symptoms or sensations; their inception; or their general cause.

(5) Recorded Recollection. A record that:
   (A) is on a matter the witness once knew about but now cannot recall well enough to testify fully and accurately;
   (B) was made or adopted by the witness when the matter was fresh in the witness's memory; and
   (C) accurately reflects the witness's knowledge. If admitted, the record may be read into evidence but may be received as an exhibit only if offered by an adverse party.

(6) Records of a Regularly Conducted Activity. A record of an act, event, condition, opinion, or diagnosis if:
   (A) the record was made at or near the time by—or from information transmitted by—someone with knowledge;

(B) the record was kept in the course of a regularly conducted activity of a business, organization, occupation, or calling, whether or not for profit;
(C) making the record was a regular practice of that activity;
(D) all these conditions are shown by the testimony of the custodian or another qualified witness, or by a certification that complies with Rule 902(11) or (12) or with a statute permitting certification; and
(E) neither the source of information nor the method or circumstances of preparation indicate a lack of trustworthiness.

(7) Absence of a Record of a Regularly Conducted Activity. Evidence that a matter is not included in a record described in paragraph (6) if:
(A) the evidence is admitted to prove that the matter did not occur or exist;
(B) a record was regularly kept for a matter of that kind; and
(C) neither the possible source of the information nor other circumstances indicate a lack of trustworthiness.

(8) Public Records. A record or statement of a public office if:
(A) it sets out:
(i) the office's activities;
(ii) a matter observed while under a legal duty to report, but not including, in a criminal case, a matter observed by law-enforcement personnel; or
(iii) in a civil case or against the government in a criminal case, factual findings from a legally authorized investigation; and
(B) neither the source of information nor other circumstances indicate a lack of trustworthiness.

(9) Public Records of Vital Statistics. A record of a birth, death, or marriage, if reported to a public office in accordance with a legal duty.

(10) Absence of a Public Record. Testimony—or a certification under Rule 902—that a diligent search failed to disclose a public record or statement if the testimony or certification is admitted to prove that:

(A) the record or statement does not exist; or
(B) a matter did not occur or exist, if a public office regularly kept a record or statement for a matter of that kind.

(11) Records of Religious Organizations Concerning Personal or Family History. A statement of birth, legitimacy, ancestry, marriage, divorce, death, relationship by blood or marriage, or similar facts of personal or family history, contained in a regularly kept record of a religious organization.

(12) Certificates of Marriage, Baptism, and Similar Ceremonies. A statement of fact contained in a certificate:
(A) made by a person who is authorized by a religious organization or by law to perform the act certified;
(B) attesting that the person performed a marriage or similar ceremony or administered a sacrament; and
(C) purporting to have been issued at the time of the act or within a reasonable time after it.

(13) Family Records. A statement of fact about personal or family history contained in a family record, such as a Bible, genealogy, chart, engraving on a ring, inscription on a portrait, or engraving on an urn or burial marker.

(14) Records of Documents That Affect an Interest in Property. The record of a document that purports to establish or affect an interest in property if:
(A) the record is admitted to prove the content of the original recorded document, along with its signing and its delivery by each person who purports to have signed it;
(B) the record is kept in a public office; and
(C) a statute authorizes recording documents of that kind in that office.

(15) Statements in Documents That Affect an Interest in Property. A statement contained in a document that purports to establish or affect an interest in property if the matter stated was relevant to the document's purpose—unless later dealings with the property are inconsistent with the truth of the statement or the purport of the document.

(16) Statements in Ancient Documents. A statement in a document that is at least 20 years old and whose authenticity is established.

(17) Market Reports and Similar Commercial Publications. Market quotations, lists, directories, or other compilations that are generally relied on by the public or by persons in particular occupations.

(18) Statements in Learned Treatises, Periodicals, or Pamphlets. A statement contained in a treatise, periodical, or pamphlet if:

(A) the statement is called to the attention of an expert witness on cross-examination or relied on by the expert on direct examination; and

(B) the publication is established as a reliable authority by the expert's admission or testimony, by another expert's testimony, or by judicial notice.

If admitted, the statement may be read into evidence but not received as an exhibit.

(19) Reputation Concerning Personal or Family History. A reputation among a person's family by blood, adoption, or marriage—or among a person's associates or in the community—concerning the person's birth, adoption, legitimacy, ancestry, marriage, divorce, death, relationship by blood, adoption, or marriage, or similar facts of personal or family history.

(20) Reputation Concerning Boundaries or General History. A reputation in a community—arising before the controversy—concerning boundaries of land in the community or customs that affect the land, or concerning general historical events important to that community, state, or nation.

(21) Reputation Concerning Character. A reputation among a person's associates or in the community concerning the person's character.

(22) Judgment of a Previous Conviction. Evidence of a final judgment of conviction if:

(A) the judgment was entered after a trial or guilty plea, but not a nolo contendere plea;

(B) the conviction was for a crime punishable by death or by imprisonment for more than a year;

(C) the evidence is admitted to prove any fact essential to the judgment; and

(D) when offered by the prosecutor in a criminal case for a purpose other than impeachment, the judgment was against the defendant.

The pendency of an appeal may be shown but does not affect admissibility.

(23) Judgments Involving Personal, Family, or General History, or a Boundary. A judgment that is admitted to prove a matter of personal, family, or general history, or boundaries, if the matter:
  - (A) was essential to the judgment; and
  - (B) could be proved by evidence of reputation.

*Rule 804. Exceptions to the Rule against Hearsay—When the Declarant Is Unavailable as a Witness*

(a) Criteria for Being Unavailable. A declarant is considered to be unavailable as a witness if the declarant:
  - (1) is exempted from testifying about the subject matter of the declarant's statement because the court rules that a privilege applies;
  - (2) refuses to testify about the subject matter despite a court order to do so;
  - (3) testifies to not remembering the subject matter;
  - (4) cannot be present or testify at the trial or hearing because of death or a then-existing infirmity, physical illness, or mental illness; or
  - (5) is absent from the trial or hearing and the statement's proponent has not been able, by process or other reasonable means, to procure:
    - (A) the declarant's attendance, in the case of a hearsay exception under Rule 804(b)(1) or (6); or
    - (B) the declarant's attendance or testimony, in the case of a hearsay exception under Rule 804(b)(2), (3), or (4).

But this subdivision (a) does not apply if the statement's proponent procured or wrongfully caused the declarant's unavailability as a witness in order to prevent the declarant from attending or testifying.

(b) The Exceptions. The following are not excluded by the rule against hearsay if the declarant is unavailable as a witness:

(1) Former Testimony. Testimony that:
   (A) was given as a witness at a trial, hearing, or lawful deposition, whether given during the current proceeding or a different one; and
   (B) is now offered against a party who had—or, in a civil case, whose predecessor in interest had—an opportunity and similar motive to develop it by direct, cross-, or redirect examination.

(2) Statement under the Belief of Imminent Death. In a prosecution for homicide or in a civil case, a statement that the declarant, while believing the declarant's death to be imminent, made about its cause or circumstances.

(3) Statement against Interest. A statement that:
   (A) a reasonable person in the declarant's position would have made only if the person believed it to be true because, when made, it was so contrary to the declarant's proprietary or pecuniary interest or had so great a tendency to invalidate the declarant's claim against someone else or to expose the declarant to civil or criminal liability; and
   (B) is supported by corroborating circumstances that clearly indicate its trustworthiness, if it is offered in a criminal case as one that tends to expose the declarant to criminal liability.

(4) Statement of Personal or Family History. A statement about:
   (A) the declarant's own birth, adoption, legitimacy, ancestry, marriage, divorce, relationship by blood, adoption, or marriage, or similar facts of personal or family history, even though the declarant had no way of acquiring personal knowledge about that fact; or
   (B) another person concerning any of these facts, as well as death, if the declarant was related to the person by blood, adoption, or marriage or was so intimately associated with the person's family that the declarant's information is likely to be accurate.

(5) [Other Exceptions.] [Transferred to Rule 807.]

(6) Statement Offered against a Party That Wrongfully Caused the Declarant's Unavailability. A statement offered against a

party that wrongfully caused—or acquiesced in wrongfully causing—the declarant's unavailability as a witness, and did so intending that result.

*Rule 805. Hearsay within Hearsay*

Hearsay within hearsay is not excluded by the rule against hearsay if each part of the combined statements conforms with an exception to the rule.

*Rule 806. Attacking and Supporting the Declarant's Credibility*

When a hearsay statement—or a statement described in Rule 801(d)(2)(C), (D), or (E)—has been admitted in evidence, the declarant's credibility may be attacked, and then supported, by any evidence that would be admissible for those purposes if the declarant had testified as a witness. The court may admit evidence of the declarant's inconsistent statement or conduct, regardless of when it occurred or whether the declarant had an opportunity to explain or deny it. If the party against whom the statement was admitted calls the declarant as a witness, the party may examine the declarant on the statement as if on cross-examination.

*Rule 807. Residual Exception*

(a) In General. Under the following circumstances, a hearsay statement is not excluded by the rule against hearsay even if the statement is not specifically covered by a hearsay exception in Rule 803 or 804:
   (1) the statement has equivalent circumstantial guarantees of trustworthiness;
   (2) it is offered as evidence of a material fact;
   (3) it is more probative on the point for which it is offered than any other evidence that the proponent can obtain through reasonable efforts; and
   (4) admitting it will best serve the purposes of these rules and the interests of justice.

(b) Notice. The statement is admissible only if, before the trial or hearing, the proponent gives an adverse party reasonable notice of the intent to offer the statement and its particulars, including the declarant's name and address, so that the party has a fair opportunity to meet it.

## Article IX. Authentication and Identification

### *Rule 901. Authenticating or Identifying Evidence*

(a) In General. To satisfy the requirement of authenticating or identifying an item of evidence, the proponent must produce evidence sufficient to support a finding that the item is what the proponent claims it is.
(b) Examples. The following are examples only—not a complete list—of evidence that satisfies the requirement:
  (1) Testimony of a Witness with Knowledge. Testimony that an item is what it is claimed to be.
  (2) Nonexpert Opinion about Handwriting. A nonexpert's opinion that handwriting is genuine, based on a familiarity with it that was not acquired for the current litigation.
  (3) Comparison by an Expert Witness or the Trier of Fact. A comparison with an authenticated specimen by an expert witness or the trier of fact.
  (4) Distinctive Characteristics and the Like. The appearance, contents, substance, internal patterns, or other distinctive characteristics of the item, taken together with all the circumstances.
  (5) Opinion about a Voice. An opinion identifying a person's voice—whether heard firsthand or through mechanical or electronic transmission or recording—based on hearing the voice at any time under circumstances that connect it with the alleged speaker.
  (6) Evidence about a Telephone Conversation. For a telephone conversation, evidence that a call was made to the number assigned at the time to:
    (A) a particular person, if circumstances, including self-identification, show that the person answering was the one called; or

(B) a particular business, if the call was made to a business and the call related to business reasonably transacted over the telephone.

(7) Evidence about Public Records. Evidence that:

(A) a document was recorded or filed in a public office as authorized by law; or

(B) a purported public record or statement is from the office where items of this kind are kept.

(8) Evidence about Ancient Documents or Data Compilations. For a document or data compilation, evidence that it:

(A) is in a condition that creates no suspicion about its authenticity;

(B) was in a place where, if authentic, it would likely be; and

(C) is at least 20 years old when offered.

(9) Evidence about a Process or System. Evidence describing a process or system and showing that it produces an accurate result.

## Article X. Contents of Writings, Recordings, and Photographs

### *Rule 1001. Definitions That Apply to This Article*

In this article:

(a) A "writing" consists of letters, words, numbers, or their equivalent set down in any form.

(b) A "recording" consists of letters, words, numbers, or their equivalent recorded in any manner.

(c) A "photograph" means a photographic image or its equivalent stored in any form.

(d) An "original" of a writing or recording means the writing or recording itself or any counterpart intended to have the same effect by the person who executed or issued it. For electronically stored information, "original" means any printout—or other output readable by sight—if it accurately reflects the information. An "original" of a photograph includes the negative or a print from it.

(e) A "duplicate" means a counterpart produced by a mechanical, photographic, chemical, electronic, or other equivalent process or technique that accurately reproduces the original.

*Rule 1002. Requirement of the Original*

An original writing, recording, or photograph is required in order to prove its content unless these rules or a federal statute provides otherwise.

*Rule 1003. Admissibility of Duplicates*

A duplicate is admissible to the same extent as the original unless a genuine question is raised about the original's authenticity or the circumstances make it unfair to admit the duplicate.

*Rule 1004. Admissibility of Other Evidence of Content*

An original is not required and other evidence of the content of a writing, recording, or photograph is admissible if:

(a) all the originals are lost or destroyed, and not by the proponent acting in bad faith;
(b) an original cannot be obtained by any available judicial process;
(c) the party against whom the original would be offered had control of the original; was at that time put on notice, by pleadings or otherwise, that the original would be a subject of proof at the trial or hearing; and fails to produce it at the trial or hearing; or
(d) the writing, recording, or photograph is not closely related to a controlling issue.

*Rule 1005. Copies of Public Records to Prove Content*

The proponent may use a copy to prove the content of an official record—or of a document that was recorded or filed in a public office as authorized by law—if these conditions are met: the record or document is otherwise admissible; and the copy is certified as correct in accordance with Rule 902(4) or is testified to be correct by a witness who has compared it with the original. If no such copy can be obtained by reasonable diligence, then the proponent may use other evidence to prove the content.

*Rule 1006. Summaries to Prove Content*

The proponent may use a summary, chart, or calculation to prove the content of voluminous writings, recordings, or photographs that cannot be conveniently examined in court. The proponent must make the originals or duplicates available for examination or copying, or both, by other parties at a reasonable time and place. And the court may order the proponent to produce them in court.

*Rule 1007. Testimony or Statement of a Party to Prove Content*

The proponent may prove the content of a writing, recording, or photograph by the testimony, deposition, or written statement of the party against whom the evidence is offered. The proponent need not account for the original.

*Rule 1008. Functions of the Court and Jury*

Ordinarily, the court determines whether the proponent has fulfilled the factual conditions for admitting other evidence of the content of a writing, recording, or photograph under Rule 1004 or 1005. But in a jury trial, the jury determines—in accordance with Rule 104(b)—any issue about whether:

(a) an asserted writing, recording, or photograph ever existed;
(b) another one produced at the trial or hearing is the original; or
(c) other evidence of content accurately reflects the content.

# NOTES

INTRODUCTION

1 This notion is not original with your authors. Writing before the close of the nineteenth century, James Bradley Thayer observed that "the law [is] a human contrivance or outgrowth . . . resting, as if by gravity, on human nature, human experience, and the principles that regulate human thought." James Thayer, *The Present and Future of the Law of Evidence*, 12 HARVARD LAW REVIEW 71, 77 (1898). An evidence scholar writing early in the twentieth century had this to say: "The various rules of evidence in serving their diverse policies all reflect certain assumptions which have been made by the judicial or legislative makers of the rules about human psychology. The test to apply to any rule of evidence, either to support its validity, or to argue for change, or to make for more efficient learning, is whether the psychological assumption implicit in the instant rule is a valid one." John Strahorn, *Extra-Legal Materials and the Law of Evidence*, 29 ILLINOIS LAW REVIEW 300 (1934). More recently, an Australian evidence scholar noted, "Of all other disciplines, it would seem that psychology would be the most fruitful for any exponent of the law of evidence to explore." Eilis Magner, *Wigmore Confronts Munsterberg: Present Relevance of a Classic Debate*, 13 SYDNEY LAW REVIEW 121, 122 (1991).

2 These kinds of issues implicate cognitive psychology. Cognitive psychology is the scientific study of the mental processes by which people perceive, store, process, retrieve, and use information.

3 These kinds of issues implicate social psychology. Social psychology is the scientific study of how people's thoughts, feeling, and behavior are influenced by (the words, conduct, and creations of) other people.

4 Including the adversarial process and the existence of the jury.

5 These issues somewhat expand the concerns of evidence law to organizational psychology and sociology.

6 For example, if perception and memory were flawless, if truth telling occurred with every utterance, if decision makers applied the law correctly to evidence they recalled perfectly and to which they had applied optimal weights to reach accurate understandings of "what happened" in the disputed transaction—we would have different rules than the ones we have. Another part of why we have the rules we have is that the rulemakers, too, are human—in possession of incomplete information about how the minds of others work, and armed with certain kinds of intuitions ready to fill the gaps in knowledge.

7 JOHN THIBAUT AND LAURENS WALKER, PROCEDURAL JUSTICE: A PSYCHOLOGICAL ANALYSIS (1975).
8 Linda J. Skitka and David A. Houston, *When Due Process Is of No Consequence: Moral Mandates and Presumed Defendant Guilt or Innocence*, 14 SOCIAL JUSTICE RESEARCH 305 (2001).
9 See 6 WIGMORE ON EVIDENCE §1747. As stated in the Advisory Committee Note to Rule 803(2): "circumstances may produce a condition of excitement which temporarily stills the capacity of reflection and produces utterances free of conscious fabrication."
10 Which, by the way, is quite likely. The effects of stress on perception, memory, and performance approximately trace an inverted U-shaped function: at moderate levels of stress, human ability is enhanced; at higher levels of excitement, it degrades. This is the Yerkes-Dodson law. If levels of stress and excitement become high enough, serious degradation of performance generally occurs. See, e.g., Donald Norman and Daniel Bobrow, *On Data-Limited and Resource-Limited Processes*, 7 COGNITIVE PSYCHOLOGY 44 (1975); P.E. Lehner et al., *Cognitive Biases and Time Stress in Team Decision Making*, 27 IEEE TRANSACTIONS ON SYSTEMS, MAN, AND CYBERNETICS PART A: SYSTEMS AND HUMANS 698 (1997).
11 Unless, of course, the rulemakers thought that people were sensitive to the problem of degraded perception and cognition under stress and could appropriately discount the out-of-court witness's report—then the rule might endure despite the testimony's defects.
12 Similarly, when a trial judge makes a ruling in a particular case.
13 See, e.g., the work of Kahneman and Tversky on cognitive heuristics, discussed later in this book.
14 Though the rulemakers apparently think that they often draw different inferences from laypersons, and that the cognitive skills of judges are superior on factual matters compared to those of laypersons, a common finding is that judges and jurors draw much the same inferences. Further discussion can be found in Chapter 1.
15 JAMES B. THAYER, A TREATISE ON EVIDENCE AT COMMON LAW (1898), suggesting that evidence law was "the child of the jury system."
16 Id.
17 Simeon Baldwin, *The Artificiality of Our Law of Evidence*, 21 YALE LAW JOURNAL 105 (1911). Baldwin was, among other things, a justice of Connecticut's supreme court, governor of Connecticut, and professor of law at Yale Law School. His article went on to say that the rules have become unnecessary, and in the U.S. were never necessary, due to our system of public education that produces much better educated citizens and jurors than had been true in England.
18 Thomas P. Gallanis, *The Rise of Modern Evidence Law*, 84 IOWA LAW REVIEW 499 (1999); Stephan Landsman, *The Rise of the Contentious Spirit: Adversary Procedure in Eighteenth Century England*, 75 CORNELL LAW REVIEW 497 (1990); John H. Langbein, *Historical Foundations of the Law of Evidence: A View from the Ryder Sources*, 96 COLUMBIA LAW REVIEW 1168 (1996).

19 Richard O. Lempert et al., *A Brief History of the Codification of Evidence Law*, in A MODERN APPROACH TO EVIDENCE, 3d edition (Richard O. Lempert et al., eds., 2000).

20 If lawyers appreciate what a rule is designed to achieve and on what rationale, in circumstances where application of the rule is unlikely to serve its purpose, an exception to the rule can be requested, and judges who have a similar appreciation are more likely to grant the request than to woodenly apply the rule whether it makes sense to do so or not.

21 2 WIGMORE ON EVIDENCE §576.

22 In *Respublica v. Keating*, 1 U.S. 110, 1 Dall. 110 (1784), for example, the court allowed the victim of an allegedly forged promissory note to testify as to whether the document was fraudulent. The decision was based partly on the reasoning that "the probability was, that Meng's testimony would be favourable to the prisoner; for if Meng swears the note to be false, he can gain nothing; but if he proves it to be true, he testifies against his own interest."

23 Anglo-American evidence law in its present form came into being after the middle of the eighteenth century. John Langbein, *Historical Foundations of the Law of Evidence*, 96 COLUMBIA LAW REVIEW 1168 (1996).

24 An illustration of this process of change is the development of the hearsay, or second-hand evidence, rule, which began to be regularly discussed in common law courts in the sixteenth century as live witnesses appeared with greater frequency. Early in the development of the hearsay concept the main focus, though inconsistently articulated, was whether the scrutinized statement had been made under oath—reflecting assumptions about the power of oaths to ensure truthful statements—or whether it had been appropriately corroborated. If either or both of those conditions were satisfied, hearsay was likely to be accepted; otherwise it might be successfully challenged. The hearsay concept underwent substantial alteration and expansion during the turbulent period stretching from the middle 1600s to the 1770s. In this era, concern shifted from the oath and corroboration to the in-court testing of witnesses by cross-examination, as the rising tide of adversarial, advocate-led processes came to dominate proceedings—a shift emphasizing important assumptions about the power of questioning to test and secure truth. Things shifted again in the nineteenth and early twentieth centuries as hearsay doctrine was reworked to reflect concerns about increasingly heterogeneous juries. Even in our own day, change has continued as hearsay rules are slowly being relaxed by courts and rule drafters alike in response to perceived shifts in juror and adjudicator sophistication. The underlying issue of hearsay now involves more finely graded questions about the ability (or lack of ability) of jurors to adjust the weight they give to hearsay testimony depending upon circumstances surrounding the out-of-court declaration.

25 James B. Thayer, *The Present and Future of the Law of Evidence*, 12 HARVARD LAW REVIEW 71 (1898).

26 Edward Cleary, *Evidence as a Problem in Communicating*, 5 VANDERBILT LAW REVIEW 277, 279 (1952).

27 Roger C. Park, *Evidence Scholarship, Old and New*, 75 MINNESOTA LAW REVIEW 849 (1991).

28 Edward Cleary, *Evidence as a Problem in Communicating*, 5 VANDERBILT LAW REVIEW 277, 278 (1952) (suggesting that communications research was likely to provide the illumination that evidence law needed).

29 Id., at 278.

30 We will not delve into the complexities and pitfalls of different research designs. Interested readers can find a more detailed, but highly accessible, discussion of the scientific method for lawyers in Michael J. Saks, *Scientific Method: The Logic of Drawing Inferences from Empirical Evidence*, in MODERN SCIENTIFIC EVIDENCE: THE LAW AND SCIENCE OF EXPERT TESTIMONY (David L. Faigman et al., eds., 2010).

31 Linda J. Demaine, *In Search of an Anti-Elephant: Confronting the Human Inability to Forget Inadmissible Evidence*, 16 GEORGE MASON LAW REVIEW 99 (2008). See Chapter 3 for more details.

32 In modern science, "theory" refers to a well-developed explanation of real-world phenomena, susceptible to empirical testing, and often well tested or in the process of being tested. The empirical testing either provides support (verification) or contradicts (falsification) the theory. A "theory" in science contrasts with the more common uses of the word, which imply something unproven or speculative.

33 Barbara A. Spellman, *Individual Reasoning*, in INTELLIGENCE ANALYSIS: BEHAVIORAL AND SOCIAL SCIENTIFIC FOUNDATIONS (Baruch Fischhoff and Cherie Chauvin, eds., 2011).

34 Timothy D. Wilson and Nancy Brekke, *Mental Contamination and Mental Correction: Unwanted Influences on Judgments and Evaluations*, 16 PSYCHOLOGICAL BULLETIN 117 (1994).

35 JANET METCALFE AND ARTHUR P. SHIMAMURA (eds.), METACOGNITION: KNOWING ABOUT KNOWING (1996).

36 Chris Guthrie, Jeffrey J. Rachlinski, and Andrew J. Wistrich, *Inside the Judicial Mind*, 86 CORNELL LAW REVIEW 777 (2000–2001).

37 Frederick Schauer, *On the Supposed Jury-Dependence of Evidence Law*, 155 UNIVERSITY OF PENNSYLVANIA LAW REVIEW 165 (2006–2007).

38 See Jeffrey J. Rachlinski, *A Positive Psychological Theory of Judging in Hindsight*, 65 UNIVERSITY OF CHICAGO LAW REVIEW 571 (1998), for a review of the hindsight bias as related to law literature and the surprising thesis that the law already takes the bias into account. See Scott A. Hawkins and Reid Hastie, *Hindsight: Biased Judgments of Past Events after the Outcomes Are Known*, 107 PSYCHOLOLOGICAL BULLETIN 311 (1990), for the classic "early" review and Neal J. Roese and Kathleen D. Vohs, *Hindsight Bias*, 7 PERSPECTIVES ON PSYCHOLOGICAL SCIENCE 411 (2012), for a more recent theoretical review of psychological research on the hindsight bias.

39 See http://www.smartekusa.com/pdffiles/ST-1200.pdf, page 3, number 2—"Steam Iron Operating Instructions," which include the manufacturer's warning against

exactly that action. Also: http://ec1.images-amazon.com/media/i3d/01/A/man-migrate/MANUAL000006529.pdf, page 2, "Consumer Safety Information."

40 See the classic collection of early papers demonstrating and describing various heuristics and biases: DANIEL KAHNEMAN, PAUL SLOVIC, AND AMOS TVERSKY (eds.), JUDGMENT UNDER UNCERTAINTY: HEURISTICS AND BIASES (1982).

41 This point was made by Tversky and Kahneman in their early paper in *Science*—that heuristics are shortcuts that usually work and that they reveal much about thinking. Amos Tversky and Daniel Kahneman, *Judgment under Uncertainty: Heuristics and Biases*, 185 SCIENCE 1124 (1974). But those messages were often lost in the 1980s. See Barbara A. Spellman and Simone Schnall, *Embodied Rationality*, 35 QUEEN'S LAW JOURNAL 117 (2009), for a summary of rationality research relevant to law.

42 For example, researchers discovered that people use two different kinds of information processing when receiving persuasive communications: central and peripheral (discussed in greater detail in Chapter 7). Peripheral processing appears to be a particular instance of System 1 reasoning and central processing appears to be a particular instance of System 2 reasoning.

43 Eliot R. Smith and Jamie DeCoster, *Dual-Process Models in Social and Cognitive Psychology: Conceptual Integration and Links to Underlying Memory Systems*, 4 PERSONALITY AND SOCIAL PSYCHOLOGY REVIEW 108, 124 (table) (2000).

44 Chris Guthrie, Jeffrey J. Rachlinski, and Andrew J. Wistrich, *Blinking on the Bench: How Judges Decide Cases*, 93 CORNELL LAW REVIEW 1 (2007–2008).

45 See Jonathan St. B. T. Evans and Keith E. Stanovich, *Dual-Process Theories of Higher Cognition: Advancing the Debate*, 8 PERSPECTIVES ON PSYCHOLOGICAL SCIENCE 223 (2013), for a summary of dual-process theorizing and the subsequent commentaries for other views.

46 For a useful critique, see P. Greg Mitchell, *Mapping Evidence Law*, 4 MICHIGAN STATE LAW REVIEW 1065 (2003).

47 GERALD L. CLORE, KAREN GASPER, AND ERIKA GARVIN, AFFECT AS INFORMATION (2001).

48 To say that people are generally better at a skill after they have mastered it than before is not to say that experts do not make errors, or that those errors do not result from understandable, also psychologically based, causes. The factors contributing to expert errors have been studied in such areas as health care, forensic science, transportation (trains, planes, cars, and spacecraft), and manufacturing. Indeed, some researchers have invested considerable energy in trying to improve our understanding of the systematic factors that contribute to expert errors. See, e.g., Itiel Dror and David Charlton, *Why Experts Make Errors*, 56 JOURNAL OF FORENSIC IDENTIFICATION 600 (2006); JAMES REASON, HUMAN ERROR (1990); JOHN W. SENDERS AND NEVILLE P. MORAY, HUMAN ERROR: CAUSE, PREDICTION, AND REDUCTION (1991); DAVID D. WOODS, SIDNEY DEKKER, RICHARD COOK, AND LEILA JOHANNESEN, BEHIND HUMAN ERROR (2012). An important paper elucidating the factors that affect the quality

of expert intuitive judgments is Daniel Kahneman and Gary Klein, *Conditions for Intuitive Expertise: A Failure to Disagree*, 64 AMERICAN PSYCHOLOGIST 515 (2009).

49 See, e.g., BRANDON GARRETT, CONVICTING THE INNOCENT: WHERE CRIMINAL PROSECUTIONS GO WRONG (2012); Michael J. Saks and Jonathan J. Koehler, *The Coming Paradigm Shift in Forensic Identification Science*, 309 SCIENCE 892 (2005). See also the cases described on www.innocenceproject.org.

50 HUGO MÜNSTERBERG, ON THE WITNESS STAND (1908).

51 John H. Wigmore, *Professor Müensterberg* [sic] *and the Psychology of Testimony*, 3 UNIVERSITY OF ILLINOIS LAW REVIEW 399 (1909). Wigmore's unusual stylistic device was to describe a mock trial in which members of the bar brought a claim of libel against Professor Münsterberg for overstating the usefulness of psychologists as experts at trial.

52 Roger C. Park and Michael J. Saks, *Evidence Scholarship Reconsidered: Results of the Interdisciplinary Turn*, 47 BOSTON COLLEGE LAW REVIEW 949 (2006).

53 Id.

54 Theirs was a brief, but highly prolific, collaboration. More than a few events could account for its ending: the Great Depression, Hutchins moving to the Yale Law School deanship and then to the presidency of the University of Chicago, as well as Hutchins's interests shifting away from empirical social science and toward philosophy and literature.

55 Robert M. Hutchins and Donald Slesinger, *Some Observations on the Law of Evidence—Spontaneous Exclamations*, 28 COLUMBIA LAW REVIEW 432 (1928).

56 Robert M. Hutchins and Donald Slesinger, *Some Observations on the Law of Evidence—Memory*, 41 HARVARD LAW REVIEW 860 (1928).

57 Robert M. Hutchins and Donald Slesinger, *Some Observations on the Law of Evidence—Family Relations*, 13 MINNESOTA LAW REVIEW 675 (1929).

58 Robert M. Hutchins and Donald Slesinger, *Some Observations on the Law of Evidence—The Competency of Witnesses*, 37 YALE LAW JOURNAL 1017 (1928).

59 Robert M. Hutchins and Donald Slesinger, *Some Observations on the Law of Evidence—State of Mind to Prove an Act*, 38 YALE LAW JOURNAL 283 (1929).

60 Robert M. Hutchins and Donald Slesinger, *Some Observations on the Law of Evidence—State of Mind in Issue*, 29 COLUMBIA LAW REVIEW 147 (1929).

61 Robert M. Hutchins and Donald Slesinger, *Some Observations on the Law of Evidence—Consciousness of Guilt*, 6 PENNSYLVANIA LAW REVIEW 725 (1929).

62 Robert M. Hutchins and Donald Slesinger, *Legal Psychology*, 36 PSYCHOLOGICAL REVIEW 13 (1929).

63 Id., at 13–14.

64 See Brian Leiter, *American Legal Realism*, *in* THE BLACKWELL GUIDE TO PHILOSOPHY OF LAW AND LEGAL THEORY (William Edmundson and Martin Golding, eds., 2003); John Henry Schlegel, *American Legal Realism and Empirical Social Science: From the Yale Experience*, 28 BUFFALO LAW REVIEW 459 (1979).

65 Underhill Moore, whose controversial work is described in John Henry Schlegel, *American Legal Realism and Empirical Social Science: The Singular Case of Underhill Moore*, 29 BUFFALO LAW REVIEW 195 (1980).

66 Charles Clark, a prominent legal realist, succeeded Robert Hutchins as dean of Yale Law School, served as a federal appellate judge, and was the principal drafter of the Federal Rules of Civil Procedure.

67 Karl Llewellyn, a prominent legal realist at Columbia University, was the principal drafter of the Uniform Commercial Code.

68 B. Michael Dann and George Logan III, *Jury Reform: The Arizona Experience*, 79 JUDICATURE 280 (1996).

69 See Shari Seidman Diamond et al., *Juror Discussions during Civil Trials: Studying an Arizona Innovation*, 45 ARIZONA LAW REVIEW 1 (2003); Valerie Hans et al., *The Arizona Jury Reform Permitting Civil Jury Trial Discussions: The Views of Trial Participants, Judges and Jurors*, 32 UNIVERSITY OF MICHIGAN JOURNAL OF LAW REFORM 349 (1999). These studies are discussed in Chapter 1. Also see B. MICHAEL DANN ET AL., TESTING THE EFFECTS OF SELECTED JURY TRIAL INNOVATIONS ON JUROR COMPREHENSION OF CONTESTED MTDNA EVIDENCE, FINAL TECHNICAL REPORT (2004, unpublished), https://www.ncjrs.gov/pdffiles1/nij/grants/211000.pdf; further described in David H. Kaye et al., *Statistics in the Jury Box: How Jurors Respond to Mitochondrial DNA Match Probabilities*, 4 JOURNAL OF EMPIRICAL LEGAL STUDIES 797 (2007) (describing jurors' cognitive errors in interpreting the statistics of mitochondrial DNA).

70 Itiel Dror et al., *Contextual Information Renders Experts Vulnerable to Make Erroneous Identifications*, 156 FORENSIC SCIENCE INTERNATIONAL 74 (2006); D. Michael Risinger et al., *The* Daubert/Kumho *Implications of Observer Effects in Forensic Science: Hidden Problems of Expectation and Suggestion*, 90 UNIVERSITY OF CALIFORNIA LAW REVIEW 1 (2002).

71 The need for such improvements has long been recognized. Errors by eyewitnesses are associated with erroneous convictions of innocent defendants more than any other factor. See, e.g., Brandon L. Garrett, *Judging Innocence*, 108 COLUMBIA LAW REVIEW 55 (2008).

72 Gary L. Wells, *Eyewitness Identification*, in MODERN SCIENTIFIC EVIDENCE: THE LAW AND SCIENCE OF EXPERT TESTIMONY (David L. Faigman et al., eds., 2010).

73 Id.

74 Specific examples of these procedural improvements are discussed later in this book.

75 See the opinion and order of the Supreme Court of New Jersey in *State v. Henderson*, 27 A.3d 872 (N.J. 2011), and the Report of the Special Master, prepared pursuant to an order of the Court, A-8-08 September Term 2008. See also EYEWITNESS WORKING GROUP, EYEWITNESS EVIDENCE: A GUIDE FOR LAW ENFORCEMENT (1999).

76 *Michelson v. United States*, 335 U.S. 469 (1948).

## CHAPTER 1. JUDGES VERSUS JURIES

1 The classroom analogy described is borrowed from the film *Order in the Classroom*, produced by the Institute of the International Association of Defense Counsel, as part of its National Jury Trial Innovations Project (1998). Reforms are gradually spreading among the nation's courts designed to create an environment that facilitates the jury's performing its task—allowing note taking, question-asking, discussion among jurors as the trial is underway, and other modifications. Many of these reforms were pioneered by the Arizona courts, which were informed partly by psychological research on learning and on juries. See Arizona Supreme Court Orders, Nos. R-94–0031, R-92–004 (1995) (launching a sweeping set of procedural reforms to assist juries in better performing their functions); Michael Dann and George Logan III, *Jury Reform: The Arizona Experience*, 79 JUDICATURE 280 (1996).

2 Barbara A. Spellman and Frederick Schauer. *Legal Reasoning*, in THE OXFORD HANDBOOK OF THINKING AND REASONING 719 (Keith J. Holyoak and Robert G. Morrison, eds., 2012).

3 Shari Seidman Diamond et al., *Blindfolding the Jury*, 52 LAW AND CONTEMPORARY PROBLEMS 247 (1989); Shari Seidman Diamond and Jay Casper, *Blindfolding the Jury to Verdict Consequences: Damages, Experts and the Civil Jury*, 26 LAW AND SOCIETY REVIEW 513 (1992).

4 Id.

5 See reviews of the research in DENNIS J. DEVINE, JURY DECISION MAKING: THE STATE OF THE SCIENCE 51–55 (2012); Shari Seidman Diamond, *Scientific Jury Selection: What Social Scientists Know and Do Not Know*, 73 JUDICATURE 178 (1989); VALERIE HANS AND NEIL VIDMAR, JUDGING THE JURY (1986).

6 Variables vary, and the amount is referred to generically as "variation." For example, grades on exams range from high to low, and how much they vary is their "variation." Researchers often measure the impact of an independent variable (cause; e.g., amount of studying) on a dependent variable (effect; e.g., exam grade) in terms of the amount of variation in the latter that is influenced by the former. If an effect is completely under the control of a cause, the cause would account for 100% of the variation in the effect. If changes in the cause have no impact at all on the effect, then the cause accounts for 0% of the variation in the effect. Usually, as in this example, the result is somewhere in between.

7 Partly or largely in recognition of this fact, what was once an industry of jury selection firms is now an industry of trial consulting firms, which place as much or more emphasis on shaping evidence presentation.

8 HARRY KALVEN AND HANS ZEISEL, THE AMERICAN JURY (1966).

9 "Rape myths" are mental sets or representations (called *schemas* by psychologists) that people typically have about rape, some of which blame the victim while others focus blame on the accused. A "rape myth" is therefore a form of mental

contamination—prior knowledge that affects the way one interprets present information. See discussion of such contamination in the Introduction.

10 See, e.g., Jeffrey Lehman et al., *The Effects of Graduate Training on Reasoning: Formal Discipline and Thinking about Everyday-life Events*, 43 AMERICAN PSYCHOLOGIST 431 (1988); MICHAEL J. SAKS, SMALL-GROUP DECISION-MAKING AND COMPLEX INFORMATION TASKS (1981); N. J. Schweitzer and Michael J. Saks, *Jurors and Scientific Causation: What Don't They Know, and What Can Be Done About It?*, 52 JURIMETRICS JOURNAL 433 (2012).

11 THE STAFF OF THE LOS ANGELES TIMES, UNDERSTANDING THE RIOTS: LOS ANGELES BEFORE AND AFTER THE RODNEY KING CASE (1996)

12 ROBERT CIALDINI, INFLUENCE: THE PSYCHOLOGY OF PERSUASION (2006).

13 More details on these problems can be found in Chapter 4, which discusses examination and cross-examination.

14 DANIEL KAHNEMAN, PAUL SLOVIC, AND AMOS TVERSKY (eds.), JUDGMENT UNDER UNCERTAINTY: HEURISTICS AND BIASES (1982); THOMAS GILOVICH, DALE GRIFFIN, AND DANIEL KAHNEMAN, HEURISTICS AND BIASES: THE PSYCHOLOGY OF INTUITIVE JUDGMENT (2001); MARK KELMAN, THE HEURISTICS DEBATE (2011). The Kelman book is specifically addressed to the implications and applications of decision heuristics to law.

15 IRVING JOHN GOOD, GOOD THINKING: THE FOUNDATIONS OF PROBABILITY AND ITS APPLICATIONS (2009); Michael J. Saks and William C. Thompson, *Assessing Evidence: Proving Facts*, in HANDBOOK OF PSYCHOLOGY IN LEGAL CONTEXTS, 2d edition (David Carson and Ray Bull, eds., 2003). The Saks and Thompson chapter discusses legal applications.

16 On Rule 401 (Definition of Relevance), see Richard O. Lempert, *Modeling Relevance*, 75 MICHIGAN LAW REVIEW 1021 (1977). For a brief overview of Bayesian applications to evidence law, see Roger C. Park and Michael J. Saks, *Evidence Scholarship Reconsidered: Results of the Interdisciplinary Turn*, 47 BOSTON COLLEGE LAW REVIEW 949 (2006).

17 REID HASTIE ET AL., INSIDE THE JURY (1983); Nancy Pennington and Reid Hastie, *The Story Model for Juror Decision Making*, in INSIDE THE JUROR (Reid Hastie, ed., 1993).

18 Lola Lopes, *Two Conceptions of the Juror*, in INSIDE THE JUROR (Reid Hastie, ed., 1993).

19 Pennington and Hastie, *supra* note 17; Elizabeth R. Tenney, Haley M. D. Cleary, and Barbara A. Spellman, *Unpacking the Doubt in "Beyond a Reasonable Doubt": Plausible Alternative Stories Increase Not Guilty Verdicts*, 31 BASIC AND APPLIED SOCIAL PSYCHOLOGY 1 (2009).

20 Phoebe Ellsworth, *Are Twelve Heads Better than One?*, 52 LAW AND CONTEMPORARY PROBLEMS 205 (1989).

21 Stephan Landsman et al., *Be Careful What You Wish For: The Effects of Bifurcating Claims for Punitive Damages in Product Liability Cases*, 1998 WISCONSIN LAW

REVIEW 297 (1998). Using the most realistic trial simulation in the literature, a large sample of jury-eligible adults, in the context of a toxic tort trial, Landsman et al. found that "deliberations resulted in significantly *reduced* comprehension on three of the four questions about judicial instructions" compared to individual performance.

22 See Introduction for a discussion of System 1 and System 2 thinking.

23 IVAN STEINER, GROUP PROCESS AND PRODUCTIVITY (1972).

24 REID HASTIE ET AL., INSIDE THE JURY (1983).

25 HARRY KALVEN AND HANS ZEISEL, THE AMERICAN JURY (1966).

26 James H. Davis, *Group Decision and Social Interaction: A Theory of Social Decision Schemes*, 80 PSYCHOLOGICAL REVIEW 97 (1983); Norbert L. Kerr, *Social Transition Schemes: Charting the Group's Road to Agreement*, 41 JOURNAL OF PERSONALITY AND SOCIAL PSYCHOLOGY 684 (1981); Robert J. McCoun and Norbert Kerr, *Asymmetric Influence in Mock Jury Deliberation: Jurors' Bias for Leniency*, 54 JOURNAL OF PERSONALITY AND SOCIAL PSYCHOLOGY 21 (1988); Dennis J. Devine et al., *Jury Decision-Making: 45 Years of Empirical Research on Deliberating Groups*, 7 PSYCHOLOGY, PUBLIC POLICY AND LAW 632 (2001).

27 ROBERT CIALDINI, INFLUENCE: THE PSYCHOLOGY OF PERSUASION (2006), Chapter 4.

28 If you have seen the film *Twelve Angry Men*, where an initial 11–1 vote in favor of conviction gradually reverses, through dramatic discussion and debate, into a 12–0 vote for acquittal, you may need to be reminded that the film is fiction. Such a turnaround can happen, but it would be very, very, very rare.

29 Michael J. Saks, *What Do Jury Experiments Tell Us about How Juries (Should) Make Decisions?*, 6 SOUTHERN CALIFORNIA INTERDISCIPLINARY LAW JOURNAL 1 (1998).

30 Jessica M. Salerno and Shari Seidman Diamond, *The Promise of a Cognitive Perspective on Jury Deliberation*, 17 PSYCHONOMIC BULLETIN AND REVIEW 174 (2010).

31 Daniel J. Isenberg, *Group Polarization: A Critical Review and Meta-Analysis*, 50 JOURNAL OF PERSONALITY AND SOCIAL PSYCHOLOGY 1141 (1986); David G. Myers and Helmut Lamm, *The Group Polarization Phenomenon*, 83 PSYCHOLOGICAL BULLETIN 602 (1976); David Schkade et al., *Deliberating about Dollars: The Severity Shift*, 100 COLUMBIA LAW REVIEW 1139 (2000).

32 SOURCEBOOK OF CRIMINAL JUSTICE STATISTICS, at http://www.albany.edu/sourcebook/

33 BUREAU OF JUSTICE STATISTICS, CIVIL AND BENCH TRIALS IN STATE COURTS, 2005 (2008). Importantly, the number of civil trials in state courts has fallen by more than half between 1992 and 2005. For further discussion, see Marc Galanter, *The Vanishing Trial*, 1 JOURNAL OF EMPIRICAL LEGAL STUDIES 459 (2004).

34 Id. Some kinds of civil cases, however, are required by law to be tried only to judges, and therefore the 32% does not reflect only the choices of litigants in individual cases.

35 SOURCEBOOK OF CRIMINAL JUSTICE STATISTICS, online at http://www.albany.edu/sourcebook/1995/wk1/t522.wk1.

36 Barbara A. Spellman, *On the Supposed Expertise of Judges in Evaluating Evidence*, 155 UNIVERSITY OF PENNSYLVANIA LAW REVIEW PENNUMBRA 1, 5 (2006). See also Jennifer K. Robbennolt, *Evaluating Juries by Comparison to Judges: A Benchmark for Judging*, 32 FLORIDA STATE UNIVERSITY LAW REVIEW 469 (2004–2005), and Paul H. Robinson and Barbara A. Spellman, *Sentencing Decisions: Matching the Decisionmaker to the Decision Nature*, 105 COLUMBIA LAW REVIEW 1124 (2005).

37 See, e.g., Jeffrey J. Rachlinski, *Heuristics and Biases in the Courts: Ignorance or Adaptation?*, 79 OREGON LAW REVIEW 61 (2000).

38 Charles F. Bond, Jr., and Bella DePaulo, *Individual Differences in Detecting Deception*, 134 PSYCHOLOGICAL BULLETIN 477 (2008); Charles F. Bond, Jr., and Bella DePaulo, *Accuracy of Deception Judgments*, 10 PERSONALITY AND SOCIAL PSYCHOLOGY REVIEW 214 (2006); Maria Hartwig and Charles F. Bond, Jr., *Why Do Lie-Catchers Fail?: A Lens Model Meta-Analysis of Human Lie Judgments*, 137 PSYCHOLOGICAL BULLETIN 643 (2011).

39 As noted in the Introduction, jurors, too, are more willing to follow a judicial instruction (such as to disregard evidence ruled inadmissible) when they are given certain types of explanation for the rule. Also see Chapter 3.

40 E.g., Stephan Landsman and Richard Rakos, *A Preliminary Inquiry into the Effect of Potentially Biasing Information on Judges and Jurors in Civil Litigation*, 12 BEHAVIORAL SCIENCES AND LAW 113 (1994)

41 See, e.g., Chris Guthrie et al., *Inside the Judicial Mind*, 86 CORNELL LAW REVIEW 777 (2001); Jeffrey J. Rachlinski, *Heuristics and Biases in the Courts: Ignorance or Adaptation?*, 79 OREGON LAW REVIEW 61 (2000); Chris Guthrie et al., *Blinking on the Bench: How Judges Decide Cases*, 93 CORNELL LAW REVIEW 1 (2007).

42 See the discussion of Kalven and Zeisel's work, and recent replication of it, in the following paragraphs. Also see, e.g., Gary Wells, *Naked Statistical Evidence of Liability: Is Subjective Probability Enough?*, 62 JOURNAL OF PERSONALITY AND SOCIAL PSYCHOLOGY 739 (1992); Roselle L. Wissler et al., *Decisionmaking about General Damages: A Comparison of Jurors, Judges, and Lawyers*, 98 MICHIGAN LAW REVIEW 751 (1999).

43 HARRY KALVEN AND HANS ZEISEL, THE AMERICAN JURY (1966).

44 Such as: scientists deciding the merits of research proposals, doctors diagnosing skin diseases, employment interviewers evaluating qualifications for hiring, and Navy pilots rating the technical effectiveness of aircraft. Roselle L. Wissler et al., *Decisionmaking about General Damages: A Comparison of Jurors, Judges, and Lawyers*, 98 MICHIGAN LAW REVIEW 751 (1999), at Table 5.

45 Theodore Eisenberg et al., *Judge-Jury Agreement in Criminal Cases: A Partial Replication of Kalven and Zeisel's* The American Jury, 2 JOURNAL OF EMPIRICAL LEGAL STUDIES 171 (2005).

46 Harry Kalven, *The Jury, the Law, and the Personal Injury Damage Award*, 19 OHIO STATE LAW JOURNAL 158 (1958).

CHAPTER 2. BALANCING ACTS

1 FRE 803(2) (excluding excited utterances from the general rule against hearsay).

2 Richard D. Friedman, *A Close Look at Probative Value*, 66 BOSTON UNIVERSITY LAW REVIEW 733 (1986). We also suspect that relevance is in the eye of the beholder. As described in prior chapters, people have a tendency to overconnect information—we are pattern seekers and perceive causation when it does not exist (think of superstitions or astrology). And because determinations of relevance are made in hindsight (i.e., during a trial, after the events in question have happened), it should be easy to make events seem as if they were connected, even if they were not. Lawyers sometimes say that if your evidence is being thrown out based on lack of relevance alone, your imagination isn't good enough.

3 GEORGE FISHER, EVIDENCE, 3d edition, 43–44 (2013).

4 See generally Raymond S. Nickerson, *How We Know—and Sometimes Misjudge—What Others Know: Imputing One's Own Knowledge to Others*, 125 PSYCHOLOGICAL BULLETIN 737 (1999).

5 Shari Seidman Diamond, Mary R. Rose, Beth Murphy, and Sven Smith, *Juror Questioning During Trial: A Window into Juror Thinking*, 59 VANDERBILT LAW REVIEW 1927, 1932 (2006).

6 Colleen Curry, *Jodi Arias Jurors Show Skepticism in Questions to Arias*, ABC News (Mar. 6, 2013), http://abcnews.go.com/US/jodi-arias-answer-100-questions-murder-jury/story?id=18665931 This program includes some examples of juror questions in the Jody Arias case.

7 See generally NEAL FEIGENSON AND CHRISTINA SPIESEL, LAW ON DISPLAY (2009).

8 For a summary of the studies addressing this question, see DENNIS J. DEVINE, JURY DECISION MAKING: THE STATE OF THE SCIENCE 147–149 (2012).

9 David A. Bright and Jane Goodman-Delahunty, *Gruesome Evidence and Emotion: Anger, Blame, and Jury Decision-Making*, 30 LAW AND HUMAN BEHAVIOR 183, 199 (2006).

10 See Jessica M. Salerno and Bette L. Bottoms, *Emotional Evidence and Jurors' Judgments: The Promise of Neuroscience for Information Psychology and Law*, 27 BEHAVIORAL SCIENCES & THE LAW 273 (2009).

11 The journal COGNITION AND EMOTION began in 1987 and is a good source for tracking how attitudes towards emotion have changed. LAW AND HUMAN BEHAVIOR ran a special issue (Vol. 30, No. 2) on "Emotion in Legal Judgment and Decision Making" in April 2006.

12 Heat of passion is technically not a "defense" to a crime but is an argument for a defendant not having premeditation.

13 See generally Susan A. Bandes and Jeremy A. Blumenthal, *Emotion and the Law*, 8 ANNUAL REVIEW OF LAW AND SOCIAL SCIENCE 161 (2012); Terry A. Maroney, *Law and Emotion: A Proposed Taxonomy of an Emerging Field*, 30 LAW AND HUMAN BEHAVIOR 119 (2006); Jessica M. Salerno and Bette L. Bottoms, *Emotional Evidence and Jurors' Judgments: The Promise of Neuroscience for Information Psychology and Law*, 27 BEHAVIORAL SCIENCES & THE LAW 273 (2009); Brian H. Bornstein and Richard L. Wiener (eds.), EMOTION AND THE LAW: PSYCHOLOGICAL PERSPECTIVES (2010).

14 Karen Gaspar and Gerald L. Clore, *Attending to the Big Picture: Mood and Global versus Local Processing of Visual Information*, 13 PSYCHOLOGICAL SCIENCE 33 (2002).

15 Hanah A. Chapman and Adam K. Anderson, *Things Rank and Gross in Nature: A Review and Synthesis of Moral Disgust*, 139 PSYCHOLOGICAL BULLETIN 300, 311 (2013).

16 See Jennifer S. Lerner and Larissa Z. Tiedens, *Portrait of the Angry Decision Maker: How Appraisal Tendencies Shape Anger's Influence on Cognition*, 19 JOURNAL OF BEHAVIORAL DECISION MAKING 115 (2006).

17 Jessica M. Salerno and Liana C. Peter-Hagene, *The Interactive Effect of Anger and Disgust on Moral Outrage and Judgments*, 24 PSYCHOLOGICAL SCIENCE 2069 (2013).

18 People do differ. When we described the cognitive errors revealed in the judgment and decision-making research, we noted that people differ in Need for Cognition, which predicts how susceptible they are to making those errors. There are similar individual differences in emotion, e.g., people differ in Need for Affect.

19 David Schkade, Cass R. Sunstein, and Daniel Kahneman, *Deliberating about Dollars: The Severity Shift*, 100 COLUMBIA LAW REVIEW 1139 (2000).

20 See DENNIS J. DEVINE, JURY DECISION MAKING: THE STATE OF THE SCIENCE 152–180 (2012).

21 Susan A. Bandes and Jessica Salerno, *Emotion, Proof and Prejudice: The Cognitive Science of Gruesome Photos and Victim Impact Statements*, 46 ARIZONA STATE LAW JOURNAL (2014).

22 See Norbert Schwarz and Gerald. L. Clore, *Mood, Misattribution, and Judgments of Well-Being: Informative and Directive Functions of Affective States*, 45 JOURNAL OF PERSONALITY AND SOCIAL PSYCHOLOGY 513 (1983).

23 Jeremy A. Blumenthal, *Law and the Emotions: The Problem of Affective Forecasting*, 80 INDIANA LAW JOURNAL 155 (2005).

24 This example is analogous to Problem 1.8 from GEORGE FISHER, EVIDENCE, 3d edition, 48 (2013), which is based on *United States v. Hitt*, 891 F.2d 422 (9th Cir. 1992).

25 See the discussion of character evidence in Chapter 5.

26 See *United States v. Brewer*, 451 F. Supp. 50 (E.D. Tenn. 1978), for a good explication of the factors to be considered.

27 H. R. Rep. No. 93–1597, at 9 (1974).
28 See similar arguments about privileges in Chapter 4.
29 See Baruch Fischhoff and Ruth Beyth, *I Knew It Would Happen: Remembered Probabilities of Once-Future Things*, 13 ORGANIZATIONAL BEHAVIOR AND HUMAN PERFORMANCE 1 (1975).
30 Kim A. Kamin and Jeffrey J. Rachlinski, *Ex Post ≠ Ex Ante: Determining Liability in Hindsight*, 19 LAW AND HUMAN BEHAVIOR 89, 99–100 (1995).
31 J.J. Christensen-Szalanski and Cynthia Fobian Willham, *Hindsight Bias: A Meta-Analysis*, 48 ORGANIZATIONAL BEHAVIOR AND HUMAN DECISION PROCESSES 147 (1991); Rebecca L. Guilbault et al., *A Meta-Analysis of Research on Hindsight Bias*, 26 BASIC AND APPLIED SOCIAL PSYCHOLOGY 103 (2004); for an overview, see Neal J. Roese and Kathleen D. Vohs, *Hindsight Bias*, 7 PERSPECTIVES ON PSYCHOLOGICAL SCIENCE 411 (2012).
32 See, e.g., WEINSTEIN'S EVIDENCE §407[02] at 407–15.
33 Dan M. Kahan, *The Economics—Conventional, Behavioral, and Political—of "Subsequent Remedial Measures" Evidence*, 110 COLUMBIA LAW REVIEW 1616 (2010).
34 Vin Green, *Federal Rule of Evidence 407 versus Rhode Island's Rule 407: Public Policy versus Relevance*, 16 ROGER WILLIAMS UNIVERSITY LAW REVIEW 633, 645 (2011).
35 See generally SUSAN T. FISKE AND SHELLEY E. TAYLOR, SOCIAL COGNITION, 2d edition, 22–92 (1991).
36 Making attributions to intentions or personality rather than situations is a bias in the U.S. and in other Western cultures. In Asian cultures, people tend to take the two factors into account more equally.
37 See Shari Seidman Diamond et al., *Blindfolding the Jury*, 52 LAW AND CONTEMPORARY PROBLEMS 247–67 (1989); Shari Seidman Diamond and Neil Vidmar, *Jury Room Ruminations on Forbidden Topics*, 87 VIRGINIA LAW REVIEW 1857 (2001).
38 See Chapter 3.
39 Shari Seidman Diamond and Jonathan D. Casper, *Blindfolding the Jury to Verdict Consequences: Damages, Experts, and the Civil Jury*, 26 LAW AND SOCIETY REVIEW 513 (1992).

## CHAPTER 3. INSTRUCTIONS TO DISREGARD AND TO LIMIT USE

1 We do not address pre-trial publicity in this chapter. There are no relevant Federal Rules of Evidence, or, indeed, rules of evidence in general, about pre-trial publicity. Nevertheless, pre-trial publicity creates many of the same problems as evidence that needs to be disregarded or limited in use.
2 For a meta-analysis including 48 studies, see Nancy Steblay et al., *The Impact on Juror Verdicts of Judicial Instruction to Disregard Inadmissible Evidence*, 30 LAW AND HUMAN BEHAVIOR 469 (2006). But, as for all meta-analyses, we must doubt whether the researchers found all of the relevant studies that had been conducted or whether many studies, particularly those that showed no differences between groups, were never published (known as the "file drawer problem").

3 It is important to note that because studies report aggregate data, we usually cannot tell whether each individual juror is disregarding the inadmissible evidence a little bit or whether there is variation, with some doing it fully and others not at all. The latter is more likely closer to the truth.

4 See Barbara H. Basden and David R. Basden, *Directed Forgetting: A Contrast of Methods and Interpretations*, in INTENTIONAL FORGETTING: INTERDISCIPLINARY APPROACHES 139 (Jonathan M. Golding and Colin M. MacLeod, eds., 1998).

5 Tom Trabasso and Paul van den Broek, *Causal Thinking and the Representation of Narrative Events*, 24 JOURNAL OF MEMORY AND LANGUAGE 612 (1985).

6 See DANIEL M. WEGNER, WHITE BEARS AND OTHER UNWANTED THOUGHTS (1994), for a readable account of this research, and Daniel M. Wegner, *Ironic Processes of Mental Control*, 101 PSYCHOLOGICAL REVIEW 34 (1994), for a technical one.

7 Nancy Pennington and Reid Hastie, *A Cognitive Theory of Juror Decision Making: The Story Model*, 13 CARDOZO LAW REVIEW 519 (1991).

8 Daniel T. Gilbert, *How Mental Systems Believe*, 46 AMERICAN PSYCHOLOGIST 107 (1991).

9 Colleen M. Seifert, *The Continued Influence of Misinformation in Memory: What Makes a Correction Effective?*, 41 PSYCHOLOGY OF LEARNING AND MOTIVATION: ADVANCES IN RESEARCH AND THEORY 265 (2002). For a more recent review of the broader literature, see Stephan Lewandowsky, Ullrich K. H. Ecker, Colleen M. Seifert, Norbert Schwarz, and John Cook, *Misinformation and Its Correction: Continued Influence and Successful Debiasing*, 13 PSYCHOLOGICAL SCIENCE IN THE PUBLIC INTEREST 106 (2012).

10 For slightly different accounts, see Craig A. Anderson, Mark R. Lepper, and Lee Ross, *Perseverance of Social Theories: The Role of Explanation in the Persistence of Discredited Information*, 39 JOURNAL OF PERSONALITY AND SOCIAL PSYCHOLOGY 1037 (1980); Saul M. Kassin and Christina A. Studebakers, *Instructions to Disregard and the Jury: Curative and Paradoxical Effects*, in INTENTIONAL FORGETTING: INTERDISCIPLINARY APPROACHES 413 (Jonathan M. Golding and Colin M. MacLeod, eds., 1998).

11 Baruch Fischhoff, *Hindsight Is Not Equal to Foresight: The Effect of Outcome Knowledge on Judgment Under Uncertainty*, 1 JOURNAL OF EXPERIMENTAL PSYCHOLOGY: HUMAN PERCEPTION AND PERFORMANCE 288 (1975).

12 Kim A. Kamin and Jeffrey J. Rachlinski, *Ex Post ≠ Ex Ante: Determining Liability in Hindsight*, 19 LAW AND HUMAN BEHAVIOR 89 (1995).

13 Timothy D. Wilson and Nancy Brekke, *Mental Contamination and Mental Correction: Unwanted Influences on Judgments and Evaluations*, 116 PSYCHOLOGICAL BULLETIN 117 (1994).

14 Saul M. Kassin and Samuel R. Sommers, *Inadmissible Testimony, Instructions to Disregard, and the Jury: Substantive Versus Procedural Considerations*, 23 PERSONALITY AND SOCIAL PSYCHOLOGY BULLETIN 1046 (1997).

15 Kerri L. Pickel, *Inducing Jurors to Disregard Inadmissible Evidence: A Legal Explanation Does Not Help*, 19 LAW AND HUMAN BEHAVIOR 407 (1995).
16 Saul M. Kassin and Samuel R. Sommers, *Inadmissible Testimony, Instructions to Disregard, and the Jury: Substantive Versus Procedural Considerations*, 23 PERSONALITY AND SOCIAL PSYCHOLOGY BULLETIN 1046 (1997).
17 E.g., Shari Seidman Diamond and Jonathan D. Casper, *Blindfolding the Jury to Verdict Consequences: Damages, Experts, and the Civil Jury*, 26 LAW AND SOCIETY REVIEW 513 (1992), gave a policy reason for disregarding reliable information about treble damages. See Linda J. Demaine, *Realizing the Potential of Instructions to Disregard*, in MEMORY AND LAW 185 (Lynn Nadel and Walter P. Sinnott-Armstrong, eds., 2012).
18 Sharon Wolf and David A. Montgomery, *Effects of Inadmissible Evidence and Level of Judicial Admonishment to Disregard on the Judgments of Mock Jurors*, 7 JOURNAL OF APPLIED SOCIAL PSYCHOLOGY 205 (1977).
19 Linda J. Demaine, *In Search of an Anti-Elephant: Confronting the Human Inability to Forget Inadmissible Evidence*, 16 GEORGE MASON LAW REVIEW 99 (2008).
20 Molly J. Walker-Wilson, Barbara A. Spellman, and Rachel M. York, *Beyond Instructions to Disregard: When Objections Backfire and Interruptions Distract*, retrieved from http://papers.ssrn.com/sol3/papers.cfm?abstract_id=2432527
21 Mark Travers, Leaf Van Boven, and Charles Judd, *The Secrecy Heuristic: Inferring Quality from Secrecy in Foreign Policy Contexts*, 35 POLITICAL PSYCHOLOGY 97 (2014).
22 Molly J. Walker-Wilson, Barbara A. Spellman, and Rachel M. York, *Beyond Instructions to Disregard: When Objections Backfire and Interruptions Distract*, retrieved from http://papers.ssrn.com/sol3/papers.cfm?abstract_id=2432527; Nancy Steblay et al., *The Impact on Juror Verdicts of Judicial Instruction to Disregard Inadmissible Evidence*, 30 LAW AND HUMAN BEHAVIOR 469 (2006).
23 Nancy Steblay et al., *The Impact on Juror Verdicts of Judicial Instruction to Disregard Inadmissible Evidence*, 30 LAW AND HUMAN BEHAVIOR 469 (2006).
24 The short amount of time means that jurors are less likely to mix up which piece of evidence they were supposed to disregard.
25 Thomas R. Carretta and Richard L. Moreland, *Direct and Indirect Effects of Inadmissible Evidence*, 13 JOURNAL OF APPLIED SOCIAL PSYCHOLOGY 291 (1983); Shari Seidman Diamond and Neil Vidmar, *Jury Room Ruminations on Forbidden Topics*, 87 VIRGINIA LAW REVIEW 1857 (2001). For post-deliberation juries disregarding inadmissible evidence, see also Kamala London and Narina Nuñez, *The Effect of Jury Deliberations on Jurors' Propensity to Disregard Inadmissible Evidence*, 85 JOURNAL OF APPLIED PSYCHOLOGY 932 (2000).
26 For an early use of video technology for this purpose, see [Judge] James L. McCrystal, *Videotape Trials: Relief for Our Congested Courts*, 49 DENVER LAW JOURNAL 463 (1973); James L. McCrystal, *Ohio's First Video Tape Trial*, 45 OHIO BAR 1 (1972).
27 Allowing a witness to testify in a separate room is sometimes allowed for victim-children testifying in child abuse cases. See *Maryland v. Craig*, 497 U.S. 836 (1990).

In that case the child, prosecutor, and defense attorney were in another room; the defendant could see the child and the jury could see both the child and the defendant. The Supreme Court allowed the set up in a 5–4 ruling; Justice Scalia's dissent (joined by the liberals Brennan, Marshall, and Stevens) was on the grounds that such testimony denies the defendant the Sixth Amendment right to confront the witnesses against him, 497 U.S. at 860 (Scalia, J., dissenting). See also *Marx v. Texas*, 528 U.S. 1034 (1999) (Scalia, J., dissenting from denial of certiorari); *Danner v. Kentucky*, 525 U.S. 1010 (1998) (Scalia, J., dissenting from denial of certiorari). Taping, and editing, testimony is likely to raise some similar and some different concerns. Given the more recent interpretations of the Confrontation Clause, a challenge to videotaping would be likely.

28 Linda J. Demaine, *Realizing the Potential of Instructions to Disregard*, in MEMORY AND LAW 185 (Lynn Nadel and Walter P. Sinnott-Armstrong, eds., 2012); Linda J. Demaine, *In Search of an Anti-Elephant: Confronting the Human Inability to Forget Inadmissible Evidence*, 16 GEORGE MASON LAW REVIEW 99 (2008).

29 Id.

30 Roselle L. Wissler and Michael J. Saks, *On the Inefficacy of Limiting Instructions: When Jurors Use Prior Conviction Evidence to Decide on Guilt*, 9 LAW AND HUMAN BEHAVIOR 37 (1985). The similarity between the current and past crimes is one of the factors considered in whether the prior conviction is unduly prejudicial. *Gordon v. U.S.*, 383 F. 2d 936, 940–41 (D.C. Cir. 1967).

31 Joel D. Lieberman and Jamie Arndt, *Understanding the Limits of Limiting Instructions: Social Psychological Explanations for the Failures of Instructions to Disregard Pretrial Publicity and Other Inadmissible Evidence*, 6 PSYCHOLOGY, PUBLIC POLICY, AND LAW 667, 691 (2000).

32 *U.S. v. Spikes*, 158 F.3d 913, 929 (6th Cir. 1998).

33 *U.S. v. Barnes*, 586 F.2d 1052, 1059 (5th Cir. 1978).

34 On the phenomenon, with examples and references to judicial defenses of the practice, see Frederick Schauer, *On the Supposed Jury-Dependence of Evidence Law*, 155 UNIVERSITY OF PENNSYLVANIA LAW REVIEW 165, 165–166, and notes 2–4 (2006).

35 In the state court studies, judges reported what they would have decided in cases that juries were actually deciding. HARRY KALVEN, JR. AND HANS ZEISEL, THE AMERICAN JURY (1966). See also Theodore Eisenberg et al., *Judge-Jury Agreement in Criminal Cases: A Partial Replication of Kalven & Zeisel's* The American Jury, 2 JOURNAL OF EMPIRICAL LEGAL STUDIES 171 (2005). A study of federal courts shows that judges acquit substantially more often than juries. This research compares what judges do with the cases they've heard versus what juries do with cases they've heard. So some of the difference is likely due to the fact that judges and juries hear different types of cases. But perhaps some of the difference is a consequence of judges' knowing what the potential sentences would be if they convict and being affected (consciously or unconsciously) by that knowledge. Andrew D. Leipold, *Why Are Federal Judges So Acquittal Prone?*, 83 WASHINGTON UNIVERSITY LAW REVIEW 151 (2005).

36 HARRY KALVEN, JR. AND HANS ZEISEL, THE AMERICAN JURY 124 (1966).

37 N. J. Schweitzer, Douglas J. Sylvester, and Michael J. Saks, *Rule Violations and the Rule of Law: A Factorial Survey of Public Attitudes*, 56 DEPAUL LAW REVIEW 615 (2006–2007). However, some unpublished research suggests that those with legal training may be more likely to prefer to follow a rule (even if unjust) than would non–legally trained people, although even for those with legal training there remains a preference for the just result over the rule-based one. N. J. Schweitzer et al., *The Effect of Legal Training on Judgments of Rule of Law Violations* (paper presented to the American Psychology-Law Association, March 5, 2008), http://www.allacademic.com/meta/p229442_index.html. For an overview of the psychology research on rule following, see generally Barbara A. Spellman and Frederick Schauer, *Legal Reasoning*, in THE OXFORD HANDBOOK OF THINKING AND REASONING, 2d edition, 719 (Keith J. Holyoak and Robert G. Morrison, eds., 2012).

38 Shari Seidman Diamond et al., *Juror Discussions during Civil Trials: Studying an Arizona Innovation*, 45 ARIZONA LAW REVIEW 1 (2003) (reporting observations of actual trials in Pima County, Arizona [Tucson]).

39 Stephan Landsman and Richard F. Rakos, *A Preliminary Inquiry into the Effect of Potentially Biasing Information on Judges and Jurors in Civil Litigation*, 12 BEHAVIORAL SCIENCES AND LAW 113 (1994).

40 Andrew J. Wistrich, Chris Guthrie, and Jeffrey J. Rachlinski, *Can Judges Ignore Inadmissible Information? The Difficulty of Deliberately Disregarding*, 153 UNIVERSITY OF PENNSYLVANIA LAW REVIEW 1251 (2005).

41 Id. See also Jennifer Mnookin, *Bifurcation and the Law of Evidence*, 155 UNIVERSITY OF PENNSYLVANIA LAW REVIEW PENNUMBRA 134 (2006).

42 See Frederick Schauer, *On the Supposed Jury-Dependence of Evidence Law*, 155 UNIVERSITY OF PENNSYLVANIA LAW REVIEW 165, 165–166 notes 2–4 (2006).

43 *Chapman v. California*, 386 US 18 (1967).

44 Although *Chapman* and the harmless error standards are a matter of federal constitutional law applicable in all states, the Supreme Court has allowed the states some discretion in exactly how they may specify the test and its presumptions. See *Premo v. Moore*, 131 S. Ct. 733 (2011). And of course an even more permissive version of the harmless error standard is applicable in civil case appeals.

45 We agree with many of the suggestions of Linda J. Demaine, *Realizing the Potential of Instructions to Disregard, in* MEMORY AND LAW 185 (Lynn Nadel and Walter P. Sinnott-Armstrong, eds., 2012), and Shari Seidman Diamond and Neil Vidmar, *Jury Room Ruminations on Forbidden Topics*, 87 VIRGINIA LAW REVIEW 1857 (2001).

46 Shari Seidman Diamond and Neil Vidmar, *Jury Room Ruminations on Forbidden Topics*, 87 VIRGINIA LAW REVIEW 1857, 1884 (2001).

## CHAPTER 4. WITNESS THE WITNESS

1 Gary Wells in the television show segment "Eyewitness, Part 2," *60 Minutes* (CBS News), at 2:50. The segment is about the DNA exoneration case of Ronald Cotton;

Wells demonstrates how eyewitnesses can be mistaken even when confident in their memories.

2 The following data come from an early paper on this topic. Elizabeth F. Loftus and John C. Palmer, *Reconstruction of Automobile Destruction: An Example of the Interaction Between Language and Memory*, 13 JOURNAL OF VERBAL LEARNING AND VERBAL BEHAVIOR 585 (1974). For a review of the more recent work on the misinformation effect, see Steven J. Franda, Rebecca M. Nichols, and Elizabeth F. Loftus, *Current Issues and Advances in Misinformation Research*, 20 CURRENT DIRECTIONS IN PSYCHOLOGICAL SCIENCE 20 (2011).

3 Id. See also Marcia K. Johnson, John D. Bransford, and Susan K. Solomon, *Memory for Tacit Implications of Sentences*, 98 JOURNAL OF EXPERIMENTAL PSYCHOLOGY 203 (1973).

4 Suparna Rajaram and Luciane P. Pereira-Pasarin, *Collaborative Memory: Cognitive Research and Theory*, 5 PERSPECTIVES ON PSYCHOLOGICAL SCIENCE 649 (2010).

5 "Incompetence" here is a technical term—certain witnesses were deemed not competent to testify, for reasons noted in the text, but this was not a judgment about their mental competence in the more ordinary sense.

6 STEWART RAPALJE, A TREATISE ON THE LAW OF WITNESSES (1887).

7 There is case law, research, and much written about child witnesses. Questions include things like: How do you know if they understand the oath and know what it means to lie? Are child witnesses more easily influenced than adults? How and do adults try to manipulate them (both outside and inside the courtroom)? When do they need to be protected from alleged perpetrators of events they have witnessed or been victims of? See, e.g., Gail S. Goodman and Bette L. Bottoms (eds.), CHILD VICTIMS, CHILD WITNESSES: UNDERSTANDING AND IMPROVING TESTIMONY (1993); Stephen J. Ceci and Maggie Bruck, *Suggestability of the Child Witness: A Historical Review & Synthesis*, 113 PSYCHOLOGICAL BULLETIN 403 (1993); STEPHEN J. CECI AND MAGGIE BRUCK, JEOPARDY IN THE COURTROOM: A SCIENTIFIC ANALYSIS OF CHILDREN'S TESTIMONY (1995).

8 *United States v. Turner*, 558 F.2d 46, 50 (2d Cir. 1977).

9 The studies described here are from Nina Mazar, On Amir, and Dan Ariely, *The Dishonesty of Honest People: A Theory of Self-Concept Maintenance*, 45 JOURNAL OF MARKETING RESEARCH 633 (2008). For an overview of the related research see DAN ARIELY, THE HONEST TRUTH ABOUT DISHONESTY: HOW WE LIE TO EVERYONE—ESPECIALLY OURSELVES (2013).

10 Some jurisdictions have solved at least part of the problem by asking a witness: "Do you swear or affirm that the testimony you are about to give . . . ," without mentioning either a deity or a holy book.

11 And that is why witnesses who choose to affirm rather than swear may not be cross-examined about their reasons for doing so. *United States v. Kalaydjian*, 784 F.2d 53, 57 (2d Cir. 1986).

12 In-group biases refer to the general tendency for people to prefer members of their own "group"—who they like more, trust more, would spend time with, etc. There is a lot of research on the types of biases and the groups that hold such biases; for a review of in-group favoritism in religion, see Luke W. Galen, *Does Religious Belief Promote Prosociality? A Critical Examination*, 5 PSYCHOLOGICAL BULLETIN, 876, 878–79 (2012).

13 The requirement of first-hand knowledge and the prohibition on hearsay are related but not identical. When witness A testifies about what B said, witness A has first-hand knowledge of what B said even if she has no first-hand knowledge of the matters about which B was speaking.

14 Are witnesses allowed to testify that someone was drunk? Generally, yes. See *State v. Sweet*, 949 A.2d 809, 813 (N.J. 2008). The standard view is that these are the kinds of judgments that people make regularly, and allowing testimony about what are in effect "collective facts" will be more informative than requiring witnesses to break it down into particulars.

15 Overall, potential jurors disagreed with the experts on 87% of the issues, whereas judges disagreed with the experts on 60% of the issues. Tanja Rapus Benton, David F. Ross, Emily Bradshaw, W. Neil Thomas, and Gregory S. Bradshaw, *Eyewitness Memory Is Still Not Common Sense: Comparing Jurors, Judges and Law Enforcement to Eyewitness Experts*, 20 APPLIED COGNITIVE PSYCHOLOGY 115 (2006).

16 A good and up-to-date summary, with many references to cases, is CHRISTOPHER B. MUELLER AND LAIRD C. KIRKPATRICK, EVIDENCE §7.21, 5th edition, 715–18 (2012).

17 See *State v. Bealor*, 902 A.2d 226, 233–234 (N.J. 2006).

18 See Frederick Schauer and Barbara A. Spellman, *Is Expert Evidence Really Different?*, 89 NOTRE DAME LAW REVIEW 1 (2013).

19 See George Fisher, *The Jury's Rise as Lie Detector*, 107 YALE LAW JOURNAL 575 (1997). In the civil law system, experts may and do provide this service.

20 See, for example, Charles F. Bond, Jr. and Bella DePaulo, *Individual Differences in Detecting Deception*, 134 PSYCHOLOGICAL BULLETIN 477 (2008); Charles F. Bond, Jr. and Bella DePaulo, *Accuracy of Deception Judgments*, 10 PERSONALITY AND SOCIAL PSYCHOLOGY REVIEW 214 (2006); Maria Hartwig and Charles F. Bond, Jr., *Why Do Lie-Catchers Fail?: A Lens Model Meta-Analysis of Human Lie Judgments*, 137 PSYCHOLOGICAL BULLETIN 643 (2011).

21 For a good description of various techniques for studying lie detection, see Aldert Vrij, Par Anders Granhag, and Stephen Porter, *Pitfalls and Opportunities in Nonverbal and Verbal Lie Detection*, 11 PSYCHOLOGICAL SCIENCE IN THE PUBLIC INTEREST 89, 91–93 (2010).

22 ALDERT VRIJ, DETECTING LIES AND DECEIT: PITFALLS AND OPPORTUNITIES (2008).

23 Bella M. DePaulo et al., *Cues to Deception*, 129 PSYCHOLOGICAL BULLETIN 74 (2003); Maria Hartwig and Charles F. Bond, Jr., *Why Do Lie-Catchers Fail?: A Lens*

*Model Meta-Analysis of Human Lie Judgments*, 137 PSYCHOLOGICAL BULLETIN 643 (2011).

24 See Bella M. DePaulo and Wendy L. Morris, *Discerning Lies from Truths: Behavioral Cues to Deception and the Indirect Pathway of Intuition*, in THE DETECTION OF DECEPTION IN FORENSIC CONTEXTS 15 (Pär Anders Granhag and Leif A, Strömwall, eds., 2004) (on rating ambivalence); Leanne ten Brinke, Dayna Stimson, and Dana R. Carney, *Some Evidence for Unconscious Lie Detection*, 25 PSYCHOLOGICAL SCIENCE 1098 (2014) (using the Implicit Association Test or IAT).

25 Aldert Vrij, Pär Anders Granhag, and Stephen Porter, *Pitfalls and Opportunities in Nonverbal and Verbal Lie Detection*, 11 PSYCHOLOGICAL SCIENCE IN THE PUBLIC INTEREST 89 (2010). See also Maria Hartwig and Charles F. Bond, Jr., *Why Do Lie-Catchers Fail?: A Lens Model Meta-Analysis of Human Lie Judgments*, 137 PSYCHOLOGICAL BULLETIN 643 (2011), for other ideas.

26 Charles F. Bond, Jr. and Bella M. DePaulo, *Accuracy of Deception Judgments*, 10 PERSONALITY AND SOCIAL PSYCHOLOGY REVIEW 214, 231 (2006). See also Maria Hartwig and Charles F. Bond, Jr., *Why Do Lie-Catchers Fail?: A Lens Model Meta-Analysis of Human Lie Judgments*, 137 PSYCHOLOGICAL BULLETIN 643 (2011).

27 *Frye v. United States*, 293 F. 1013 (D.C. Cir. 1923). The standard for admissibility of scientific evidence is discussed more in Chapter 7.

28 See, e.g., *United States v. Benavidez-Benavidez*, 217 F.3d 720 (9th Cir. 2000); *United States v. Gilliard*, 133 F.3d 809 (11th Cir. 1998); State v. Porter, 698 A.2d 739 (Conn. 1997); *Commonwealth v. Duguay*, 720 N.E.2d 458 (Mass. 1999).

29 N.M. R. Evid. §11–707; *State v. Dorsey*, 539 P.2d 204 (N.M. 1975).

30 See DAVID L. FAIGMAN ET AL., MODERN SCIENTIFIC EVIDENCE: THE LAW AND SCIENCE OF EXPERT TESTIMONY §40 (2011); PAUL C. GIANELLI AND EDWARD J. IMWINKELREID, SCIENTIFIC EVIDENCE, 4th edition, §8.04 (2007); *United States v. Nelson*, 207 Fed. App'x 291 (4th Cir. 2006); *People v. Richardson*, 183 P.2d 1146 (Cal. 2008); *State v. Castaneda*, 842 N.W.2d 740 (Neb. 2014).

31 See Nobohito Abe, *How the Brain Shapes Deception: An Integrated Review of the Literature*, 17 NEUROSCIENTIST 560 (2011); Daniel D. Langleben, *Detection of Deception with fMRI: Are We There Yet?*, 13 LEGAL AND CRIMINOLOGICAL PSYCHOLOGY 1 (2008); George T. Monteleone, et al., *Detection of Deception Using fMRI: Better than Chance, But Well Below Perfection*, 4 SOCIAL NEUROSCIENCE 528 (2009); Anthony Wagner, *Can Neuroscience Identify Lies?*, in A JUDGE'S GUIDE TO NEUROSCIENCE: A CONCISE INTRODUCTION 13 (Michael S. Gazzaniga and Jed S. Rakoff, eds., 2010).

32 NATIONAL RESEARCH COUNCIL, THE POLYGRAPH AND LIE DETECTION (2003). And see also www/polygraph.org/section/resources/polygraph-validity-research.

33 See Henry T. Greely and Judy Illes, *Neuroscience-Based Lie Detection: The Urgent Need for Regulation*, 33 AMERICAN JOURNAL OF LAW AND MEDICINE 377 (2007); Nancy Kanwisher, *The Use of fMRI in Lie Detection: What Has Been Shown*

*and What Has Not*, in USING IMAGING TO IDENTIFY DECEIT: SCIENTIFIC AND ETHICAL QUESTIONS 7 (Emilio Bizzi and Steven E. Hyman, eds., 2007); Elizabeth A. Phelps, *Lying Outside the Laboratory: The Impact of Imagery and Emotion on the Neural Circuitry of Lie Detection*, in Bizzi and Hyman, id., at 14.

**34** See Cephos Corp., http://www.cephoscorp.com; NoLie MRI, http://www.noliemri.com.

**35** See Neal Feigenson, *Brain Imaging and Courtroom Evidence: On the Admissibility and Persuasiveness of fMRI*, 2 INTERNATIONAL JOURNAL OF LAW IN CONTEXT 233 (2006); Leo Kittay, Note, *Admissibility of fMRI: The Cultural Bias against "Mind Reading" Devices*, 72 BROOKLYN LAW REVIEW 1351 (2007).

**36** See F. Andrew Kozel, et al., *Detecting Deception Using Functional Magnetic Imaging*, 58 BIOLOGICAL PSYCHIATRY 605 (2005); F. Andrew Kozel, et al., *Functional MRI Detection of Deception after Committing a Mock Sabotage Crime*, 54 JOURNAL OF FORENSIC SCIENCE 220 (2009); Daniel D. Langleben, *Telling Truth from Lie in Individual Subjects with Fast Event-Related fMRI*, 26 HUMAN BRAIN MAPPING 262 (2005); Sean A. Spence et al., *A Cognitive Neurobiological Account of Deception: Evidence from Functional Neuroimaging*, 359 PHILOSOPHICAL TRANSACTIONS OF THE ROYAL SOCIETY OF LONDON 1755 (2004).

**37** A good and recent but generally skeptical treatment is Martha J. Farah, J. Benjamin Hutchinson, Elizabeth Phelps, and Anthony D. Wagner, *Functional MRI-based Lie Detection: Scientific and Social Challenges*, 115 NATURE REVIEWS—NEUROSCIENCE 122 (2014).

**38** *United States v. Semrau*, 2010 WL 6845092 (W.D. Tenn., June 1, 2010), *aff'd*, 693 F.3d 510 (6th Cir. 2012); *Wilson v. Corestaff Services*, LLP, 900 N.Y.S.2d 639 (Sup. Ct. 2010).

**39** David P. McCabe and Alan D. Castel, *Seeing Is Believing: The Effect of Brain Images on Judgments of Scientific Reasoning*, 107 COGNITION 343 (2008); David P. McCabe et al., *The Influence of fMRI Lie Detection Evidence on Juror Decision-Making*, 29 BEHAVIORAL SCIENCES & THE LAW 566 (2011).

**40** N. J. Schweitzer et al., *Neuroimages as Evidence in a Mens Rea Defense: No Impact*, 17 PSYCHOLOGY, PUBLIC POLICY, AND LAW 357 (2011).

**41** Martha J. Farah and Cayce J. Hook, *The Seductive Allure of "Seductive Allure,"* 8 PERSPECTIVES ON PSYCHOLOGICAL SCIENCE 88 (2013). See also Frederick Schauer, *Neuroscience, Lie-Detection and the Law: A Contrarian View*, 14 TRENDS IN COGNITIVE SCIENCE 101 (2010). It is, of course, possible that fMRI had been viewed as superior evidence but as it has become more familiar has lost some of its "seductive allure."

**42** Joshua D. Greene and Joseph M. Paxton, *Patterns of Neural Activity Associated with Honest and Dishonest Moral Decisions*, 106 PROCEEDINGS OF THE NATIONAL ACADEMY OF SCIENCES 12506 (2009). See generally Kamila E. Sip et al., *Detecting Deception: The Scope and Limits*, 12 TRENDS IN COGNITIVE SCIENCE 48 (2008).

43 And thus it has long been claimed that the jury is the lie detector in the courtroom. See *United States v. Thompson*, 615 F.2d 329 (5th Cir. 1980); *United States v. Barnard*, 490 F.2d 907 (9th Cir. 1973); *State v. Myers*, 382 N.W.2d 91 (Iowa 1986). See generally George Fisher, *The Jury's Rise as Lie Detector*, 107 YALE LAW JOURNAL 575 (1997).

44 5 WIGMORE ON EVIDENCE §1367 (James Chadbourn rev., 1974).

45 Laurence H. Tribe, *Triangulating Hearsay*, 87 HARVARD LAW REVIEW 957 (1974). This framing appears in many casebooks but sometimes the terms used are different. We adopt the terms of Justin Sevier, *Testing Tribe's Triangle: Juries, Hearsay, and Psychological Distance*, 103 GEORGETOWN LAW JOURNAL 879 (2015). We like the neutral framing (e.g., "memory" rather than "erroneous memory"; "sincerity" rather than "insincerity") because the infirmities are only potential not necessarily actual. We also like the abbreviation SPAM (sincerity, perception, ambiguity, memory)—which would not have evoked the same meaning 40 years ago. Note that we add "confidence" and "judgment" to Table 4.1 because, as we describe, we believe that cross-examination is a good tool for determining whether a witness's confidence is warranted and judgment is sound.

46 Laurence H. Tribe, *Triangulating Hearsay*, 87 HARVARD LAW REVIEW 957, 958 (1974).

47 Jennifer S. Hunt and Thomas Lee Budesheim, *How Jurors Use and Misuse Character Evidence*, 89 JOURNAL OF APPLIED PSYCHOLOGY 347 (2004).

48 DENNIS J. DEVINE, JURY DECISION MAKING: THE STATE OF THE SCIENCE 127–29 (2012).

49 See LARRY POZNER AND ROGER J. DODD, CROSS-EXAMINATION: SKILL FOR LAW STUDENTS, §1.13. The book advocates keeping witnesses anxious but does not (and need not) refer to the psychology literature.

50 See *Manson v. Braithwaite*, 432 U.S. 98 (1977).

51 For a review see Barbara A. Spellman and Elizabeth R. Tenney, *Credible Testimony in and out of Court*, 17 PSYCHONOMIC BULLETIN & REVIEW 168 (2010).

52 Gary L. Wells, Amina Memon, and Steven D. Penrod, *Eyewitness Evidence: Improving Its Probative Value*, 7 PSYCHOLOGICAL SCIENCE IN THE PUBLIC INTEREST 45, 65–67 (2006). Many police departments have adopted the procedure of making sure not to give such feedback after lineups. And when relevant, New Jersey gives jurors instructions about feedback given to witnesses after making an identification, noting that it may affect the witnesses's confidence (http://www.jerseyjusticemonitor.com/2012/07/24/new-jersey-courts-taking-the-lead-to-inform-jurors-about-the-fallability-of-eyewitness-testimony/).

53 Elizabeth R. Tenney, Barbara A. Spellman, and Robert J. MacCoun, *The Benefits of Knowing What You Know (and What You Don't): How Calibration Affects Credibility*, 44 JOURNAL OF EXPERIMENTAL SOCIAL PSYCHOLOGY 1368 (2008).

54 R. C. L. Lindsay, Robert Lim, Louis Marando, and Deborah Cully, *Mock-Juror Evaluations of Eyewitness Testimony: A Test of Metamemory Hypotheses*, 16 JOURNAL OF APPLIED SOCIAL PSYCHOLOGY 447 (1986).

55 Summarized in DENNIS J. DEVINE, JURY DECISION MAKING: THE STATE OF THE SCIENCE 127–129 (2012).

56 Saul M. Kassin, Lorri N. Williams, and Courtney L. Saunders, *Dirty Tricks of Cross-Examination: The Influence of Conjectural Evidence on the Jury*, 14 LAW AND HUMAN BEHAVIOR 373 (1990).

57 *Jaffee v. Redmond*, 518 U.S. 1 (1996).

58 *Trammel v. United States*, 445 U. S. 40 (1980).

59 We do not discuss journalist-source privilege further. See Paul M. Smith and Jessica Ring Amunson, *Chapter 8. The Journalist's Privilege*, in 2 TESTIMONIAL PRIVILEGES, 3d edition, § 8:6 (2005–2009).

60 Catherine Chiantella Stern, Note, *Don't Tell Mom the Babysitter's Dead: Arguments for a Federal Parent—Child Privilege and a Proposal to Amend Article V*, 99 GEORGETOWN LAW JOURNAL 605 (2010–2011).

61 Erin R. Schrantz, *Chapter 7. The Physician-Patient, Psychotherapist-Patient, and Related Privileges*, in 2 TESTIMONIAL PRIVILEGES, 3d edition, § 7:4 (2005-2009). The coverage of this privilege varies across states.

62 *Jaffee v. Redmond*, 518 U.S. 1, 22 (1996).

63 *Tarasoff v. Regents of the University of California*, 551 P.2d 334 (Cal. 1976). A majority of states have adopted some type of similar rule.

64 Catherine Chiantella Stern, Note, *Don't Tell Mom the Babysitter's Dead: Arguments for a Federal Parent—Child Privilege and a Proposal to Amend Article V*, 99 GEORGETOWN LAW JOURNAL 605 (2010–2011).

65 Daniel W. Shuman and Myron S. Weiner, *The Privilege Study: An Empirical Examination of the Psychotherapist-Patient Privilege*, 60 NORTH CAROLINA LAW REVIEW 893 (1981–1982). Note that for reasons of various biases, one has to be very skeptical of claims by people that what they did had not hurt others.

66 A 1980 survey about *Tarasoff*, with responses from 1,722 psychiatrists, psychologists, and social workers (out of 2,875 sampled), revealed that most were knowledgeable about the case and its applications, especially those in California, where *Tarasoff* was decided. The respondents believed that they would be good at predicting the future dangerousness of patients. Daniel J. Givelber, William J. Bowers, and Carolyn L. Blitch, *Tarasoff, Myth and Reality: An Empirical Study of Private Law in Action*, 1984 WISCONSIN LAW REVIEW 445 (1984); Vincent C. Alexander, *The Corporate Attorney-Client Privilege: A Study of the Participants*, 63 ST. JOHN'S LAW REVIEW 191 (1988–1989).

## CHAPTER 5. CHARACTER EVIDENCE

1 H. Richard Uviller, *Evidence of Character to Prove Conduct: Illusion, Illogic, and Injustice in the Courtroom*, 130 UNIVERSITY OF PENNSYLVANIA LAW REVIEW 845 (1982).

2 As one state supreme court justice wrote in an opinion not long ago: "I am unable to do what all the text-writers and other legal authorities have failed to do. I am un-

able to outline the contours of the term 'character.' . . ." *State v. Williams*, 874 P.2d 12, 25 (N.M. 1994) (Montgomery, C. J., specially concurring).

3 1A WIGMORE ON EVIDENCE §55, at 1159.

4 CHARLES T. MCCORMICK, HANDBOOK OF THE LAW OF EVIDENCE, 1st edition, 340–41 (1954), quoted in FRE 406 Advisory Committee Note.

5 "[E]vidence offered to prove a victim's sexual predisposition" as well as sexual history have been made generally inadmissible by Rule 412(a) and, with certain exceptions, Rule 412(b). Similar rules exist now in almost every state.

6 *Michelson v. United States*, 335 U.S. 469 (1948).

7 Because of its radical departure from centuries of evidence theory and doctrine, when enacted by Congress the Judicial Conference of the United States overwhelmingly opposed the new rules and urged Congress to reconsider, but these rules nevertheless became part of the evidence code. Unsurprisingly, courts subsequently read into these rules a requirement to balance probativeness and prejudice, under Rule 403.

8 See Chapter 4.

9 STEWART RAPALJE, A TREATISE ON THE LAW OF WITNESSES (1887).

10 Among the critiques of common law impeachment rules, for which reforms were proposed and adopted by the Federal Rules, was impeachment by attack on a witness's religious beliefs. See MCCORMICK ON EVIDENCE, 2d edition, 107–8 (Edward W. Cleary et al., eds.,1972).

11 1 WIGMORE ON EVIDENCE §55, at 122.

12 *R. v. Rowton*, 169 Eng. Rep. 1497 (1865).

13 *Michelson v. United States*, 335 U.S. 469 (1948).

14 H. Richard Uviller, *Evidence of Character to Prove Conduct: Illusion, Illogic, and Injustice in the Courtroom*, 130 UNIVERSITY OF PENNSYLVANIA LAW REVIEW 845 (1982).

15 Richard O. Lempert et al., A MODERN APPROACH TO EVIDENCE, 4th edition, 323 (2000).

16 For at least three centuries, suggests Wigmore. 1 WIGMORE ON EVIDENCE §58.2, at 1213 (Tillers rev., 1983).

17 BIBB LATANÉ AND JOHN M. DARLEY, THE UNRESPONSIVE BYSTANDER: WHY DOESN'T HE HELP? (1970).

18 Why? When other strangers are present, each is less likely to notice anything, because we look around less in the presence of strangers, in part to avoid making eye contact. If noticed, the situation is less likely to be defined as an emergency because the more that others do not react, the more that all of us interpret the situation as nothing to be alarmed about. If interpreted as an emergency, each individual is less likely to feel responsible for taking action because we assume someone else will intervene. If someone does feel responsible to intervene, the presence of others makes them feel more restrained by their lack of knowledge of what to do; when alone we are less reserved. In short, the presence of others promotes pluralistic ignorance

and diffusion of responsibility. In order for bystanders to intervene, they have to get through all of these steps successfully, and the presence of others impedes in various ways.

19 John M. Darley and C. Daniel Batson, *From Jerusalem to Jericho: A Study of Situational and Dispositional Variables in Helping Behavior*, 27 JOURNAL OF PERSONALITY AND SOCIAL PSYCHOLOGY 100 (1973).

20 STANLEY MILGRAM, OBEDIENCE TO AUTHORITY: AN EXPERIMENTAL VIEW (1974).

21 Similarly, when the "right" procedures are employed—all of them even more subtle than the manipulations in Milgram's experiments—virtually any family member will agree to donate an organ to a relative in need, no matter what the donor's initial attitudes were, no matter the donor's personality characteristics. Michael J. Saks, *Social Psychological Contributions to a Legislative Subcommittee on Organ and Tissue Transplants*, 33 AMERICAN PSYCHOLOGIST 680 (1978).

22 A correlation measures the extent to which two or more variables are associated with each other.

23 WALTER MISCHEL, PERSONALITY AND ASSESSMENT (1968). For comparison, consider that the SAT, a measure of cognitive ability, gets as high as .62 in predicting first-year college performance. S. A. Hezlett et al., *The Effectiveness of the SAT in Predicting Success Early and Late in College: A Comprehensive Meta-Analysis* (paper presented at the annual meeting of the National Council on Measurement in Education, April 2001). The LSAT correlation goes as high as .56, and when combined with undergraduate GPA can get as high as .62. LAW SCHOOL ADMISSION COUNCIL PREDICTIVE VALIDITY OF THE LSAT (LSAT Technical Report 11–02) (2011).

24 Later work increased the upper limit of the correlations, though not by much.

25 WALTER MISCHEL, PERSONALITY AND ASSESSMENT 177 (1968).

26 See, e.g., DAN P. MCADAMS, THE PERSON: AN INTRODUCTION TO THE SCIENCE OF PERSONALITY PSYCHOLOGY, 5th edition (2009).

27 KURT LEWIN, A DYNAMIC THEORY OF PERSONALITY (1935).

28 For a recent detailed discussion, see John Kihlstrom, *The Person-Situation Interaction*, *in* OXFORD HANDBOOK OF SOCIAL COGNITION 786 (Donal E. Carlston, ed., 2013). Also see Walter Mischel and Yuichi Shoda, *A Cognitive-Affective System Theory of Personality: Reconceptualizing Situations, Dispositions, Dynamics, and Invariance in Personality Structure*, 102 PSYCHOLOGICAL REVIEW 246 (1995).

29 Understanding of this self-awareness has been developed by self-complexity theory. See Patricia W. Linville, *Self-Complexity and Affective Extremity: Don't Put All Your Eggs in One Cognitive Basket*, 3 SOCIAL COGNITION 94 (1985); Patricia W. Linville, *Self-Complexity as a Cognitive Buffer against Stress-Related Illness and Depression*, 52 JOURNAL OF PERSONALITY AND SOCIAL PSYCHOLOGY 663 (1987). See also Allen R. McConnell, *The Simple Life: On the Benefits of Low Self-Complexity*, 35 PERSONALITY AND SOCIAL PSYCHOLOGY BULLETIN 823 (2009).

30 See Susan M. Davies, *Evidence of Character to Prove Conduct: A Reassessment of Relevancy*, 27 CRIMINAL LAW BULLETIN 504 (1991).

31 Some empirical research has found that the interaction of person and situation adds independently to the predictive power of a statistical model, over and above that provided by personality measures and by situational variables. But the relative power of these elements varies from study to study, depending on the persons and the situations.

32 See Gerd Gigerenzer, *Fast and Frugal Heuristics: The Tools of Bounded Rationality*, in BLACKWELL HANDBOOK OF JUDGMENT AND DECISION MAKING 62 (Derek Koehler and Nigel Harvey, eds., 2004).

33 See SUSAN T. FISKE AND SHELLEY E. TAYLOR, SOCIAL COGNITION: FROM BRAINS TO CULTURE, 2d edition (2013).

34 See, most prominently, DANIEL KAHNEMAN, THINKING, FAST AND SLOW (2011).

35 Concerning causal attributions, see also Chapter 2. Concerning filling in gaps, see Chapter 3, on instructions to disregard. Also see the discussion of the story model in Chapter 1.

36 *People v. Zackowitz*, 172 N.E. 466, 468 (N.Y. 1930).

37 But it turns out not to be fundamental. Research on cross-cultural reasoning shows that people raised in North America and Europe tend to make dispositional attributions, whereas people raised in more collectivist cultures (typically in the Far East) tend to make more situational attributions than Westerners, demonstrating more sensitivity to person-situation interactions. Incheol Choi, Richard E. Nisbett, and Ara Norenzayan, *Causal Attribution across Cultures: Variation and Universality*, 125 PSYCHOLOGICAL BULLETIN 47 (1999).

38 EDWARD E. JONES AND RICHARD E. NISBETT, THE ACTOR AND THE OBSERVER: DIVERGENT PERCEPTIONS OF THE CAUSES OF BEHAVIOR (1971); SUSAN T. FISKE AND SHELLEY E. TAYLOR, SOCIAL COGNITION, 2d edition (1991) (finding research evidence for the actor-observer asymmetry to be abundant).

39 You might recognize in this description an analogy to what jurors try to do with the disparate and conflicting evidence that is offered to them in a trial: they try to fit it into the most coherent story they can of what most likely actually took place in the dispute they are asked to decide about. (See the discussion of the story model in Chapter 1.)

40 Consider the advice elders give to their children to "make a good first impression."

41 For an example of error produced by rapid trait inferences and stereotyping, made famous by the film *A Cry in the Dark*, starring Meryl Streep, see Julia Baird, *She's Innocent. We're Guilty*, NEW YORK TIMES (June 15, 2012). At a campground in the Australia Outback, infant Azaria Chamberlain disappeared. Her mother, Lindy Chamberlain, shouted when she saw an Australian wild dog, known as a dingo, swipe the baby from the family tent. But her report was not believed, and Lindy and her husband were accused of killing the child and hiding her body. The public's strong belief in Lindy's guilt was the product of impressions of her character, resulting from her appearance (too sexy, tanned, and wearing large sunglasses and

an extensive wardrobe) and her behavior (said to appear cold, stoic, belonging to a little-known religion, not weeping in court). It took officials 32 years of trials, convictions, appeals, reversals, commissions, and tens of millions of dollars before officials finally and fully concluded that a dingo killed the child, and issued a death certificate so indicating.

**42** A dramatic example is provided by a study in which teachers were told that elementary students (chosen at random by the researchers) would blossom during the current school year, and they did. ROBERT ROSENTHAL AND LENORE JACOBSON, PYGMALION IN THE CLASSROOM: TEACHER EXPECTATION AND PUPILS' INTELLECTUAL DEVELOPMENT (1992).

**43** See Richard J. Ofshe and Richard A. Leo, *The Social Psychology of Police Interrogation: The Theory and Classification of True and False Confessions*, 16 STUDIES IN LAW, POLITICS, AND SOCIETY 189 (1997).

**44** Does this sound like one aspect of "thinking like a lawyer"?

**45** See Dan Simon, *A Third View of the Black Box: Cognitive Coherence in Legal Decision Making*, 71 UNIVERSITY OF CHICAGO LAW REVIEW 511 (2004).

**46** ROBERT SAPOLSKY, BIOLOGY AND HUMAN BEHAVIOR: THE NEUROLOGICAL ORIGINS OF INDIVIDUALITY (2005).

**47** In contrast to the professionally managed or distorted images of public figures.

**48** Douglas T. Kenrick and David O. Stringfield, *Personality Traits and the Eye of the Beholder: Crossing Some Traditional Philosophical Boundaries in The Search for Consistency in All of the People*, 87 PSYCHOLOGICAL REVIEW 88 (1980).

**49** See Roger C. Park, *Character at the Crossroads*, 49 HASTINGS LAW JOURNAL 717 (1998).

**50** Most civil law and non-U.S. common law countries are already there. They permit character evidence to be admitted whenever the judge finds it to be highly probative. Thus, only the United States maintains a strong allegiance to the traditional prohibitions on propensity evidence.

**51** Wendy Wood and David T. Neal, *A New Look at Habits and the Habit-Goal Interface*, 114 PSYCHOLOGICAL REVIEW 843 (2007).

**52** F. Gregory Ashby, Benjamin O. Turner, and Jon C. Horvitz, *Cortical and Basal Ganglia Contributions to Habit Learning and Automaticity*, 14 TRENDS IN COGNITIVE SCIENCES 208 (2010).

**53** To the extent that police practices have the effect of focusing attention on potential perpetrators who have previously committed the same crime being investigated, the probability increases that the person who becomes the defendant will have a prior conviction for the same offense.

**54** Because of doubts about the ability of jurors to restrict their use of prior convictions to evaluating credibility (as opposed to drawing an impermissible propensity inference), courts are reluctant to allow use of prior crimes to impeach a defendant-witness's credibility when the prior crime is highly similar to the crime for which the defendant is now on trial. The authoritative source for the factors to be considered in such circumstances remain the opinion of then Judge (later Chief Justice of the United States) Warren Burger in *Gordon v. United States*, 383 F.2d 936, 940–41 (D.C. Cir. 1967).

55 For a brief review of these studies, see NEIL VIDMAR AND VALERIE P. HANS, AMERICAN JURIES: THE VERDICT 161–63 (2007).

56 Roselle L. Wissler and Michael J. Saks, *On the Inefficacy of Limiting Instructions: When Jurors Use Prior Conviction Evidence to Decide on Guilt*, 9 LAW AND HUMAN BEHAVIOR 37 (1985)

57 On a 10-point scale, defendant witnesses were rated between 3.0 and 3.7. Other witnesses were rated in the mid-7.0s.

58 At least one state supreme court has taken heed of such research findings to narrow the kinds of prior convictions that may be used for impeachment purposes. *People v. Allen*, 420 N.W.2d 499 (Mich. 1988).

59 The procedure for these inquiries is somewhat complicated. But the concept is simple.

60 DAN ARIELY, THE (HONEST) TRUTH ABOUT DISHONESTY: HOW WE LIE TO EVERYONE—ESPECIALLY OURSELVES (2012). See also Nina Mazar and Dan Ariely, *Dishonesty in Everyday Life and Its Policy Implications*, 25 JOURNAL OF PUBLIC POLICY AND MARKETING (2006); Bella M. DePaulo et al., *Lying in Everyday Life*, 70 JOURNAL OF PERSONALITY AND SOCIAL PSYCHOLOGY 979 (1996); Bella M. DePaulo et al., *Everyday Lies in Close and Casual Relationships*, 74 JOURNAL OF PERSONALITY AND SOCIAL PSYCHOLOGY 93 (1998).

61 And that is what the sponsors of the legislation in Congress argued, though they offered no empirical evidence that it is true. An interesting discussion of the politics, arguments, and evidence behind the adoption of Rules 413, 414, and 415 can be found in RICHARD O. LEMPERT ET AL., A MODERN APPROACH TO EVIDENCE, 4th edition, 457–62 (2000).

62 Again, see discussion in Lempert et al. Also, see *Report of the Judicial Conference of the United States on the Admission of Character Evidence in Certain Sexual Misconduct Cases*, reprinted in 56 CRIMINAL LAW REPORTER (BNA) No. 129, at 2140 (Feb. 15, 1995), stating: "The overwhelming majority of judges, lawyers, law professors and legal organizations who responded [to the Judicial Conference's request for comments] opposed the new Evidence Rules 413, 414, and 415. . . It is important to note the highly unusual unanimity of members of the Standing and Advisory Committees [of the Judicial Conference] . . . in taking the view that Rules 413–415 are undesirable."

63 One reason for this might be that while burglars, for example, engage in crime as teams or a criminal network, lending group support and structure to the enterprise, sexual offenders are much more likely to act as individuals.

64 Frank E. Zimring, Alex R. Piquero, and Wesley G. Jennings, *Sexual Delinquency in Racine: Does Early Sex Offending Predict Later Sex Offending in Youth and Adulthood?*, 6 CRIMINOLOGY AND PUBLIC POLICY 507 (2007).

65 Studies varied in their measure of whether an offense was committed or recidivism occurred. Usually, the measure is whether a juvenile was "adjudicated" delinquent

for an offense or an adult was found "guilty" (which usually occurred by a guilty plea). But some studies employed less official judicial measures, such as being charged. To have a range of measures leading to much the same conclusions should add to one's confidence in the general conclusion.

66 A study that analyzed classifications and registration of youthful sex offenders under recent federal legislation—the Adam Walsh Child Protection and Safety Act of 2006 (Pub. L. 109–248, codified at 42 U.S.C. §§ 16911 et seq. (2012))—found similar errors of over- and under-identification. Ashley B. Batastini et al., *Federal Standards for Community Registration of Juvenile Sex Offenders: An Evaluation of Risk Prediction and Future Implications*, 17 PSYCHOLOGY, PUBLIC POLICY AND LAW 451 (2011).

67 Patrick Lussier and Garth Davies, *A Person-Oriented Perspective on Sexual Offenders, Offending Trajectories, and Risk of Recidivism: A New Challenge for Policymakers, Risk Assessors, and Actuarial Prediction*, 17 PSYCHOLOGY, PUBLIC POLICY AND LAW 530 (2011).

68 Charles H. Rose III, *Should the Tail Wag the Dog?: The Potential Effects of Recidivism Data on Character Evidence Rules*, 36 NEW MEXICO LAW REVIEW 341 (2006).

69 For more narrowly defined categories, the data are: homicide: 1.2–6.6; rape: 2.5–7.7; other sexual assaults: 3.3–5.5; motor vehicle theft: 11.5–18.6; robbery: 13.4–19.6; burglary: 23.4–31.9; larceny/theft: 33.5–33.9; drug offenses: 24.8–41.2. Much the same pattern of findings was reported in earlier studies. See FRANK O. BECK (BUREAU OF JUSTICE STATISTICS, UNITED STATES DEPARTMENT OF JUSTICE), RECIDIVISM OF PRISONERS RELEASED IN 1983 (1989).

70 This should not be surprising considering that these new rules were driven by ideology and political preference—undergirded by mere assertions rather than evidence—to discard a rule that had been in place for centuries. See *supra* notes 58 and 59.

## CHAPTER 6. HEARSAY AND EXCEPTIONS

1 Experiments using "rumor chains" like this game of telephone are reported by Gordon W. Allport and Leo Postman, *The Basic Psychology of Rumor*, 11 TRANSACTIONS OF THE NEW YORK ACADEMY OF SCIENCES 61 (1945), and in their subsequent book. In those studies, the first person saw a picture and described it to the second person (who did not see it), the second person described it to the third person, and so on down the line. The final person sometimes supplied inaccurate descriptions biased in the direction of stereotypes of the people in the pictures. These experimental findings have been exaggerated and mischaracterized over the years as showing the dangers of eyewitness testimony. We believe that they are much more relevant to showing the dangers of (transmitted) hearsay evidence. For an explanation of the studies and attempted replications see Molly Treadway and Michael McCloskey, *Effects of Racial Stereotypes on Eyewitness Performance: Implications of the Real and the Rumoured Allport and Postman Studies*, 3 APPLIED COGNITIVE PSYCHOLOGY 53 (1989).

2 Laurence H. Tribe, *Triangulating Hearsay*, 87 HARVARD LAW REVIEW 957 (1974).

3 Rule 803 contains 23 exceptions and Rule 804 contains 5, totaling 28. But Rule 801(d) lists 8 types of hearsay evidence to be considered as "statements that are *not* hearsay"—which are then treated the same as exceptions. And Rule 807, the residual exception, states that other types of hearsay evidence may be admissible if sufficiently trustworthy and necessary. Also, it should be noted that just because something falls into one of the exceptions does not mean it *will* necessarily be admitted; that is just a first step. For example, the evidence may be subject to other rules, including a balancing test.

4 For some rules the witness may also be the declarant, testifying about what she said earlier. See, e.g., Rule 801(d)(1) (A Declarant-Witness's Prior Statement).

5 See *supra* note 1 and John D. Bransford and Marcia K. Johnson, *Contextual Prerequisites for Understanding: Some Investigations of Comprehension and Recall*, 11 JOURNAL OF VERBAL LEARNING AND VERBAL BEHAVIOR 717 (1972).

6 For example, compare the exceptions allowed by Rule 803 versus those allowed by Rule 804. The latter exceptions are thought of as less reliable but more necessary.

7 Nancy Steblay et al., *The Impact on Juror Verdicts of Judicial Instruction to Disregard Inadmissible Evidence*, 30 LAW AND HUMAN BEHAVIOR 469 (2006). This meta-analysis is described more fully in the chapter on instructions to disregard.

8 Michael E. Lamb, Yael Orbach, Kathleen J. Sternberg, Irit Hershkowitz, and Dvora Horowitz, *Accuracy of Investigators' Verbatim Notes of Their Forensic Interviews with Alleged Child Abuse Victims*, 24 LAW AND HUMAN BEHAVIOR 699 (2000).

9 Amye Warren, Narina Nuñez, Jennifer M. Keeney, Julie A. Buck, and Beverly Smith, *The Believability of Children and Their Interviewer's Hearsay Testimony: When Less Is More*, 87 JOURNAL OF APPLIED PSYCHOLOGY 846 (2002).

10 Narina Nuñez, Jennifer Gray, and Julie A. Buck, *Educative Expert Testimony: A One-Two Punch Can Affect Jurors' Decisions*, 42 JOURNAL OF APPLIED SOCIAL PSYCHOLOGY 525 (2011).

11 Justin Sevier, *Testing Tribe's Triangle: Juries, Hearsay, and Psychological Distance*, 103 GEORGETOWN LAW JOURNAL 879 (2015).

12 See the Advisory Committee Notes to Rule 803, especially to Exceptions (1) and (2). Edward J. Imwinkelried, *The Need to Resurrect the Present Sense Impression Hearsay Exception: A Relapse in Hearsay Policy*, 52 HOWARD LAW JOURNAL 319, 319 (2009).

13 Imwinkelried, id., at 322.

14 See Imwinkelried, id., for interesting commentary that provides the basis for most of the following historical discussions.

15 Robert M. Hutchins and Donald Slesinger, *Some Observations on the Law of Evidence*, 28 COLUMBIA LAW REVIEW 432, 439 (1928).

16 Aldert Vrij, Par Anders Granhag, and Stephen Porter, *Pitfalls and Opportunities in Nonverbal and Verbal Lie Detection*, 11 PSYCHOLOGICAL SCIENCE IN THE PUBLIC INTEREST 89 (2010).

17 Charles A. Morgan III et al., *Accuracy of Eyewitness Memory for Personas Encountered during Exposure to Highly Intense Stress*, 27 INTERNATIONAL JOURNAL OF LAW AND PSYCHIATRY 265 (2004). Charles A. Morgan III, Anthony Doran, George Steffian, Gary Hazlett, and Steven M. Southwick, *Stress-Induced Deficits in Working Memory and Visuo-Constructive Abilities in Special Operations Soldiers*, 60 BIOLOGICAL PSYCHIATRY 722 (2006). Charles A. Morgan III, Steven M. Southwick, George Steffian, Gary Hazlett, and Elizabeth F. Loftus, *Misinformation Can Influence Memory for Recently Experienced, Highly Stressful Events*, 36 INTERNATIONAL JOURNAL OF LAW AND PSYCHIATRY 11 (2013).

18 See Tanja Rapus Benton, David F. Ross, Emily Bradshaw, W. Neil Thomas, and Gregory S. Bradshaw, *Eyewitness Memory Is Still Not Common Sense: Comparing Jurors, Judges and Law Enforcement to Eyewitness Experts*, 20 APPLIED COGNITIVE PSYCHOLOGY 115 (2006).

19 Richard E. Nisbett and Timothy D. Wilson, *Telling More than We Can Know: Verbal Reports on Mental Processes*, 84 PSYCHOLOGICAL REVIEW 231 (1977). The article lacks a description of what the subjects did give as reasons. See also the descriptions of the cognitive dissonance literature in this article.

20 *Mutual Life Insurance Co. v. Hillmon*, 145 U.S. 285 (1892). Your authors share the view that the principle for which the *Hillmon* doctrine stands is silly. See Marianne Wesson, *The* Hillmon *Case, The Supreme Court, and the McGuffin (FRE 803(3): Statements of Existing Mental Conditions/Intent)*, in EVIDENCE STORIES 277 (Richard Lempert, ed., 2006).

21 Nira Liberman and Yaacov Trope, *The Role of Feasibility and Desirability Considerations in Near and Distant Future Decisions: A Test of Temporal Construal Theory*, 75 JOURNAL OF PERSONALITY AND SOCIAL PSYCHOLOGY 5 (1998).

22 Nicholas Epley and David Dunning, *Feeling "Holier than Thou": Are Self-Serving Assessments Produced by Errors in Self- or Social Prediction?*, 79 JOURNAL OF PERSONALITY AND SOCIAL PSYCHOLOGY 861 (2000).

23 Of course the real problem with admitting tweets, e-mails, etc., is that of authentication—e.g., making sure communications really are from whom they are alleged to be from.

24 *Crawford v. Washington*, 541 U.S. 36 (2004); *Davis v. Washington*, 547 U.S. 813 (2006).

## CHAPTER 7. SCIENTIFIC AND OTHER EXPERT EVIDENCE

1 *CSI* stands for Crime Scene Investigation; *NCIS* stands for Naval Criminal Investigative Service; *Bones* is a crime comedy-drama involving forensic anthropology and archaeology.

A cautionary note about these television programs and their forensic science comes from the following exchange, which appears on Yahoo Answers at https://answers.yahoo.com/question/index?qid=20110416125717AAIZGYa. A student beginning a course on forensic science posted the following question online:

[M]y tutor has suggested for recreation to watch some Forensic Science shows as some are based on real procedure. But which is the best, as I don't really watch those sort of shows but would like to get a "head start" on the course as much as possible.

A forensic scientist responded with this answer:

As a forensic scientist, I can tell you they are ALL c**p. They are all fiction for entertainment value only and shouldn't be watched in the hopes that they can contribute ANYTHING helpful in understanding the real world of forensic science. They start from real tests and tests in the research and hypothetical phase, then completely twist them into something that is too far removed from fact to be educational.

2 John Monahan and Laurens Walker, *Social Authority: Obtaining, Evaluating, and Establishing Social Science in Law*, 134 UNIVERSITY OF PENNSYLVANIA LAW REVIEW 477 (1987); Laurens Walker and John Monahan, *Social Frameworks: A New Use of Social Science in Law*, 73 VIRGINIA LAW REVIEW 559 (1987).

3 *Dunagin v. City of Oxford*, 718 F.2d 738 (5th Cir. 1983).

4 See David Parker, *Policing Procedure Before Substance: Reforming Judicial Review of the Factual Predicates to Legislation*, 99 VIRGINIA LAW REVIEW 1327 (2013).

5 *Furman v. Georgia*, 408 U.S. 238 (1972).

6 See, e.g., JAMES REASON, HUMAN ERROR (1990); DANIEL KAHNEMAN ET AL. (eds.), JUDGMENT UNDER UNCERTAINTY: HEURISTICS AND BIASES (1982); JONATHAN BARON, THINKING AND DECIDING (2007); GERD GIGERENZER, CALCULATED RISKS: HOW TO KNOW WHEN NUMBERS DECEIVE YOU (2003).

7 *Williams v. Florida*, 399 U.S. 78 (1970) (emphasis added).

8 An easy way to calculate these results is to begin by thinking about the probability that every juror on a jury will be from the majority group. Juror 1 chosen at random from the 90/10 population described in the text has a .90 probability of being from the majority group. The probability of two jurors both being from the majority group is .90 x .90. And so on. So, for a 6-person jury, the probability of all 6 being from the majority is .90 x .90 x .90 x .90 x .90 x .90, which is the same as $.90^6$, which equals .53. Therefore, the probability of a jury of 6 being constituted of something *other than* all members of the majority group would be 1-.53 =.47. If we do the same calculation for a 12-person jury, we get $.90^{12} = .28$ as the probability of having an all-majority jury. And 1-.28 =.72 is the probability of a 12-person jury having one or more non-majority members.

9 Daniel C. Murrie et al., *Are Forensic Experts Biased by the Side That Retained Them?*, 24 PSYCHOLOGICAL SCIENCE 1398 (2013).

10 VALERIE HANS AND NEIL VIDMAR, AMERICAN JURIES 173–74 (2007).

11 Rule 706. See also *General Electric Co. v. Joiner*, 522 U.S. 136, 146 (1997) (Breyer, J., concurring) (summarizing the range of tools available to district judges to "help them overcome the inherent difficulty of making determinations about complicated scientific or otherwise technical evidence"); JOE CECIL AND THOMAS WILL-

GING, COURT-APPOINTED EXPERTS: DEFINING THE ROLE OF EXPERTS APPOINTED UNDER FEDERAL RULE OF EVIDENCE 706 (1993).

12 Sheila Jasanoff, *What Judges Should Know about the Sociology of Science*, 32 JURIMETRICS JOURNAL 345 (1992).

13 Daniel C. Murrie et al., *Are Forensic Experts Biased by the Side That Retained Them?*, 24 PSYCHOLOGICAL SCIENCE 1398 (2013).

14 See more detailed description of "weapons of influence" in Chapter 1.

15 Ziva Kunda, *The Case for Motivated Reasoning*, 108 PSYCHOLOGICAL BULLETIN 480 (1990).

16 MILTON LODGE AND CHARLES TABER, THE RATIONALIZING VOTER (2013); David Redlawsk et al., *The Affective Tipping Point: Do Motivated Reasoners Ever "Get It"?*, 31 POLITICAL PSYCHOLOGY 563 (2010).

17 Chris Mooney, *The Science of Why We Don't Believe Science*, MOTHER JONES (May/June 2011) (paraphrasing the main point being made in Jonathan Haidt, *The Emotional Dog and its Rational Tail: A Social Intuitionist Approach to Moral Judgment*, 108 PSYCHOLOGICAL REVIEW 814 [2001]), puts it this way: "We may think we're being scientists, but we're actually being lawyers. Our 'reasoning' is a means to a predetermined end—winning our 'case'—and is shot through with biases. They include 'confirmation bias,' in which we give greater heed to evidence and arguments that bolster our beliefs, and 'disconfirmation bias,' in which we expend disproportionate energy trying to debunk or refute views and arguments that we find uncongenial."

18 RICHARD FEYNMAN, CARGO CULT SCIENCE (1974) (commencement address to California Institute of Technology).

19 See Scott Bales, *Turning the Microscope on Forensic Science*, 26 LITIGATION 51 (2000).

20 Joseph Peterson et al., *The Role and Impact of Forensic Evidence in the Criminal Justice Process*, Revised Final Report to National Institute of Justice (2010).

21 Brandon L. Garrett and Peter J. Neufeld, *Invalid Forensic Science Testimony and Wrongful Convictions*, 95 VIRGINIA LAW REVIEW 1 (2009). Michael J. Saks and Jonathan J. Koehler, *The Coming Paradigm Shift in Forensic Identification Science*, 309 SCIENCE 892 (2005).

22 People who watch too much television will think this means they are a "match" and that a match means they were made by the same person. But that is incorrect. After deciding that they are indistinguishably alike, then a decision needs to be made about the frequency of those characteristics in the population—something about which we have nothing like complete data. Because "match" can be so misleading, properly trained forensic examiners do not use the term.

23 Itiel Dror et al., *Contextual Information Renders Experts Vulnerable to Make Erroneous Identifications*, 156 FORENSIC SCIENCE INTERNATIONAL 74 (2006). The experiment described involved only five examiners. Later experiments reached similar conclusions with larger sample sizes. See Itiel Dror and Rebecca Bucht, *Psychological Perspectives on Problems with Forensic Science*, in CONVICTION OF

THE INNOCENT (Brian L. Cutler, ed., 2011); see also Itiel Dror and Simon Cole, *The Vision in 'Blind' Justice: Expert Perception, Judgment and Visual Cognition in Forensic Pattern Recognition*, 17 PSYCHONOMIC BULLETIN & REVIEW 161 (2010).

24 See chapters on these fields in DAVID L. FAIGMAN ET AL. (eds.), MODERN SCIENTIFIC EVIDENCE: THE LAW AND SCIENCE OF EXPERT TESTIMONY (2010).

25 NATIONAL RESEARCH COUNCIL, COMMITTEE ON IDENTIFYING THE NEEDS OF THE FORENSIC SCIENCE COMMUNITY, STRENGTHENING FORENSIC SCIENCE IN THE UNITED STATES: A PATH FORWARD (2009) (stating that "[f]orensic science professionals have yet to establish either the validity of their approach or the accuracy of their conclusions"); DAVID L. FAIGMAN ET AL. (eds.), MODERN SCIENTIFIC EVIDENCE: THE LAW AND SCIENCE OF EXPERT TESTIMONY (2010) (see chapters on forensic pattern matching sciences); Michael Saks and Jonathan Koehler, *The Coming Paradigm Shift in Forensic Identification Science*, 309 SCIENCE 892 (2005); Mark Page et al., *Uniqueness in the Forensic Identification Sciences—Fact or Fiction?*, 206 FORENSIC SCIENCE INTERNATIONAL 12 (2011); Bruce Budowle et al., *Review of the Scientific Basis for Friction Ridge Comparisons as a Means of Identification: Committee Findings and Recommendations*, 8 FORENSIC SCIENCE COMMUNICATIONS (2006), www.fbi.gov/hqllab/fsc/backissuljan2006/research/2006_01_research02.htm (concluding that "[e]mpirical studies can never prove absolutely the hypothesis of uniqueness"); Michael Saks and Jonathan Koehler, *The Individualization Fallacy in Forensic Science*, 61 VANDERBILT LAW REVIEW 199 (2008).

26 Sheila Jasanoff, *What Judges Should Know about the Sociology of Science*, 32 JURIMETRICS JOURNAL 345 (1992).

27 *Frye v. U.S.*, 293 F. 1013 (D.C. Cir. 1923).

28 This is, in fact, exactly what happened in courts. In virtually every case where a court evaluated voiceprints using a narrow-field *Frye* test, the court ended up *admitting* the testimony; and in virtually every case where a court evaluated voiceprints using a broad-field *Frye* test, the court ended up *excluding* the testimony. See DAVID L. FAIGMAN ET AL. (eds.), MODERN SCIENTIFIC EVIDENCE: THE LAW AND SCIENCE OF EXPERT TESTIMONY (2010), at Chapter 38, "Talker Identification," Sec. 38:1.

29 *Daubert v. Merrell Dow Pharmaceuticals, Inc.*, 509 U.S. 579 (1993).

30 As of this writing, at least 27 states have adopted the essential principles of *Daubert*, while about 10 have rejected *Daubert* in favor of *Frye*. Some of the states that do not follow *Daubert* are, however, populous ones: California, New Jersey, New York, and Pennsylvania.

31 *General Electric v. Joiner*, 522 U.S. 136 (1997); *Kumho Tire Ltd. v. Carmichael*, 526 U.S. 137 (1999)

32 Roselle L. Wissler et al., *Dual Processing Models of Admissibility: Legal Tests for the Admissibility of Scientific Evidence Resemble Cognitive Science's System 1 and System 2*, 17 VIRGINIA JOURNAL OF LAW, SCIENCE AND TECHNOLOGY 11 (2012).

33 David E. Bernstein, *The* Daubert *Counterrevolution*, 89 NOTRE DAME LAW REVIEW 27 (2013) (documenting and discussing reasons for considerable evasion by judges of the Supreme Court's *Daubert* revolution).

34 LLOYD DIXON AND BRIAN GILL, CHANGES IN THE STANDARDS FOR ADMITTING EXPERT EVIDENCE IN FEDERAL CIVIL CASES SINCE THE DAUBERT DECISION (2001).

35 Carol Krafka et al., *Judge and Attorney Experiences, Practices, and Concerns Regarding Expert Testimony in Federal Civil Trials*, 8 PSYCHOLOGY, PUBLIC POLICY, AND LAW 309 (2002).

36 D. Michael Risinger, *Navigating Expert Reliability: Are Criminal Standards of Certainty Being Left on the Dock?*, 64 ALBANY LAW REVIEW 99 (2000).

37 MICHAEL J. SAKS ET AL., ANNOTATED REFERENCE MANUAL ON SCIENTIFIC EVIDENCE—SECOND (WEST) (2005) (see notes of decisions in chapters on economics, engineering, survey research, epidemiology, toxicology, and medicine).

38 D. Michael Risinger, *Navigating Expert Reliability: Are Criminal Standards of Certainty Being Left on the Dock?*, 64 ALBANY LAW REVIEW 99 (2000).

39 As to the four specific subfields: testimony was limited or excluded in response to 21.3% of the challenges to handwriting examiners, 17.9% of those to firearms and toolmark examiners, 16.7% of those to forensic dentists, and 6.8% of those to fingerprint examiners. Mark Page et al., *Forensic Identification Science Evidence since* Daubert: *Part I—A Quantitative Analysis of the Exclusion of Forensic Identification Science Evidence*, 56 JOURNAL OF FORENSIC SCIENCES 1180 (2011).

40 Michael J. Saks and David L. Faigman, *Evidence after* Daubert, in 1 ANNUAL REVIEW OF LAW AND SOCIETY (2005).

41 One study of 450 judges from all 50 states found that although the judges generally viewed themselves as competent to assess scientific evidence, only 6% were able to give adequate answers to basic questions concerning the evaluation of scientific procedures. S. I. Gatowski et al., *Asking the Gatekeepers: A National Survey of Judges on Judging Expert Evidence in a Post-*Daubert *World*, 25 LAW AND HUMAN BEHAVIOR 433 (2001).

42 These fields are voice spectrography, indicators of arson used by fire investigators, and comparative bullet lead analysis. NATIONAL ACADEMY OF SCIENCES, COMMITTEE ON EVALUATION OF SOUND SPECTROGRAMS, ON THE THEORY AND PRACTICE OF VOICE IDENTIFICATION (1979); NATIONAL FIRE PROTECTION ASSOCIATION, NFPA 921, GUIDE FOR FIRE AND EXPLOSION INVESTIGATIONS (2011); NATIONAL ACADEMY OF SCIENCES, COMMITTEE ON SCIENTIFIC ASSESSMENT OF BULLET LEAD ELEMENTAL COMPOSITION COMPARISON, FORENSIC ANALYSIS: WEIGHING BULLET LEAD EVIDENCE (2004).

43 NATIONAL RESEARCH COUNCIL, COMMITTEE ON IDENTIFYING THE NEEDS OF THE FORENSIC SCIENCE COMMUNITY, STRENGTHENING FORENSIC SCIENCE IN THE UNITED STATES: A PATH FORWARD (2009).

44 Id., at 53 (emphasis added).

45 N. J. Schweitzer and Michael J. Saks, *The Gatekeeper Effect: Judges' Influence on the Persuasiveness of Expert Testimony*, 15 PSYCHOLOGY, PUBLIC POLICY AND LAW 1 (2009).

46 BIBB LATANÉ AND JOHN M. DARLEY, THE UNRESPONSIVE BYSTANDER: WHY DOESN'T HE HELP? (1970).

47 See Chapter 1.

48 RICHARD E. PETTY AND JOHN T. CACIOPPO, COMMUNICATION AND PERSUASION: CENTRAL AND PERIPHERAL ROUTES TO ATTITUDE CHANGE (1986). Note the similarity to System1 versus System 2 dual processing, discussed in the Introduction.

49 See, e.g., Sanja Kutnjak Ivkovic and Valerie Hans, *Jurors' Evaluations of Expert Testimony: Judging the Messenger and the Message*, 28 LAW AND SOCIAL INQUIRY 441 (2003); Anthony Champagne and Daniel Shuman, *Removing the People from the Legal Process: The Rhetoric and Research on Judicial Selection and Juries*, 3 PSYCHOLOGY, PUBLIC POLICY AND LAW 242 (1997); Joseph Sanders, *The Jury Deliberation in a "Complex Case":* Havener v. Merrell Dow Pharmaceuticals, 16 JUSTICE SYSTEM JOURNAL 45 (1993); Valerie Hans et al., *The Arizona Jury Reform Permitting Civil Jury Trial Discussions: The Views of Trial Participants, Judges and Jurors*, 32 UNIVERSITY OF MICHIGAN JOURNAL OF LAW REFORM 349 (1999).

50 Shari Seidman Diamond and Jay Casper, *Blindfolding the Jury to Verdict Consequences: Damages, Experts and the Civil Jury*, 26 LAW AND SOCIETY REVIEW 513 (1992).

51 For additional examples of studies testing peripheral and central processing by jurors, see Joel Cooper et al., *Complex Scientific Testimony: How Do Jurors Make Decisions?*, 20 LAW AND HUMAN BEHAVIOR 379 (1996); Joel Cooper and Isaac Neuhaus, *The "Hired Gun" Effect: Assessing the Effect of Pay, Frequency of Testifying, and Credentials on the Perception of Expert Testimony*, 24 LAW AND HUMAN BEHAVIOR 149 (2000). For a different interpretation of the findings, see Neil Vidmar and Shari Seidman Diamond, *Juries and Expert Evidence*, 66 BROOKLYN LAW REVIEW 1121 (2001).

52 Scholars and some courts recommend that the drawing of the conclusion from the major and minor premises (from the general finding of the science and the case-specific facts) is the job of the factfinder and should not be drawn for the jury by the expert. See Laurens Walker and John Monahan, *Social Frameworks: A New Use of Social Science in Law*, 73 VIRGINIA LAW REVIEW 559 (1987). Expert witnesses on the psychology of eyewitness identification have long adhered to that practice. As we shall see, however, that is not the customary practice with most kinds of expert witnesses.

53 Nancy Brekke and Eugene Borgida, *Expert Psychological Testimony in Rape Trials: A Social-Cognitive Analysis*, 55 JOURNAL OF PERSONALITY AND SOCIAL PSYCHOLOGY 372 (1988).

54 Gary Wells, *Naked Statistical Evidence of Liability: Is Subjective Probability Enough?*, 62 JOURNAL OF PERSONALITY AND SOCIAL PSYCHOLOGY 739 (1992). In

addition, note that there is a body of attitude-change research that addresses the effects of the implicit versus explicit drawing of conclusions as part of a persuasive communication.

**55** Rule 704(b) contains an exception that retains the old rule: opinions about a defendant's mental state or condition are inadmissible when they constitute an element of the crime charged or a defense.

**56** See Chapter 4, which discusses eyewitness memory. See also Laurens Walker and John Monahan, *Social Frameworks: A New Use of Social Science in Law*, 73 VIRGINIA LAW REVIEW 559 (1987).

**57** William C. Thompson and Edward Schumann, *Interpretation of Statistical Evidence in Criminal Trials: The Prosecutor's Fallacy and the Defense Attorney's Fallacy*, 11 LAW AND HUMAN BEHAVIOR 167 (1987); William C. Thompson, *Are Juries Competent to Evaluate Statistical Evidence?*, 52 LAW AND CONTEMPORARY PROBLEMS 9 (Autumn 1989).

When trait frequencies are presented as simple percentages of the population, a small proportion of jurors fall victim to the prosecutor's or the defense attorney's fallacy. When the data are given as conditional probabilities (mock jurors are told that *if* the defendant were innocent *then* there is a 2% chance that his trait would match the perpetrator's), more jurors commit the prosecutor's fallacy and fewer commit the defense attorney's fallacy. When the trait frequencies are given as a percentage along with an incidence rate (2% of people have hair that would be indistinguishable, and in a city of one million there would be approximately 20,000 such individuals), then fewer jurors commit the prosecutor's fallacy and more commit the defense attorney's fallacy. When both counsel make invalid arguments on behalf of the two fallacies, many more jurors commit the errors, especially the defense attorney's fallacy. Mock jurors' decisions about guilt reflect their having been talked into believing the fallacious arguments.

**58** Jonathan J. Koehler, *When Are People Persuaded by DNA Match Statistics?*, 25 LAW AND HUMAN BEHAVIOR 493 (2001).

**59** Additional discussion of the role of emotion in the rules of evidence and decision making can be found in other chapters in this book.

**60** MOLLY TREADWAY-JOHNSON, AN INVESTIGATION OF JUROR COMPREHENSION OF STATISTICAL PROOF OF CAUSATION (1990) (unpublished doctoral dissertation, Johns Hopkins University, Baltimore).

**61** Ulrich Hoffrage et al., *Communicating Statistical Information*, 290 SCIENCE 2261 (2000).

**62** MOLLY TREADWAY-JOHNSON, AN INVESTIGATION OF JUROR COMPREHENSION OF STATISTICAL PROOF OF CAUSATION (1990) (unpublished doctoral dissertation, Johns Hopkins University, Baltimore).

**63** Ulrich Hoffrage et al., *Communicating Statistical Information*, 290 SCIENCE 2261 (2000).

**64** Gerd Gigerenzer et al., *Helping Doctors and Patients Make Sense of Health Statistics*, 8 PSYCHOLOGICAL SCIENCE IN THE PUBLIC INTEREST 53 (2008).

65 Daniel Krauss and Bruce Sales, *The Effects of Clinical and Scientific Expert Testimony on Juror Decision Making in Capital Sentencing*, 7 PSYCHOLOGY, PUBLIC POLICY AND LAW 267 (2001).
66 Id., at 286–87.
67 The story model is explained in Chapter 1.
68 Daniel Krauss and Bruce Sales, *The Effects of Clinical and Scientific Expert Testimony on Juror Decision Making in Capital Sentencing*, 7 PSYCHOLOGY, PUBLIC POLICY AND LAW 267 (2001).
69 Shari Seidman Diamond et al., *Juror Reactions to Attorneys at Trial*, 87 JOURNAL OF CRIMINAL LAW AND CRIMINOLOGY 17 (1996).
70 Weak cross: 47% voted for death. Strong cross: 51%. Strong cross plus opposing expert: 50%.
71 In this condition, 39% of the juries favored death. See also Margaret Bull Kovera et al., *Expert Testimony in Child Sexual Abuse Cases: Effects of Expert Evidence Type and Cross-Examination*, 18 LAW AND HUMAN BEHAVIOR 653 (1994), with similar results in the context of child sexual abuse prosecutions.
72 Joseph Sanders, *The Merits of the Paternalistic Justification for Restrictions on the Admissibility of Expert Evidence*, 33 SETON HALL LAW REVIEW 881(2003).
73 B. Michael Dann et al., *Testing the Effects of Selected Jury Trial Innovations on Juror Comprehension of Contested MtDNA Evidence*, Final Technical Report (2004, unpublished) , https://www.ncjrs.gov/pdffiles1/nij/grants/211000.pdf; further described in David H. Kaye et al., *Statistics in the Jury Box: How Jurors Respond to Mitochondrial DNA Match Probabilities*, 4 JOURNAL OF EMPIRICAL LEGAL STUDIES 797 (2007) (describing jurors' cognitive errors in interpreting the statistics of mitochondrial DNA).
74 Gerd Gigerenzer et al., *Helping Doctors and Patients Make Sense of Health Statistics*, 8 PSYCHOLOGICAL SCIENCE IN THE PUBLIC INTEREST 53 (2008). See also GERD GIGERENZER, RISK SAVVY: HOW TO MAKE GOOD DECISIONS (2014).
75 Transparency can be facilitated by (a) using frequency statements rather than single-event probabilities, (b) using absolute risks rather than relative risks, (c) using mortality rates (how many people die), rather than survival rates (how many live), and (d) using natural frequencies rather than conditional probabilities.
76 Either way, the result should be .09. That is, the probability that a woman with a positive mammogram actually has breast cancer is about .09, or about 9%, or about 9 chances in 100.
77 For a fascinating look at other ways to present data that are designed to be more clear and understandable—and rather dramatic—visit the website of Hans Rosling, at www.gapminder.org.
78 Richard E. Nisbett et al., *Teaching Reasoning*, 238 SCIENCE 625 (1987); Geoffrey T. Fong et al., *The Effects of Statistical Training on Thinking about Everyday Problems*, 18 COGNITIVE PSYCHOLOGY 253 (1986).

79 N. J. Schweitzer and Michael J. Saks, *Jurors and Scientific Causation: What Don't They Know and What Can Be Done about It?*, 52 JURIMETRICS JOURNAL 433 (2012).

80 On remand of *Daubert* back to the Court of Appeals for a decision consistent with the Supreme Court's requirement that judges determine the validity of proffered science, Judge Kozinski introduced his opinion with this lament:

> As we read the Supreme Court's teaching in *Daubert* . . . , though we are largely untrained in science and certainly no match for any of the witnesses whose testimony we are reviewing, it is our responsibility to determine whether those experts' proposed testimony amounts to "scientific knowledge," constitutes "good science," and was "derived by the scientific method." Our responsibility, then, unless we badly misread the Supreme Court's opinion, is to resolve disputes among respected, well-credentialed scientists about matters squarely within their expertise, in areas where there is no scientific consensus as to what is and what is not "good science," and occasionally to reject such expert testimony because it was not "derived by the scientific method." Mindful of our position in the hierarchy of the federal judiciary, we take a deep breath and proceed with this heady task.

*Daubert v. Merrell Dow Pharmaceuticals, Inc.*, 43 F.3d 1311 (9th Cir. 1995).

81 NATIONAL RESEARCH COUNCIL, COMMITTEE ON IDENTIFYING THE NEEDS OF THE FORENSIC SCIENCE COMMUNITY, STRENGTHENING FORENSIC SCIENCE IN THE UNITED STATES: A PATH FORWARD 53 (2009).

# INDEX

admissibility. *See* gatekeeping
adversarial system, 207, 211; versus inquisitorial, 11
Advisory Committee Notes, 63, 70, 74, 75, 79, 80, 165–166, 192, 194, 195–196, 203
allegiance bias, 207–208
Ariely, D., 118–119, 171
assimilation, 158
attribution, 5, 79, 142; actor-observer effect, 158; dispositional, 157; fundamental attribution error, 157–158; non-Western cultures, 305n37
attribution theory, 79

balancing tests, 18, 57–84, 100, 115, 148, 165, 234–235
Baldwin, S., 11
Bayes' Theorem, 44, 61, 161–162
bench trials, 11, 19
blindfolding the jury, 35–36, 82, 83
bottom-up knowledge, 17

Cardozo, B., 157
Casper, J., 218
categorical exclusions, 19, 58, 72–83; behavioral dimension, 74–75; cognitive dimension, 73–74; limited use, 101; other dimensions, 75–76. *See also* Rules 407, 408, 409, 410, 411
causation. *See* statistics
character evidence, 5, 142–175, 237–238; character for truthfulness, 130–131, 143, 148, 167, 169–170; perception of trait-behavior consistency, 156–159; policy and psychology, 149–162; predictive power, 151–154. *See also* reputation evidence
character in issue, 145
Chicago Jury Project, 53
Cialdini, R., 40, 208
Cleary, E., 14
cognitive capacity, 4, 113–115, 156, 193–195
coherence, 17, 45
confirmation bias, 209. *See also* motivated reasoning
Confrontation Clause/Sixth Amendment, 97, 128–129, 193, 200–201
context effects, 210
cross-examination, 112–113, 128–136, 141, 148, 170, 181, 189–191, 194, 224–225, 236
cultural truism, 210
curse of knowledge, 18, 57, 62–63, 97, 104–105

damages, 35, 77, 81–83, 218
Dann, M., 226
Darley, J., 151–152
*Daubert v. Merrell Dow Pharmaceuticals*. *See* gatekeeping
debiasing, 47, 97
Demaine, L., 97
demeanor, 112–113, 122–123, 129, 181, 236
Diamond, S. S., 49, 218
diffusion of responsibility, 216
disregarding inadmissible evidence, 15–17, 85–97, 235–236; empirical research, 87–90; hearsay, 187; inability to disregard, 91–93; instructions, 85, 96–97; judges, 52–53, 103–107; unwillingness to disregard, 93–95

Dror, I., 26
dual processing: System 1 versus System 2, 20–22, 66, 69, 86, 124, 156, 205, 214–215; central versus peripheral, 283n42, 217–218

emotion, 21, 22, 48, 57–58, 63–69, 192–195, 222, 225
empirical questions: designing study to answer, 15–17, 22; drawing on basic research to answer, 17–18, 22
erroneous convictions, 22–23, 25–26
evidence rules: codification, 12; history of, 9–14, 281n24; purpose, 10–12
expert witnesses, 162, 205–230; basic principles, 205–207; *Daubert* hearing, 86; educating the jury about, 229–230; experts versus non-experts, 120–122; eyewitness experts, 121, 220; improving understanding of, 225–230; psychology of—civil cases, 207–209; psychology of—criminal cases, 209–211; problems of understanding, 217–220. *See also* statistics; testimony
eyewitness identification, 23, 26, 121, 219

Feynman, R., 209
Fischhoff, B., 93
forensic science, 209, 210, 310n1, 312n22, 313n25; deceased techniques, 216; DNA, 22, 44, 202, 221–222; fingerprints, 26, 209–210; National Research Council Report on, 216
foreseeability, 19
framing. *See* heuristics
*Frye v. United States*. *See* gatekeeping

gatekeeping, 202, 205–216; civil cases, 215; criminal cases, 215; *Daubert v. Merrell Dow Pharmaceuticals*, 213, 215, 318n80; *Frye v. United States*, 125, 212; *General Electric v. Joiner*, 214; *Kumho Tire v. Carmichael*, 213, 214; marketplace test, 212; Rule 104, 214; Rule 702, 213
Gigerenzer, G., 227, 228
Greenleaf, S., 13
groups: decision-making, 22, 38, 46–49, 65, 67–68, 226–227; group polarization, 49, 67; in-group bias, 119, 298n12
Guthrie, C., 51

habit, 147, 155, 162, 165–167
harmless error, 19, 86, 106–107, 236
hearsay, 69, 129, 181–201, 238–239, 281n24; definition, 181–184; hearsay within hearsay, 188, 190–191; reasons for exceptions, 185; "testimonial infirmities," 129, 181, 186, 188–191
hearsay exceptions, 184, 191–200, 309n3; dying declaration, 193, 198–199; excited utterance, 4, 192–196; motive, intent, plan, 197–198; present sense impression, 192–194; residual exception, 185–186; statement against interest, 200; then-existing conditions, 193, 196–198
heuristics, 20–21, 43, 44, 51; anchoring, 43, 51; framing, 43, 51, 221; gain-loss, 51
*Hillmon, Mutual Life Insurance Co. v.*, 197
hindsight bias, 19, 76–77, 86, 89, 92–93, 107, 235, 290n2
Hutchins, R. 24, 194

impeachment: declarants, 191; witnesses, 72, 100, 112–113, 129–135, 148
individual differences, 50, 151, 154. *See also* character evidence
inferences, 2, 4–5, 7–9, 18, 33–34, 43–45, 57, 69, 79, 93, 102, 126, 129, 144–145, 147, 149–150, 157, 161, 168–169, 170, 172, 232. *See also* attribution theory; spontaneous trait inference
influence, weapons of, 40, 208, 240; authority, 40; commitment and consistency, 40, 197; liking, 41; reciprocation, 40; scarcity, 41, 95; social proof, 40, 48

influence and persuasion, 12, 37, 39–42, 63, 86, 93, 95, 158, 207–209, 210, 233
instructions to disregard. *See* disregarding inadmissible evidence
insurance, 35, 75, 81–83, 91, 102, 108
integrating information, 43–46, 91
interactionism, 155

James, W., 23
judges: decisions, compared to juries, 50–55, 104–105, 234, 295n35; role of, 34–36; trial judges, 2, 59, 86, 105, 235–236
juries/jurors: as reason for rules of evidence, 10–11, 233; blindfolding, 35–36, 82, 83; compared to judges, 50–55, 295n35; decision-making by juries, 46–49; decision-making by jurors, 42–45; deliberations, 22, 46–49, 65, 67–68, 226–227; experience of being 33–34; influence of attributes (traits, biases) on decisions, 36–39, 234; influence of evidence on decisions, 36, 41–42, 234; influence by lawyers, 39–41; selection (by exclusion), 37. *See also* disregarding inadmissible evidence

Kahneman, D., 21, 43
Kalven, H., 48, 53–55
*Kumho Tire v. Carmichael. See* gatekeeping

Latane, B., 151–152
law and psychology, history of, 22–25
lawyers, ability to influence, persuade, 39–41
leading questions, 114, 135–136
legal realism, 25
legislative facts, 203
lie detection, 122–133; accuracy (human), 123–124; fMRI, 126–128; polygraphs, 122, 125–126
limited use evidence: categorical exclusion rules, 101–102; limiting instructions, 19, 85, 97–103, 165; prior convictions, 100
Loftus, E., 114, 136
limiting instructions. *See* limited use evidence

McCormick, C., 165–166
memory, 85, 89–90, 105, 112–115, 121, 133–134, 195–196. *See also* source confusion
*Menendez, California v.*, 99
mental contamination, 17–19, 25–26, 62, 69, 76, 86, 89–90, 92, 98, 106–107, 113, 235
metacognition, 8, 18, 22, 59, 62–64, 83–84, 107, 227, 232, 235
Milgram, S., 153
Mischel, W., 154
motivated reasoning, 159, 208, 222, 312n17
Münsterberg, H., 23

need for cognition, 21
negotiations (settlements/plea bargains), 50

oath, 112–113, 116–119, 181, 236
observer effects, 26, 210
*On the Witness Stand*, 23
overconfidence, 161

Park, R., 23–24
personality. *See* character evidence
predictive power, 37
pre-trial publicity, 85, 102, 292n1
prior convictions, 58, 69, 70–72, 100
privileges, 6, 11, 136–141, 237; attorney-client, 137–138; clergy, 139; medical, therapist, 138–139; spousal and family, 139–140; self-incrimination/Fifth Amendment, 137
probability. *See* statistics
probative value, 18, 57–61, 65, 70–74, 79, 99, 151, 164. *See also* relevance
propensity. *See* character evidence; Rule 404

province of the jury, 120, 121, 128
psychopathy, 160

Rachlinski, J., 51
recidivism rates, 175
relevance, 9, 57–60, 74–75, 81, 197; statistical concepts, 161–162
reputation evidence, 130–131, 146, 148, 170, 199–200
Rule 101—Purpose, 34
Rule 103—Preventing the Jury from Hearing Inadmissible Evidence, 86–87
Rule 104—Preliminary Questions, 213, 214
Rule 105—Limiting Evidence, 70, 98, 100
Rule 401—Test for Relevant Evidence, 9–10, 44, 59
Rule 402—General Admissibility of Relevant Evidence, 10, 59–60
Rule 403—Exclusion of Relevant Evidence, 18, 57–58, 61–63, 70–72, 164
Rule 404—Character Evidence, 5, 100, 144–145; exceptions to, 146–14; other acts evidence, 163–165
Rule 405—Methods of Proving Character, 145–146
Rule 406—Habit; Routine Practice, 147, 165–167
Rule 407—Subsequent Remedial Measures, 19, 69, 73–78, 101, 183; criticisms of policy rationale, 77–78
Rule 408—Compromise Offers and Negotiations, 78–80
Rule 409—Payment of Medical Expenses, 80–81
Rule 410—Pleas, Plea Discussions, and Related Statements, 80
Rule 411—Liability Insurance, 75, 81–83
Rule 412(a)—Sex-Offense Cases: Victim's Sexual Behavior or Predisposition, 143
Rules 413, 414, 415—Similar Conduct Exceptions: Sexual Crimes, 147, 172–175, 303n7, 307n62
Rule 501—Privilege in General, 6, 137
Rule 601—Competency to Testify in General, 117
Rule 602—Lack of Personal Knowledge, 120
Rule 603—Oath or Affirmation to Testify Truthfully, 118
Rule 607—Who May Impeach a Witness, 130
Rule 608—A Witness's Character for Truthfulness or Untruthfulness, 130–131, 148, 169–172
Rule 609—Impeachment by Evidence of a Criminal Conviction, 58, 69, 70–72, 100, 130, 148, 167–169, 183
Rule 610—Religious Belief or Opinions, 119, 149
Rule 611—Mode and Order of Examining Witnesses, 111–112, 114
Rule 613—Witness's Prior Statement, 131
Rule 615—Excluding Witnesses, 115
Rule 701—Opinion Testimony by Lay Witnesses, 120
Rule 702—Testimony by Expert Witnesses, 213
Rule 801—Definitions . . . Exclusions from Hearsay, 184
Rule 802—The Rule against Hearsay, 184
Rule 803(1)—Present Sense Impression Exception, 192–194
Rule 803(2)—Excited Utterance Exception, 4, 192–196
Rule 803(3)—Then-Existing Mental, Emotional of Physical Condition Exception, 196–198
Rule 803(21)—Reputation Concerning Character, 199–200
Rule 804(2)—Dying Declarations, 193, 198–199
Rule 804(3)—Statement against Interest, 200
Rule 805—Hearsay within Hearsay, 188, 190–191

Rule 806—Attacking and Supporting the Declarant, 191–192
Rule 807—Residual Exception, 185–186
rulemakers / rulemaking: as applied psychologists, 1–3, 150, 165, 222, 232; at common law, 13; psychology of, 7–9; using scientific evidence, 202–205

Saks, M., 23–24
Salerno, J., 49
scientific evidence, 239–240; factfinding using, 205–230; use in rulemaking, 202–205, 233
scientific method, 16
self-complexity theory, 304n29
self-fulfilling prophecy, 159
Sevier, J., 188, 301n45
situation, 5, 24, 89, 114, 142, 149, 151–155, 157–158, 159, 160, 162, 166, 171–172
Slesinger, D., 24, 194
source confusion, 98, 113, 135–136, 141, 236, 245
spontaneous trait inference, 157, 305n41
statistics, 221–225: causation, 222–223; clinical versus actuarial, 223–225; defense attorney's fallacy, 221, 316n57; improving presentation of, 227–229, 317n75; prosecutor's fallacy, 221, 316n57
stereotyping, 158, 308n1
story model, 45–46, 61, 90–92, 224
stress, effects of on perception, memory, 4, 152, 193, 195–196, 199, 280n10
syllogistic analysis, 219
System 1/System 2. *See* dual processing

*Tarasoff v. Regents of the University of California*, 139, 141
temperament, 159–160
testimony: evaluating truthfulness of, 122–136; experts versus non-experts, 120–121; infirmities, 129, 181–182, 188–191; opinion testimony (of experts), 120–122, 205–207, 213, 219–220, 223–225, 231; personal knowledge, 120–122, 180–182, 187–188, 199, 206. *See also* expert witnesses; reputation evidence
Thayer, J. B., 13, 14
theory, definition of, 282n32
top-down knowledge, 17
traits. *See* character evidence
trial procedure, reforms of, 25, 26, 62, 286n1
trial values, 3, 6, 34, 61, 104, 111, 240; fairness, 3, 80, 129, 237; public policy, 34, 74–75, 77, 81, 101, 103, 106, 237; relationships, 34, 111, 136, 237; trial efficiency, 34, 61–62, 74, 111
Tribe, L., 129, 181, 188
Tversky, A., 21
*Twelve Angry Men*, 288n28

unfair prejudice, 57, 63–70

variance accounted for, 286n6
Violence Risk Assessment Guide (VRAG), 223
visual evidence, 64–65

weapons of influence. *See* influence, weapons of
Wells, G., 112, 220
Wigmore, J. H., 4, 23–24, 128, 149, 194, 195
Wistrich, A., 51
witnesses, 116–141; accuracy, 26, 132–133; calibration, 133–134; children, 116–117, 177–178, 294–295n27, 297n7; competence, 116–117; confidence, 133–134; credibility, 51–52, 112, 117, 119, 122, 128–136; disqualifications, 116–117. *See also* expert witnesses; privileges
Wundt, W., 23

Zeisel, H., 48, 53–55

# ABOUT THE AUTHORS

Michael J. Saks is Regents Professor at Arizona State University, where he is on the faculties of the Sandra Day O'Connor College of Law and the Department of Psychology. He holds a Ph.D. in social psychology from the Ohio State University and an M.S.L. from Yale Law School. His research has addressed a range of topics at the intersection of behavioral science and law.

Barbara A. Spellman is Professor of Law (and former Professor of Psychology) at the University of Virginia. She received a J.D. (1982) from NYU and a Ph.D. (Psychology, 1993) from UCLA. Her research has moved from basic questions about memory and reasoning to their applications to law, intelligence analysis, and public policy.